Urban Design Ecologies

READER

Urban Design Ecologies
Edited by Brian McGrath

A John Wiley and Sons Ltd, Publication

The editor and the publisher gratefully acknowledge the people who gave their permission to reproduce material in this book. While every effort has been made to contact copyright holders for their permission to reprint material, the publishers would be grateful to hear from any copyright holder who is not acknowledged here and will undertake to rectify any errors or omissions in future editions.

Registered office
John Wiley & Sons Ltd, The Atrium, Southern Gate, Chichester, West Sussex, PO19 8SQ, United Kingdom

For details of our global editorial offices, for customer services and for information about how to apply for permission to reuse the copyright material in this book please see our website at www.wiley.com.

This is a collective work. The copyright ownership of individual extracts is indicated in a copyright notice at the end of each extract.

Wiley publishes in a variety of print and electronic formats and by print-on-demand. Some material included with standard print versions of this book may not be included in e-books or in print-on-demand. If this book refers to media such as a CD or DVD that is not included in the version you purchased, you may download this material at http://booksupport.wiley.com. For more information about Wiley products, visit www.wiley.com.

Designations used by companies to distinguish their products are often claimed as trademarks. All brand names and product names used in this book are trade names, service marks, trademarks or registered trademarks of their respective owners. The publisher is not associated with any product or vendor mentioned in this book.

ISBN 978-0-470-97405-6 (paperback)
ISBN 978-0-470-97406-3 (hardback)
ISBN 978-1-118-48741-9 (ebk)
ISBN 978-1-118-48742-6 (ebk)
ISBN 978-1-118-48743-3 (ebk)

Executive Commissioning Editor: Helen Castle
Project Editor: Miriam Swift
Assistant Editor: Calver Lezama

Design by Artmedia, London
Printed in Spain by Grafos

Front cover images: Photographs Brian McGrath © Brian McGrath

To Mary R McGrath

Acknowledgements

The term urban design ecologies emerged during a multiyear discussion with my colleagues at Parsons The New School for Design: Lisa DeBenedittis, Miodrag Mitrasinovic and Joel Towers, with the leadership of Tim Marshall. Together we created one new undergraduate and two new graduate degree programmes in Urban Design that bridge the gap between urban design, urban studies and urban ecology. The small group followed the work of a broad committee chaired by Mitrasinovic and Towers that brought together faculty from across The New School around a new curriculum in Environmental and Urban Studies. This joining together of environmental and urban thinking within Parsons, a design school located within a university dedicated to social research, was a unique and important undertaking. This anthology is structured by writings embedded in different urban ecologies: the city, the metropolis, the megalopolis, the megacity and the metacity. The idea that the contemporary city is an assemblage of various urban morphologies came from a collaboration with David Grahame Shane as section co-editors and co-authors of an essay for the *Handbook of Architectural Theory* edited by C Greig Crysler, Stephen Cairns and Hilde Heynen.

Editorial Note on Presentation and Editing of Texts

This anthology aims to be inclusive, therefore some texts must appear in abbreviated form in the course of presenting others in their entirety. Some texts have been edited to shorten them, to exclude references that require more space for a full explanation and to preserve the flow of argument. Information for the sources of the edited and complete texts is given in the copyright line after each text. The term 'From' preceding a copyright line signifies that a specific extract or extracts has been taken from a longer text. Otherwise texts are given in their entirety or edited to indicate the argument of the whole. Texts have been clearly marked to show where they have been edited. The following conventions have been used throughout. Suspended points '…' are used to denote omissions of words or phrases within a sentence. Suspended points within a square bracket […] are used to denote omissions extending from a complete sentence to a paragraph. Three asterisks '***' mark omissions of more than one paragraph, and may denote exclusion of a complete subdivision of the original text. A paragraph may end […] if the last sentences of that paragraph are omitted or if the following paragraph is omitted. A paragraph may also start with […] if one or more sentences at the beginning of the paragraph have been omitted or if a previous paragraph has been omitted. Typographical errors and errors of transcription have been corrected when discovered in the anthologised texts but otherwise idiosyncrasies of spelling or punctuation remain unchanged. Notes and references have been included only where judged to be necessary to the text as printed.

Contents

Introduction

Brian McGrath

The title of this reader puts together three key words: *urban*, *design* and *ecology*. Standing alone, each word marks a specific territory within the broad debate around the challenges of globalisation, urbanisation, sustainability and climate change. However, when lined in succession, the title *Urban Design Ecologies* evokes a more complex way of thinking and new forms of practice beyond the limits of the autonomous fields of 'urban design' or 'ecology'. *Urban Design Ecologies* collects 23 chapters that together point the way for reconciling the often conflicting concerns of urbanism and environmentalism.

UN-Habitat's fourth session of the World Urban Forum during November 2008, in Nanjing, China, marked the 21st century as the urban age when it identified a fundamental demographic tipping point in 2008: humans are no longer a rural dwelling species, but predominantly inhabit cities.[1,2] The trend in global urbanisation will only escalate in the coming years, as we increasingly inhabit urban ecosystems that vary greatly in size, density and composition across the world. On an urbanised planet is the conceptual distinction between the rural and the urban or nature and culture still productive? The first misconception that must be addressed in this introduction is the value of the term urban as a space set apart from nature, and **urban design** as an autonomous discipline patrolling that obsolete divide.

The ecological impact from the historical shift towards carbon fuel-based industrial urbanisation is undeniable, but human-impacted urban systems rather than a lost 'natural wilderness' is the most important site for ecology, not as metaphor but as science. Jennifer Light has carefully critiqued the misuse of the term 'ecology' as a metaphor by social scientists from the University of Chicago in the 1920s.[3] Light demonstrates how the pioneers of the new discipline of urban studies used ecological concepts such as natural communities, succession and blight in analysing American cities, yet never pursued collaborations with ecologists to achieve a deeper understanding of complex biophysical processes in cities. The second important misconception to be overcome is that there exists an insurmountable divide between the scientific discipline and quantitative demands of **urban ecology** as science rather than metaphoric qualitative, experiential and socio-aesthetic pursuits of design iteration as **urban ecologies**.

Solutions to the complex set of 'wicked problems' surrounding rapid urbanisation and climate change have vexed normative modes of rational thinking and problem solving. Traditional modes of top-down governance, policy and planning, as well as growth-only oriented financial and business models have both proven inadequate. Today's unprecedented problems have generated new arenas for politics, art, media and design practices, adding new actors and scales of engagement within urban design. Examples in New York include the various artists who occupied the SoHo district in the 1970s, the establishment of community gardens in the Lower East Side in the 1980s, advocates for bicycle mobility such as Transportation Alternatives in the 1990s and the Friends of the High

Line in this decade. This legacy can be seen in cities such as Phnom Penh today, where art festivals such as 'Our City' place art in the context of urban displacement and eviction.

Established design disciplines based on the fashioning of industrially-designed objects have refocused on relationships between people's fundamental desires and needs, concentrating on by-products rather than products of consumer society. An example is the work of Ezio Manzini in Milan, and the international network he established called the DESIS network (Design for Social Innovation and Sustainability). In the words of sociologist Ulrich Beck, focusing on the 'bads' rather than the 'goods' of industrial society.[4] The discipline of urban design is in urgent need of engagement with these broader modes of design thinking beyond architecture and physical planning. The third misconception addressed in this volume is that urban design can maintain autonomy outside the new and expanding fields of **design ecologies**.

The use of the plural 'ecologies' frustrates scientists who see the field as in pursuit of singularly-defined quantifiable truths rather than qualitative and contingent human constructs (see Pickett, pages 162–71). As a critique of technocratic and scientific environmentalism, psychoanalyst Félix Guattari, in *The Three Ecologies*, identifies three ecological *registers*. First, there is the ecological register of the environment itself; second, is the ecological register of social relations; and finally there is the ecological register of human subjectivity. Borrowing from Gregory Bateson's concept of the ecology of the mind, Guattari argues that human society cannot respond to the environmental degradation of the planet without first acknowledging the loss of social relations in the breakdown of family, tribe, community, kinship, etc as well as the 'poison' of advertising, media and mass consumption at a global scale which has led to the deterioration of the human psyche.[5]

It is within the wide bandwidth of these three ecological registers that increasingly urban, design and ecological thinking emerge as important disciplinary threads that need to be intertwined. *Urban Design Ecologies* refers to both a radical revision of the theories and practices of the discipline of urban design, but also an expansion of the field through a range of sites and conditions that constitute the urban to include environmentally-impacted hinterlands, social relations and the urban subjectivity itself. The introduction to this anthology will first frame the range of issues which surround these three key words before proceeding to unpack the possibilities in their realignment, triggering creative engagement with new ways of living together within the limited resources of an urbanised planet.

Urban

While only occupying 3 per cent of the Earth's surface, urban areas consume most of the world's resources and release the most waste to our air, water and soils.[6] Urban life increasingly requires a global logistical network of people, information, money, matter and fuel. Additionally, information and knowledge generated from the materially-concentrated urban metabolism is dispersed and interconnected through a web of complex communication and transport technologies. We crowd in dense cities or drive across dispersed ones, but all urban areas are increasingly connected through transport systems and communication devices. A vast and increasingly depopulated and depleted countryside supplies cities with cheap food, water and labour, but also provides the spaces of retreat from the city in dormitory suburbs or weekend resorts. Disconnection from urban society through these escapes has become an expensive luxury rather than privation.

The demographic definition of urban varies greatly across multiple political jurisdictions and there is no precise count of urban dwellers nor is there a uniform line that can be drawn between the urban and the rural. The UN's *Demographic Yearbook* outlines the legal definition of 'urban' for all the nation states of the world. Definitions vary from 'Agglomeration of 5000 or more inhabitants where 75 per cent of the economic activity is non-agricultural', in Botswana, to '2500 or more inhabitants, generally having population densities of 1000 persons per square mile [2.59 square kilometres] or more' in the United States. In Peru, urban areas are defined as 'populated centres with 100 or more dwellings', while in hyper-urban Japan the city (*shi*) is defined as 'having 50,000 or more inhabitants with 60 per cent or more of the houses located in the main built-up areas and 60 per cent or more of the population engaged in manufacturing, trade or other urban type of business'. National urban populations range from Singapore with an urban population of 100 per cent to Bhutan with 9 per cent.[7]

Counting people in cities is also unreliable. Every 10 years municipal officials in New York City contest the national census figures. The 2010 census has again been challenged as population figures amount to 8,175,133 people living in the city, while new home construction and other records lead city officials to believe there are at least 8,400,000 residents.[8] While it is extremely difficult to account for all the residents of a city like New York with its large immigrant and transient young adult population, many national censuses count people according to their household residence rather than their actual dwelling place. Rural migrants living in Shenzhen, Lagos and Bangkok are statistically living in the villages of their birth rather than the cities in which they currently live. The urban remains an elusive moving target for quantitative tabulation.

The structural legibility of a historic city as a complete and holistic work of art draws hordes of tourists, but contemporary megacities defy logics of cognition or knowing. The expansion of the reach, dependencies and interconnectivities of contemporary cities has also been accompanied by a rise in the diversity of urban dwellers now living cheek by jowl, passing in close proximity if not socially interacting. If the compact city with its agricultural hinterland charms us with its walkability, convivial microclimates, self sufficiency and ease in navigation, the contemporary city awes with its spatial intricacy, social pulse and endless material and sensorial offerings. The question of the urban today must cover this vast range of interest and issues from its architecture and image to its ecologies of social and natural metabolic flows and pulses as well as the unpredictability of human desire.

The distinction between urban and rural, while more and more difficult to disentangle today, has been historically useful for an urban elite to exert political power. The urban as a discursive space encompasses urbanism, urban studies, urban theory, urban planning, as well as urban design. While in Europe urbanism is understood as the design of cities through architecture and planning, in American social science it has been defined as the social life of urban inhabitants. Today we must expand these definitions to include the metabolic consequences of those design decisions and social habits when much practical environmental knowledge is possessed by former rural dwellers living in cities. In urban studies, the city has served as a laboratory for the study of social habits, mobility, crime, health, gender, race, sexuality and power relations, and now often includes art, design, media, visual and spatial studies in addition to architecture, planning and ecology. Urban theory is a field for both classical and modern social theories as well as architectural scholarship.

The professional field of urban design and its first academic programmes were opportunistically born in the United States to take advantage of the enormous resources of a post-Second World War industrial economy redirected towards redeveloping an urban frontier neglected since the Great Depression. Whole areas of cities were appropriated for urban renewal, and the American Interstate Highway system was under construction, not just loops and networks connecting cities, but arteries crossing through the hearts of previously dense urban centres. The scale of urban renewal in the US was slowed by activism and protest from the 1960s. District-scale urban design took the place of large-scale urban renewal until a new phase of urban redevelopment was created by the neo-liberal deregulations of the market economy beginning in the 1980s, and a global boom of urbanisation. Yet this was the period of the rise of the US as a 'suburban nation' and a subsequent lack of any urban policy at the turn of the 21st century, other than the removal of public housing, on a national level.

Across the world, urban design is even less uniformly codified and understood as a discipline, and often has negative connotations given the reactionary neo-conservative practices of so-called New Urbanism. As David Grahame Shane has shown in his *Urban Design Since 1945 – a Global Perspective*, the Cold War split into Soviet and US blocs resulted in two opposing urban design models for the developing world – one which involved heavy state planning and design controls, and another that promoted deregulation and private market development. Urban design has consequently struggled to keep pace with the changing definition of what constitutes and structures the urban, its various disciplinary branches and its various forms of governance and policy.[9]

Ecology

The Cary Institute of Ecosystem Studies' definition of ecology integrates several successive advances in ecological thinking since the term was originally defined in the mid-19th century. Ecology is 'the scientific study of the processes influencing the distribution and abundance of organisms, the interactions among organisms, and the interactions between organisms and the transformation and flux of energy and matter'.[10] German biologist Ernst Haeckel (1834–1919) coined the term 'ecology' in his book titled *Natürliche Schöpfungsgeschichte*, published in 1868, and translated into English as *The History of Creation* in 1876. Following the work of Darwin, he described ecology as the study of the relationship between organisms and their environment. Haeckel was an artist as well as a biologist, and his drawings of the genealogical tree of life (1866) offer lush illustrations of the multiple life forms that constituted various branches. His illustrated books popularised Darwin's concept of evolution and natural selection, and influenced thinking more broadly as evident in Friedrich Nietzsche's philosophical tract *On the Genealogy of Morals* of 1887. Haeckel's influence in urban design can be seen in German architect OM Ungers' exhibition and book *Morphologie: City Metaphors*, a classification of various city forms as biological species (see Ungers, pages 36–47).

According to the Cary Institute website, 'the mid-19th century, with its largely macroscopic view of the world, neglected inconspicuous organisms, such as microbes, the chemical products of organisms in the environment, and ecological systems at larger scales or higher hierarchical levels than organisms'. This blind spot may be the result of the abundance of life studied by European biologists. In the more biologically sparse and isolated Australia, ecologists Herbert Andrewartha and Louis Birch formulated the science of population ecology in 1954. Instead of seeing a populated environment as an arena for competition and the 'survival of the fittest', their theory of metapopulation dynamics explained the overall persistence of species, survival within the harsh and fragmented habitats of Australia.[11] The two Australians provided a model to explain the distribution and abundance of organisms in all environments: 'A natural population occupying any considerable area will be made up of a number of ... local populations or colonies. In different localities the [demographic] trends may be going in different directions at the same time.' Modern ecological concepts such as patch dynamics and metacommunity derive from this thinking of survival through distribution and diffusion.

A second refinement that added another dimension to the definition of ecology is based on the integrative experimental ecosystem model designed by Howard T Odum in Silver Springs, Florida. Between the years 1951 and 1956, Odum conducted the first complete analysis of a natural ecosystem by measuring all the flows coming in and out of this spring-fed stream. His experiment helped our understanding of the productivity of an ecosystem in maintaining a constant temperature and chemical composition. Odum 'mapped in detail all the flow routes to and from the stream. He measured the energy input of sun and rain, and of all organic matter – even those of the bread the tourists threw to the ducks and fish – and then measured the energy that gradually left the spring. In this way he was able to establish the stream's energy budget'.[12] Odum established a new area of ecosystem ecology that added functional analysis of budgets and flows, inputs and outputs, to the structural analysis of the distribution and abundance of metapopulation dynamics. Odum is also important in having created a diagrammatic model of feedback loops and homeostasis, a discovery that influenced early concepts of urban design emerging in the same period.

Urban ecology endeavours to translate all these dimensions of ecology into the human-dominated realm of cities of all shapes and forms. Cutting-edge urban ecology uses an ecosystem approach that adds humans as a major actor in the functioning, dynamics and feedbacks in the system. Urban ecosystems are studied structurally as dynamic and heterogeneous land-cover patches (see Cadenasso, pages 272–81) and functionally as basins or sub-catchments of watersheds – where like, in Silver Springs, inputs and outputs can be measured. A recent definition of urban ecology by Steward Pickett is 'the distribution and abundance of organisms in and around cities and the biogeochemical budgets of urban areas'.[13] This is quite different from the metaphorical use of the term by social scientists, especially in the Chicago School of the 1920s which sought to 'naturalise' urban succession from growth to blight.

One of the primary goals of this volume is to establish more than a metaphorical understanding of ecology as an essential part of this expanded notion of urban design. The Cary Institute's robust definition of ecology, with its structural, relational and transformational dimensions, establishes standards of performance for urban design in this century beyond those previously defined by mechanistic aesthetic, social and developmental imperatives. By understanding *the processes influencing the distribution and abundance of organisms, the interactions among organisms, and the interactions between organisms and the transformation and flux of energy and matter*, urban designers will have a more robust set of analytical and creative tools and a way of seeing the world, not just as patterns and forms in space, but as relationships between organisms, energy flows and the environment.

Design

Through the writing of Leon Battista Alberti, urbanism was inaugurated as a modern humanist discipline to be undertaken by architects retained by the princes of the city-states in Renaissance Europe.[14] The 19th-century École des Beaux-Arts formalised modern metropolitan urbanism, made legible through monumental architecture, which spread internationally via the colonial world system. The disciplines of product design and advertisement accompanied mass industrialisation in the 20th century, and immediately addressed individual human needs and desires rather than national or institutional power as in Beaux-Arts architecture and urbanism. As industrial design gained greater importance it challenged the authority of Classical architecture, which in turn influenced both Modernist urbanism and architecture based on the utopian promise of an industrialised society. The Bauhaus introduced the idea of an integration of the design disciplines for a new industrial society, however urban design was not yet part of the new mix and remained an outdated Beaux-Arts discipline.

While design history has considered any human-made object a subject of aesthetic, social and cultural interest, design studies have turned away from the production and consumption of objects to a consideration of how all human activity itself is 'designed' as such. Broadly examining both material and visual culture, design thinkers such as Victor Papanek describe design as the conscious effort to create order in all human activity – it is how we *perceive* and feel about the world, how we act in that world, and how we reflect about that action, continuously at all times.[15]

Paul Ralph and Yair Wand from the University of British Columbia propose a multi-dimensional definition of design: 'Design is a specification of object, manifested by an agent, intended to accomplish goals, in a particular environment, using a set of primitive components, satisfying a set of requirements, subject to constraints.'[16] These seven dimensions – objects, agents, goals, environments, primitives, requirements and constraints – situate design between people, contexts, things and resources in a cybernetic feedback system rather than merely the aesthetic production of objects. Physical artefacts, processes, symbolic systems, scripts, laws, rules and policies, as well as human activity systems all can be integrated in design.

For John Thackara, designing in a complex world is a matter of finding a way out of the environmental problems created in large part by the design of industrially produced 'things'. He calculates that 80 per cent of the environmental impact of any product – including the built environment – is determined at the design stage.[17] According to Victor Margolin and Richard Buchanan, design is an integrative discipline constituted of diverse practitioners joined by the common theme of conceiving and planning the artificial. It therefore differs from science, which focuses on highly specific subject matters.[18] Horst Rittel and Melvin Webber introduced the 'wicked problem' approach in the 1970s as an alternative to the linear, step-by-step rational or scientific process of problem solving. Wicked problems are a 'class of social system problems which are ill-formulated, where the information is confusing, where there are many clients and decision makers with conflicting values, and where the ramifications in the whole system are thoroughly confusing'.[19] Design problems are by nature indeterminate, and urban design encompasses the most 'wicked' design problems. Urban design needs to more broadly engage politics, art, design and media practices in order to address the complex problems of the consequences of industrial society. It is new ways of design thinking through sensing, archiving, tagging, mapping, communicating and networking technologies that has the greatest potential of moving urban design into the 21st century.

Urban Design Ecologies

The chapters in this anthology are structured within different urban design ecologies: from the city to the metropolis, the megalopolis, the megacity and the metacity. Urban design texts will be considered as part of discursive ecologies which need to address the following questions: how does a theory of urban design frame a specific type of ecology? How is this theory represented and communicated through design? How, when built, does an urban design create a particular urban metabolism comprising socio-natural relationships? Who are the actors and agents who design the city? And finally, what is the particular role designers play in shaping these theories, relationships, participants and metabolisms?

The first urban design ecology explores the shift **From the Architecture of the City to Metropolitan Architecture.** The art of traditional city making teaches us much about convivial public space and the creation of artificial microclimates, yet is far removed from the ability of metropolitan architecture to compress and stack multiple social functions with efficient energy and transport systems, as the urban population continues to dramatically grow. The second section of chapters is titled **Megalopolis: The Nature of Sprawl.** The distributed and diffuse conurbation comprising the megalopolis forms an integral part of the future of urban design ecologies, as the lower density mix of built and vegetated environments are important for biodiversity, food security and water management. While currently a car-based city dependent on oil, the megalopolis of the future will have new forms of mobility.

The third section takes in various views from around the globe on informality and sustainability in **The Megacity**. The informal megacity's efficiency of resource use, recycling and frugality provides an example for all types of sustainable urbanisation. The final section seeks a way of looking at urban design beyond the previous categories and is titled **The Metacity**. The metacity's integration of community activism, smart technologies and a vibrant and mobile society are all important dimensions of the human ecology of the future city.

From Venice, to Berlin, New York, Hong Kong, Los Angeles, Baltimore, Las Vegas, Houston, Mumbai, Bangalore, Johannesburg, São Paulo, Bangkok, London, Paris, Tokyo, the following chapters experiment with multiple urban design ecologies reflecting the conflicting desires of billions of urban residents who must learn to live sensibly within the limits of the earth's natural resources. Through metacity thinking, all forms of urbanisation can be locally responsive to larger networks and systems, and it is the comprehensive knowledge gained by examining the recent history of an expanded urban design discourse that can produce the metacity of the future.

Notes

1   http://www.unhabitat.org/content.asp?cid=4613&catid=535&typeid=24&subMenuId=0
2   http://www.un.org/esa/population/publications/wup2007/2007WUP_ExecSum_web.pdf
3   JS Light, *The Nature of Cities*, Johns Hopkins University Press (Baltimore), 2009.
4   U Beck, *Risk Society*, Sage Publications (London), 1992.
5   F Guattari, *The Three Ecologies*, Athlone Press (London), 2000.
6   http://www.livescience.com/6893-cities-cover-earth-realized.html
7   http://unstats.un.org/unsd/demographic/products/dyb/dyb2.htm
8   http://2010.census.gov/2010census/
9   D Grahame Shane, *Urban Design Since 1945*, John Wiley & Sons (London), 2011.
10 http://www.ecostudies.org/definition_ecology.html
11 HG Andrewartha and LC Birch, *The Distribution and Abundance of Animals*, University of Chicago Press (Chicago), 1954.
12 The Crafoord Prize 1987 for EP Odum and HT Odum, with an overview of HT Odum's career, 23 September 1987.
    http://www.kva.se/en/pressroom/press-releases-1990-1982/The-Crafoord-Prizewinners-1987-Eugene-P-Odum-and-Howard-T-Odum/
13 STA Pickett, 'Urban Ecological Systems: Scientific Foundations and a Decade of Progress', *Journal of Environmental Management*, vol 92(3), 2011, pp 331–62.
14 F Choay, *The Rule and the Model*, MIT Press (Cambridge, MA), 1997.
15 V Papanek, *Design for the Real World: Human Ecology and Social Change*, Academy Chicago Publishers (Chicago), 2005.
16 P Ralph and Y Wand, 'A Proposal for a Formal Definition of the Design Concept', in K Lyytinen, P Loucopoulos, J Mylopoulos and W Robinson, (eds), *Design Requirements Workshop*, Springer-Verlag (Berlin, Heidelberg), 2009, pp 103–36.
17 J Thackara, *In the Bubble: Designing for a Complex World*, MIT Press (Cambridge, MA), 2006.
18 V Margolin and R Buchanan, *The Idea of Design*, MIT Press (Cambridge, MA), 1996.
19 H Rittel, 'On the Planning Crisis: Systems Analysis of the "First and Second Generations"', *Bedriftsøkonomen*, vol 8, 1972.

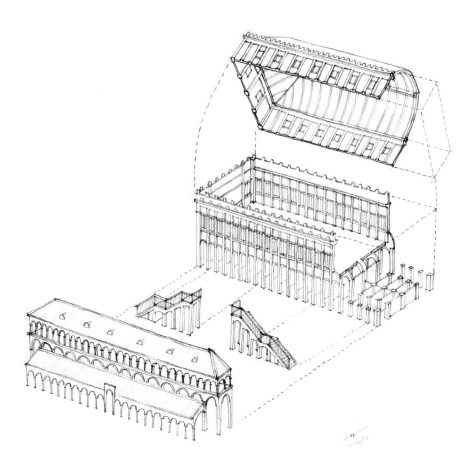

Rossi identifies the Palazzo della Ragione in Padua as an example of an urban artefact. It was constructed from 1172 to 1219 as the town hall. Its large roof, covering three large rooms without columns, was completed at the beginning of the 14th century. The three rooms were combined into one large meeting hall, and a front arcade with connecting stairs were added after a fire in the mid-15th century. For Rossi it is an example of how a multiplicity of functions can be accommodated over time, including an informal market on the ground floor, while the overall form of the structure remains intact, giving the figure a sense of permanence in changing times.

The Architecture of the City

Aldo Rossi

Aldo Rossi's insertion of the preposition 'of' between architecture and the city constitutes a powerful critique of Modernist urbanism and the fixation on the architecture of individual buildings *in* rather than *of* the city. Rossi defines the architecture of the city as the persistence and change evident in the physical fabric of the city as an artefact in time. Rossi finds that urban artefacts can serve multiple functions over time, independent of their function. For Rossi, the architecture of the city can be read in its *morphology* and *typology*. Urban morphology is a description of the form of an urban artefact, while urban typology identifies the sets of rules or structuring principles and is located in the transformation and adaptations of forms and types of habitation, such as in the creation of microclimates. This chapter offers brief selections from Rossi's description of the morphology of urban artefacts, typology, classification systems and the process of transformation of the architecture of the city in time.

The Individuality of Urban Artefacts

Our description of the city will be concerned primarily with its form. This form depends on real facts, which in turn refer to real experiences: Athens, Rome, Paris. The architecture of the city summarises the city's form, and from this form we can consider the city's problems.

By architecture of the city we mean two different things: first, the city seen as a gigantic man-made object, a work of engineering and architecture that is large and complex and growing over time; second, certain more limited but still crucial aspects of the city, namely urban artefacts, which like the city itself are characterised by their own history and thus by their own form. In both cases architecture clearly represents only one aspect of a more complex reality, of a larger structure; but at the same time, as the ultimate verifiable fact of this reality, it constitutes the most concrete possible position from which to address the problem.

We can understand this more readily by looking at specific urban artefacts, for immediately a series of obvious problems opens up for us. We are also able to perceive certain problems that are less obvious: these involve the quality and the uniqueness of each urban artefact.

In almost all European cities there are large palaces, building complexes or agglomerations that constitute whole pieces of the city and whose function now is no longer the original one. When one visits a monument of this type, for example the Palazzo della Ragione in Padua, one is always surprised by a series of questions intimately associated with it. In particular, one is struck by the multiplicity of functions that a building of this type can contain over time and how these functions are entirely independent of the form. At the same time, it is precisely the form that impresses us; we live it and experience it, and in turn it structures the city.

Where does the individuality of such a building begin and on what does it depend? Clearly it depends more on its form than on its material, even if the latter plays a substantial role; but it also depends on being a complicated entity that has developed in both space and time. We realise, for example, that if the architectural construction we are examining had been built recently, it would not have the same value. In that case the architecture in itself would be subject to judgement, and we could discuss its style and its form; but it would not yet present us with that richness of its own history characteristic of an urban artefact.

In an urban artefact, certain original values and functions remain, others are totally altered; about some stylistic aspects of the form we are certain, others are less obvious. We contemplate the values that remain – I am also referring to spiritual values – and try to ascertain whether they have some connection with the building's materiality, and whether they constitute the only empirical facts that pertain to the problem. At this point, we might discuss what our idea of the building is, our most general memory of it as a product of the collective, and what relationship it affords us with this collective.

It also happens that when we visit a palazzo like the one in Padua or travel through a particular city, we are subjected to different experiences, different impressions. There are people who do not like a place because it is associated with some ominous moment in their lives; others attribute an auspicious character to a place. All these experiences, their sum, constitute the city. It is in this sense that we must judge the *quality* of a space – a notion that may be extremely difficult for our modern sensibility. This was the sense in which the ancients consecrated a place, and it presupposes a type of analysis far more profound than the simplistic sort offered by certain psychological interpretations that rely only on the legibility of form.

We need, as I have said, only consider one specific urban artefact for a whole string of questions to present themselves; for it is a general characteristic of urban artefacts that they return us to certain major themes: individuality, locus, design, memory. A particular type of knowledge is delineated along with each artefact, a knowledge that is more complete and different from that with which we are familiar. It remains for us to investigate how much is real in this complex of knowledge.

I repeat that the reality I am concerned with here is that of the architecture of the city – that is, its form, which seems to summarise the total character of urban artefacts, including their origins. Moreover, a description of form takes into account all of the empirical facts we have already alluded to and can be quantified through rigorous observation. This is in part what we mean by urban morphology: a description of the forms of an urban artefact. On the other hand, this description is nothing but one moment, one instrument. It draws us closer to a knowledge of structure, but it is not identical with it.
***

Typological Questions

The city as above all else a human thing is constituted of its architecture and of all those works that constitute the true means of transforming nature. Bronze Age men adapted the landscape to social needs by constructing artificial islands of brick, by digging wells, drainage canals and watercourses. The first houses sheltered their inhabitants from the external environment and furnished a climate that man could begin to control; the development of an urban nucleus expanded this type of control to the creation and extension of a microclimate. Neolithic villages already offered the first transformations of the world according to man's needs. The 'artificial homeland' is as old as man.

In precisely this sense of transformation the first forms and types of habitation, as well as temples and more complex buildings, were constituted. The *type* developed according to both needs and aspirations to beauty; a particular type was associated with a form and a way of life, although its specific shape varied widely from society to society. The concept of type thus became the basis of architecture, a fact attested to both by practice and by the treatises.

It therefore seems clear that typological questions are important. They have always entered into the history of architecture, and arise naturally whenever urban problems are confronted. Theoreticians such as Francesco Milizia never defined type as such, but statements like the following seem to be anticipatory: 'The comfort of any building consists of three principal items: its site, its form and the organization of its parts.'[1] I would define the concept of type as something that is permanent and complex, a logical principle that is prior to form and that constitutes it.

One of the major theoreticians of architecture, Quatremère de Quincy, understood the importance of these problems and gave a masterly definition of type and model:

The word 'type' represents not so much the image of a thing to be copied or perfectly imitated as the idea of an element that must itself serve as a rule for the model ... The model, understood in terms of the practical execution of art, is an object that must be repeated such as it is; type, on the contrary, is an object according to which one can conceive works that do not resemble one another at all. Everything is precise and given in the model; everything is more or less vague in the type. Thus we see that the imitation of types involves nothing that feelings or spirit cannot recognize ...

We also see that all inventions, notwithstanding subsequent changes, always retain their elementary principle in a way that is clear and manifest to the senses and to reason. It is similar to a kind of nucleus around which the developments and variations of forms to which the object was susceptible gather and mesh. Therefore a thousand things of every kind have come down to us, and one of the principal tasks of science and philosophy is to seek their origins and primary causes so as to grasp their purposes. Here is what must be called 'type' in architecture, as in every other branch of human inventions and institutions.[2] [...]

In the first part of this passage, the author rejects the possibility of type as something to be imitated or copied because in this case there would be, as he asserts in the second part, no 'creation of the model' – that is, there would be no making of architecture. The second part states that in architecture (whether model or form) there is an element that plays its own role, not something to which the architectonic object conforms but something that is nevertheless present in the model. This is the *rule*, the structuring principle of architecture.

In fact, it can be said that this principle is a constant. Such an argument presupposes that the architectural artefact is conceived as a structure and that this structure is revealed and can be recognised in the artefact itself. As a constant, this principle, which we can call the typical element, or simply the type, is to be found in all architectural artefacts. It is also then a cultural element and as such can be investigated in different architectural artefacts; typology becomes in this way the analytical moment of architecture, and it becomes readily identifiable at the level of urban artefacts.

Thus typology presents itself as the study of types of elements that cannot be further reduced, elements of a city as well as of an architecture. The question of monocentric cities or of buildings that are or are not centralised, for example, is specifically typological; no type can be identified with only one form, even if all architectural forms are reducible to types. The process of reduction is a necessary, logical operation, and it is impossible to talk about problems of form without this presupposition. In this sense all architectural theories are also theories of typology, and in an actual design it is difficult to distinguish the two moments. [...]

Ultimately, we can say that type is the very idea of architecture, that which is closest to its essence. In spite of changes, it has always imposed itself on the 'feelings and reason' as the principle of architecture and of the city.

While the problem of typology has never been treated in a systematic way and with the necessary breadth, today its study is beginning to emerge in architecture schools and seems quite promising. I am convinced that architects themselves, if they wish to enlarge and establish their own work, must again be concerned with arguments of this nature.[3] Typology is an element that plays its own role in constituting form; it is a constant. The problem is to discern the modalities within which it operates and, moreover, its effective value.

Certainly, of the many past studies in this field, with a few exceptions and save for some honest attempts to redress the omission, few have addressed this problem with much attention. They have always avoided or displaced it, suddenly pursuing something else – namely *function*. Since this problem of function is of absolutely primary importance in the domain of our inquiry, I will try to see how it emerges in studies of the city and urban artefacts in general and how it has evolved. Let us say immediately that the problem can be addressed only when we have first considered the related problems of description and classification. For the most part, existing classifications have failed to go beyond the problem of function.

***

Problems of Classification

In my summary of functionalist theory I have deliberately emphasised those aspects that have made it so predominant and widely accepted. This is in part because functionalism has had great success in the world of architecture, and those who have been educated in this discipline over the past 50 years can detach themselves from it only with difficulty. One ought to inquire into how it has actually determined modern architecture, and still inhibits its progressive evolution today; but this is not an issue I wish to pursue here.

* * *

The task of human geography is to study the structures of the city in connection with the form of the place where they appear; this necessitates a sociological study of place. But before proceeding to an analysis of place, it is necessary to establish a priori the limits within which place can be defined. Tricart[4] thus establishes three different orders or scales:

1   The scale of the street, including the built areas and empty spaces that surround it.
2   The scale of the district, consisting of a group of blocks with common characteristics.
3   The scale of the entire city, considered as a group of districts.

The principle that renders these quantities homogeneous and relates them is social content.

On the basis of Tricart's thesis, I will develop one particular type of urban analysis which is consistent with his premises and takes a topographical point of view that seems quite important to me. But before doing so, I wish to register a fundamental objection to the scale of his study, or the three parts into which he divides the city. That urban artefacts should be studied solely in terms of place we can certainly admit, but what we cannot agree with is that places can somehow be explained on the basis of different scales. Moreover, even if we admit that the notion is useful either didactically or for practical research, it implies something unacceptable. This has to do with the *quality* of urban artefacts.

Therefore while we do not wholly deny that there are different scales of study, we believe that it is inconceivable to think that urban artefacts change in some way as a result of their size. The contrary thesis implies accepting, as do many, the principle that the city is modified as it extends, or that urban artefacts in themselves are different because of the size at which they are produced. As was stated by Richard Ratcliff:

> To consider the problems of locational maldistribution only in the metropolitan context is to encourage the popular but false assumption that these are the problems of size. We shall see that the problems to be viewed crop up in varying degrees of intensity in villages, towns, cities, and metropolises, for the dynamic forces of urbanism are vital wherever men and things are found compacted, and the urban organism is subject to the same natural and social laws regardless of size. To ascribe the problems of the city to size is to imply that solutions lie in reversing the growth process, that is, in deconcentration; both the assumption and the implication are questionable.[5]

At the scale of the street, one of the fundamental elements in the urban landscape is the inhabited real estate and thus the structure of urban real property. I speak of inhabited real estate and not the house because the definition is far more precise in the various

European languages. Real estate has to do with the deed registry of land parcels in which the principal use of the ground is for construction. The usage of inhabited land in large measure tends to be residential, but one could also speak of specialised real estate and mixed real estate, although this classification, while useful, is not sufficient.

To classify this land, we can begin with some considerations that are apparent from plans. Thus we have the following:

1   A block of houses surrounded by open space.
2   A block of houses connected to each other and facing the street, constituting a continuous wall parallel to the street itself.
3   A deep block of houses that almost totally occupies the available space.
4   Houses with closed courts and small interior structures.

A classification of this type can be considered descriptive, geometric or topographic. We can carry it further and accumulate other classificatory data relative to technical equipment, stylistic phenomena, the relationship between green and occupied spaces, etc. The questions this information gives rise to can lead us back to the principal issues which are, roughly speaking, those that deal with:

1   Objective facts.
2   The influence of the real-estate structure and economic data.
3   Historical-social influences.

The real-estate structure and economic questions are of particular importance and are intimately bound up with what we call historical-social influences. [...] For now, we will continue with the subject of real-estate structure and economic data, even if the second is given summary treatment.

The shape of the plots of land in a city, their formation and their evolution, represents a long history of urban property and of the classes intimately associated with the city. Tricart has stated very clearly that an analysis of the contrasts in the form of plots confirms the existence of a class struggle. Modifications of the real-estate structure, which we can follow with absolute precision through historical registry maps, indicate the emergence of an urban bourgeoisie and the phenomenon of the progressive concentration of capital. [...]

Real estate, which we considered earlier from a topographic point of view, also offers other possibilities of classification when seen in a socio-economic context.

We can distinguish the following:

1   The 'pre-capitalist' house, which is established by a proprietor without exploitative ends.
2   The 'capitalist' house, which is meant for rental and in which everything is subordinated to the production of revenue. Initially it might be intended either for the rich or the poor, but in the first case, following the usual evolution of needs, the house drops rapidly in class status in response to social changes.

These changes in status create blighted zones, one of the most typical problems of the modern capitalist city and as such the object of particular study in the United States, where they are more evident than in Italy.

3   The 'para-capitalist' house, built for one family with one floor rented out.

4   The 'socialist' house, which is a new type of construction appearing in socialist countries where there is no longer private land ownership and also in advanced democratic countries. Among the earliest European examples are the houses constructed by the city of Vienna after the First World War.

When this analysis of social content is applied with particular attention to urban topography, it becomes capable of providing us with a fairly complete knowledge of the city; such an analysis proceeds by means of successive syntheses, causing certain elementary facts to come to light, which ultimately encompass more general facts. In addition, through the analysis of social content, the formal aspect of urban artefacts takes on a reasonably convincing interpretation, and a number of themes emerge that play an important role in the urban structure.

* * *

Processes of Transformation

The relationship between the dwelling areas and the primary elements of a city is responsible for configuring that city in a specific way. If this can be demonstrated in cities in which historical events have always acted to unify disparate elements, it is even more apparent in the case of cities that have never managed to integrate in an overall form the urban artefacts that constitute them: thus London, Berlin, Vienna, Rome, Bari and many other cities.

In Bari,[6] for example, the ancient city and the walled city constitute two extremely different, almost unrelated artefacts. The ancient city has never been enlarged; its nucleus is completely defined as a form. Only its principal street, which served to link it to the surrounding region, emerges intact and permanent in the texture of the walled city. In cases of this type there is always a close connection between primary elements and the area; often this connection becomes an urban artefact so absolutely predominant that it constitutes a characteristic of the city, for the city is invariably the sum of its artefacts.

Morphological analysis, one of the most important instruments for studying the city, brings these aspects into full view. Amorphous zones do not exist in the city, or where they do, they are moments of a process of transformation; they represent inconclusive times in the urban dynamic. Where phenomena of this type appear very frequently, as in the suburbs of the American city, the processes of transformation have usually been accelerated, since high density puts greater pressure on land usage. These transformations are realised through the definition of a precise area, and this is when the process of *redevelopment* occurs.

A distinctive characteristic of all cities, and thus also of the urban aesthetic, is the tension that has been, and still is, created between areas and primary elements and

The Lower East Side in Manhattan shows traces of the four historical periods outlined by Rossi. The area was first cultivated as farms from the Bowery (Dutch for farm) to the East River in the pre-capitalist period. The land was cut into blocks defined by streets and avenues and the blocks were subdivided into building lots for row house construction and property speculation in the capitalist period. Tenement and apartment buildings later replaced row houses. In the para-capitalist phase, row houses were subdivided and rented out as flats. Finally, during the socialist phase, large areas along the East River were declared blighted and cleared to create public housing, a park and highway. In the 1970s and 1980s, a number of abandoned lots became a network of community gardens, while more recently the neighbourhood has been the site of intensive gentrification. (Map overlay from *Transparent Cities*, 1994, SITES Books.)

between one sector of the city and another. This tension arises from the differences between urban artefacts existing in the same place and must be measured not only in terms of space but also of time. By time I mean both the historical process, in which phenomena of a permanent kind are present with all their implications, and a purely chronological process, in which such phenomena can be measured against urban artefacts of successive periods.

In this way, formerly peripheral parts of large cities in transformation often appear beautiful: London, Berlin, Milan and Moscow reveal entirely unexpected perspectives, aspects and images. The different *times* more than the immense spaces of the Moscow periphery, by virtue of an aesthetic pleasure that resides in the very nature of the artefacts, give us the real image of a culture in transformation, of a modification taking place in the social structure itself.

Of course, we cannot so easily entrust the values of today's cities to the natural succession of artefacts. Nothing guarantees an effective continuity. It is important to know the mechanism of transformation and above all to establish how we can act in this situation – not, I believe, through the total control of this process of change in urban artefacts, but through the control of the principal artefacts emerging in a certain period. Here the question of scale, and of the scale of intervention, comes to the fore.

The transformation of particular parts of the city over time is very closely linked to the objective phenomenon of the decay of certain zones. This phenomenon, generally referred to in the English and American literature as 'obsolescence', is increasingly evident in large modern cities, and it has special characteristics in the large American cities, where it has been closely studied. For our purposes, we will define this phenomenon as characterised by a group of buildings – which may be in the neighbourhood of a certain street or may constitute an entire district – that has outlived the dynamics of land use in the surrounding area (this definition has a much broader scope than some others). Such areas of the city do not follow life; often they remain islands for a long time with respect to the general development, bearing witness to different periods in the city and at the same time configuring large areas of 'reserve'. This phenomenon of obsolescence illustrates the validity of studying areas of the city as urban artefacts; we can then relate the transformations of such areas to the study of specific events.

The hypothesis of the city as an entity constituted of many parts which are complete in themselves is, it seems to me, one which truly permits freedom of choice; and *freedom of choice* becomes a fundamental issue because of its implications. For example, we do not believe that questions concerning values can be decided in terms of abstract architectural and typological formulations – for example, high-rise or low-rise housing. Such questions can only be resolved at the concrete level of urban architecture. We are fully convinced that in a society where choices are free, the real freedom of the citizen rests in being able to choose one solution rather than another.

Notes

1 F Milizia, *Principi di Architettura Civile*, cit no 4 of the introduction to this book; the phrase quoted is from the beginning of the second part, 'Della comodità', p 221.

2 A-C Quatremère de Quincy, *Dictionnaire historique d'architecture comprenant dans son plan les notions historiques, descriptives, archaeologiques, biograhiques, théoriques, didactiques et pratiques de cet art*, 2 vols (Paris), 1982. The passage quoted is from vol 2, the selection on 'Type'. Quatremère's definition of type has recently been picked up by Giulio Carlo Argan in a particularly interesting way, in Argan, 'Sul concetto di tipologia architettonica', in *Progetto e destino*, Casa editrice Il Saggiatore (Milan), 1965, pp 75–81. See also Louis Hautecoeur, *Histoire de l'architecture classique en France*, 7 vols, A et J Picard (Paris), 1943–57, in particular vol V, *Révolution et Empire 1792–1815* (1953), where Hautecoeur writes, 'As Schneider noted, Quatremère affirmed that there is a "correlation between scale, forms, and the impressions that our spirit receives from them"' (p 122).

3 Among the new aspects of the research by architects on the problems of typology, the lectures given by Carlos Aymonino at the Istituto Universitario di Architettura di Venezia are particularly interesting. In one of them, 'The Formation of a Concept of Building Typology', he states, 'We can thus attempt to distinguish some "characteristics" of building typologies which allow us to identify them better: a) singleness of theme, even if [the type is] subdivided into one or more activities in order to derive a reasonable elementarity or simplicity from the organism; this also applies in more complex cases; b) indifference – in theoretical formulations – to context, that is, to a precise urban location (does a significant interchangeability derive from this?) and the formation of a relationship concerned only with its own plan as the single relevant boundary (an incomplete relationship); c) the overcoming of building code regulations to the extent that the type is characterised precisely by its own architectural form. The type in fact is also conditioned by codes (of hygiene, security, etc) but not *only* by them' (p 9). Aymonino's lectures are found in two volumes published by the Istituto Universitario di Architettura di Venezia, *Aspetti e problemi della tipologia edilizia. Documenti del corso di caratteri distributivi degli edifici. Anno accademico 1963–1964 (Venice), 1964; and La formazione del concetto di tipologia edilizia. Atti del corso di caratteri distributivi degli edifici. Anno accademico 1964–1965* (Venice), 1965. Some of these lectures are also republished with revisions in C Aymonino, *Il significato della città*, Editori Laterza (Bari), 1975.

4 J Tricart, *Cours de géographie humaine*, 2 vols: vol I, *L'habitat rural*; vol II, *L'habitat urbain*, Centre de Documentation Universitaire (Paris), 1963. Tricart observes, 'Like every study of artifacts considered in themselves, urban morphology presupposes a convergence of givens customarily drawn from different disciplines: urbanism, sociology, history, political economy, law itself. It is sufficient that this convergence has as its aim the analysis and explanation of a concrete artifact, of a landscape, for us to be able to state that it has its place in the framework of geography' (vol II, p 4).

5 R Updegraff Ratcliff, 'The Dynamics of Efficiency in the Locational Distribution of Urban Activities', in Harold Melvin Mayer and Clyde Frederick Kohn (eds), *Readings in Urban Geography*, University of Chicago Press (Chicago), 1959, pp 299–324; the passage cited is on p 299.

6 V Rizzi, *I cosiddetti Statuti Murattiani per la città di Bari. Regolamenti edilizi particolari*, Leonardo da Vinci (Bari), 1959.

From Aldo Rossi, *The Architecture of the City*, excerpts from pp 29–32, 35–41, 48–51, 95–6. Notes have been renumbered. © 1982 Massachusetts Institute of Technology, by permission of The MIT Press. Images: p 16 drawing Agkarat Atiprasertkul and Brian McGrath © Brian McGrath; p 24 drawing Brian McGrath 1994 © Brian McGrath.

Collage City

Colin Rowe and Fred Koetter

Colin Rowe and Fred Koetter's critique of the modern city is most clearly represented through the abstract concept of figure-ground. Figure-ground is based on the idea from gestalt psychology that there is an essential experience that comes from a shape or form. For Rowe and Koetter, it is the loss of the formal legibility of the traditional city, and its replacement by modern architecture's idealised view of nature – object buildings floating above an Arcadian landscape – that was the primary cause of the crisis of the 'object' of the Modernist city. The authors see the role of the architect as the formal mediator between inside and outside, modernity and tradition, utopia and the everyday. For them *Collage City* is a technique in recreating an open city, rich with perceptions, consciousness and experience of the new and old – the conquest of time through urban design. This chapter offers selections from the description of figure-ground. Texture and the crisis of the object is followed by a discussion of *poché*, a design methodology in which buildings can take on a complex plan figuration in order respond to both internal programmatic needs, and the creation of figural urban space outside the building.

* * *

Crisis of the Object: Predicament of Texture

… (M)odern architecture's object fixation … is our present concern only insofar as it involves the city, the city which was to become evaporated. For, in its present and unevaporated form, the city of modern architecture as a congeries of conspicuously disparate objects has become quite as problematical as the traditional city, which it has sought to replace.

Let us, first of all, consider the theoretical desideratum that the rational building is obliged to be an object and, then, let us attempt to place this proposition in conjunction with the evident suspicion that buildings, as man-made artefacts, enjoy a meretricious status, in some way, detrimental to an ultimate spiritual release. Let us further attempt to place this demand for the rational materialisation of the object and this parallel need for its disintegration alongside the very obvious feeling that space is, in some way, more sublime than matter, that, while the affirmation of matter is inevitably gross, the affirmation of a spatial continuum can only facilitate the demands of freedom, nature and spirit. And then let us qualify what became a widespread tendency to space worship with yet another prevalent supposition: that, if space is sublime, then limitless naturalistic space must be far more so than any abstracted and structured space; and, finally, let us upstage this whole implicit argument by introducing the notion that, in any case, space is far less important than time and that too much insistence – particularly upon delimited space – is likely to inhibit the unrolling of the future and the natural becoming of the 'universal society'.

Such are some of the ambivalences and fantasies which were, and still are, embedded in the city of modern architecture. But, though these could seem to add up to a cheerful and exhilarating prescription, as already noticed, even when realisations of this city, though pure, were only partial, doubts about it began very early to be entertained. Perhaps these were scarcely articulated doubts and whether they concerned the necessities of perception or the predicament of the public realm is difficult to determine; but, if, in the Athens Congress of 1933 CIAM had spelled out the ground rules for the new city, then by the mid-1940s there could be no such dogmatic certainty. For neither the state nor the object had vanished away; and, in CIAM's *Heart of the City* conference of 1947,[1] lurking reservations as to their continuing validity began, indecisively, to surface. Indeed, a consideration of the 'city core', in itself, already indicates a certain hedging of bets and, possibly, the beginnings of a recognition that the ideal of indiscriminate neutrality or inconspicuous equality was hardly attainable or even desirable.

But, if a renewed interest in the possibilities of focus and hence of confluence seems, by this time, to have been developing, while the interest was there, the equipment to service it was lacking; and the problem presented by the revisionism of the late 1940s might best be typified and illustrated by Le Corbusier's plan for St Dié where modified standard elements of Athens Charter specification are loosely arranged so as to insinuate some notions of centrality and hierarchy, to simulate some version of 'town centre' or structured receptacle. And might it be said that, in spite of the name of its author, a built St Dié would, probably, have been the reverse of successful; that St Dié illustrates, as clearly as possible, the dilemma of the free-standing building, the space occupier attempting to act as space definer? For, if it is to be doubted whether this 'centre' would facilitate confluence, then, regardless of the desirability of this effect, it seems that what we are here provided with is a kind of, unfulfilling schizophrenia – an acropolis of sorts which is attempting to perform as some version of an agora!

However, in spite of the anomaly of the undertaking, the re-affirmation of centralising themes was not readily to be relinquished; and, if the 'core of the city' argument might easily be interpreted as a seepage of townscape strategies into the CIAM city diagram, a point may now be made by bringing the St Dié city centre into comparison with that of the approximately contemporaneous Harlow new town which, though evidently 'impure', may not be quite so implausible as, sometimes, has appeared to be the case.

At Harlow, where there is absolutely no by-play with metaphors of acropolis, there can be no doubt that what one is being offered is a 'real' and literal marketplace; and, accordingly, the discrete aspects of the individual buildings are played down, the buildings themselves amalgamated, to appear as little more than a casually haphazard defining wrapper. But, if the Harlow town square, supposed to be the authentic thing itself, a product of the vicissitudes of time and all the rest, may be a little over-ingratiating in its illusory appeal, if one might be just a little fatigued with quite so enticing a combination of instant 'history' and overt 'modernity', if its simulation of medieval space may still appear believable as one stands inside it, then, as curiosity becomes aroused, even this illusion quickly disappears.

For an overview or quick dash behind the immediately visible set-piece rapidly discloses the information that what one has been subjected to is little more than a stage set. That is, the space of the square, professing to be an alleviation of density, the relief of an impacted context, quickly lends itself to be read as nothing of the kind. It exists without essential back up or support, without pressure, in built or human form, to give credibility or vitality to its existence; and, with the space thus fundamentally 'unexplained', it becomes apparent that, far from being any outcropping of a historical or spatial context (which it would seem to be), the Harlow town square is, in effect, a foreign body interjected into a garden suburb without benefit of quotation marks.

But, in the issue of Harlow versus St Dié, one is still obliged to recognise a coincidence of intention. In both cases the object is the production of a significant urban foyer; and, given this aim, it seems perfectly fair to say that, whatever its merits as architecture, the Harlow town square provides a closer approximation to the imagined condition than ever St Dié might have done. Which is neither to endorse Harlow nor condemn St Dié; but is rather to allow them both, as attempts to simulate the qualities of 'solid' city with the elements of 'void' to emerge as comparable gestures of interrogation.

Now, as to the relevance of the questions which they propound, this might be best examined by once more directing attention to the typical format of the traditional city which, in every way, is so much the inverse of the city of modern architecture that the two of them together might, sometimes, almost present themselves as the alternative reading of some Gestalt diagram illustrating the fluctuations of the **figure-ground phenomenon**. Thus, the one is almost all white, the other almost all black; the one an accumulation of solids in largely unmanipulated void, the other an accumulation of voids in largely unmanipulated solid; and, in both cases, the fundamental ground promotes an entirely different category of figure – in the one *object,* in the other *space.*

However, not to comment upon this somewhat ironical condition; and simply, in spite of its obvious defects, to notice very briefly the apparent virtues of the traditional city: the solid and continuous matrix or texture giving energy to its reciprocal condition, the specific space; the ensuing square and street acting as some kind of public relief valve and providing some condition of legible structure; and, just as important, the very great versatility of the supporting texture or ground. For, as a condition of virtually continuous building of incidental make up and assignment, this is not under any great pressure for self-completion or overt expression of function; and, given the stabilising effects of public facade, it remains relatively free to act according to local impulse or the requirements of immediate necessity.

Perhaps these are virtues which scarcely require to be proclaimed; but, if they are, every day, more loudly asserted, the situation so described is still not quite tolerable. If it offers a debate between solid and void, public stability and private unpredictability, public figure and private ground which has not failed to stimulate, and if the object building, the soap bubble of sincere internal expression, when taken as a universal proposition, represents nothing short of a demolition of public life and decorum, if it reduces the public realm, the traditional world of visible civics to an amorphic remainder, one is still largely

Black and white figure-ground drawings of Le Corbusier's plan of St Dié, on the left, and the city of Parma, on the right. If Le Corbusier's plan represents the Modernist city of objects in a green field, Parma can be seen as a city where public spaces form a series of figural voids, and most of the buildings, aside from churches and other public monuments, recede to the background.

impelled to say: so what? And it is the logical, defensible presuppositions of modern architecture – light, air, hygiene, aspect, prospect, recreation, movement, openness – which inspire this reply.

So, if the sparse, anticipatory city of isolated objects and continuous voids, the alleged city of freedom and 'universal' society will not be made to go away and if, perhaps, in its essentials, it is more valuable than its discreditors can allow, if, while it is felt to be 'good', nobody seems to like it, the problem remains: what to try to do with it?

There are various possibilities. To adopt an ironical posture or to propound social revolution are two of them; but, since the possibilities of simple irony are almost totally pre-empted and since revolution tends to turn into its opposite, then, in spite of the persistent devotees of absolute freedom, it is to be doubted whether either of these are very useful strategies. To propose that more of the same, or more of approximately the same, will – like old-fashioned *laissez-faire* – provide self-correction? This is just as much to be doubted as is the myth of the unimpaired capacities of self-regulating capitalism; but, all of these possibilities apart, it would seem, first of all, to be reasonable and plausible to examine the threatened or promised city of object fixation from the point of view of the possibility of its perception.

* * *

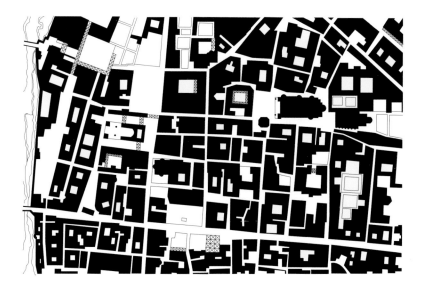

Certainly, in considering the modern city from the point of view of perceptual performance, by gestalt criteria it can only be condemned. For, if the appreciation or perception of object or figure is assumed to require the presence of some sort of ground or field, if the recognition of some sort of however closed field is a prerequisite of all perceptual experience and, if consciousness of field precedes consciousness of figure, then, when figure is unsupported by any recognisable frame of reference, it can only become enfeebled and self-destructive. For, while it is possible to imagine – and to imagine being delighted by – a field of objects which are legible in terms of proximity, identity, common structure, density, etc, there are still questions as to how much such objects can be agglomerated and of how plausible, in reality, it is to assume the possibility of their exact multiplication. Or, alternatively, these are questions relative to optical mechanics, of how much can be supported before the trade breaks down and the introduction of closure, screening, segregation of information, becomes an experiential imperative.

Presumably this point has not, as yet, quite been reached. For the modern city in its cut-price versions (the city in the park becomes the city in the parking lot), for the most part still exists within the closed fields which the traditional city supplies. But, if, in this way – not only perceptually but also sociologically parasitic – it continues to feed off the organism which it proposes to supplant, then the time is now not very far remote when this sustaining background may finally disappear.

Such is the incipient crisis of more than perception. The traditional city goes away; but even the parody of the city of modern architecture refuses to become established. The public realm has shrunk to an apologetic ghost but the private realm has not been significantly enriched; there are no references – either historical or ideal; and, in this atomised society, except for what is electronically supplied or is reluctantly sought in print, communication has either collapsed or reduced itself to impoverished interchange of ever more banal verbal formulae.

* * *

A proposal which, for practical purposes, demands a willingness to imagine the present dispensation as inverted, the idea of such inversion is most immediately and succinctly to be explained by the comparison of a void and a solid of almost identical proportions. And, if to illustrate prime solid nothing will serve better than Le Corbusier's Unité, then, as an instance of the opposite and reciprocal condition, Vasari's Uffizi could scarcely be more adequate. The parallel is, of course, transcultural; but, if a 16th-century office building become a museum may, with certain reservations, be brought into critical proximity with a 20th-century apartment house, then an obvious point can be made. For, if the Uffizi is Marseilles turned outside in, or if it is a jelly mould for the Unité, it is also void become figurative, active and positively charged; and, while the effect of Marseilles is to endorse a private and atomised society, the Uffizi is much more completely a 'collective' structure. And, to further bias the comparison; while Le Corbusier presents a private and insulated building which, unambiguously, caters to a limited clientele, Vasari's model is sufficiently two-faced to be able to accommodate a good deal more. Urbanistically it is far more active. A central void-figure, stable and obviously planned, with, by way of entourage, an irregular back up which may be loose and responsive to close context. A stipulation of an ideal world and an engagement of empirical circumstance, the Uffizi may be seen as reconciling themes of self-conscious order and spontaneous randomness; and, while it accepts the existing, by then proclaiming the new the Uffizi confers value upon both new and old.

* * *

(T)he Palazzo Borghese, located upon its highly idiosyncratic site, contrives both to respond to this site and to behave as a representative palace of the Farnese type. The Palazzo Farnese provides its reference and meaning. It contributes certain factors of central stability, both of facade and plan; but, with the 'perfect' *cortile* now embedded in a volume of highly 'imperfect' and elastic perimeter, with the building predicated on a recognition of both archetype and accident, there follows from this duplicity of evaluation an internal situation of great richness and freedom.

Now this type of strategy which combines local concessions with a declaration of independence from anything local and specific could be indefinitely illustrated; but, perhaps, one more instance of it will suffice. Le Pautre's Hôtel de Beauvais, with its ground floor of shops, is externally something of a minor Roman palazzo brought to Paris; and, as an even more elaborate version of a category of free plan, it might possibly prompt comparison with the great master and advocate of the free plan himself. But Le Corbusier's technique

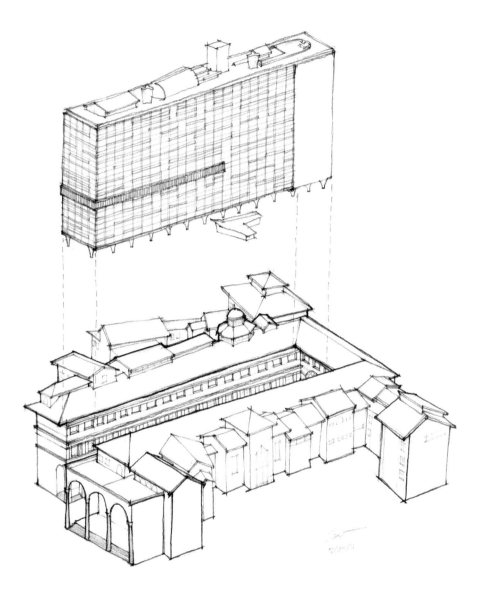

Le Corbusier's Marseilles Unité
d'Habitation is an object building
that, quite literally, is the inverse
of Vasari's banking offices for
the Medici in Florence (now the
Uffizi Museum).

is, of course, the logical opposite to that of Le Pautre; and, if the 'freedoms' of the Villa Savoye depend on the stability of its indestructible perimeter, the 'freedoms' of the Hôtel de Beauvais are derived from the equivalent stability of its central *cour d'honneur*.

In other words, one might almost write an equation: Uffizi: Unité = Hôtel de Beauvais: Villa Savoye; and, as a simple convenience, this equation is of completely crucial importance, for on the one hand at the Villa Savoye, as at the Unité, there is an absolute insistence upon the virtues of primary solid, upon the isolation of the building as object and the urbanistic corollary of this insistence scarcely requires further commentary; and, on the other, in the Hôtel de Beauvais, as at the Palazzo Borghese, the built solid is allowed to assume comparatively minor significance, indeed, in these last cases, the built solid scarcely divulges itself; and, while unbuilt space (courtyard) assumes the directive role, becomes the predominant idea, the building's perimeter is enabled to act as no more than a 'free' response to adjacency. On the one side of the equation building becomes prime and insulated, on the other the isolation of identifiable space reduces (or elevates) the status of building to infill.

But building as infill! The idea *can* seem to be deplorably passive and empirical – though such need not be the case. For, in spite of their spatial preoccupations neither the Hôtel de Beauvais nor the Palazzo Borghese are, finally, flaccid. They, both of them, assert themselves by way of representational facade, by way of progression from facade-figure (solid) to courtyard-figure (void); and, in this context, although the Villa Savoye is by no means the simplistic construct which we have here made it appear (although it too, to some extent, operates as its opposite) for present purposes its arguments are not central.

For, far more clearly than at Savoye, at the Hôtel de Beauvais and the Palazzo Borghese the gestalt condition of ambivalence – double value and double meaning – results in interest and provocation. However, though speculation may thus be incited by the fluctuations of the figure-ground phenomenon (which may be volatile or may be sluggish), the possibilities of any such activity – especially at an urban scale – would seem very largely to depend upon the presence of what used to be called *poché*.

Frankly, we had forgotten the term, or relegated it to a catalogue of obsolete categories; and were only recently reminded of its usefulness by Robert Venturi.[2] But if *poché*, understood as the imprint upon the plan of the traditional heavy structure, acts to disengage the principal spaces of the building from each other, if it is a solid matrix which frames a series of major spatial events, it is not hard to acknowledge that the recognition of *poché* is also a matter of context and that, depending on perceptual field, a building itself may become a type of *poché*, for certain purposes a solid assisting the legibility of adjacent spaces. And thus, for instance, such buildings as the Palazzo Borghese may be taken as types of habitable *poché* which articulate the transition of external voids.
* * *

To summarise: it is here proposed that, rather than hoping and waiting for the withering away of the object (while, simultaneously manufacturing versions of it in profusion unparalleled), it might be judicious, in most cases, to allow and encourage the object to become digested in a prevalent texture or matrix. It is further suggested that neither object nor space fixation are, in themselves, any longer representative of valuable attitudes. The one may, indeed, characterise the 'new' city and the other the old; but, if these are situations which must be transcended rather than emulated, the situation to be hoped for should be recognised as one in which both buildings *and* spaces exist in an equality of sustained debate. A debate in which victory consists in each component emerging undefeated, the imagined condition is a type of solid-void dialectic which might allow for the joint existence of the overtly planned and the genuinely unplanned, of the set-piece and the accident, of the public and the private, of the state and the individual. It is a condition of alerted equilibrium which is envisaged; and it is in order to illuminate the potential of such a contest that we have introduced a rudimentary variety of possible strategies. Cross-breeding, assimilation, distortion, challenge, response, imposition, superimposition, conciliation; these might be given any number of names and, surely, neither can nor should be too closely specified; but if the burden of the present discussion has rested upon the city's morphology, upon the physical and inanimate, neither 'people' nor 'politics' are assumed to have been excluded. Indeed, both 'politics' and 'people' are, by now, clamouring for attention; but, if their scrutiny can barely be deferred, yet one more morphological stipulation may still be in order.

Ultimately, and in terms of figure-ground, the debate which is here postulated between solid and void is a debate between two models and, succinctly, these may be typified as acropolis and forum.

Notes

1   JL Sert and EN Rogers (eds), J Tyrwhitt (trans), *The Heart of the City Towards the Humanisation of Urban Life*, Pellegrini and Cudahy (New York), 1952; Lund Humphries (London), 1952.
2   R Venturi, *Complexity and Contradiction in Architecture*, The Museum of Modern Art Papers on Architecture I (New York), 1966.

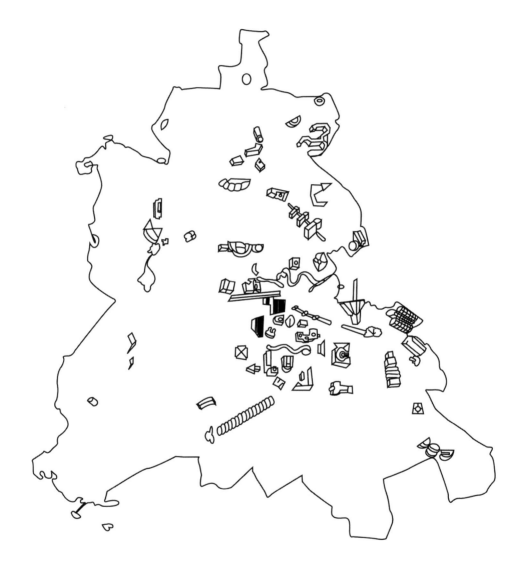

Cities Within the City

Oswald Mathias Ungers

OM Ungers establishes a link between Rossi's architecture of the city and Rem Koolhaas's idea of metropolitan architecture. Ungers is a transatlantic figure, teaching at Cornell and practising in Germany, and it is the fragmented metropolis of Berlin that serves as the site of his most important urban design thinking. *Planning Criteria* is a description of Ungers' work as based in 'reality as found' – in all its plurality, contradictions, accidents and changes over time. For Ungers, urban design is creating a set of rules, yet allowing accidents to happen. The designer's primary goals are complemented by local spontaneity and the design of systems adaptable to multiple needs and change over time. *Cities Within the City* theorises a summer academy in Berlin with Cornell University from 1977. The case is an ideal example of the criteria Ungers established in a specific historical urban context. The text is present as islands of thought – like the urban design model of the archipelago city itself – for Ungers' Berlin and later for Koolhaas' Manhattan.

***

Planning Criteria
The first criterion of my design is the dialectical process with a reality as found:

a) The impulse of the design comes usually from a permanent confrontation with the environment as it exists as well as the acceptance of specific economic, social and historical conditions.
b) The design process as a continuous experiment of knitting and fitting the elements into a complex grown and sometimes simply banal reality. The design is determined by the specific building task, by the integration into an existing context and also by the intensification of the place. [...]

The proposed *city as a green archipelago* concentrates development in the shrunken city of West Berlin, isolated within East Germany by a wall, as islands of urbanity within a 'green lagoon'.

The second criterion has to do with the problem of planning and accident in several ways. First, that accidents are sometimes turned into planning intentions or to put in better terms into an architectural event. Second, that the plan has at least two levels of definition, a primary and a secondary. The primary level determines the framework of the basic structure which organises the space for a secondary event which can be more accidental, spontaneous and if necessary temporary. Part of it is also the necessity to create planning-fields for a more individualistic architecture within a set of fixed rules, or to develop a design strategy for every specific solution.

The third criterion that I want to demonstrate with the design is the plurality of solutions or the wide spectrum of the architectural interpretation of one and the same element. As far as it is possible the spectrum is conceived as a continuum of interpretations which represent steps in-between two extremes. Implicit in this criterion is a catalogue of alternatives, in contrast to the usual attempts at an ideal solution. The projects are better characterised as fragments and partial solutions of a very specific area, than ideal realisations of a platonic idea. [...]

The fourth criterion is the concept of architecture as an environment or as one could also put it, the urban characteristics of architecture. Opposed to this is the usual concern with architecture as an object. The projects demonstrate in several cases how the object-character of architecture can be diminished in favour of an architecture concept, which accomplishes a higher degree of quality than only a simple organisation of a given programme. Under this aspect architecture can become an urban element, which is conditioned to incorporate environmental functions. [...]

The last criterion. [...] The principle of adaptability should be made one of the basic conditions of design. [...] Any building project which extends through a period of time is facing this problem and has to come to grips with a solution for an organisational system which permits additions and adaptations. [...] In a deterministic plan, adaptations and changes are usually blocked as soon as they contradict a preconceived formal order. [...] A design concept with an orientation toward adaptable systems of order searches for a minimal design in which the organisation of elements in space will be minimised to allow or even to provoke a maximum participation of those who are using the space. Such a concept requires the exploration of a design matrix for an open-ended and self-generated process; which responds to a constructive participation of different interests. [...] The design process becomes infinitely more complex and will not be stabilised into one permanent fact. In reality, adaptability in architectural design means a transformation from an authoritarian act into an act of participation.
***

Cities Within the City

Thesis 1: Berlin's population drop

The following evaluations predict a drop in the population of Berlin during the 1980s equal to more than 10 per cent of the present figure which is between 2 and 1.7 million inhabitants.

Comment

If we start from the assumption that these estimates are fairly exact, then it must be borne in mind that the real figures may exceed the estimated reduction because when the decrease is in progress it ends up in causing a bigger effect. A certain percentage of anxiety-prone inhabitants in fact allow themselves to be caught up in the end by an exodus psychosis with the result that the population slips below the estimated figure. Experience, however, has shown that this figure will subsequently tend to swing back upwards on the assumption that a simultaneous improvement in the quality of life occurs and that the city becomes a more congenial place to live in after a reorganisation of the urban environment. In fact, without a radically improved offer no one will want to stay of his own accord in a decommercialised city, or still less, to go back there.

Conclusions

Any future planning for Berlin must therefore come to grips with the problem of a city in the process of depopulation. Since Berlin occupies a limited territory and political reality is such that it can be neither reduced nor increased, future strategies have got to be devised that will take into account a controlled decrease in the population density, without jeopardising the general quality of the urban environment.

Thesis 2: Criticism of current design theories

The current opinion whereby the historic quarters of the city can be preserved and saved only through additional and integrant building stems from erroneous assumptions and is therefore illusory.

Comment

There are two urban design tendencies to be avoided on the theoretic and operative plane, due to their illusory character: one is that of starting from the assumption that the city can be restored to its former historic substance and configuration. Programmes of this kind are, in the best of instances, the result of a misunderstood wave of nostalgia. As the statistic forecasts seem to indicate, it will not be possible in this way to make up for future necessities. The depopulation process, however, cannot be left to chance. The inevitably untidy development that would ensue not only spells chaos but would ultimately have disastrous consequences for the city. The realisation of the idea of 'repairing' the city which, if wrongly interpreted, may in practice be transformed into a destruction of the city, implies an inevitable thrust towards an increase in buildings, homes, shops, social services and so on. The concept of repairing the city denies an established fact, namely, that most areas have by now ended in ruins precisely because, in almost all cases and especially in Berlin, there was never any real necessity to increase their density. [...]

Conclusions
In Berlin in particular the consequences of the theory of a restored city, in the sense of a historic reconstruction, would be the reverse of those expected, since the inexorable depopulation process would only be camouflaged and all action taken to improve reality would be pointlessly deferred, to the consequent disadvantage of the city.

Thesis 3: The problem of the population drop
At Frankfurt a number of social democratic councillor politicians met recently to discuss the problem of the population drop in big cities and to draw up the necessary countermeasures. In the majority of big German cities this tendency is regressive. As in America, here too the exodus to suburban areas is mounting. The consequence of this constant efflux is a general impoverishment and, in a broader perspective, a partial decay of the city centre. The depopulation process in some major cities like Cologne, Frankfurt and Berlin, which have a high percentage of foreign labour, is already in progress.

Comment
Clearly, however, the reasons for this flight from the city also result from a changed way of life. As shown by a recent survey by the Demoscopic Bureau of Allensbach, big cities are steadily losing their residential value. The enquiry shows that 74 per cent of the population prefer an apartment in the country to an apartment in the city. Country life seems to offer more attractions. The car and television play an important role in this respect. Moving to the country is much more than a flight from society. With the improvement of transport both the spatial and the psychological distance has been considerably reduced. This process of depopulation does not apply only to Berlin either. Most of the big cities of the world, with very few exceptions, have been hit by the same phenomenon.
* * *

Conclusions
Since ... this fall-off is not a local phenomenon but, rather, a sign of a much more general tendency, the future task is going to be not only to plan the growth of cities but also to develop new proposals and concepts for dealing with this exodus by protecting the better aspects of cities. Faced with this assignment, urban planners today are unprepared and certainly incapable of solving the problem with the means that have been employed hitherto. Berlin, which has such radical and idiosyncratic features, is particularly well suited, within this problematic, for use as a workshop.

Thesis 4: The differentiated urban structure
Large cities are characterised by an overlapping of many opposite and divergent conceptions. Therein lies the difference between them and villages, rural populated areas,

urban districts, and small or medium towns. Here the chief characteristic is expressed in the predominance of a single basic principle or, if there is more than one, these will nevertheless be complementary to each other. The ideal would be to find an order for the city in which there is both a convergence of principles and a climate of functionality.

Comment

★ ★ ★

Although it is difficult to establish what the reasonable size of a city is, it is still clear that a convenient size is somewhere around 250,000 inhabitants. Zurich, Florence, Trier or Freiburg are places in which the atmosphere that one breathes far exceeds the commercial aspect. These examples show that size does not mean an improvement in the quality of life. In Tokyo, New York or London the millions of inhabitants do not raise the effective value of these cities; and instead they create enormous technical and organisational problems, while basically only ruining the human environment. Today we suffer from a sense of universal respect for giantism, perhaps because we think that what is big must be better. Reality has instead shown that reduction and diminution also make for better quality, and not least in the quality of life itself. For this reason small, restricted units ought to be created. This applies to production and the way of life as well as to any other environment.

Conclusions

These considerations suggest that if within the context of a selective programme for the reduction of urban over-population, or even of a partial demolition of those districts that are superfluous and work badly, the reduction of the population in Berlin may not perhaps provide an outstanding opportunity to redevelop zones that no longer satisfy technical, social and structural demands. Simultaneously those zones that deserve to be preserved should be identified, or, at the outside, their characteristics should be underlined and, if incomplete, completed. These enclaves liberated from the anonymity of the city would, in their quality of quasi-islands, form a green urban archipelago in a natural lagoon.

Thesis 5: The idea of the city in the city

The idea of the city in the city is the basic concept for a future urban replanning of Berlin. It is substantiated in the image; Berlin as a city-archipelago. The urban islands will have an identity in keeping with their history, social structure and environmental characteristics. The city as a whole will be a federation of all these single towns with different structures, developed in a deliberately antithetic manner. A decisive factor in the choice ought to be the degree of clarity and comprehensibility of the existing basic and design principles.

Comment

The first step to be taken ought to be to pick out and select those districts of the city that possess clearly identifiable features likely to justify their preservation and accentuation. These so-called identity-spaces should not be established on the basis of a particular taste or of aesthetic conceptions. The second step towards a redevelopment is the completion of fragments to be preserved which in the course of this process must receive their architectural and definitive urban planned form. This first step leads to the development of a whole series of integrative and complementary measures of a clearly not sentimental kind. In quarters having a high building density, the existing bulk building ought to be diminished through the creation of fine spaces, as city parks, public gardens and squares; while districts having a low density, for example, the western parts of the city, could be intensified by the integration of residential centres. The architectural and planning intentions for the future consist solely in enucleating the true configuration of each single island-in-the-city on the basis of which it was first chosen. [...] Each part of the city taken in itself will receive an identity of its own that will differentiate it from that of the others. [...]

Conclusions
The pluralistic project for a city within the city is in this respect in antithesis to the current planning theory which stems from a definition of the city as a single whole. This corresponds to the contemporary structure of society which is developed more as a society of individuality with different demands, issues and conceptions.

The project also involves an individualisation of theme and therefore a moving away from typisation and standardisation. This should be applied on the one hand to all possible openings and on the other to the multiplicity that springs from them.

Thesis 6: Establishment of the area of city-islands
The phase of the establishment of the area of so-called islands-in-the-city is both the result of a programme and a formal urban design job. Not all the new integrations have to be planned afresh. With analogisms and confrontations it is possible to acquire knowledge than can be employed in a typological sense.

Comment
Upon a preliminary analytical examination a number of zones in the city leap to the eye; they stand out from the others by their characteristics and importance. Areas of the city that are exemplary by their closed structure are the southern area of Friedrichstadt, Görlitz Station, the Schlosstrasse, Siemensstadt and Spandau, what is known as the 'city', but also the Märkisches Viertel, the Gropiusstadt and centres like the Tempelhofer Feld, the Hufeisen Siedlung, Onkel Toms Hütte, but also the cultural zone around Kemperplatz which is a reproduction of the historic Museuminsel. The zones just mentioned represent a compound of extremely different structures in content and form; they contain buildings in blocks but also single, radial, linear and reticular forms, open and closed systems, a network of regular and irregular streets, while also having different graphic, spatial, functional and social characteristics.

Conclusions

To establish the characteristics of the city a number of typical cases might be taken into consideration, which were designed at other times for other occasions and may have comparable typological features. For example, the ideal project of Karlsruhe, with its radial axis, might serve as an example for a configuration of the southern part of Friedrichstadt, or the project for Manhattan's Central Park might be transferred just as it is into the Görlitz Station zone. The urban planning structure of the Schlosstrasse is identical to the Baroque structure of Mannheim. The linear design of Leonidow for Magnitogorsk is similar from a typological point of view to the structure of the buildings along the Unter den Eichen.

Thesis 7: The green archipelago

The project for the city in the city, formed by a group of different units, is completed antithetically, by the surfaces in-between the islands-in-the-city. In fact, the structures here, by now valueless, ought to be allowed to be gradually retransformed into natural zones and pastures, without any rebuilding. This concerns in particular the areas of Kemperplatz, the stations of Görlitz and Potsdam, and at a later stage, the Tempelhofer airport zone.

These islands-in-the-city would, in other words, be divided from each other by strips of green, thus defining the framework of the city in the city and thereby explaining the metaphor of the city as a green archipelago.

Comment

The green interspaces form a system of modified nature and preserve a series of characteristics that range from suburban zones to parks and to wooded areas up to the urban developed zones or those for agricultural use (*Schrebergärten*).

The surfaces earmarked for agriculture could penetrate all parts of the city and at the same time create an additional source of industry and employment ... The natural grid ought also to welcome the infrastructure of this technologicalised age in which we live, that is to say, it should embrace a motorway extended network to link up the islands-within-the-city to one another; it ought also to include supermarkets, drive-in cinemas, drive-in banks and similar services connected with the car just as any other typology of the 20th century which depends not only on space but on mobility.

Next to suburban zones with a different density, wooded areas, shooting preserves, natural parks, gardens, family allotments, urban agriculture and infrastructural services of the modern age, it should also be possible to rely on green zones for 'parking' temporary mobile facilities. What is hoped for here is a new type of town in which the main interest is that of the employment of leisure time and which will show a predilection for living in tent-houses and in mobile units. These inhabitants, then, do not remain attached to any fixed spot, but their existence is indeed stimulated by a transitory way of life.

Conclusions

In the open zones between the blocks projects should be realised to improve urban characteristics, viz:

- the building of areas for detached dwellings with a low density in accordance with Hilberseimer's recommendations for Chicago
- the building of zones for temporary inhabitation with mobile homes to replace living in the city centre and as an alternative to living in green areas and to a certain way of experiencing leisure time
- the building of sports facilities, recreation and free time facilities, beginning with park and play areas and extending to shooting preserves and to artificial landscapes, and to amusement zones of the Disneyland type and National Parks for the friends of nature
- the setting aside of production areas in the 'industrial parks' style of American cities with leisure-time facilities and for play and sport for the workers.

Thesis 8: The urban villa as a form of residential building

Residential building in general has hitherto been limited to two types of buildings: the detached dwelling and the apartment block. Leaving aside the transformation of the detached home into series-houses, we are left essentially with these two types. To an ever-growing extent the apartment block is seen as a renunciation of the detached dwelling. Various researches have shown that nearly 70 per cent of the population prefers a detached home to one in a block.

Comment

In the last few years the tendency towards detached homes has risen in step with the increased affluence, although in this way considerable troubles and higher costs, longer streets and poorer services perhaps have to be accepted. At the same time, however, precious areas for recreation, particularly on the outskirts of the city, are occupied by detached houses, thereby preventing that land from being enjoyed by the community. The real underlying reason for this aspiration to have one's own house is not so much the fruit of commercial reflections as, rather, the desire for independence and the need to develop one's personality more freely, in other words, a greater need for individualisation and for an improvement in the quality of life. The apartment block cannot fulfil this wish because it imposes certain obligations upon those who live in it and cuts down their living space. ... The problem therefore is whether between these two extreme forms of dwelling there may be one that offers the advantages of a detached home while avoiding the disadvantages of the apartment block. The answer is that the old rented villa type of home is the one fitted to this purpose. It is a type of house with four to eight homes of different structures within it. On account of its limited volume and of its consequent adaptability to the particular wishes of its occupants, this type of house allows an absolutely individual structure ...

Conclusions

In residential building the construction of town houses as rent-villas ought to be encouraged more than before. The transformation of historic villas for the reduced requirements of today has demonstrated that this type of home is not suited only for residential purposes but also lends itself to other functions. It satisfies both the desire of those who use it for a stronger individualisation of the environment in an ideal way, as well as the interest of the collectivity in the measure in which this concerns the social infrastructures and concentration. Houses similar to these villas with a limited number of dwellings and with an individual structure are fairly easily fitted into a historic pattern of a city that has been enlarged. While the building of big blocks does in any case result in a redevelopment of the surface concerned with all the ensuing social, economic and planning disadvantages, in the case of the urban villa all this is avoided because it is more an integrative than a substitutive element.

Thesis 9: Transformation of the city in the course of history

The history of Berlin shows us the development of a city into many different zones. The difference and multiplicity of its history of quarters express the importance of Berlin and are its main urban design feature. It is a city in which contrasting elements, that have always been articulated in an attempt at cohesion, did not manage to blend together under one single principle. Berlin has never followed one idea alone, but has been formed on divergent ideas. Theses and antitheses coincide here like breathing in and breathing out.

Comment

The history of Berlin is the history of the transformation from one type of city into another. In the course of 700 years Berlin has been several different cities. It began by being two cities, Berlin and Kölln, the one for fishermen and the other for traders. It soon became a market city, then a residential one, a capital and in the 19th century an industrial city. Finally it became a metropolis and ultimately once again a double city. Already in the 18th century Berlin was formed by several different cities: Berlin, Kölln, Friedrichswerder, Dorotheenstadt, Friedrichstadt and the eastern suburbs. The different quarters had their own administration, different planning structures and independent functions. [...]

From a historic point of view this model also transforms the project drawn up by William IV for the Havel landscape between Berlin and Potsdam. Here in the 19th century a humanistic cultural landscape was formed with historic commemorative monuments of different epochs ... inserted as places in themselves, thus forming an archipelago of architectonic phenomena. The architecture of the Havel landscape in itself encloses the key to regarding Berlin as an archipelago of many different places.

Conclusions

The superimposition of ideas, concepts, decisions, casualties and reality across the arc of seven centuries have given the city its present form. The current plan is a book of events in which the traces of history have remained clearly visible. It is not a unitary image but a living collage, a union of fragments. The contemporary vicinity of contrasting elements is from a historic point of view the expression of the dialectic process in which the city has always found itself and still does. [...]

Thesis 10: Standards and definition of objectives for the future

The inevitable drive towards the reduction, improvement of planning characteristics, the preservation of the historic substance, the individualisation of architecture, the humanisation of living space in the city and the improvement of the environment bring themes barely mentioned, which will need to be discussed within the framework of the reconstruction of the city and for whose solution new proposals must be developed.

Comment

The problem is no longer posed as the designing of a completely new environment, but rather as the rebuilding of what already exists. Not the discovery of a new order for the city, but the improvement of what is already there; not the discovery of new conceptions, but the rediscovery of proven principles; not the construction of new cities but the re-organisation of the old ones – this is the real problem for the future.

There is no need for a new Utopia but rather to create a better reality. And this is something that applies not only to Berlin but also to the majority of other major cities. Berlin might, however, prompt other initiatives that could go beyond its own particular problems and thus assume a more general role of leadership.

Conclusions

The creation of an archipelago in the city is the answer to a series of fundamental planning necessities of the following kind:

- the solution to the problem of reduction which goes hand in hand with that of an improvement of the city in antithesis to the constant growth and unlimited enlargement with the loss in quality that ensues from it
- the improvement of the city in the sense of a vital space and of multiple and more varied activity
- the creation of a pluralistic system of reciprocally unresolved contradictions by comparison with a unitary and centralised system
- the reconstruction of an identity for the urban environment
- the close link between city and country, which means a new way of considering the relations between culture and nature
- the intensification of places as also the conservation of the collective heritage and of the historic conscious in the sense of a continuity in space and in time
- the individualisation of architecture and hence the simultaneous improved adaptability to the desires and expectations of inhabitants
- the necessity for smaller units for the creation of living spaces and for more delimited activities, in a scale with the city and its individual buildings.

The model of the city in the city was organised on a general basis during the Sommer Akademie of Berlin in 1977 by Cornell University; it was designed by the senator in charge of building and housing systems, by the IDZ and by the Künstlerhaus Bethanien. The villa as a form of town housing and the city in the city were the objects discussed at that Sommer Akademie. Cornell University architectural students drew up proposals for an urban villa during an eight-week course held at the Sommer Akademie which are contained in a specially published volume. Taking part in the rough draft and elaboration of the city in the city theme were: OM Ungers (Berlin, Cologne, Ithaca, NY), Rem Koolhaas (London), Peter Riemann (Ithaca, NY), Arthur Ovaska (Cologne, Boston).

Oswald Mathias Ungers, 'Planning Criteria', *Lotus International* 11, 1976, p 13 and 'Cities Within the City', *Lotus International* 19, 1978, pp 82–97. © Lotus International. Image: p 36 drawing Agkarat Atiprasertkul and Brian McGrath © Ungers archive Anja Sieber-Albers, original, redrawn for publication.

Chicago à la Carte

Alvin Boyarsky

**Alvin Boyarsky's postcards collected while living in Chicago form the basis
for a radically new form of urban analysis. This popular art form provides
a lens to understand the rise of the American metropolis, whose history
breaks from the slow evolution of urban form described by Rossi, Rowe
and Ungers. Boyarsky analyses a city designed, imagined and experienced
in section. The extreme height of skyscrapers and the superimposition of
layers of infrastructure produce a machine city dominating over nature.
This is an edited version of Boyarsky's essay which first appeared in
Architectural Design in 1970 and was reprinted in the book *The Idea of
the City* published in 1996 in honour of Boyarsky's 20 years as Chairman of
the Architectural Association (AA) in London. The AA between 1971 and
1990 offered an à la carte selection of alternative models for contemporary
urban design, feeding the imagination of Rem Koolhaas (pages 60–71),
Bernard Tschumi (pages 248–59), and David Grahame Shane (pages 260–
71). Boyarsky's experience of the great Midwestern metropolis of Chicago
allowed him to cultivate teachers, students and projects that celebrated
technology, popular culture and the excesses of modernity.**

1970 marks the centenary of the postcard. Deltiologists will know that it is still possible
to turn up a reasonable collection of popular picture postcards dating from 1902 (when
regulations were changed to allow messages and address to occupy one side of the card,
leaving the other side free for a picture). [...]

Connoisseurs of Americana will not be surprised to discover that early postcards
present the exotic contrasts of a primitive continental landscape in the process of
becoming. They include a catalogue of audacious engineering feats, determined by
everything that was not there to begin with, of absolute reliability, cold calculation,
maximum elasticity and lightness, necessary to harness the power and to force a link
between the isolated regions. [...]

The hastily assembled, gridded utilitarian settlements, astride the great lines of force
crossing the continent, appear to float in an ever-varying natural setting of overpowering
scale and isolation, and embody the regional breaks in transportation. The architectonic
fixes are the grain elevators, the wharves and warehouses, the mine heads, the open
seams, the sawmills, the oil rigs and the belching chimneys.

Main Street is given over to commerce, providing, among other things, a chronological
account of the spontaneous development of marketing and urban transportation, from
the trading post to the supermarket, from the burro, the lone rider, the stagecoach, the
horse-driven streetcar, the cable and electric trolleys, the elevated, to the advent of
the automobile and the Greyhound bus. The transitory and expendable suburbs, which

Greetings from Chicago; discarded postcards became a primary source for Alvin Boyarsky's analysis of the American metropolis.

extend the field uniformly to the edges of civilisation, offer the promise of unfettered growth and the possibility of each generation building its own home anew.

Representations of the great cities from New York to San Francisco, their abstract spatial fields scarcely adapted to the natural setting, suggest a similarity in quality and origin. Projecting a tough-minded, often sensationalistic pride in a bustling public domain whose dynamic equilibrium is derived solely from the contingencies of their time and place, they appear relieved of the laws of historical continuity and purely compositional activities involving good taste, harmony and delicacy of expression. Plotted with a compass whose coordination is indefinitely future, these self-regulating models of empirical efficiency appear to glean immediate benefit from science and technology.

Psychologically embraced by the overtones and associations of an aggressively assembled environment of simultaneously colliding elements, deformed and multiplied images, restrained by superimposed geometrical networks, buildings like giant machines, containing within themselves the architectonics of the environment around them, are perceived in successive states by primitives of a new sensibility that has been completely overhauled.

The residential areas, seen at their best, are grass-carpeted leafy arcadian counterpoints whose commodious and well-equipped wooden-framed houses along spacious tree-lined boulevards domesticise the symbols of local government and church, while the naturalistic park systems complement the nostalgia for a vanishing Jeffersonian myth.

These themes of new frontiers, colonisation, instant history and flexibility, linked to an easy-found manipulation of available technology, suggest a broad strategy for today's burgeoning urban populations, often without hope and totally alienated from any significant role in the reconstruction of society. The intricate *ex novo* urban mechanisms of the 19th century, in which the engineer emerges as a noble savage, suggest an urban archaeology of peeling *décollage* which continues to the present, complete with its own mechanistic cycle of growth, redundancy and replacement, quite different from the typical European experience which, at its best, represents an uninterrupted history in stone dating back to the Roman castrum at the bend of the Po, the Rhine and the Danube, and which, according to Camillo Sitte's *fin-de-siècle* analysis, revealed an art of city building whereby each generation adapted to what was found, and thus produced a continuity of space, surface and structure whose hierarchies, symbolism and ritual offered a measure of comfort and security.

Successive generations of avant-garde European designers, armed with Utopian sociologies, have drawn ideological strength from the early Futurists' cathartic attempts at transposing the facts of the American experience into an idea for the city of the future, all the while giving vent to their frustrations at the supposed static state and *passéiste* cowardice of their own culture. Topped up by such post-Second World War erotic fall-out of the ongoing American scene as, for example, the activities at Cape Kennedy, the suburbs of Los Angeles, the basements at MIT, there remains a continuing seismographic willingness to transfer the experience of the 'great mechanised individuals', however squalid the reality, into a completely renovated sensitiveness.

It is a matter of paradox, therefore, that while Marinetti in 1909 was publishing his ideological *Futurist Manifesto*, Daniel Burnham, with measured calm and with the backing of the Merchants' Club, was offering the tantalising image of a neoclassic collage, with many quotations from Haussmann's Paris, the imperial Roman fora, and other high points of European urban culture, which would provide respectability and civic pride to the frontiersman of Chicago. Born in a flash, due to the accidents of intercontinental transportation, with its destined topological organisation intact, and developed as a self-regulating interchange valve of the greatest mechanical efficiency, from the very beginning Chicago already possessed the basic hardware and Dionysian qualities of Sant'Elia's version for Milan 2000.

Circling the loop of the screeching overhead railways which branched out into the region in all directions, and looking down at the tumultuous, active, mobile and everywhere dynamic centre of a vast distribution system, which consisted of broad gridded avenues, commuting railways and expanding electric streetcar networks, on to its re-ordered crust which contained, some 410 feet (125 metres) below (so as not to interfere with future underground railways and access facilities which have since been realised), the recently opened service tunnel which was silently and automatically transferring packaged goods between the world's largest railway network and the busiest in land port facilities, delivering coal and hauling ashes from the light-framed, bold and simple skyscrapers to fill in future lakeshore parks, an early settler of the region might well reflect on Burnham's proposals. During a single lifetime he had watched a small settlement which as late as 1832 had consisted of a cabin, a store, two taverns and the derelict remains of the second Fort Dearborn, become the world's fourth largest city with a population of 2 million, surviving a great conflagration which had reduced its centre and most populated residential areas in 1871. He could reminisce with pride that, under the guidance of the

Greetings from Chicago
Gruss aus Chicago

. Jack'Knife" Bridge over Chicago River near
Jackson Blvd. built by the Scherzer Rolling
Lift Bridge Co. (Bridge open)
„Aufklapp"-Bruecke ueber den Chicago Fluss.
(Bruecke offen)

The drama of the technological display of the machine-
city metropolis are the 'jack-knife' bridges that lift to allow
freight barges to move along the Chicago River.

city engineer, Ellis S Chesbrough, he had literally helped to raise this city 8 feet (2.5 metres) out of the mud of the stagnant reeking creek named by the Indians Checagua (meaning wild onion), had reached out into the lake for a supply of fresh drinking water in a daring tunnelling feat which was the wonder of its time. He had helped straighten its river and, to avoid further pollution of the lake, had reversed its flow in a massive earth-moving venture which had rivalled that of the Panama Canal, a river which, with its systems of tunnels permitting uninterrupted access of trams, wagons and pedestrians to the business centre, with its lifting, swivelling and jack-knifing bridges, had become a vast machine. The clusters of activity which lined its banks, supported by an immense railway network, included grain elevators hovering over tracks, trains and sailing ships, rolling mills organised on an imperial scale, combing Lake Superior ore, Pennsylvania coal and Michigan limestone, and lumber distributing yards along special slips, attended by planing mills, furniture factories, wagon and shipbuilding yards. [...]

Tunnels Under The Lake
Having grown to a population of 200,000 in a single generation, Chicago was great, prosperous and happy in all things, with the paradoxical exceptions that it was set in a soggy marshland, was cut off from its hinterland, lacked culture and, with Lake Michigan's tantalisingly fresh, cool and crystal clear water constantly in view, it had not the one great essential – pure water. It was decreed in 1855 that, stuck in the mud without benefit of drainage or sewers or reliable paving, the city should jack itself up to a more salubrious level. A European traveller, marvelling at the ingenuity by which the whole city was raised,

building by building and block by block, streets re-aligned, buildings moved, drainage and new pavements laid, reported: *A gigantic hotel five storeys high of solid masonry was raised 42 feet (13 metres) and new foundations built below. People were in it all the time, coming and going, eating and sleeping; the whole business of the hotel proceeding without interruption. Never a day passed when I did not meet one or more houses shifting their quarters. One day I met nine.'*

'Parks first and museums and libraries will follow' was the motto as a greenbelt of parks and boulevards was laid out to encircle the built-up area, linked to the principal commuting stations for accessibility and thus compensating for a generation's neglect. Circa 1871 the notes of an English traveller included: *'Lincoln Park, on the North Side, is perhaps the most striking and apparently magical of all the enterprises and improvements of the city. It is already very beautiful with a variety of surface and ornamentation most wonderful, when we remember that scarcely five years ago the spot was a dreary waste of drifting sand and unsightly weeds ... the present entrance to it is a little depressing, being through a cemetery, for those old settlers are fast being unsettled and re-established elsewhere. Even the dead must "move on" in Chicago.'*

Thick and slimy, with the miles of sewage discharged into it, with the hundreds of tugs and lake craft that ploughed its surface, and the refuse and offal from numberless slaughterhouses, the currentless Chicago river discoloured the lake. To make matters worse, as cold weather approached, millions of infinitesimal fishes sought the enclosure near shore and, alive and swimming in the foul liquid, found their way into the city's reservoirs. To taste, smell and bath in fishy liquid, which made the goblets look dirty, was too great a torment to be borne. Ladies complained that avaricious milkmen forgot to take the fish out of the lactal fluid, and wicked liquor dealers were caught in the act of adulterating their goods, pickled minnows being frequently found in their best brands. Thus Chicago water became the butt for jokes all over the country, to the no small mortification of the city's citizens.

The will and determination was there and it was not long before Ellis Chesbrough, by then the city engineer, surveying all the practical alternatives, conceived the idea of constructing a tunnel 2 miles (3.2 kilometres) in length beneath the bed of Lake Michigan which would literally tap the lake bottom to ensure against the impurities from the murky influx and sheltering fish, and through which fresh water could be conveyed into the city's reservoirs. Pronounced by engineers of both hemispheres to be the greatest project ever entered upon by man, it was noted at the inauguration ceremonies on 17 March 1864: 'Every man participating feeling aware of the great undertaking upon which they were entering and the disgrace which failure would bring upon themselves and the city.' [...]

Five feet (1.5 metres) in diameter on the inside, the tunnel was just wide enough for two miners working on the excavation, followed by the masons who lined it, using 'Illinois brick of the usual size laid in cement': progressing at the rate of 14 to 20 feet (4.25 to 6 metres) per day on a 24-hour basis. Rails for a submarine railway were laid down and small cars placed upon them to carry the excavated clay, propelled by two small mules of very picturesque appearance wearing small lamps upon their collars. [...]

Meanwhile, on 24 July 1865, the 98 foot (30 metre) diameter and 40 foot (12 metre) high crib was launched, composed of three hardwood membranes, each of distinct structure, bolted together, caulked and tarred like the hulk of a vessel, with outer armour to protect it from ice and vessels to a depth of 12 feet (3.6 metres) below the surface of the water, and with no expense spared.

***

Tunnels Under The River

A distressed citizen writing in 1856 summed up the bustle and impatience of an isolated centre city whose bridges swivelled open for interminable periods as 300 vessels arrived in a single 12-hour period, passing at the rate of two a minute during the peak hours: 'People jump on and jump off as long as the policemen will let them; those that are on (the bridge), horse and foot, quietly stand still and are ground round to the other side ... While the process is going on, a row of vehicles and impatience frequently accumulates that is quite terrific. I have seen a closely packed column a quarter of a mile (400 metres) in length, every individual driver looking as if he thought he could have turned the bridge 16 times while he was waiting.'

Using their newfound tunnelling expertise, the city engineers designed and built a series of tunnels under the Chicago River, including those at Washington Street (1869) and LaSalle Street (1871): 'Both of these submarine thoroughfares have two roads each for vehicles, and one for pedestrians, the latter entirely separate from the former. They are kept constantly lighted with gas, and the passage through them is by no means unpleasant. At the time of the fire, when the bridges were swept away by the flames, great crowds of people surged through them, and thousands found shelter in their depths from the fiery element.'

Freight Tunnels

Unknown and unseen, 40 feet (12 metres) below the surface there exists a complete network of freight tunnels that covers almost every part of the downtown area. Franchised in 1899, in the early days of telephones and telegraph, it was meant to provide a means of running wires below streets without the necessity of continually tearing up the surface. An amended franchise was obtained by the Illinois Tunnel Company in 1903, permitting the tunnels to be used for transportation of merchandise and packages, including the necessary connections to loading and unloading stations along the route, linking systems with railway freight terminals, large loading commercial buildings and public freight stations. By 1909 it was substantially complete. There were 62 miles (100 kilometres) in operation, including 150 electric locomotives powered by overhead trolley and wire, and 3,300 cars on 2 foot (60 centimetre) gauge track, in oval sections bored out of blue clay with a 1 foot (30 centimetre) concrete lining and inside dimensions of 6 feet by 7.5 feet (1.8 metres by 2.28 metres), protected by an elaborate system of electric pumps, pipes and sumps, through which any accumulations of water were raised to the sewers above. It was electrically lighted and a central train dispatcher controlled all movements by means of some 300 telephones distributed at strategic points throughout the system. A signal system with automatic blocks was developed to accommodate 734 intersections, many of them four-way. Emerging from nowhere, the cars were automatically raised in elevation shafts to the basements and upper floors of the facilities served without the necessity of unloading or re-handling, and trains were made up of cars that descended from shipping rooms above. This ingenious automatic network became an integral part of Chicago's great scheme of transportation, relieving street congestion. (By the mid-1920s it was handling the equivalent of 5,000 surface truckloads of goods per day.) In addition to linking the wharves, warehouses and railway depots to each other, thus making it unnecessary to negotiate the crowded streets above, coal, mail and packaged goods were distributed to most of the buildings within the central area. Ashes, garbage and the debris from construction sites were hauled away and used to fill emerging lakeshore park areas. Many commercial buildings, hotels and theatres, tapping into the cool dry air down below, were able to air-condition their premises. [...]

Union Stock Yards

Enveloped by the rancid, sensual and strong odour, the thick, oily, black smoke from the chimneys, and the restless lowing and grunting of 20,000 head of livestock, the South Side Elevated screeched through the maze of pens and barns. The Union Stock Yards was a city in itself, occupying one square mile (300 hectares) of land laid out on a grid pattern with streets, alleys, ingenious services and a 'Broadway', served by a canal, highways and railways bringing livestock from as far away as the Rockies and Texas, and shipping the packed meat in refrigerated cars. Attended by hotels, restaurants and an exchange, the cluster of sinister packing houses where 6 million hogs alone were received in 1909, operated with terrifying efficiency, there being nothing wasted except the whistle of a beast when its throat was cut. [...]

Returning home to Packingtown through the endless vista of 'ugly and dirty little wooden buildings' which had been hastily assembled by the universal balloon frame developed to accommodate half a million new settlers every decade: 'in a cold-blooded impersonal way without a pretence at apology, like some horrible crime committed in a dungeon all unseen and unheeded, buried out of sight and of memory', our settler might be forgiven for sympathising with the hogs who had come so innocently, so very trustingly and were so very human in their protests and so perfectly within their rights, squealing as the life blood ebbed away as they vanished with a splash into a huge vat of boiling water. [...]

Surface Transit

By the time of Daniel Burnham's Plan for Chicago of 1909, transit systems were pouring 750,000 people per day into the one mile (2.6 kilometre) square of the Loop. The ability to absorb 2 million people in half a century, living in relatively low densities spread out over a vast terrain, was in no small measure due to an efficiently evolved transit system with a volatile rate of redundancy, necessary to complement the activities generated by the pressure of the intersecting national routes. [...]

Chicago   Lumber Yards and Grain Elevators on Chicago River

Nature's metropolis: lumber yards
and grain silos store the harvest from
the nation's forest and farms.

The great Chicago stock
yards – the food distribution
centre of the nation.

Wooden plank roads consisting of simple boards nailed to long timbers were laid along the marshy routes of a horse-drawn street railway which was making 400 trips per day along 18 different lines in 1856. Travelling at 6 miles (9.5 kilometres) per hour, the railway made it possible to live well removed from downtown areas by doubling the radius of settlement, and gave rise to fashionable neighbourhoods along the lakeshore and edges of the city. Constantly extending to serve the growing population, it remained in service until electric cars replaced the horses on established routes in the 1890s. But it was the cable car, developed in California by a wire manufacturer (Andrew Hallidie) as a method of climbing the alpine grades of downtown San Francisco, which, ingeniously adapted to one of the flattest cities on earth as the largest cable system America ever had, set the tone for future developments. Inaugurated in January 1882, before a crowd of 300,000 spectators, 'a team of eight horses drew a train of two grip cars and seven trailers down town to Madison Avenue ... and Chicago had become the second city in the world to be served by cable traction'.

By 1894, the river was tunnelled, 86 miles (140 kilometres) of cables were laid and 450 grip cars were driven by 11 power plants and served by storage and repair bars of ingenious design, as citizens counted their blessings: 'The value of removing from the street the voidings of 2 to 3,000 horses is a matter not to be lightly estimated in point of health. The constant clatter of hooves on the pavement is supplemented by the quiet gliding of a train scarcely audible from the sidewalk.'

The cable cars converged to make a loop around the business section before making return runs into the ever-receding residential areas at the edge of the city, their expansion carefully followed by shrewd financiers, one of whom observed: 'Only let me know six weeks in advance where the city railway intends building a cable line and I will make an independent fortune every time.'

Reaching their peak in October 1893, when 700,000 passengers were carried to the Chicago Day at the Columbian Exposition, their high cost of maintenance, resulting in inefficient service, relatively low speeds 10 to 12 miles (16 to 19 kilometres) per hour, and the advent of electric traction brought about their demise. [...]

The electric streetcar, with its characteristic overhead power line, introduced in the late 1880s, despite heavy investment in the cable car, quickly took up the load, extending the field and following the mile, half mile and principal diagonal avenues of the universal grid. Its 1,000 miles (1,600 kilometres) of track became the largest unified system ever known. Nearly everyone was within walking distance of some line or the grid of shops which lined its path. 'Early passengers often complained about the conditions of the first Elevated. The engines had extremely short range and had to make frequent stops for refuelling. The wooden open-ended coaches were badly heated in winter and seemed to collect heat in summer. Still, the elevated trains could move faster than surface cars since grade crossing dangers could be disregarded.'

The blunt sawn-off coal-burning engines, of which an 1893 commuter complained, were soon replaced by electrification. The El, cutting through old-established neighbourhoods, reached out diagonally to municipalise the prairies as a fast system superimposed on the open-ended surface net of electric trams, giving rise to densely settled corridors along its path. [...]

left: Cut-away view of Chicago's subway in the Central Business District. Shown are the main tubes: the downtown centre platform (which is 3,500 feet (1,066 metres) long); the two-way escalators to the mezzanines with store connections; and the State Street surface level. Features of the subway are ventilation, illumination, escalators, safety, comfort.

right: Marina City (1964), Bertrand Goldberg's vision of metropolitan architecture, spiralling car ramps from ship berth and street to telecommunication towers at the top.

The Loop today stands isolated, surrounded by successive rings of redundant industrial waste, random patches of slickness and deterioration, garish new rebuilding, Lake Shore Drive properties and uniform tenement districts. Not unlike a middle-aged citadel, its corners are flanked by such mega-symbols of 1920s solidity and permanence as the world's largest commercial structure (the Merchandise Mart), the busiest post office sorting station (which, sitting atop a railway siding, swallows the principal east/ west expressway and has a roof which was designed as an aeroplane landing field), the world's largest inland pier, and the Field Museum and attachments which bear witness to the continuing background tempo. Frayed edges and entrails reveal the anatomy of its multilayered section which, plunging storeys deep into the earth, has been further tuned in recent decades by lower-level expressways gathering up traffic and service vehicles, and a subway system, complete with accessible sewers, water supply, electric cables, communication lines, threaded through an already complex matrix, giving access to public and commercial buildings, and eventually to the commuting railway stations and massive underground parking facilities.

This 'city as a building' stands amid a mass of heterogeneous objects which, although no longer impacting on each other, still retain the quality of some previous mechanical and functional construction. It is a masterpiece of junk culture whose unexpected lustre, fractures, misalignments and fascinating details invoke an inverted aesthetic acceptance.

Daniel Burnham, looking over his shoulder at the river frontages at Algiers, Budapest, Geneva and Paris, and with an eye to easing the congestion, suggested: 'The boulevards should extend from the mouth of the river along the north and south branches and on both sides ... they should be raised above the normal traffic level in order to afford greater facility to circulation and to allow warehouses to be constructed below the roadway ... apart from practical advantages they would become the most delightful route to the lake.'

Wacker Drive was the only proposed double-deck avenue completed, in 1926, replacing the bustle of South Water Street (the principal centre for wholesale produce and marketing), and set the tone for further multi-purpose traffic improvements. A school textbook in 1930 described it: 'It is a two level street. The upper one is 110 feet (33.5 metres) wide and is for general traffic. The lower is 130 feet (40 metres) wide and is used by heavy commercial traffic. This level connects the warehouses and the industrial and terminal district on the west side with the boat and rail terminals and the industrial district east of Michigan Avenue.'

Lower Wacker Drive today is part of the typical experience of negotiating Chicago. Its murky subterranean quality amid lower level servicing of office buildings, newspaper plants, hotels, its parking facilities, restaurants and bars, are offset by the brightness of the river which it follows.

The underground rapid transit facility, the first phase of which was completed in 1943, and which continues to expand out from the centre of the city, is eventually meant to replace the hundred-year-old elevated system.

In 1963, a loose 3-mile (4.8-kilometre) mesh of expressways tying into the massive inter-state structure and linking with the Outer Drive 'Parkway' was begun, the objective being to overlay the hierarchical mile, half mile, quarter mile road system with rapid automobile access to every part of the metropolis. A north/south connection 6 miles (9.6 kilometres) west of the Loop, linking the two airports, is now being planned to complete the system. While the design of the expressways largely conforms to Federal Government standards, local distinctive features include a central median strip reserved for subways producing a characteristic interchange point between bus stops at the bridge level via ramped snorkel to train platform within the cut of the expressway.

Peter Smithson has spoken of the expressway fix as a river with grassy banks whose measure and interval would provide the scale and identity for a modern metropolis. The example of Chicago suggests, as in all major hardware systems, that the pleasure and freedom provided by a complete open-ended system is more than paid for by the brutal scars left on the resulting land castle.

This *fin-de-siècle* system of throw-aways, which includes mouldering warehouses, abandoned lofts, bridges which remain permanently open, wharves, basins, disused railway properties, partially filled tunnels, flop-houses, graffiti covering old walls, vacant lots and the shadowy people who flit through, contains the seed of a new beginning. Alas, save for Marina City, whose 'village green' and extraordinary section so nicely capture the ambience of the place and give some direction for the future, new development, piecemeal and mean, suggests that today's generation has not the ability to make large plans to inspire the future in keeping with the giant bones and sane topology of its original anatomy.

Chicago is only half a city. The great linear park, with its Chinese wall of affluence which offers a one-room-deep view of the broad expanse of Lake Michigan and the parallel forest preserve lands some 10 to 12 miles (16 to 19 kilometres) inland, suggests a linear structure as yet untapped. The dominant reading, however, is that of a vast tartan grid composed of hierarchical bands of services, communications, commercial and industrial land use, each with its own scale, geometry, attachments and linkages, some in the process of development, others rapidly becoming redundant, and others not as yet invented, superimposed on an abstract field of residential land use. The build-up, when seen in plan, is not unlike a series of transparent overlays suggesting a chronological catalogue of the working parts of a brave new world. The lines of energy and communication define the neighbourhoods which contain the isolated symbols of religion, education and civic authority. Marinetti's 'mechanised man', without the benefit of a Utopian socialist vision, is destined to live in an energised Boccioni field among persistent symbols of universal motion, often embittered by dissatisfaction, ranging from impatience to nihilism, at the squalor of a reality which, in rapid succession, consists of negotiating the broad tumultuous industrial bands, the vast railway marshalling yards, passing under the cacophony of the elevated railways and looking down into the expressway 'fixes' along streets of infinite length and endless repetition. The vignettes include negotiating the metal catwalks at the local E1, the high-speed conveyor belts at the subway stop, the swaying hangers on the local bus, or chancing your lot at the nearest expressway feeder lane, where, encapsulated, you move along the elevated rail, the giant tubes, the stoplight half-mile (0.8 kilometre) shopping street, or the open cuts.

* * *

From Alvin Boyarsky, 'Chicago à la Carte', *Architectural Design*, vol 11, December 1970, John Wiley & Sons Ltd (London), excerpts from pp 595– 640. The Publisher wishes to thank Nicholas Boyarsky for his assistance in relation to this article. © Alvin Boyarsky Memorial Trust. Images: pp 49, 51, 55, 57, Alvin Boyarsky Archive © Alvin Boyarsky Memorial Trust.

Life in the Metropolis or The Culture of Congestion

Rem Koolhaas

As the original leader published in *AD* states:

Rem Koolhaas uses Manhattan as a model to outline fundamental attributes of high-density, high-rise urbanity. He shows Coney Island as the test-bed for Manhattanism – a surreal environment to which New Yorkers escaped from the congestion of their city to experiment with alternative lifestyles within the same context of congestion. Entrepreneurs rapidly implemented these experiments: skyscrapers became multi-layered shells with each layer providing the opportunity for living out independent – even opposed – lifestyles. This promise of metropolitanism – a totally fabricated world within which any number of opposing views could co-exist – needlessly failed, he observes, due to a profound lack of nerve. The work of OMA attempts a recovery of that nerve.

'Why do we have a mind, if not to get our own way'

Dostoevsky

Somewhere in the 19th century certain parts of the globe – negligible in terms of surface – developed an unprecedented condition: through the simultaneous explosion of modern technologies and human population on their limited territories, they found themselves supporting the mutant form of human coexistence that is known as Metropolis. The Metropolis invalidates all the previous systems of articulation and differentiation that have traditionally guided the design of cities. The Metropolis annuls the previous history of architecture. But if the Metropolis is a true mutation, it can be assumed that it has also generated its own Urbanism: an architecture that is exclusively concerned with the 'splendeurs et misères' of the Metropolitan Condition; an architecture with its own theorems, laws, methods, breakthroughs and achievements that has remained largely outside the field of vision of official architecture and criticism, both unable to admit a fundamental rupture that would make their own existence precarious.

Manhattan

By an unspoken consensus, Manhattan is considered the archetype of the Metropolitan Condition, the point where the two are often interchangeable. Manhattan's spectacular growth coincided exactly with the definition of the concept of Metropolis itself. Manhattan represents the apotheosis of the ideal of density per se, both of population and of infrastructures; its architecture promotes a state of congestion on all possible levels, and exploits this congestion to inspire and support particular forms of social intercourse that together form a unique *culture of congestion*. The following episodes of Manhattan's history circumscribe such an Urbanism that is specifically Metropolitan.

Coney Island

Coney Island is a clitoral appendage at the mouth of New York Harbor, discovered one day before Manhattan itself. From 1600 to 1800 the shape of the peninsula changed under the combined impact of natural forces (shifting sands) and human intervention (the cutting of a canal that turned Coney actually into an island). These modifications together followed a 'design' that turned the island more and more into a miniature of Manhattan.

From the mid-19th century, the obstacles of geography that had so far ensured relative inaccessibility to the island, were one by one transcended by new transportation technologies. In 1883 the Brooklyn Bridge removed the last obstruction that had kept Manhattan's inhabitants in place. From then on they escaped to the Atlantic beach in a weekly Exodus that concentrated more than 1 million people on the minuscule island on a good day.

The virgin nature that is the destination of this frantic migration, disappeared under the onslaught of the unprecedented hyper-density. As compensation for this loss of nature, a battery of new technologies was developed to provide equivalent sensations on a scale that was commensurate with the new Metropolitan numbers. Coney Island became a laboratory of the collective unconscious: the themes and tactics of its experimentation were later to reappear in Manhattan.

Cow

The first natural element to be converted was the cow. Since no amount of real cows could deal with the insatiable thirst of the million, a machine was designed and built: the Inexhaustible Cow. Its milk is superior to the natural product in terms of quantity, regularity of flow, hygiene and controllable temperature.

Bathing

Similar conversions follow in rapid succession. Since the total surface of the beaches and the total length of the surfline were finite and given, it followed with mathematical certainty that the hundreds of thousands of visitors could not all find a place to spread out in the sand, let alone succeed in reaching the water within the limit of a single day.

Toward 1890, the introduction of electricity in this impasse made it possible to create a second daytime – intense electric lights were placed at regular intervals along the surfline, so that the sea could be enjoyed in a truly Metropolitan shift system. Those unable to reach the water in the day were given a 12-hour extension. What is unique in Coney Island – and this syndrome of the Irresistible Synthetic sets the tone for later events in Manhattan – is that this illumination was not seen as a second-rate experience, but that its very artificiality was advertised as an attraction in itself: Electric Bathing.

Horses

The preferred activity of the happy few who had enjoyed the island in its virgin state had been horseback riding. Of course, that experience was unthinkable on the scale of the new masses. Real horses in adequate numbers would require a separate infrastructure as big as the island itself. Also, the ability to ride a horse was a form of 'knowledge' not available to the proletariat that had made the island its playground. In the mid-1890s George Tilyou laid out a mechanical track that leads through Coney's natural landscapes, along the oceanfront and across a number of man-made obstacles. He named it 'Steeplechase' … 'an automatic racetrack with gravitation as its motive power … Its horses resemble in size and model the track racer. Staunchly built, they are to a certain extent under the control of the rider, who can accelerate the speed by the manner in which he utilises his weight and his position on the ascending and descending grades.'

Steeplechase combined in a single attraction the provision of entertainment with a form of emancipation through machinery – the elite experience of horseback riding democratised through technology.

Love

Two years later, even the most intimate processes of human nature were converted. It is often alleged that the Metropolis creates loneliness and alienation. Coney Island responded to this problem with the 'Barrels of Love'.

Two horizontal cylinders – mounted in line – revolve in opposite directions. At either end a narrow staircase leads up to the entrance; one feeds men into the apparatus, the other women. It is impossible to remain standing in the machine, men and women are thrown on top of each other. The unrelenting rotation then creates synthetic intimacy between couples who would never have met without its assistance.

If necessary, this intimacy could be further processed in the 'Tunnels of Love', an artificial mountain next to the couple-forming machine. The freshly formed pairs board a small boat that disappears inside a system of dark tunnels where complete obscurity ensues – or at least – visual privacy. The rocking movement of the boats on the shallow water was supposed to increase sensuality.

Conclusion: 1

With the sequence of: Cow, Electric Bathing, Steeplechase and Barrels of Love, all the natural elements that had once defined the attraction of the island, were systematically replaced – a new kind of machinery that converted the original nature into an intricate simulacrum of nature, a compensatory technical service.

This technology is not the agent of objective and quantifiable improvements – such as raising the levels of illumination, controlling temperature, etc – it is a superior substitute for the 'natural' reality that is being depleted by the sheer density of human consumers. Together, this apparatus constitutes an alternative reality that is invented and designed, instead of accidental and arbitrary.

Since this 'instrumentarium' of true modernity creates states and situations that have never existed before, it can never escape its aspect of fabrication – of being the result of human fantasy.

The Metropolis is irrevocably the resultant of such identifiable mental constructions, and that is the source of its fundamental 'otherness' from all previous Urbanisms.

Elevator

In 1853, at Manhattan's first World's Fair, the invention that would, more than any other, become the 'sign' of the Metropolitan Condition, was introduced to the public in a singularly theatrical format.

Elisha Otis, the inventor of the elevator, mounts a platform. The platform ascends. When it has reached its highest level, an assistant presents Otis with a dagger on a velvet cushion. The inventor takes the knife and attacks what appears the crucial component of his invention: the cable that has hoisted the platform upward and that now prevents its fall. Otis cuts the cable; nothing happens to platform or inventor.

Invisible safety-catches prevent the platform from rejoining the surface of the earth. They represent the essence of Otis's invention: the ability to prevent the elevator from crashing. Like the elevator, each technical invention is pregnant with a double image: the spectre of its possible failure. The way to avert that phantom disaster is as important as the original invention itself.

Otis introduced a theme which would become a leitmotif in the performance of the Metropolis: a spectacle that features a neck and neck race between an astronomical increase in the potential for disaster that is only just exceeded by a still more astronomical increase in the potential to avert disaster.

Elevator 2

From the 1870s, the elevator became the great emancipator of all the floors above the ground floor. Otis's apparatus recovered the innumerable planes that had so far been purely speculative, and revealed their superiority in the first Metropolitan paradox: the greater the distance from the earth – the more unnatural the location – the closer the communication with what remains of nature (ie, light, air, views, etc). The elevator is the ultimate self-fulfilling prophecy: the further it travels upward, the more undesirable the circumstances it leaves behind.

Through the mutual reinforcement of the elevator and the steel frame (the latter with its uncanny ability to support the newly identified territories without itself taking any space), any given site in the Metropolis could now be multiplied ad infinitum, a proliferation of floor space that was called Skyscraper, prime instrument of the architecture of density.

Theorem

In 1909 the 'layering' of the world's surface through the action of the elevator, was posited in the form of a visual theorem that appeared in the popular press. A slender steel structure supports 84 horizontal planes, all the size of the original plot. Each of these artificial levels is treated as a virgin *site* to establish a private domain around a single country house and its attendant facilities such as stables, servants' cottages, gazebos, etc, all implanted in an airborne meadow.

Emphatic permutations of the styles of the villas suggested that each of the elevator stops corresponded to a different lifestyle – an implied ideological variation – all of them supported with complete neutrality by the steel-frame rack. Life inside this building is fractured to the extent that it could not conceivably be part of a single scenario: on the 82nd floor a donkey shrinks back from the void, on the 81st a cosmopolitan couple hail a plane.

The privacy and isolation of each of the aerial plots seemingly conflicts with the fact that, together, they form a single building. In fact, the diagram implies that the structure is successful exactly to the extent that the individuality of each plot is respected. The structure 'frames' their coexistence without interfering with their contents. The Building is an accumulation of privacies.

Only five of the 84 floors are visible on the drawing. Hidden in the clouds other activities occupy other plots; the use of each platform can never be known in advance of its construction. Villas go up and collapse, other facilities replace them, but that does not affect the framework.

100 Storey Building

In 1911 a project for a '100 Storey Building' was unveiled that incorporated many of the breakthroughs which, only two years earlier, seemed entirely theoretical. The Building was a straightforward extrusion of the block it occupies multiplied by 100.

The lower third of the Building is devoted to industry, the middle part to business, the upper part to living. On every 20th storey is a public plaza that occupies a whole floor and articulates the demarcation between the different functional sectors: a 'general market' on the 20th, a cluster of theatres on the 40th, a 'shopping district' on the 60th, a hotel on the 80th, and an 'amusement park, roof garden and swimming pool' on the roof.

At first sight, the rooms inside this structure are conventional, equipped with fireplaces and wood panelling. But they are also equipped with seven outlets for 'temperature and atmosphere regulating tubes' which demonstrate once more, the anti-pragmatic, in fact, poetic usage of the Metropolitan infrastructure: 'A = salt air, B = fresh air, C = dry salt air, D = dry fresh air, E = medicated air (to suit disease), F = temperature switch, GHI = perfumes'.

The outlets of this techno-psychic battery are the keys to a scale of synthetic experiences that ranges from the hedonistic to the hyper-medical. Some rooms can be 'set' on Florida, others on the Canadian Rocky Mountains. The perfumes and the medicinal air suggest even more abstract destinations. In the 100 Storey Building each cubicle is equipped to pursue its private existential journey.

The building has become a laboratory for emotional and intellectual adventure; the fact that it is implanted in Manhattan has become – almost – immaterial.

Downtown Athletic Club

Within 20 years, the promise of the 100 Storey Building – that of a skyscraper fully conquered by higher forms of social intercourse than mere business – was realised in 1931 with the Downtown Athletic Club.

All the latent potential of the skyscraper as a Type is exploited in a masterpiece of the Culture of Congestion, a Constructivist Social Condenser materialised in Manhattan. It is one of the rare 20th-century buildings that is truly revolutionary: it offers a full inventory of the fundamental modifications – technical and psychological – that are caused by life

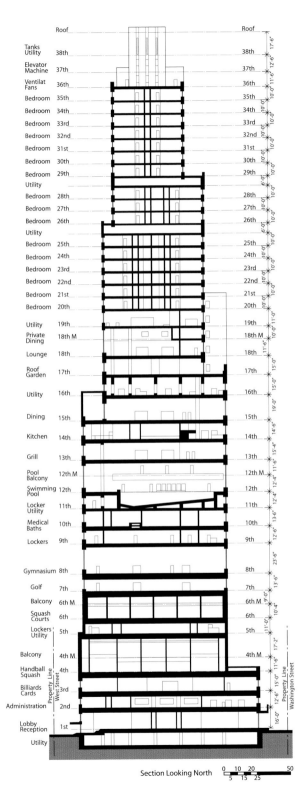

Roof ... Roof ... 17'-6"

Tanks
Utility 38th ... 38th ... 12'-6"

Elevator
Machine 37th ... 37th ... 11'-6"

Ventilat
Fans 36th ... 36th ... 10'-0"

Bedroom 35th ... 35th ... 10'-0"
Bedroom 34th ... 34th ... 10'-0"
Bedroom 33rd ... 33rd ... 10'-0"
Bedroom 32nd ... 32nd ... 10'-0"
Bedroom 31st ... 31st ... 10'-0"
Bedroom 30th ... 30th ... 10'-0"
Bedroom 29th ... 29th ... 6'-0"
Utility
Bedroom 28th ... 28th ... 10'-0"
Bedroom 27th ... 27th ... 10'-0"
Bedroom 26th ... 26th ... 6'-0"
Utility
Bedroom 25th ... 25th ... 10'-0"
Bedroom 24th ... 24th ... 10'-0"
Bedroom 23rd ... 23rd ... 10'-0"
Bedroom 22nd ... 22nd ... 10'-0"
Bedroom 21st ... 21st ... 10'-0"
Bedroom 20th ... 20th ... 10'-0"

Utility 19th ... 19th ... 11'-0"
Private
Dining 18th M ... 18th M ... 10'-0"
Lounge 18th ... 18th ... 11'-6"
Roof
Garden 17th ... 17th ... 15'-0"

Utility 16th ... 16th ... 15'-0"

Dining 15th ... 15th ... 19'-0"

Kitchen 14th ... 14th ... 14'-6"

Grill 13th ... 13th ... 15'-4"
Pool
Balcony 12th M ... 12th M ... 11'-6"
Swimming
Pool 12th ... 12th ... 12'-4"
Locker
Utility 11th ... 11th ... 12'-4"
Medical
Baths 10th ... 10th ... 13'-6"
Lockers 9th ... 9th ... 12'-6"

Gymnasium 8th ... 8th ... 23'-6"

Golf 7th ... 7th ... 13'-6"
Balcony 6th M ... 6th M ... 9'-0"
Squash
Courts 6th ... 6th ... 10'-4"
Lockers
Utility 5th ... 5th ... 11'-0"

Balcony 4th M ... 4th M ... 17'-2"
Handball
Squash 4th ... 4th ... 11'-6"
Billiards
Cards 3rd ... 3rd ... 15'-0"
Administration 2nd ... 2nd ... 12'-6"
Lobby
Reception 1st ... 16'-0"
Utility

Property Line / West Street

Property Line / Washington Street

Section Looking North

0 10 20   50
   5 15 25

Section through the
Downtown Athletic Club
shows the strange vertical
juxtaposition of a residential
hotel, swimming pool, boxing
ring, oyster bar and indoor
miniature golf course.

in the Metropolis, and that separate this century from all previous ones. Its existence allows a spectrum of experiences on a single place that was previously unthinkable.

The Club – externally indistinguishable from the other skyscrapers in the Wall Street area – is located on the Hudson near Battery Park on a lot 23 metres (75 feet) wide and 54 metres (177 feet) deep. The Club is the 1909 theorem made concrete: a sequence of superimposed platforms that each repeat the original rectangle of the site, connected by a battery of 13 elevators concentrated along the north wall of the structure.

'The plan is of primary importance, because on the floor are performed all the activities of the occupants …', that is how Raymond Hood (the most theoretical of Manhattan's architects) defined Manhattan's interpretation of Functionalism: each plan as a collage of functions that describes on the synthetic platforms an episode of Metropolitan ritual. Each of the rectangles of the Downtown Athletic Club is such a scenario with a highly suggestive – if abstract – plot.

Each floor is a separate instalment of a complex intrigue – their sequence as random as only the elevator man can make them – this form of architecture is a form of Modernistic writing: the planning of choreography of mankind through experimental techno-psychic apparatus designed by themselves to celebrate their own redesign.

The lower 15 floors of the building are accessible only to men. Their sequence from the ground to the top corresponds to an increasing refinement and artifice. From the 17th to the 18½th floor, the men, perfected in the lower floors, are allowed to communicate with the opposite sex in the dining room, the roof terrace and the dance floor. The final 20 floors are devoted to hotel accommodation.

Floors 7, 9, 11 and 12 deserve special analysis for their extreme daring. Emerging from the elevator on the 9th floor, the visitor – probably a Wall Street stockbroker – finds himself in a vestibule that leads directly to a locker room at the centre of the floor (where there is no daylight). There he undresses, puts on gloves and enters an adjoining space that is equipped for boxing and wrestling. But on the southern side, the locker room is also served by a small oyster bar.

Eating oysters with boxing gloves, naked, on the 9th floor – such is the plot of this floor – the 20th century in action.

The 10th floor is devoted to preventive medicine. On one side of a large dressing room and lounge an array of body manipulations – sections for massage and rubbing, an 8-bed station for artificial sunbathing (open to the river), a 10-bed rest area – is arranged around a Turkish bath. The south-east corner of the floor is a medical facility capable of treating five patients at once. A doctor is charged with the process of 'colonic irrigation' – the literal invasion of the human body with cultivated bacteria that modify and accelerate the natural metabolism of the human body.

This final step completes the sequence of radical intervention and voluntary self-experimentation initiated by such apparently innocent attractions as Coney Island's 'Barrels of Love'.

On the 12th floor, a swimming pool occupies almost the full rectangle. At night, it is illuminated by an underwater lighting system, so that the entire slab of water with its frenetic swimmers appears to float in space, between the electric scintillation of the Wall Street skyline.

Of all the floors, the Interior Golf Course is perhaps the most significant enterprise: an interior English garden landscape of small hills and valleys, a little river that curls across the rectangle, green grass (real), a bridge ... A mural extends the landscape toward a nebulous horizon, but the regular punctuation of the lighting fixtures on the ceiling reminds, irrevocably, of fabrication. The presence of the Golf Course argues that nature, obliterated by all the Metropolitan structures, will now be resurrected as merely one of the layers of the Metropolis. After its total eclipse, nature returns as one of the services of the Culture of Congestion.

Conclusion: 2

Through the medium of the Skyscraper, each site in the Metropolis accommodates – in theory at least – an unstable and unforeseeable combination of superimposed and simultaneous activities whose configuration is fundamentally beyond the control of architect or planner.

As a vehicle of Urbanism, the indeterminacy of the Skyscraper suggests that – in the Metropolis – no single specific *function* can be matched with a single *place*. Through this destabilisation it is possible to absorb the 'change that is life' by continuously rearranging functions on the individual platform in an incessant process of adaptation that does not affect the framework of the building itself.

Exteriors and interiors of such structures belong to two different kinds of architectures. The first – external – is only concerned with the appearance of the building as a more or less serene sculptural object, while the interior is in a constant state of flux – of themes, programmes, iconographies – with which the volatile metropolitan citizens, with their overstimulated nervous systems, combat the perpetual threat of ennui.

Radio City Music Hall

The application of technology at the service of metaphor occurs at a still more explicit level and on a larger scale than the Athletic Club in Radio City Music Hall, a theatre for 6,200.

It is 'a prototype of a strictly interior architecture inserted in the neutral envelope of Rockefeller Center. Its cosmogony was not invented by its official architects, but by their client, the impresario Samuel Rothafel, known as Roxy.

In the early 1930s a group of architects – among them Wallace Harrison – took Roxy on a European tour, all the way to Moscow, in an attempt to convert him to Modern Architecture. But Roxy remained indifferent to the antiseptic accommodations which modern architects had designed for the fundamentally irrational culture of the theatre.

---

overleaf: The *City of the Captive Globe* shows the Manhattan grid as an urban archipelago where each block acts as an artificial island of unique invention in a sea of traffic.

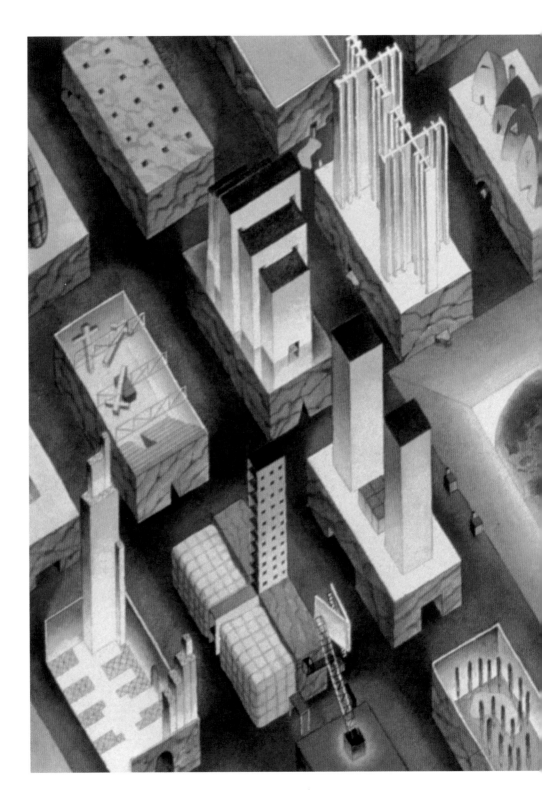

On his return to New York, he had a revelation when he watched a mid-Atlantic sunset. 'I didn't conceive of the idea. I dreamed it. I believe in creative dreams. The picture of Radio City Music Hall was complete and practically perfect in my mind before architects and artists put pen on drawing paper ... ' His theatre is to be a simulation of the spectacle he beheld from the railing of the ship: a sunset.

Roxy's architect dutifully executed the metaphorical theme. A vast ovoid space is covered with plaster 'rays' that extend across the ceiling of the entire theatre, embracing the audience like a firmament. The curtain is made of an especially developed synthetic fibre – so glittering that it outshines the real sun. When the lights are slowly dimmed, the impression of a sunset is inescapable.

But the lights have to go on again. And off again. There are three or four such cycles for each complete performance. If the metaphor is taken seriously, the audience lives through three or four accelerated days.

Then Roxy discovered that the air-conditioning system could be used for more creative purposes than simple cooling and heating – ie, to increase the density of metaphor in the auditorium. First he considered adding laughing gas to its atmosphere, so that his 6,200 clients would be transported to 'another world' where they would be more receptive to the impact of the movies. However, he desisted after urgent pleading by his lawyers, but only after substituting health-giving Ozone for the N_2O. Now his theatre combines 'Supertime' with 'Superhealth', a union that is caught perfectly in his advertisement 'A visit to Radio City Music Hall is as good as a month in the country ... '

Conclusion: 3

As in the example of Radio City Music Hall, planning in Manhattan consists of the imposition on the explosive substance of the Metropolis of metaphoric models – at once primitive and efficient – that replace literal organisation, impossible in any case, with a form of conceptual control.

Such hermetic, self-contained enclaves offer emotional shelter to the disinherited Metropolitan masses, ideal worlds removed in time and space, protected against the corrosion of everyday reality in their interior locations. These sub-Utopian fragments are all the more convincing having no territorial ambitions beyond occupying their interior allotments through a private hyper-density of symbolism and localised paroxysms of the particular. Together, such moments form a matrix of frivolity, a system of poetic formulas that replaces traditional quantifiable planning in favour of metaphoric planning.

Movement in the Metropolis becomes ideological navigation between the conflicting claims and promises of 'islands' of a metaphoric archipelago.

Postscript

The three episodes above present a provisional triangulation of a truly Metropolitan architecture. If they appear extravagant, or even unreal, that is only a sign of the narrowness of our architectural focus and of our refusal to admit that a fundamental break has occurred between traditional and modern Urbanisms.

These 'stories' describe a tradition of modernity that insists on systematically exploiting all available apparatus and all the fresh infrastructures of the age to establish fantasies as realities in the world. The cumulative effect of such scattered episodes, and no doubt the cause of the anxieties they inspire, is that they discredit the idea of reality as an immutable and indestructible presence – of reality as an ultimate safety net under our flawed acrobatic performances. Instead, the 'hysterical' structures of the Metropolis represent a free fall in the space of human imagination, a fall with unpredictable outcome, not even the certainty that it will end on the ground.

The true ambition of the Metropolis is to create a world totally fabricated by man, ie, to live *inside* fantasy. The responsibilities of a specifically Metropolitan architecture have increased correspondingly: to design those hermetic enclaves – bloated private realms – that comprise the Metropolis. Such an architecture not only creates the 'sets' of everyday life, but it also defines its contents with all possible means and disciplines such as literature, psychology, etc. Through the magical arrangement of human activities on all possible levels, it writes a scenario for the scriptless Metropolitan extras.

If that appears a form of megalomania, such a megalomania is tempered by the fact that its expressions are always localised, since they address, by definition, only a part of the total audience, never the whole. Metropolitan architecture is megalomaniac on a modest scale.

Metropolitan architecture thus defined, implies a twofold polemic: against those who believe that they can undo the damage of the Modern Age – ie, the Metropolis itself – through the artificial respiration and resuscitation of 'traditional' architecture of streets, plazas, boulevards, etc; empty spaces for dignified and decent forms of social intercourse, to be enforced in the name of a stoic good taste … and against that Modern architecture which – with its implacable aversion to metaphor – has tried to exorcise its fear of chaos through a fetish for the objective and to regain control over the volatility of the Metropolis by dispersing its bulk, isolating its components, and quantifying its functions, and render it predictable once more … Both squander the potential of the Culture of Congestion.

The Urbanism of the three episodes was subconscious and spontaneous, not the result of an explicit doctrine. It was followed by an interval in which the architecture of the Metropolis has regressed, or at least fallen under the domination of official architecture.

The New York projects of the Office for Metropolitan Architecture attempt to negotiate the transition from that early, deliberately subconscious, state of architectural production to a conscious stage.

Rem Koolhaas, 'The Culture of Congestion', *Architectural Design* (May 1977), John Wiley & Sons Ltd (London), pp 318–25. The Publisher wishes to thank Rem Koolhaas and OMA for their assistance in relation to this article. © Rem Koolhaas. Images: p 65, drawing Agkarat Atiprasertkul and Brian McGrath from Starrett & Van Vleck Architects © Brian McGrath; pp 68–9, image by Madelon Vriesendorp, courtesy of OMA © OMA. The image may not be passed to any third parties without further permission. No part of the work may be reproduced or utilised in any form or by any means, electronic or mechanical, including photocopying, recording or by any information storage retrieval system, without permission in writing from OMA.

The Making of Hong Kong

Barrie Shelton, Justyna Karakiewicz and Thomas Kvan

> Hong Kong's unique history as treaty port, British colony, and then special administrative region of China, combined with dramatic topography of the island city of steep mountainsides and reclaimed land, has produced an improbable vertical culture of congestion even beyond the densities of Manhattan. In this chapter, the authors state: 'Vertical expansion results in ever taller buildings, while intensification brings greater concentration of activities and modes of movement across more levels of the city.' They go on to describe the recent emergence in Hong Kong of a volumetric Metropolitan Architecture that redefines the ground, creates multiple paths of vertical and horizontal movement in space, and layers multiple functions in a single building.

Emerging Volumetric Components

Vertical expansion and intensification are two processes that have dominated Hong Kong's urban growth. Both follow from the need to survive through adaptation and reconfiguration. Vertical expansion results in ever taller buildings, while intensification brings greater concentration of activities and modes of movement across more levels of the city. Vertical change is something readily apparent – essentially perpendicular extrusions forming new elements in the skyline. Intensification is less obvious, as it is a process concerning use, movement and often the incremental transformation of existing space: above all, it concerns multiple levels and volume. It is therefore easy to appreciate why the popular image of urban Hong Kong is of towers and *verticality*. However, the even more defining characteristic is that of *volumetric intensity* – a condition exemplified in the seething megastructure of Kowloon's Walled City during its final decade, when some 35,000 people lived and worked in the approximately one million cubic metre (35 million cubic feet) volume over its modest 2.7 hectare site.

In this section we examine three aspects of Hong Kong's form and function that contribute to building and sustaining a successful volumetric character:

- the several ways in which ground is being redefined
- the nature of movement on and between these 'new' grounds
- the layering of functions on them.

Further, to illustrate each point, we select some examples.

Redefining Ground

With a shortage of natural land on which to build, Hong Kong has engaged in reclamation from the earliest days of British settlement. Pouring sand into the sea is not, however, the only manner in which additional ground can be created. This section sets out several ways in which usable 'grounds' have been constructed.

Duplicate Ground
Although it is often repeated that Hong Kong is one of the densest places in the world, specific spot densities in certain neighbourhoods and blocks are well beyond the norm. For example, the spot density in Sham Shui Po is greater than 4,000 people per hectare and in Mong Kok it rises above 6,000 per hectare. These figures are calculated using census data, which reflect residential figures. Any visitor to Mong Kok could assume that the spot density on a busy shopping evening is substantially higher. In many sectors of the city, the population moving through the area can readily overwhelm the capacity of the surface of the streets to carry the flow. An obvious response to this demand is to duplicate the means of access to distribute the population. An early example is the bridge constructed in the early 1990s that carries substantial traffic from Wanchai MTR station to Immigration Tower, a destination that must be visited by everyone obtaining or renewing their Identity Card (carried by every resident of Hong Kong over the age of 11), visas or Hong Kong travel documents. Adjacent to this tower is Revenue Tower, less frequently visited but, as home to the tax office, also a common destination. The narrow streets that connect the destinations – O'Brien and King Streets – do not have the necessary capacity for the flow of traffic as well as serving neighbourhood needs of vehicular access, shop frontage and local activities. A duplicate ground surface has been created to facilitate the foot traffic across this area, traversing each block as a bridge and connected back to the neighbourhood at every junction.

Wanchai Bridge: part of Central's
extensive system of duplicate ground
providing direct links to the upper floors
of adjacent buildings.

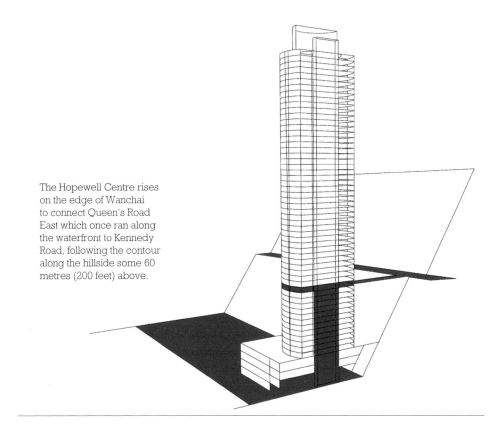

The Hopewell Centre rises on the edge of Wanchai to connect Queen's Road East which once ran along the waterfront to Kennedy Road, following the contour along the hillside some 60 metres (200 feet) above.

In a private context and at a smaller scale, we see 'ground' surfaces being reclaimed for individual use. As already noted, flower pots, sheds for additional rooms, washing lines, and the like are common roof-top sights. There are also more unusual ones. An example is the moon-viewing pavilion, which is a traditional Chinese structure for an intellectual. Here, tea or wine can be drunk while contemplating the night sky and poetry written. Tucked away in Pokfulam on the western end of Hong Kong Island, we find such a moon-viewing pavilion atop a residential building of six floors. Constructed at least as early as the 1950s, this pavilion exists at the time of writing, but the surrounding towers and night light pollution probably obscure the moon on all but a few days of each year.

Split Ground
The topography of Hong Kong poses considerable challenges to a planar understanding of a city but offers some advantages. One of these is the opportunity to create more than one 'front door'. An example of this is Hopewell Centre in Wanchai where the principal 'front door' is located on Queen's Road East but, because the building is located against the hillside, a second access is available directly to Kennedy Road approximately 60 metres (200 feet) higher. These circumstances in effect create a ground plane through Hopewell Centre that includes a 17-floor vertical translation. Access is granted to the public who use the lifts in Hopewell Centre to connect between the residential towers on Kennedy Road and the shops and offices of Wanchai below. In this example, we find an illustration of ambiguity in the concept of 'the ground floor'.

This is played out to a greater extent in Pacific Place, where the lobby of the Conrad Hotel can be accessed through its primary entrance on Justice Drive, from a lower entrance on Park Avenue (which runs on the roof of the shopping atrium) that gives access to the coffee shop, or directly from level three of Pacific Place shopping centre to the function rooms. While these two examples are the direct result of the topographic conditions, this feature can be created through design. For example, the main entrance to the Sha Tin Town Hall is from the upper podium level while service access is from the street below. This concept of a split ground expands the notion of ground level access, enhancing the porosity of the city not only horizontally but also vertically. While it increases the commercial or operational frontage of a building, it also folds functions that were limited to one plane into a volume of space.

Multiple Ground
The Shun Tak Centre, departure point for Macau, is a rich mix of activities. The closest example ever built of the aspirations of Futurists and Modernists, this building brings together the transport systems of MTR, tram, ferry and helicopter with road systems of buses, taxis and cars. Completed in 1984, this pair of towers on a four-storey podium is accessed by underground, surface and above ground links. A similar condition can be found in the complex of buildings at Exchange Square and the International Finance Centre, spanning from the Stock Exchange building to the IFC2 tower between which there are up to six levels of connection, some aligned with the urban road network and others that set up connections in new directions, such as the underground connection that links the Airport Express and MTR lines at Hong Kong Station. In Exchange Square, for example, the main public space of the notional town square is suspended over a substantial bus station that, in turn, sits adjacent to the underground trains noted earlier. In both these examples, we can find functional engagements of a ground floor at multiple levels. Visitors can traverse each of the buildings as if they were walking on the ground plane.

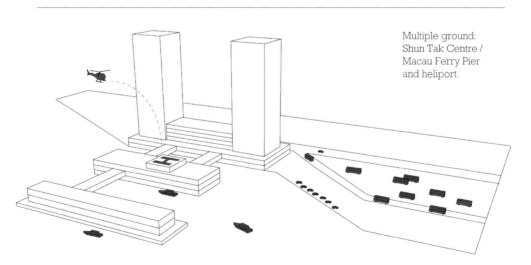

Multiple ground:
Shun Tak Centre /
Macau Ferry Pier
and heliport.

Borrowed Ground

While reclaiming land by mounding sand onto the seabed is the most obvious way to create additional space, a traditional mode of placing activities on the sea cannot be ignored. Long before the British arrived, boat-based living was common in Hong Kong. Floating communities and structures built over the sea provided accommodation for portions of the populations of those times, most commonly the Tanka people. Today we see remnants of these water-based communities. While the large floating communities that were found in bays such as Aberdeen Harbour and later moved to constructed locations such as the Causeway Bay Typhoon Shelter have disappeared, we can still see two distinctive manifestations of borrowed ground. In Tai O, on Lantau Island, the village of housing on stilts over the sea continues; communities such as these can be found throughout Asia. A more colourful alternative is regularly photographed in Aberdeen – the floating restaurants. Developing from a tradition of visiting the floating fishing community to eat seafood on board, purpose-built barges were anchored in the harbour by the middle of the 20th century. In the late 1970s the strategy was developed to an enormous scale and three interconnected two-, three- and four-storey structures were branded as Jumbo Kingdom and located a little outside the main Aberdeen Harbour. These multistorey immobile vessels are now a common tourist destination, accommodating both Chinese and Western restaurants with, collectively, several thousand seats.

Movement in Space

Having established new grounds, new modes of movement are needed to access these different grounds.

Interlocked Ladders

A scissor stair is a set of two interlocking stairways providing two separate paths of egress located within one stairwell enclosure. The stairs wind around each other, and are separated from each other within their enclosures by fire-rated construction thus providing two separate but physically intertwined paths of egress. An ingenious device, this stair design satisfies the regulatory requirement for two paths of escape from every floor without duplicating the stair tower, thus achieving the most pressing need in Hong Kong to maximise use of plot area. Apparently used first in Hong Kong in the 1960s, the scissor stair has become ubiquitous there as it facilitates the development of the small plot areas to provide maximum usable space. The device has been credited as a key invention to solving Hong Kong's housing problems (Keynote Speech by David C Lee, Chairman of the Hong Kong Housing Society, at the Inauguration of the CII-HK, 17 November 2003). So common is it, that the scissor stair was chosen to represent Hong Kong in the 2006 Venice Biennale where bamboo scaffolding, giant folding beds and a representation of the Mid Levels escalator complemented an almost full-size scissor stair rising three flights as four symbols of the way space is used intensively. Scissor stairs have been adopted by other national building agencies as a means of providing more cost-effective design for multistorey structures, for example, in New York City Construction Code Section 1014.2.1

and a modular construction of such stairs subject of US Patent 4930273 issued in 1990. Reputedly, its origins can be traced back to the wooden staircase in the Big Swallow Temple in Sian China in the Tang Dynasty (618–907 CE); a similar wooden staircase was supposed to be in the Ying Yan Temple in Shanxi in the Yuan Dynasty (1271–1368 CE).

Mechanical Ladders

Data reported for 1998 suggest that Hong Kong has the largest number of escalators per capita in the world, with one escalator for every 1,242 people. Japan, by comparison, had one per 2,801 people and Germany one per 7,017 people. With its topographical challenges and intensity of use, this is not too surprising. What is remarkable is the extent to which such systems have been put to use. Immediately upon establishing their hold on Hong Kong, the British faced the challenge of moving up and down the hillsides. With its highly unstable soils on slopes and typically high rainfall, walking or riding up slopes required some effort to stabilise or surface the slopes. With their extremely steep inclines, many slopes in the new Central District were navigated by means of granite steps, with one coming to be known as Ladder Street with reference to its structure and incline. When technology allowed, such stone ladders were replaced by what we identify as moving ladders, namely escalators. The most famous of these is now the Central to Mid Levels Escalator, which is really a series of 18 escalators and three travelators (essentially

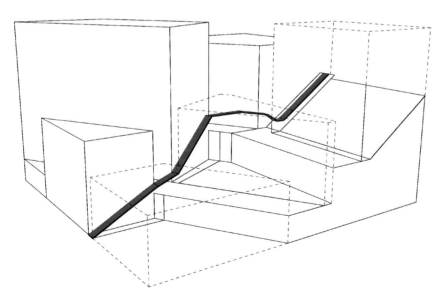

The Mid-Levels escalators thread between buildings and over streets to connect the flat ground of the former waterfront and the elevated Mid Levels.

escalators that move up gentle slopes without forming steps) linked by covered walkways and access stairs: the system carried 81,000 people per day in an estimate from 2008. Covering a distance of 800 metres (2,600 feet), the system climbs 135 metres (440 feet). Initiated as a means of reducing vehicular traffic on the congested streets accessing the lower slopes on Hong Kong Island, the project was officially labelled a failure in 1996 by the Hong Kong Government Director of Audit because it overran budgets and there was no discernible reduction in traffic on the roads. This judgement would not appear to be supported by empirical evidence of the escalator's success in regenerating the city, the introduction of a band of vitality through sections of what were difficult-to-reach areas up the hillside.

The Central to Mid-Levels Escalator is the most public example of the way in which this transport technology has redefined Hong Kong. With its open structure, the escalator facilitates the movement of pedestrians through otherwise inaccessible places or through uninviting transitions of contour without the disjuncture of a lift. By encouraging greater pedestrian traffic, the escalator has increased commercial transactions.

Elevated Pediways
Established surface transport infrastructure can be categorised by its speed of movement and access facilitated into streets, roads and motorways. Streets afford a locus for community engagement and access. Roads are distinguished by their purpose for traversing a particular site and their primacy in connecting one location to another. These different purposes will be reflected in their dimensions, the barriers (or lack of such) used to separate different modes of movement, surfacing and articulation. This then is reflected in their use; streets might be crossed by a pedestrian at any point but a road at indicated controlled crossings, for example. Within this categorisation the next level of capacity can be indicated by the motorway, a thoroughfare intended for higher speed traversal between points at longer distances on which a lack of motion is not anticipated nor encouraged. Observing Hong Kong, we can see a similar categorisation of movement systems. In describing *duplicate ground* earlier, we illustrated the replication of circulation space by way of the bridge between Wanchai Station and Immigration Tower. This bridge replicates the streets below in all except their building access; on the bridge it is common to find vendors illegally hawking their wares, acquaintances stopping to speak or people walking slowly as they observe the views within adjacent buildings or along vistas between buildings. This use of the bridge can be contrasted with that which links Mong Kok KCR station to the Mong Kok MTR station, a distance of 400 metres (1,300 feet). In this instance, the bridge runs with fewer opportunities to access the ground, running at one point 150 metres (1,300 feet) without egress. By contrast, the Wanchai pedestrian bridge has regular exits over its 300 metre (980 feet) length. The manner in which the Mong Kok connection is used is akin to that of a motorway, hence we identify it as a *pediway*. Such purposeful high-speed routes can be found across the city where densities are high and distances longer – for example in Central District running from the Shun Tak Centre to Exchange Square.

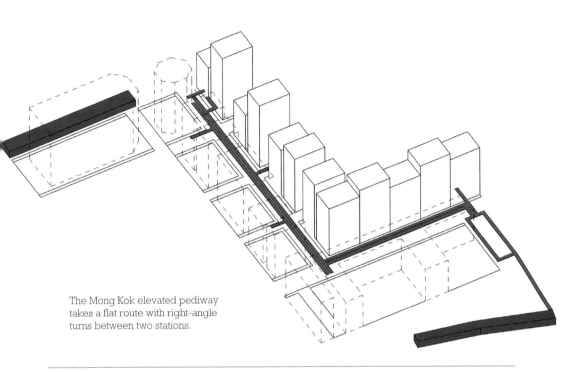

The Mong Kok elevated pediway takes a flat route with right-angle turns between two stations.

Elevated Roadways
Although Hong Kong has a comparatively low number of vehicles for its population, the need to move these through the congested areas and across challenging topographies has led to inventive solutions. While the original overpasses, or flyovers, were constructed in the 1970s to solve congestion problems at intersections, the capacity to build roadways atop columns has come to be an elegant solution to weaving roads across the topography. Of the several surprising solutions, the most extreme of these can be found taking eastbound traffic from Pokfulam Road in Western District (Sai Wan), Hong Kong Island, through the air space above Hill Road and down to the waterfront elevated dual carriageway along Connaught Road. Traffic using this 600 metre (2,000 feet) bridge descends through almost 100 metres (330 feet) with close-up views into the upper level windows of flanking apartments en route. This prosaic bridge over a congested junction has become a masterful freeform road that appears unconstrained by topography to take traffic through the city on a route freed of any ground constraints.

Layered Functions
To complement a ground that can be manipulated and multiplied, and access achieved in a variety of ways, functions can be freed from their conventional positions on the ground. Over time a variety of inventive ways have been created to accommodate such functions: here we identify a few.

Cubed Civic Centres

The government has provided Municipal Services Buildings across the territory as centres for the local community. These are composed of a distinctive combination of activities, many of which had previously taken place on the street. There is no consistent provision of functions in the building as these respond to an official reading of the community needs. The Smithfield Municipal Services Building can serve to illustrate the composition. The ground floor houses a meat and wet fish market where it can be hosed out easily and the sometimes pungent materials moved in and out with minimal impact. Rising a floor is the fruit and vegetable market, still able to be hosed down but less pungent (if you ignore the durian). The next floor is for cooked food stalls, which have been transported from their original kerbside locations into safer and less polluted surroundings. The activities on these three floors had previously been arranged in the side streets throughout Kennedy Town, which now are freed for traffic. Rising to the next level – the third floor using the British method of numbering floors – is the Smithfield Library (in some centres there will be several floors of library), on the fourth floor are administrative offices, a playroom for children, a fitness centre and a study centre for the majority of school students who do not have a quiet space at home. Above these are three more floors of sporting facilities including archery, squash, dance, basketball and badminton. In many there are also government service centres and offices.

***

Flatted Factories

With land such a scarce resource, industrial activities are subject to the same constraints as commercial and residential uses. Land noted for industrial uses has been leased by the government with similarly high plot ratios as residential land – it is common for such land to be leased with a FAR of 15. The leasor developer has therefore the pressure to generate returns by constructing a multistorey building. In this vertical arrangement of industrial activities a factory may take over all or part of a floor.

The term for these arrangements is 'flatted factories'. Derived from the British description of an apartment as a 'flat', the term is used not only in Hong Kong but also Singapore and India. Not all industrial purposes can be accommodated in such arrangements, obviously, but it is remarkable the extent to which industry is accommodated in this way: printing works, plastics moulding plants for children's toys, food production.

As Hong Kong industrialised after the 1950s, domestic industrial production became a common mode of employment. Subcontracted assembly of products paid on a piece basis supplemented many household incomes in these cottage industries. Manufacturing activities were also established in residential units or in illegal structures in squatter settlements. In the late 1950s, the government constructed buildings for light industrial uses to provide for these entrepreneurial activities, following the model of their Mark I resettlement housing. The government expanded this capacity by constructing 17 industrial estates in the late 1970s and early 1980s. Over time, the private sector has taken up the opportunity and constructed large buildings for heavier industries such as printing plants with their very heavy machines. In solving the problems of vertical access and the constraints of freight lifts, especially in the multiple handling of goods that such a form of transport demands, later buildings have included enormous ramps to allow articulated container trucks to drive directly up to the factory door on the higher levels.

By the end of 1996, over 83 per cent of all industrial space was accommodated in such multistorey facilities, with the private sector providing 17.8 million square metres (183 million square feet) of such space (Tang and Tang, 1999, 'Industrial Property, Market Initiative and Planning Policy'). The problems with such arrangements are several, including: the need for standard floor plates regardless of the various activities on each floor; limited access; limited clear span spaces; difficulty in managing industrial effluents; problems in isolating vibrations from machinery; and complexities in fire safety.

By the end of the 1980s the demand for industrial space began to drop as China opened up and welcomed industrial investments, especially in the areas lying just north of Hong Kong. A decade later, over 50 per cent of the government industrial estates were empty. With more land available, industrial facilities could be constructed with greater ease, customised to particular uses. The reduced demand for flatted factories led to an exploration of other uses, so industrial/office (IO) space came to be accepted by the government and slowly regulations were changed to allow such space. The changes, however, were additive such that the buildings had to satisfy both industrial and office requirements which resulted in more expensive space. There are few attempts at the time of writing to create residential spaces from these since the act is illegal, so the loft spaces that are so popular in North America and increasingly in Europe are not feasible in Hong Kong.
* * *

Horses in High-Rise
Under the management of the Hong Kong Jockey Club since 1884, horse racing has become a significant part of community life in Hong Kong. Nothing in Hong Kong is exempt from the need to use land more carefully, not even horses. As racing has become more popular and more horses are kept, the problem of accommodation for the horses has been addressed in the usual Hong Kong manner here – high-rise stables. The initial racetrack was built in Happy Valley in 1845 and remained the only course until the Sha Tin course was opened in 1978. With the racetrack itself occupying the only flat land in Happy Valley, space for the stables was to be found on the hillside to the south. From the 1920s onwards, horses were accommodated at the Jockey Club stables on Shan Kwong Road in Happy Valley. By the 1960s the pressure on stabling and concomitant facilities had led to the need for a high-rise solution in this congested part of town. To address these needs, a complex of buildings was erected on the steep slopes with the tallest building providing four levels of stables and seven levels of residences for the stable hands plus recreational space for the families on the roof. In the adjacent buildings linked by ramps were additional stables and roof-top exercise paddocks for the horses, providing a total of four paddock areas. Although not so constrained by space, the new facilities in Sha Tin provide 23 stables with accommodation for 1,260 horses, using multilevel stables.

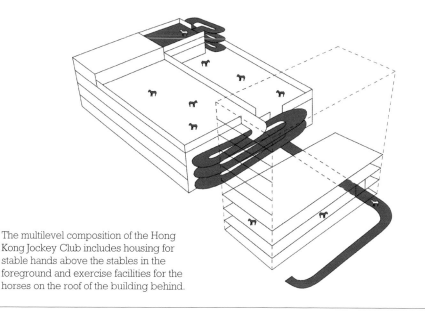

The multilevel composition of the Hong Kong Jockey Club includes housing for stable hands above the stables in the foreground and exercise facilities for the horses on the roof of the building behind.

Tiered Transport

The need for multideck transport in Hong Kong was established soon after the tramways were built. The narrow corridor of traversable flat land along the waterfront ensured that the intensity of transport needs demanded a high capacity system. Within a decade of starting their service in 1904, single-deck were replaced by double-deck trams, starting in 1910 with all removed by 1912. Although these initial double-deck trams were open to the elements on the second level, they were enclosed by 1925. While not the originator of multilevel trams, Hong Kong continues to use this form of transport as a principal and high capacity system along its 13.5 km (8.5 miles) of track.

Multilevel transport can be found in other forms. Most obvious on the streets are the double-decker buses, introduced in 1949 in Kowloon where the flatter land allowed these heavier vehicles to be used: the bus system today has over 5,000 double-decker buses in operation. Multideck ferries were introduced before the end of the 19th century, for example, the Star Ferry introduced a second level on its ferries. Yaumatei Ferries, later Hong Kong and Yaumatei Ferries, introduced two-deck car ferries in the 1960s to carry the increasing number of cars across the harbour. Until the opening of the cross harbour tunnel in 1972, this was the only means for a car to travel from Hong Kong Island to Kowloon and, on a busy day, this journey could entail a wait of many hours to obtain a space for the vehicle onboard. As the population increased and settlements on outer islands began to grow, Hong Kong and Yaumatei ferries started with triple-deck passenger ferries in the mid 1970s to accommodate the heavy demand on the inter-island routes between Hong Kong and Lantau and Cheung Chau.

Just as scissor stairs enable a single service core to provide twice the functionality, double-deck lifts have also been employed in Hong Kong in such buildings as the World Trade Centre and the International Finance Centre. Here, the building's even and odd floors are served by the two different decks in the lift.

Sky Gardens

The device of the borrowed view can be found in the Chinese tradition of gardens and is best exemplified in the exquisite urban gardens of Suzhou. These gardens illustrate the manner in which a very small piece of land can be used to create a garden with expansive intentions. The technique expands the experienced view by layering elements within it and bringing distant elements that are often not part of the garden in which you stand into the composed view. When this idea is brought into the Hong Kong capacity to layer surfaces to create land in unusual places, the notion of a sky garden emerges. In these, a garden space is provided on elevated planes as a place of refuge from the urban intensity. Gardens such as these have been created by private individuals on accessible roof surfaces, including those with structures such as the moon-viewing pavilion, as previously noted. Consistent with the pattern of legitimising individual initiatives by publicly delivering the same end, tower-based housing estates began to manifest sky gardens in the late 1990s. One example was that of Verbena Heights, Tseung Kwan O in the New Territories. In this public housing estate constructed in 1996–97, the landscaped podium covering the whole site is complemented by small pocket gardens in the tops of the towers. This approach was broadly evident in the submissions to an architectural competition held by the Hong Kong Housing Authority in 2000, 'Public Housing in a New Era', and is current in the urban design language in the region.

Stacked Warehouses/Folded Portside

The technology of bulk storage demands an ease of access and scale of provision. A common transport technology such as shipping containers, for example, is limited by the structural capacity of the container to be stacked up to eight units maximum. This constraint requires container ports to be surrounded by large areas of land. With one of the busiest container ports in the world and a severe shortage of land, Hong Kong has come up with a remarkable solution of multiplying the container land surface within stacked warehouses. These structures are misleading to observe since the obvious measure of scale, the access ramp for vehicles, appears to be a familiar circular ramp for a personal car. Instead, these ramps accommodate articulated trucks conveying single containers, a clear height of 4.2 metres (14 feet) and climb several storeys so that a single section of land can accommodate many cargo-handling activities concurrently. Additional floors are accessed by heavy-duty lifting equipment, allowing one structure at the Kwai Chung docks to replicate handling facilities across 11 floors.

* * *

From Barrie Shelton, Justyna Karakiewicz, Thomas Kvan, *The Making of Hong Kong*, excerpts from pp 131–54. © 2010 Routledge. Reproduced by permission of Taylor & Francis Books UK. Images: pp 73–5, 77, 79, 82 © Barrie Shelton, Justyna Karakiewicz and Thomas Kvan.

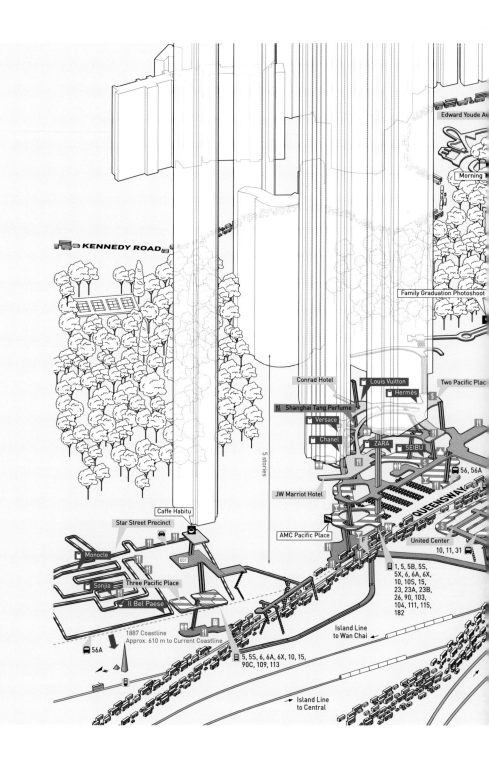

KENNEDY ROAD

Edward Youde Av

Morning

Family Graduation Photoshoot

Conrad Hotel

Louis Vuitton

Hermès

Two Pacific Plac

Shanghai Tang Perfume

Versace

Chanel

ZARA

SEIBU

5 stories

56, 56A

JW Marriot Hotel

QUEENSWAY

Caffe Habitu

Star Street Precinct

AMC Pacific Place

United Center

10, 11, 31

Monocle

Three Pacific Place

1, 5, 5B, 5S,
5X, 6, 6A, 6X,
10, 10S, 15,
23, 23A, 23B,
26, 90, 103,
104, 111, 115,
182

Sonjia

Il Bel Paese

Island Line
to Wan Chai

1887 Coastline
Approx. 610 m to Current Coastline

56A

5, 5S, 6, 6A, 6X, 10, 15,
90C, 109, 113

Island Line
to Central

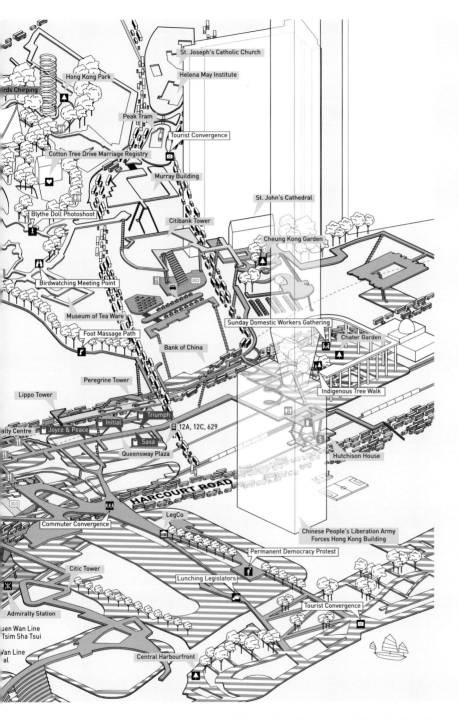

Private developments, government offices and public parks are linked in Hong Kong by elevated or submerged passages, paths along steep slopes and multistorey shopping malls. Image excerpted from *Cities Without Ground*, by Adam Frampton, Jonathan D Solomon and Clara Wong. © Adam Snow Frampton, Jonathan D Solomon, Clara Kar Wing Wong.

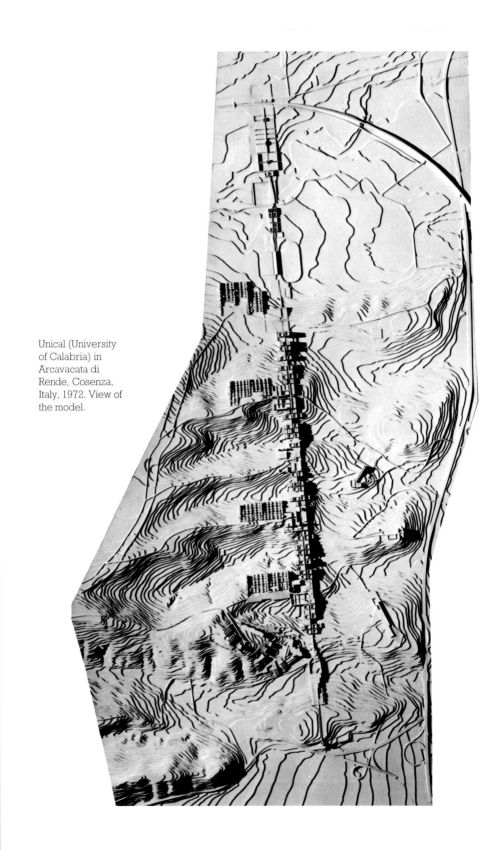

Unical (University of Calabria) in Arcavacata di Rende, Cosenza, Italy, 1972. View of the model.

The Territory of Architecture

Vittorio Gregotti

If Aldo Rossi defined the importance of *the architecture of the city*, Vittorio Gregotti defines the territory of architecture. In modern urbanism, architecture cannot be confined to the boundaries of the traditional walled city, but encompasses the larger territory of landscape, geography, transport and communication. However, for Gregotti, the form of the territory is as important to define through architecture as the form of the city, although the architecture of the territory is distinct from the architecture of building or the city. It must operate within the 'morphological dynamics' of large geographic and long timescales. This chapter includes selections of a new English translation of Gregotti's book by Giovanni Santamaria.

Landscape Geography

The purpose of this chapter is to investigate the foundations of a formal technology of the anthropogeographical landscape from an architectural perspective.[1] In other words, to investigate what problems are highlighted when seeing our work as architects as projects concerning environmental issues at differing scales. We will proceed with a list of open issues affecting the entirety of the physical space that man inhabits, not only acting in an aesthetic way on the construction of an artefact, but also giving aesthetic meaning to scenarios present in the world prior to our direct action. We use the notion of landscape here with its intentional ambiguity of meaning: the dimension of landscape at its large geographical scale represents just one example of our idea of landscape as a whole; a particularly meaningful and perhaps a new way to carry out the discourse of formal structure in architecture, analysed at all scales. This course does not claim to offer itself as the unitary one directly at the operational level, but posits a general case over the specialisation of different formal methods at several scales.

First, the anthropogeographical scale of architectural intervention and the possibility of studying the theme of architectural form need to be outlined; we need to consider the relationship between planning and architectural design on one side and the articulation of the discipline of landscape[2] on the other. Outside architecture, it is necessary to relate to the disciplinary area that historically dealt with the description of the physical environment at large scale: geography. Pierre George in his book *Active Geography* dedicates the first chapter to a general discussion about several doctrines of geography, starting from the ideas of Alexander von Humboldt, through geographical determinism, to the relationship between history and geography, then the doctrine of 'Landscape'. George proposes a scientific discipline that incorporates the comprehensive description of all the layers and relationships that define a physical environment, in the operational articulation of its geographical regions described with their potential elements.

From the statements of those same geographers, two specific areas seem germane to architecture. The first area can be understood in terms of scale: below a certain size, the spatial definition of the environment seems to become precise and particular only through the specification by other technical disciplines, and between those, architecture defines itself as the technical description of 'environment' and 'construction'. The second area is not related to problems of scale, but illuminates the whole approach of the two disciplines, making the first a descriptive one and the second a design one. Geography doesn't build proposals, it is a science of the spatial present even though it investigates relations and their constitution; besides, geography seems to ignore the formal aspects of this present related to meaning and character, in other words, to use semiotic terminology, even though geography works as an environmental measure in both syntagmatic and paradigmatic sense, it seems not to give in any way a value of aesthetic communication.

Landscape as Aesthetic Object

The second disciplinary area that needs to be taken into consideration concerns changes of communication tools and new possibilities of structuring the visual forms proposed by modern artists, that are able to cope with the dynamic of temporal and spatial development proposed by a geographic dimension. The investigation in this area makes sense on two conditions. The first one is to consider that in some way the anthropogeographical landscape can be the reading and evaluation of an existing aesthetic object; the second one is the verification of the differences in terms of specificity between the aesthetic transactions regarding the shape of the territory and what we usually call visual aesthetic operations, to bring the existing from one meaning to another or from one level to another. As in the case of language, the environment is the product of the imagination and collective memory materialised through the works that the subject and society build in meeting the world.

From this comes a further question of great interest to architects: how does our perception of landscape become an aesthetic perception? How is it possible to be aware of the figural quality of the landscape? Essentially, we believe, in two different ways. To the first (very rare) can be ascribed all the direct ways that can be summarised by the idea of myth: whenever a social group elects a site as a symbolic place, it recognises a value in it, apart from nature even though dedicated to it. This directs the place to become an object, to define itself as a figure in an environment. Whether it appears in terms of a monument, as a sacred wood or even as a forbidden place, it underlines, by being in that specific location, a special relationship with territory as well as with the ground. The figural quality makes visible the whole geographical surroundings.

The second way is indirect, constituted by evidence of removing pieces of landscape from the context through specific representational instruments, overloading it with an almost-objectivity made recognisable as a figure. We refer here to the role that the representation of landscape plays as quality, and then evidence, and as quantity and thus, as common knowledge. Painting, photography, film, photogrammetry are fundamental tools of knowledge of landscape as representation. They tend to reveal structural characteristics by means of interpretation or the exceptionality of vision, as well as by reproduction and quantitatively large distribution; resulting in the degradation to a stereotype that, compared with our urban life, for example, allows us to falsely gain the landscape as other and different, such as a personal adventure, a personal encounter with natural values considered to be stable.

The reproduction of landscape as an aesthetic object in painting, novels, poetry, as well as the literary description of a novel, of poetry and prose, places the knowledge of the landscape itself at an 'improper' level and in some way it conceals and diverts, but also reveals. But on a different level, the achievements of arts are achievements of new points of view towards reality, and in this sense they change our perceptual structures of the world as a more and more complex articulation, as a more and more comprehensive framework.

If nothing else, the territory always historically constructs our perception of it and, as a consequence, geography is continually refounded by the cultural experience of users: the conquest of new points and new dynamics of observation, new communications systems, new strategies of desire of groups and subjects, of several meanings with which a figure is charged through the transformations of the conceptions of science, about nature, matter, space and through the artistic invention of new and different figurative optics on the surrounding reality. In a more technical way, even though the problem of the architectural form of things has its own separate specificity, the visual organisation of things is shifted by the organisations proposed for the visual arts.

Morphological Dynamics of Territory

The transformational elements of landscape in the course of time range from climate and seasonal change to the processes of colonisation, from the controlled organisation of the consequences of natural phenomena, the desert that buries the city or the flooding of large areas, from wars of destruction to political, economic, or administrative changes, but more extensively, to the figures that, completely unintentionally, the productive exploitation determines, starting from the modifier of technological intervention. The last hundred years has been subjected not just to a movement of territorial expansion but also of time acceleration, and this is the most characteristic aspect of the morphological dynamics of territory.

In five years it is possible to build Dutch 'polders' or colonise the desert; a hydroelectric reservoir transforms the configuration of an entire valley in a few years; it is possible to cut an isthmus in a few months; to transport energy everywhere in almost unlimited quantities; it is possible to think of future air-conditioning systems that will guarantee much more accelerated and extensive changes. The population can move, know and compare in an ever more rapid way, bringing about a direct and coincident relationship between places, production and consumption.

We move here from the observation of a situation of gradual reduction of nature to culture at the hands of humanity, to exploit that same nature functionally and productively. Then from the consequent progressive universalisation of value systems of nature as a heritage to profit from, we move from the reduction of the importance of 'place' for

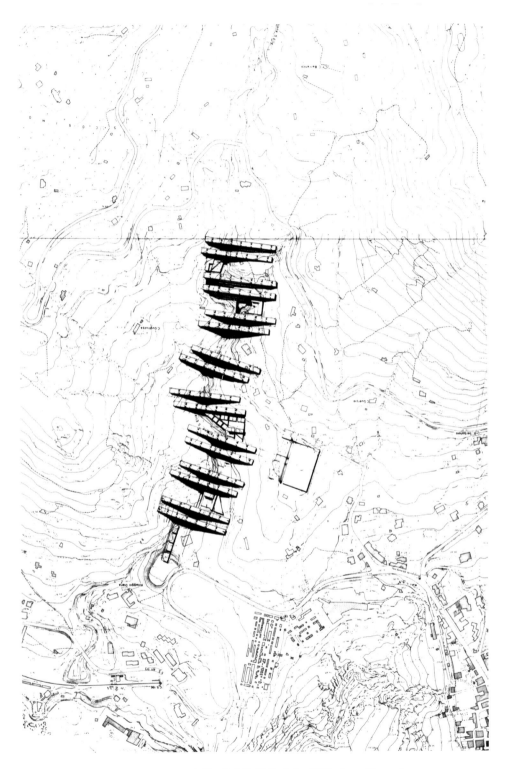

Public housing project in Vallone S Elia-Cefalù, Sicily, Italy, 1976, viewed from above.

the construction of collective value, through the technologising of landscape, in other words, through the reduction from an operational point of view, of the character of place because of its increasing connection with localised economies. We watch the increase of areas involved in anthropogeographic operations and settlement systems to arrive at the problem of the formal consequences of this attitude on the landscape itself, in which the urban environment becomes just one aspect with special features.

All of these phenomena of acceleration and expansion of environmental change at every dimensional scale, and particularly at the geographic one, made it necessary for architects to formulate design tools mostly ignored until now. Today, architects are often forced to defer to other disciplines the control or effects of these territorial measures. Currently, an adequate and specific formal instrumentation of structuring intervention techniques does not correspond to this spatial expansion and temporal acceleration of process, except through shifting or enlarging fields. On the contrary, we often witness a progressive reduction of formal organisation systems which were present, even though at the level of 'urban decoration', within 19th-century urban planning, in the tradition of garden art – that consistent design relationship between city and nature, carried out through the history of architecture from the Baroque age.[3]

Landscape Tradition and Environmental Defence

The architecture field dealt with the problem of landscape as a specific approach and not just as a pure background in which to structure its own figures. Landscape as material manipulable by architecture, going beyond the concept of 'garden', was founded in the late 16th century and powerfully used as a structuring element of the Baroque city. So here we are no longer facing the idea of nature manipulated as an architectural extension or as an aesthetic and symbolic place subjected to a complete objectification through design, but as a dialectical element with which the construction must present itself as a possibility. Basic to this idea, in a different ideological context, of course, is the foundation of 'Landscape' as a discipline. It has its origins in a modern sense, in the rejection by the Anglo-Saxon culture of the 'formal garden' (William Kent, Capability Brown) during the second half of the 18th century.

This controversy, which provided the elements to work at a large scale of influence during the Romantic period, is nourished by many factors: the Enlightenment myth of the noble savage, the discovery of the Chinese and Japanese cultures, travel literature. Colonialism afforded a supernatural quality – the memory of forest, of the wild place – to domestic nature itself. Finally, all of this is summarised in the recognition of the value to search for the 'genius loci' of the picturesque, typical place. All this makes it possible for architects to recognise nature as an inherent value and to correlate the notion of nature with characteristic landscapes.

Upon this understanding is grafted the expansion and degeneration of the historical city determined by the industrial age. Open and green spaces are lacking in the industrial city, so increasing the value of both. On the one hand, nature becomes a public park, on the other, the city tends to emerge in nature as a garden city, to ideally, as well as hygienically, regenerate itself.[4] Along with the examination of building and land speculation stimulated by mass movements, such as tourism – a way of profiting from landscape – lies the public need to defend the characterisation, distinction and protection of the existing landscape through legislation, almost always inadequate, in the creation of the first national parks (Hot Springs, USA, 1832; Gran Paradiso, Italy, 1922), while 'Landscape' as an art to regulate the 'unbuilt' continues and is articulated until it creates its own professional arena and therefore its specialists.

Architectural and urban culture, because it doesn't have the scope, abilities and inclination to design, limits itself to defence against real estate pressures. If the territory is not subject to constraint, there are no rules, except those sometimes related to mere density and behaviours, and proposals are evaluated on a case by case basis, rather than as part of the bigger picture to intensify meaning and quality of the same landscape. Moreover, each territory is divided into special areas, because of a specific historical and natural value attributed to them, and this value is simply defended against destructive forces. 'Non-landscapes', such as those having no important historical or natural value, are allowed to disintegrate rather than being structured according to figurative objectives. Their meaning starts from a reading of their formal characteristics. They are not traditionally beautiful but are often very rich and have the most dynamic morphology. This approach to nature, as only a distinctive aesthetic element, merely leads to a conservation perspective.

Figure of Territory in the Italian Tradition
These problems are schematically achievable starting from three different kinds of considerations from inside architecture today:

1   The recognition of a double condition of crisis: on the one hand related to the moment of discontinuity in the creative process as a method of linear correspondence of form-function, analysis-synthesis, as has been established in the tradition of modern architecture; on the other hand concerning the architecture itself which is no longer recognisable at just the building level and at that level is perhaps no more characteristically operational.
2   The need to establish the architect as creative formaliser with the specific role of introducing figurative goals into the spatial realisation of services from the beginning of the planning process. Disciplinary specificity, that is, that doesn't relegate the architect to the role of available technician or pure decorator, but helps properly to place his activities within the whole of the disciplines that converge in the provision of service. Of course we are well aware that the territorial reality is defined following a series of complex and interacting layers which are settled in differentiated spatial patterns (geographic, administrative, demographic, economic, etc) as physical realities that must be organised in relation to common goals and that will materialise in a new 'form of territory', and that within these models there is the need of figure. This means that there are distinct operations of territorial planning between location and formalisation.

The gardens of Arezzo, Italy, 1984. Aerial view of the
design proposal from the historic centre of the city.

3   The possibility to recognise a field of specific architectonic expertise in the construction of the landscape, starting with the suspension of a judgement of functional distinction, and which aims at the construction of a voluntary geography that offers itself as a meaningful image of the environment in which we move. This is, in other words, the idea of considering the total and functionally indistinct environment as a formal reality to know and organise according to the goals of a continued expansion of the opportunities to use its materiality.

The first question we should ask is whether this hypothesis does not tend to regain a privileged position 'outside the planet' which allows the architect to exercise his demiurgic vocation. I believe it is exactly the opposite: it is about the recognition of the presence of compelling situations and then the placement of our activities in the most appropriate areas, although technically more restricted, well aware that this location is included in the historical dialectic.

It is important to emphasise, however, that this richness and breadth of operations facilitated by the idea of landscape construction is not, as one might think, only related to the large physical size of the intervention, but its deeper quality is the recognition and assumption of the world as matter operated by architecture through the invention of the landscape as a whole; and this gives the architectural gestures at other scales new meaning. The same design can be understood throughout as control in the process of continuous replacement of the environment operated by production, of the constant invention of its geography.

Nature of Drawing at a Geographical Scale

But when it comes to design or geographical invention, what are the temporal and spatial design limits? What should the nature of design be, to match the process of growth and change in infinitesimal displacements by which the living world of things transforms itself? In what way are the figural operations proper to this dimensional level, differentiated from those traditionally associated with the figurative arts and yet, do they also have connections with attitudes and results of linguistic operations related to the tradition of the Modern Movement in architecture? Or rather, which elements that we recognise as structural to this tradition, are somehow recoverable as valuable for the operations established by our working hypothesis?

This possibility of design is probably no longer recognisable in traditional terms and we should in future take into consideration design tools widely symbolising landscape processes of self-determination through stratification of natural pulses, or those formalising the phases themselves of programming more and more totally decisive processes. It has to do with finding a design process continuously open to the construction of several configurations oscillating in an oriented field, the structure of which is defined by a series of figures working on differentiated areas able to give meaning to the whole environment through its stronger characterisation and definition, or to consider the relationship itself as the only way to regulate the quality of the environment.

A specific structure of the architectonic space of the concept of landscape as a whole environment could likely be favoured by both the use of formal studies about relationships and connections, such as graph theory, and the concepts introduced by spatial topology, such as field, set, iteration, etc. From this we can try to identify through the matter-scale relationship, a method of formability of environmental sets considered as almost-objects, collections of operable matter in a particular field. In any case, since landscape per se is not about the total transformation of the environment as all elements in a defined field, but about its total resumption in relation to formation of meaning, the point will be to operate in the slightest way possible, with the highest figurative efficiency of intervention.

In front of the overwhelming presence of nature, it was easier to read the scale of the efficiency of the human gesture on earth. The first way to intervene in the environment coincided with the opportunity to work through minimum shifts that have the minimum resistance; the results of these shifts are hardly discernible, although related to the most important points. But even in relation to a highly manipulated geographical space, the problem remains the identification of a sensitive point, the minimal operation. It has to do with the definition of the degree of congruence between the geographic material and the organisation introduced to orient the elements of the field towards an intention of figure and to know whether in practice it is possible to find a connection that links the typology of operational approaches to the formal ones, according to a system with the highest creative performance and the slightest effort.

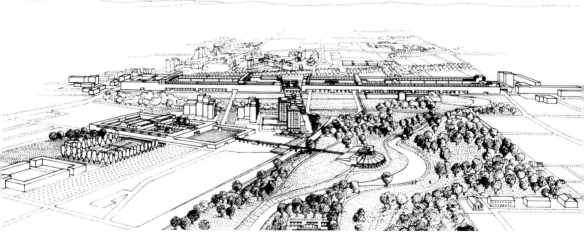

Masterplan of Corassori-Modena, Italy, 1983–4. Aerial
view of the project and its territorial context.

Architecture, Environment, Nature

We are perfectly aware that these considerations are simple directions, which are particularly oriented towards artistic operations, not scientific ones. But beyond the answers to these disciplinary questions, it seems clear that the problem of the formal structure of the anthropogeographic environment requires a revision of the concept of nature as value, as it has been made in the tradition of modern architecture: both as a social good to redistribute, and as a value to adapt the meaning itself of construction as growth and process. The two extreme positions can be identified on the one hand in Le Corbusier's idea of nature that arrives in the city through architecture, admirably represented not only in the Plan Voisin but especially in some extraordinary 'geographic' sketches such as those for Rio de Janeiro and São Paulo; and on the other hand in Frank Lloyd Wright's theory documented in *Living City* and in the design of Broadacre City where city and countryside are two blurred elements subjected to laws of creativity of the organic nature.[5]

For humanity, nature has always represented an indomitable force. Mother yet unreasonable enemy, unpredictable fury but also benefactor: most of all it coincides with the heart, with soil as the producer of direct nourishment for the community occupying the land. It has also been seen as a measure of fertility, a stable link between inhabitant and place; agriculture has been a fundamental way to regulate and give a rational form to nature. Then, during the industrial age, man kept digging the earth for its treasures; production and consumption became detached from place.

Fighting nature, organising it in geometries or transforming it through the ideal nature of the garden, an elected one, a cosmological fence, heaven on earth, nature conducive to humanity living against a wild nature or on the contrary, to be pedagogically referred to as a mirror of truth and goodness of man, all these are attitudes to which from time to time we have responded with precise and distinct answers in an architectural way.

We have tried in this chapter to offer to architecture the idea of landscape as a total environmental whole, which should move towards the recognition of the materiality of the interior anthropogeographic environment as operational and continuously subject to intention, rather than towards the preservation or reconstruction of natural separated values, to refer to its total usability as an indispensable value, recognisable as a structure of the environment beyond the same model of culture. Partially, this is about the challenge of technological values as a foundation for the image of the surroundings, to instead regenerate in its full physicality, the living body of nature to which we belong, as communication and knowledge of new possibilities. It is not about claiming the construction of a physical environment from which to influence or direct human behaviour, we simply want to make the physical environment more available.

The defining instruments of the ways anthropology as general science of man can summarise sociological, ethnological and psychological elements, with their several meanings, give foundations for a theme of human behaviour, of the strategy of his desire for expansion over the Earth's surface. The task that our discipline should face in this regard needs in large part to be explored: this should be primarily a task of clarification and reduction, aimed at the simplification, schematisation and unification of terminology, of symbols of representation, of process design schemes.[6] It should move from a lengthy practice-based design process characterised by experimental work, to establish from experience, patterns of communicable behaviour. And at the same time it should try to contradict those same results continuously comparing them with the historical dialectic: as always, the construction of the scheme should come together with the hope for its future debate.

Notes

1   In 1882, Friedrich Ratzel published the first of two volumes of his fundamental work as geographer entitled *Anthropogeographie* (Berlin), 1891. It was a study of the activities of human groups according to their geographical environments. The use we make here of the term 'anthropogeography' is completely different and indicates 'the environment modified by the actions and presence of human beings'.

2   Landscape is defined, by the *Chambers Etymological Dictionary* as 'The shape or appearance of that portion of Land which the eye can view at once; the aspect of a Country; a picture representing the aspect of a country.'

3   This discourse on 'urban decoration' was alive and present during the Neo-Classical age in the formation of 'Committees of Decoration' concerned with the perspective of the city. One of the fundamental books on the subject is Camillo Sitte's *The Art of Building the City*, Vallardi (Milan), 1953 (orig ed Vienna, 1889). Regarding the relationship between city and nature in the urban structure, see the chapters 'Sixtus V and the Master Plan of Baroque Rome' and 'The Organization of Exterior Space' in Siegfried Giedion's book, *Space, Time, Architecture*, Hoepli (Milan), 1954 (original edition Harvard University Press, 1951).

4   A very interesting thesis about the use of green, is the one developed by Lewis Mumford, *The Highway and the City*, Secker & Warburg (London), 1964, about the need to restructure the land not starting from hygienic problems, but from those of 'leisure' whose centres, instead of being concentrated in some places, will be disseminated to constitute one of the framing devices for the regeneration of the urban fringes and the integration of town and country.

5   Le Corbusier, *Manière de penser l'urbanisme* (Paris), 1946; Frank Lloyd Wright, *Living City*, Einaudi (Turin), 1966 (original edition Horizon Press (New York), 1958).

6   An interesting notational system is that proposed by Lawrence Halprin in his book *Cities*, Reinhold Publ Corp, 1963, and drawn on in an edition of *Progressive Architecture* from July 1965, where he proposes a system (largely inspired by dance and contemporary music) that he called 'Montation', for the notation of the movement of urban structures.

From Vittorio Gregotti, *The Territory of Architecture*, excerpt from pp 59–98, Feltrinelli Editore (Milan), 1966, English translation by Giovanni Santamaria for this publication, by permission of Vittorio Gregotti.
© Vittorio Gregotti. Images: pp 86, 90, 93, 95 courtesy of Vittorio Gregotti
© Vittorio Gregotti.

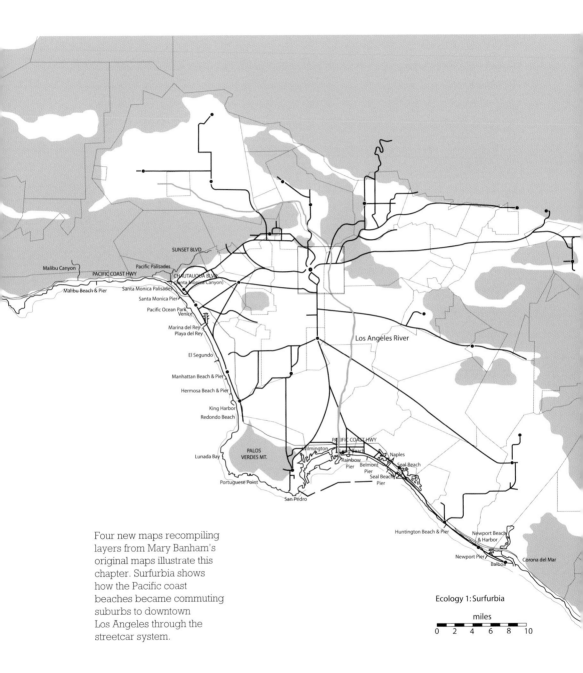

Malibu Canyon

PACIFIC COAST HWY

Pacific Palisades

SUNSET BLVD

CHAUTAUQUA BLVD
(Santa Monica Canyon)

Malibu Beach & Pier

Santa Monica Palisades

Santa Monica Pier

Pacific Ocean Park

Venice

Marina del Rey
Playa del Rey

El Segundo

Manhattan Beach & Pier

Hermosa Beach & Pier

King Harbor
Redondo Beach

Lunada Bay

PALOS
VERDES MT.

Portuguese Point

San Pedro

Los Angeles River

PACIFIC COAST HWY

Wilmington

Long Beach

Rainbow
Pier

Belmont
Pier

Naples

Seal Beach

Seal Beach
Pier

Huntington Beach & Pier

Newport Beach
& Harbor

Newport Pier

Balboa

Corona del Mar

Four new maps recompiling
layers from Mary Banham's
original maps illustrate this
chapter. Surfurbia shows
how the Pacific coast
beaches became commuting
suburbs to downtown
Los Angeles through the
streetcar system.

Ecology 1: Surfurbia

miles

0   2   4   6   8   10

Los Angeles
The Architecture of Four Ecologies

Reyner Banham

Reyner Banham's book *Los Angeles: The Architecture of Four Ecologies* turns Rossi's architecture of the city on its head – or rather leaves it behind in the rear-view mirror as the author learns to drive in order to love Los Angeles as an ecology of 'instant architecture' made comprehensible in relation to its climate, geography and infrastructure rather than through historical continuity. Banham pluralises the scientific term ecology to describe how modern architecture thrives in the various 'ecological niches' of Los Angeles' four ecologies: Surfurbia, Autopia, the Plains of Id and the Foothills. Ungers' notion of an urban archipelago of green lagoons resonates in the lush irrigated landscape of LA. However, rather than the megaform of architecture clarifying the 'territory of architecture', the architecture of Banham's Autopia is relegated to a secondary role of providing microclimates within the larger scale orders of mountains, sea and plains, and the movement of cars and water.

In the Rear-view Mirror

A city 70 miles (110 kilometres) square but rarely 70 years deep, apart from a small downtown not yet two centuries old and a few other pockets of ancientry, Los Angeles is instant architecture in an instant townscape. Most of its buildings are the first and only structures on their particular parcels of land; they are couched in a dozen different styles, most of them imported, exploited and ruined within living memory. Yet the city has a comprehensible, even consistent, quality to its built form, unified enough to rank as a fit subject for a historical monograph.

Historical monograph? Can such an old-world, academic and precedent-laden concept claim to embrace so unprecedented a human phenomenon as this city of Our Lady Queen of the Angels of Porciúncula? – otherwise known as Internal Combustion City, Surfurbia, Smogville, Aerospace City, Systems Land, the Dream-factory of the Western world. It's a poor historian who finds any human artefact alien to his professional capacities, a poorer one who cannot find new bottles for new wine. In any case, the new wine of Angeleno architecture has already been decanted into one of the older types of historical bottle with a success that I will not even try to emulate.

Architecture in Southern California by David Gebhard and Robert Winter is a model version of the classical type of architectural gazetteer – erudite, accurate, clear, well-mapped, pocket-sized. No student of the architecture of Los Angeles can afford to stir out of doors without it. But there is no need to try and write it again; all I wish to do here is to record my profound and fundamental debt to the authors, and echo their admission of even more fundamental indebtedness – to Esther McCoy and her 'one-woman crusade' to get Southern California's modern architectural history recorded and its monuments appreciated.

Yet even the professed intention of Gebhard and Winter to cover 'a broad cross-section of the varieties of Angeleno architecture', is inhibited by the relatively conventional implicit definition of 'architecture' accepted by these open-minded observers; their spectrum includes neither hamburger bars and other Pop ephemeridae at one extreme, nor freeway structures and other civil engineering at the other. However, both are as crucial to the human ecologies and built environments of Los Angeles as are dated works in classified styles by named architects.

In order to accommodate such extremes, the [four ecologies] will have to deviate from accepted norms for architectural histories of cities. What I have aimed to do is to present the architecture (in a fairly conventional sense of the word) within the topographical and historical context of the total artefact that constitutes Greater Los Angeles, because it is this double context that binds the polymorphous architectures into a comprehensible unity that cannot often be discerned by comparing monument with monument out of context.

So when most observers report monotony, not unity, and within that monotony, confusion rather than variety, this is usually because the context has escaped them; and it has escaped them because it is unique (like all the best unities) and without any handy terms of comparison. It is difficult to register the total artefact as a distinctive human construct because there is nothing else with which to compare it, and thus no class into which it may be pigeonholed. And we historians are too prone to behave like Socrates in Paul Valéry's *Eupalinos*, to reject the inscrutable, to hurl the unknown in the ocean. How then to bridge this gap of comparability. One can most properly begin by learning the local language; and the language of design, architecture and urbanism in Los Angeles is the language of movement. Mobility outweighs monumentality there to a unique degree, as Richard Austin Smith pointed out in a justly famous article in 1965, and the city will never be fully understood by those who cannot move fluently through its diffuse urban texture, cannot go with the flow of its unprecedented life. So, like earlier generations of English intellectuals who taught themselves Italian in order to read Dante in the original, I learned to drive in order to read Los Angeles in the original.

But whereas knowledge of Dante's tongue could serve in reading other Italian texts, full command of Angeleno dynamics qualifies one only to read Los Angeles, the uniquely mobile metropolis. Again that word 'uniquely' ... I make no apology for it. The splendours and miseries of Los Angeles, the graces and grotesqueries, appear to me as unrepeatable as they are unprecedented. I share neither the optimism of those who see Los Angeles as the prototype of all future cities, nor the gloom of those who see it as the harbinger of universal urban doom. Once the history of the city is brought under review, it is immediately apparent that no city has ever been produced by such an extraordinary mixture of geography, climate, economics, demography, mechanics and culture; nor is it likely that an even remotely similar mixture will ever occur again. The interaction of these factors needs to be kept in constant historical view – and since it is manifestly dangerous to face backwards while at the steering wheel, the common metaphor of history as the rear-view mirror of civilisation seems necessary, as well as apt, in any study of Los Angeles.

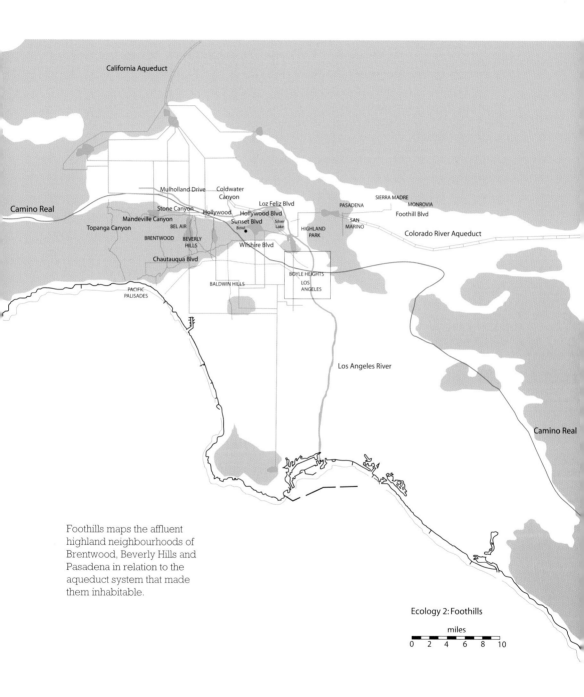

California Aqueduct

Mulholland Drive   Coldwater
                   Canyon
                                  Loz Feliz Blvd   SIERRA MADRE
Camino Real   Stone Canyon   PASADENA   MONROVIA
                         Mandeville Canyon   Hollywood   Hollywood Blvd   Foothill Blvd
           Topanga Canyon   BEL AIR   Sunset Blvd   Silver   SAN
                       BRENTWOOD   Bowl   Lake   HIGHLAND MARINO
                                 BEVERLY   PARK   Colorado River Aqueduct
                                 HILLS   Wilshire Blvd
           Chautauqua Blvd
                                                                 BOYLE HEIGHTS
                            BALDWIN HILLS   LOS
         PACIFIC   ANGELES
         PALISADES

                                                                                   Camino Real

                                                 Los Angeles River

Foothills maps the affluent
highland neighbourhoods of
Brentwood, Beverly Hills and
Pasadena in relation to the
aqueduct system that made
them inhabitable.

Ecology 2: Foothills

miles
0   2   4   6   8   10

First, observe an oddity in the 'Yellow Pages' of the local phone books; many firms list, in the same size type and without comment, branches in Hawaii, New Zealand and Australia. This is neither a picturesque curiosity nor commercial bragging – it is simply the next natural place to have branches, a continuation of the great westward groundswell of population that brought the Angelenos to the Pacific shore in the first place, a groundswell that can still be felt throughout the life of the city.

Los Angeles looks naturally to the Sunset, which can be stunningly handsome, and named one of its great boulevards after that favourite evening view. But if the eye follows the sun, westward migration cannot. The Pacific beaches are where young men stop going west, where the great waves of agrarian migration from Europe and the Middle West broke in a surf of fulfilled and frustrated hopes. The strength and nature of this westward flow need to be understood; it underlies the differences of mind between Los Angeles and its sister-metropolis to the north.

San Francisco was plugged into California from the sea; the Gold Rush brought its first population and their culture round Cape Horn; their prefabricated Yankee houses and prefabricated New England (or European) attitudes were dumped unmodified on the coast. Viewed from Southern California it looks like a foreign enclave, like the Protestant Pale in Ireland, because the Southern Californians came, predominantly, overland to Los Angeles, slowly traversing the whole North American land-mass and its evolving history.

They brought with them – and still bring – the prejudices, motivations and ambitions of the central heartland of the USA. The first major wave of immigration came from Kansas City on excursion tickets after 1885; later, they came in second-hand cars out of the dustbowl – not for nothing is Mayor Yorty known (behind his back) as the Last of the Okies, and Long Beach as the Main Seaport of Iowa! In one unnervingly true sense, Los Angeles is the Middle West raised to flash-point, the authoritarian dogmas of the Bible Belt and the perennial revolt against them colliding at critical mass under the palm trees. Out of it comes a cultural situation where only the extreme is normal, and the Middle Way is just the unused reservation down the centre of the Freeway.

Yet these extremes contrive to co-exist with only sporadic flares of violence – on Venice Beach, in Watts, or whatever is the fashionable venue for confrontations. Miraculously the city's extremes include an excessive tolerance. Partly this is that indifference which is Los Angeles' most publicised vice, but it is also a heritage from the extraordinary cultural mixture with which the city began. If Los Angeles is not a monolithic Protestant moral tyranny – and it notoriously is not! – it is because the Mid-Western agrarian culture underwent a profound transformation as it hit the coast, a sun-change that pervades moral postures, political attitudes, ethnic groupings and individual psychologies. This change has often been observed, and usually with bafflement, yet one observer has bypassed the bafflement and gone straight to an allegory of Californiation that seems to hold good from generation to generation – Ray Bradbury in the most fundamental of his Martian stories, *Dark they were, and Golden Eyed*, where the earth-family are subtly transformed, even against their wills, into tall, bronzed, gold-eyed Martians who abandon their neat Terran cities and the earthly cares and duty they symbolise, and run free in the mountains.

In one sense, this Martian transformation was forced upon the arriving agriculturalists by their daily occupations. Whereas a wheat-farming family relocating itself in the Central Valley, around Stockton in mid California, might expect to continue wheat-farming, those who went to Southern California could hardly hope even to try. Where water was available, Mediterranean crops made better sense and profit, olives, vines and – above all – citrus fruits, the first great source of wealth in Southern California after land itself. Horny-handed followers of the plough and reaper became gentlemen horticulturalists among their 'groves and fountains'.

The basic plants and crops for this transformed rural culture were already established on the land before the Mid-Westerners and North Europeans arrived, for the great wave of westward migration broke across the backwash of a receding wave from the south – the collapsing Mexican regime that was in itself the successor to the original Spanish colonisation of California. The two currents swirled together around some very substantial Hispanic relics: the Missions, where the fathers had introduced the grape, olive and orange as well as Christianity, the military communication line of the Camino Real and the Presidio forts, the very Pueblo de Nuestra Señora Reina de Los Angeles de Porciúncula.

And, above all, a system of ranching whose large scale, openhandedness and alfresco style were infectious, and whose pattern of land-holding still gives the ultimate title to practically every piece of land in Greater Los Angeles. Most of the original titles granted by the kings of Spain and by the Mexican governors were confirmed by patents granted by the US after 1848 (often a long while after; land-grant litigation became almost a national sport in California) and thus bequeathed to the area a pattern of property lines, administrative boundaries and place-names that guarantee a kind of cultural immortality to the Hispanic tradition.

So the predominantly Anglo-Saxon culture of Los Angeles ('Built by the British, financed by the Canadians') is deeply entangled with remnants of Spain, and has been so ever since an early-arriving *Yanqui* like Benjamin Wilson could translate himself into a 'Don Benito' by marrying into the Yorba clan, and thus into a ranching empire that spread over vast acreages to the east of the Pueblo. This ancient entanglement is still deeply felt, even if it is not officially institutionalised (as in the Spanish *Fiesta* in Santa Barbara, up the coast). It still provides psychological support for the periodical outbursts of pantiled roofs, adobe construction, arcaded courtyards, that constitute the elusive but ever-present Spanish Colonial Revival style, in all its variants from the simplest stuccoed shed to fantasies of fully fledged Neo-Churrigueresque. Such architecture should never be brushed off as mere fancy-dress; in Los Angeles it makes both ancestral and environmental sense, and much of the best modern architecture there owes much to its example.

As this architecture shows, the mixture of Hispanic and Anglo-Saxon traditions could have provided the basis for an interesting culture, even if its economic basis had remained agrarian. But the Yankees were coming because they knew a better trick with land than just ranching it; they stormed in on the crest of a wave of technological self-confidence and entrepreneurial abandon that left simple ranching little hope of survival. Land was acquired from the grant holders by every means in the rule book and some outside it, was subdivided, watered, put down to intensive cropping, and ultimately offered as residential plots in a landscape that must have appeared to anyone from east of the Rockies like an earthly Paradise.

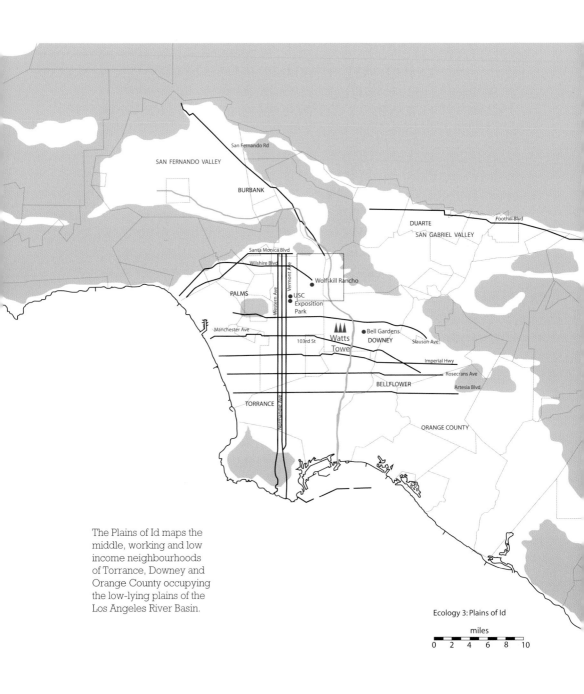

The Plains of Id maps the middle, working and low income neighbourhoods of Torrance, Downey and Orange County occupying the low-lying plains of the Los Angeles River Basin.

Ecology 3: Plains of Id

miles
0 2 4 6 8 10

Whatever man has done subsequently to the climate and environment of Southern California, it remains one of the ecological wonders of the habitable world. Given water to pour on its light and otherwise almost desert soil, it can be made to produce a reasonable facsimile of Eden. Some of the world's most spectacular gardens are in Los Angeles, where the southern palm will literally grow next to northern conifers, and it was this promise of an ecological miracle that was the area's first really saleable product – the 'land of perpetual spring'.

But to produce instant Paradise you have to add water – and keep on adding it. Once the scant local sources had been tapped, wasted and spoiled, the politics of hydrology became a pressing concern, even a deciding factor in fixing the political boundaries of Los Angeles. The City annexed the San Fernando Valley, murdered the Owens Valley in its first great raid on hinterland waters under William Mulholland, and its hydrological frontier is now on the Colorado River. Yet fertile watered soil is no use if it is inaccessible; transportation was to be the next great shaper of Los Angeles after land and water. From the laying of the first railway down to the port at Wilmington just over a century ago, transport has been an obsession that grew into a way of life.

Lines were hardly laid before commuting began along them; scattered communities were joined in a diffuse and unprecedented super-community, whose empty interstices filled up with further townships, vineyards, orchards, health resorts and the fine tracery of the second generation of railways – the inter-urbans. By 1910 when amalgamations and rationalisations had unified these inter-urban commuter lines into the Pacific Electric Railway, the map of its network was a detailed sketch for the whole Los Angeles that exists today. In part this must have been due to the way in which any major investment in transport tends to stabilise a new pattern more permanent than the old one which was disrupted by the investment, but it must have been at least equally due to the coincidence in time of the construction of the PE and a new phase of economic and industrial development.

In the decades on either side of 1900 the economic basis of Angeleno life was transformed. While land and field-produce remained the established basis of wealth, an important new primary industry was added – oil. Its existence had been long known from the natural seepages at the La Brea tar-pits in what is now Hancock Park, but commercial working did not begin until the mid-'nineties and large-scale exploitation grew throughout the first quarter of the 20th century as new fields were discovered. Nowadays drilling rigs or nodding pumps are liable to be found almost anywhere on the plains or along the coast, and the olfactory evidence of the existence of the oil industry is as ubiquitous as the visual.

In those same years of the full florescence of the Pacific Electric, Los Angeles also acquired a major secondary industry and a most remarkable tertiary one. The secondary was its port. There had always been harbour facilities on its coast, but the building of the Point Fermin breakwater to enclose the harbour at Wilmington/San Pedro from 1899 onwards was in good time to catch the greatly expanded trade promoted by the opening of the short sea-route from coast to coast through the Panama Canal after 1914. Within the breakwater now are a spreading complex of artificial islands and basins that constitute the largest man-made harbour in the world, clearing three billion dollars worth of goods a year.

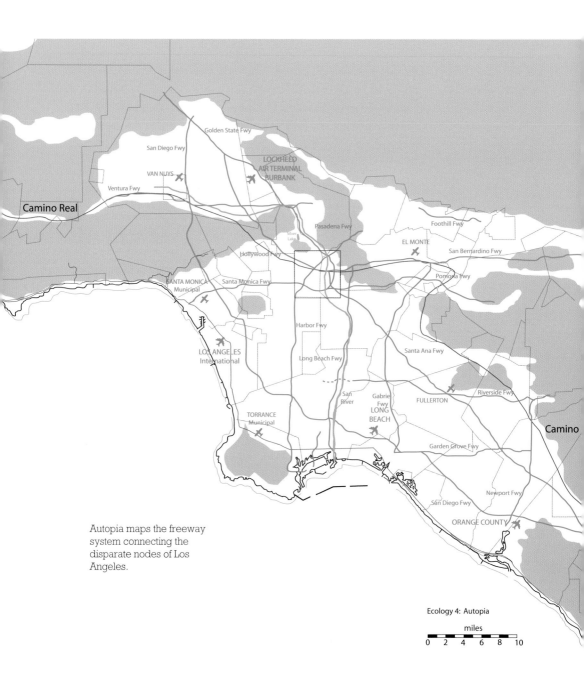

Camino Real

Golden State Fwy

San Diego Fwy

VAN NUYS

Ventura Fwy

LOCKHEED
AIR TERMINAL
BURBANK

Pasadena Fwy

Foothill Fwy

EL MONTE

San Bernardino Fwy

Silver
Lake

Hollywood Fwy

SANTA MONICA
Municipal

Santa Monica Fwy

Pomona Fwy

Harbor Fwy

LOS ANGELES
International

Long Beach Fwy

Santa Ana Fwy

San
River

Gabriel
Fwy

FULLERTON

Riverside Fwy

Camino

TORRANCE
Municipal

LONG
BEACH

Garden Grove Fwy

Newport Fwy

San Diego Fwy

ORANGE COUNTY

Autopia maps the freeway
system connecting the
disparate nodes of Los
Angeles.

Ecology 4: Autopia

miles

0   2   4   6   8   10

And in 1910, the tertiary industry that sets Los Angeles apart even from other cities that now possess the same tertiary, was founded, when the first Hollywood movie was made in a barn at the corner of Sunset and Gower. The movies seem to have been the great imponderable in the history of the area; their economic consequences were undoubtedly great, but it was mad money that the film industry brought in, and in any case it is the cultural consequences that now seem most important. Hollywood brought to Los Angeles an unprecedented and unrepeatable population of genius, neurosis, skill, charlatanry, beauty, vice, talent and plain old eccentricity, and it brought that population in little over two decades, not the long centuries that most metropolitan cities have required to accumulate a cultured and leisured class. So Hollywood was also the end of innocence and provincialism – the movies found Los Angeles a diffuse fruit-growing super-village of some 800,000 souls, and handed it over to the infant television industry in 1950 a world metropolis of over four million.

Now all these economic and cultural developments tended to go with the flow of urbanisation that the Pacific Electric both served and stimulated. Oil was struck all over the area, the harbour was spatially expansive and promoted other developments in the south of the central plain, Hollywood populated the foothills and established colonies as far afield as Malibu, while its need for vast areas of studio space indoors and out made it almost a major land-user on sites ever further from Sunset Boulevard.

The motor age, from the mid-twenties onwards, tended to confirm the going pattern, and the freeway network that now traverses the city, which has since added major aerospace industries to its economic armoury, conspicuously parallels the five first railways out of the Pueblo. Indeed the freeways seem to have fixed Los Angeles in canonical and monumental form, much as the great streets of Sixtus V fixed Baroque Rome, or the *Grands Travaux* of Baron Haussmann fixed the Paris of *la belle époque*. Whether you regard them as crowns of thorns or chaplets of laurels, the freeways are what the tutelary deity of the City of Angels should wear upon her head instead of the mural crowns sported by civic goddesses of old.

But while we drive along the freeways that are its crowning glory or prime headache, and con the rear-view mirror for historical illumination, what shall be our route? Simply to go from the oldest monument to the newest could well prove a short, boring and uninstructive journey, because the point about this giant city, which has grown almost simultaneously all over, is that all its parts are equal and equally accessible from all other parts at once. Everyday commuting tends less and less to move by the classic systole and diastole in and out of downtown, more and more to move by an almost random or Brownian motion over the whole area. The [four ecologies] are intended to invite the reader to do the same; only the history of modern architecture is treated in anything like chronological order, and can be read in historical sequence. The rest is to be visited at the reader's choice or fancy, with that freedom of movement that is the prime symbolic attribute of the Angel City.

From Reyner Banham, *Los Angeles: The Architecture of Four Ecologies*, excerpt from pp 21–36, Harper & Row (New York), 1971, by permission of the Estate of Reyner Banham. © Estate of Reyner Banham. Images: pp 98, 101, 104, 106 drawings Brian McGrath and Agkarat Atiprasertkul compiled from various maps by Mary Banham © Brian McGrath.

Learning From Las Vegas

Robert Venturi, Denise Scott Brown and Steven Izenour

Venturi, Scott-Brown and Izenour's, romp in Las Vegas with their Yale students in 1968 represents a cultural watershed; it both expanded the tools at hand with which to analyse the city, and what can be legitimately called the architecture of the city itself – now termed the 'architecture of persuasion'. What happens to urban design when the architecture of the city is primarily highway signs, casinos, supermarkets mediated by the ad-man? The team's stated goal was adapting design representational systems for the new patterns of the strip and sprawl. Ethnographic fieldwork, movie cameras, Pop Art and poetry were added to the established set of tools – such as the Nolli map – to produce a new method of urban analysis that still resonates and is widely emulated today.

A Significance For A&P Parking Lots, or Learning From Las Vegas

Substance for a writer consists not merely of those realities he thinks he discovers; it consists even more of those realities which have been made available to him by the literature and idioms of his own day and by the images that still have vitality in the literature of the past. Stylistically, a writer can express his feeling about this substance either by imitation, if it sits well with him, or by parody, if it doesn't.[1]

Learning from the existing landscape is a way of being revolutionary for an architect. Not the obvious way, which is to tear down Paris and begin again, as Le Corbusier suggested in the 1920s, but another, more tolerant way; that is, to question how we look at things.

The commercial strip, the Las Vegas Strip in particular – the example par excellence – challenges the architect to take a positive, non-chip-on-the-shoulder view. Architects are out of the habit of looking non-judgementally at the environment, because orthodox Modern architecture is progressive, if not revolutionary, utopian and puristic; it is dissatisfied with existing conditions. Modern architecture has been anything but permissive: architects have preferred to change the *existing* environment rather than enhance what is there.

But to gain insight from the commonplace is nothing new: fine art often follows folk art. Romantic architects of the 18th century discovered an existing and conventional rustic architecture. Early Modern architects appropriated an existing and conventional industrial vocabulary without much adaptation. Le Corbusier loved grain elevators and steamships; the Bauhaus looked like a factory; Mies refined the details of American steel factories for concrete buildings. Modern architects work through analogy, symbol and image – although they have gone to lengths to disclaim almost all determinants of their forms except structural necessity and the programme – and they derive insights, analogies and stimulation from unexpected images. There is a perversity in the learning process: we look backward at history and tradition to go forward; we can also look downward to go upward. And withholding judgement may be used as a tool to make later judgement more sensitive. This is a way of learning from everything.

Commercial Values and Commercial Methods

Las Vegas is analysed here only as a phenomenon of architectural communication. Just as an analysis of the structure of a Gothic cathedral need not include a debate on the morality of medieval religion, so Las Vegas's values are not questioned here. The morality of commercial advertising, gambling interests and the competitive instinct is not at issue here, although, indeed, we believe it should be in the architect's broader, *synthetic* tasks of which an analysis such as this is but one aspect. The analysis of a drive-in church in this context would match that of a drive-in restaurant, because this is a study of method, not content. Analysis of one of the architectural variables in isolation from the others is a respectable scientific and humanistic activity, so long as all are resynthesised in design. Analysis of existing American urbanism is a socially desirable activity to the extent that it teaches us architects to be more understanding and less authoritarian in the plans we make for both inner-city renewal and new development. In addition, there is no reason why the methods of commercial persuasion and the skyline of signs analysed here should not serve the purpose of civic and cultural enhancement. But this is not entirely up to the architect.

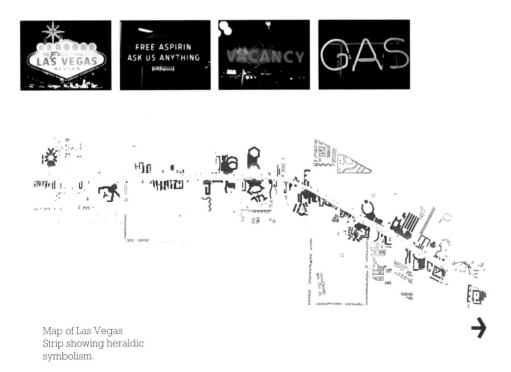

Map of Las Vegas
Strip showing heraldic
symbolism.

Billboards are Almost All Right

Architects who can accept the lessons of primitive vernacular architecture, so easy to take in an exhibit like 'Architecture without Architects', and of industrial, vernacular architecture, so easy to adapt to an electronic and space vernacular as elaborate neo-Brutalist or neo-Constructivist megastructures, do not easily acknowledge the validity of the commercial vernacular. For the artist, creating the new may mean choosing the old or the existing. Pop artists have relearned this. Our acknowledgement of existing, commercial architecture at the scale of the highway is within this tradition.

Modern architecture has not so much excluded the commercial vernacular as it has tried to take it over by inventing and enforcing a vernacular of its own, improved and universal. It has rejected the combination of fine art and crude art. The Italian landscape has always harmonised the vulgar and the Vitruvian: the *contorni* around the *duomo*, the *portiere's* laundry across the *padrone's portone*, *Supercortemaggiore* against the Romanesque apse. Naked children have never played in our fountains, and IM Pei will never be happy on Route 66.

Architecture as Space

Architects have been bewitched by a single element of the Italian landscape: the piazza. Its traditional, pedestrian-scaled and intricately enclosed space is easier to like than the spatial sprawl of Route 66 and Los Angeles. Architects have been brought up on Space, and enclosed space is the easiest to handle. During the last 40 years, theorists of Modern architecture (Wright and Le Corbusier sometimes excepted) have focused on space as the essential ingredient that separates architecture from painting, sculpture and literature. Their definitions glory in the uniqueness of the medium; although sculpture and painting may sometimes be allowed spatial characteristics, sculptural or pictorial architecture is unacceptable – because Space is sacred.

Purist architecture was partly a reaction against 19th-century eclecticism. Gothic churches, Renaissance banks and Jacobean manors were frankly picturesque. The mixing of styles meant the mixing of media. Dressed in historical styles, buildings evoked explicit associations and romantic allusions to the past to convey literary, ecclesiastical, national or programmatic symbolism. Definitions of architecture as space and form at the service of programme and structure were not enough. The overlapping of disciplines may have diluted the architecture, but it enriched the meaning.

Modern architects abandoned a tradition of iconology in which painting, sculpture and graphics were combined with architecture. The delicate hieroglyphics on a bold pylon, the archetypal inscriptions of a Roman architrave, the mosaic processions in Sant'Apollinare, the ubiquitous tattoos over a Giotto chapel, the enshrined hierarchies around a Gothic portal, even the illusionistic frescoes in a Venetian villa, all contain messages beyond their ornamental contribution to architectural space. The integration of the arts in Modern architecture has always been called a good thing. But one did not paint *on* Mies. Painted panels were floated independently of the structure by means of shadow joints; sculpture was in or near but seldom on the building. Objects of art were used to reinforce architectural space at the expense of their own content. The Kolbe in the Barcelona Pavilion was a foil to the directed spaces: the message was mainly architectural. The diminutive signs in most Modern buildings contained only the most necessary messages, like LADIES, minor accents begrudgingly applied.

Architecture as Symbol

Critics and historians, who documented the 'decline of popular symbols' in art, supported orthodox Modern architects, who shunned symbolism of form as an expression or reinforcement of content: meaning was to be communicated, not through allusion to previously known forms, but through the inherent, physiognomic characteristics of form. The creation of architectural form was to be a logical process, free from images of past experience, determined solely by programme and structure, with an occasional assist, as Alan Colquhoun has suggested,[2] from intuition.

But some recent critics have questioned the possible level of content to be derived from abstract forms. Others have demonstrated that the functionalists, despite their protestations, derived a formal vocabulary of their own, mainly from current art movements and the industrial vernacular; and latter-day followers such as the Archigram group have turned, while similarly protesting, to Pop Art and the space industry. However, most critics have slighted a continuing iconology in popular commercial art, the persuasive heraldry that pervades our environment from the advertising pages of *The New Yorker* to the super billboards of Houston. And their theory of the 'debasement' of symbolic architecture in 19th-century eclecticism has blinded them to the value of the representational architecture along highways. Those who acknowledge this roadside eclecticism denigrate it, because it flaunts the cliché of a decade ago as well as the style of a century ago. But why not? Time travels fast today.

The Miami Beach Modern motel on a bleak stretch of highway in southern Delaware reminds jaded drivers of the welcome luxury of a tropical resort, persuading them, perhaps, to forgo the gracious plantation across the Virginia border called Motel Monticello. The real hotel in Miami alludes to the international stylishness of a Brazilian resort, which, in turn, derives from the International Style of middle Corbu. This evolution from the high source through the middle source to the low source took only 30 years. Today, the middle source, the neo-Eclectic architecture of the 1940s and the 1950s, is less interesting than its commercial adaptations. Roadside copies of Ed Stone are more interesting than the real Ed Stone.

Symbol in Space before Form in Space: Las Vegas as a Communication System

The sign for the Motel Monticello, a silhouette of an enormous Chippendale tallboy, is visible on the highway before the motel itself. This architecture of styles and signs is antispatial; it is an architecture of communication over space; communication dominates space as an element in the architecture and in the landscape. But it is for a new scale of landscape. The philosophical associations of the old eclecticism evoked subtle and complex meanings to be savoured in the docile spaces of a traditional landscape.

The commercial persuasion of roadside eclecticism provokes bold impact in the vast and complex setting of a new landscape of big spaces, high speeds and complex programmes. Styles and signs make connections among many elements, far apart and seen fast. The message is basely commercial; the context is basically new.

A driver 30 years ago could maintain a sense of orientation in space. At the simple crossroad a little sign with an arrow confirmed what was obvious. One knew where one was. When the crossroads becomes a cloverleaf, one must turn right to turn left, a contradiction poignantly evoked in the print by Allan D'Arcangelo. But the driver has no time to ponder paradoxical subtleties within a dangerous, sinuous maze. He or she relies on signs for guidance – enormous signs in vast spaces at high speeds.

The dominance of signs over space at a pedestrian scale occurs in big airports. Circulation in a big railway station required little more than a simple axial system from taxi to train, by ticket window, stores, waiting room, and platform – all virtually without signs. Architects object to signs in buildings: 'If the plan is clear, you can see where to go.' But complex programmes and settings require complex combinations of media beyond the purer architectural triad of structure, form and light at the service of space. They suggest an architecture of bold communication rather than one of subtle expression.

The Architecture of Persuasion

The cloverleaf and airport communicate with moving crowds in cars or on foot for efficiency and safety. But words and symbols may be used in space for commercial persuasion. The Middle Eastern bazaar contains no signs; the Strip is virtually all signs. In the bazaar, communication works through proximity. Along its narrow aisles, buyers feel and smell the merchandise, and the merchant applies explicit oral persuasion. In the narrow streets of the medieval town, although signs occur, persuasion is mainly through the sight and smell of the real cakes through the doors and windows of the bakery. On Main Street, shop-window displays for pedestrians along the sidewalks and exterior signs, perpendicular to the street for motorists, dominate the scene almost equally.

On the commercial strip the supermarket windows contain no merchandise. There may be signs announcing the day's bargains, but they are to be read by pedestrians approaching from the parking lot. The building itself is set back from the highway and half hidden, as is most of the urban environment, by parked cars. The vast parking lot is in front, not at the rear, since it is a symbol as well as a convenience. The building is low because air conditioning demands low spaces, and merchandising techniques discourage second floors; its architecture is neutral because it can hardly be seen from the road. Both merchandise and architecture are disconnected from the road. The big sign leaps to connect the driver to the store, and down the road the cake mixes and detergents are advertised by their national manufacturers on enormous billboards inflected toward the highway. The graphic sign in space has become the architecture of this landscape. Inside, the A&P has reverted to the bazaar except that graphic packaging has replaced the oral persuasion of the merchant. At another scale, the shopping centre off the highway returns in its pedestrian malls to the medieval street.

Vast Space in the Historical Tradition and at the A&P

The A&P parking lot is a current phase in the evolution of vast space since Versailles. The space that divides high-speed highway and low, sparse buildings produces no enclosure and little direction. To move through a piazza is to move between high enclosing forms. To move through this landscape is to move over vast expansive texture: the megatexture of the commercial landscape. The parking lot is the *parterre* of the asphalt landscape. The patterns of parking lines give direction much as the paving patterns, kerbs, borders and *tapis vert* give direction in Versailles; grids of lamp posts substitute for obelisks, rows of urns and statues as points of identity and continuity in the vast space. But it is the highway signs, through their sculptural forms or pictorial silhouettes, their particular positions in space, their inflected shapes and their graphic meanings, that identify and unify the megatexture. They make verbal and symbolic connections through space, communicating a complexity of meanings through hundreds of associations in few seconds from far away. Symbol dominates space. Architecture is not enough. Because the spatial relationships are made by symbols more than by forms, architecture in this landscape becomes symbol in space rather than form in space. Architecture defines very little: the big sign and the little building is the rule of Route 66.

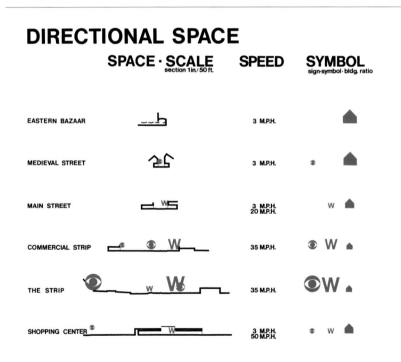

DIRECTIONAL SPACE

SPACE · SCALE · SPEED · SYMBOL

Sections through differently
scaled commercial spaces based
on the speed of experience.

The sign is more important than the architecture. This is reflected in the proprietor's budget. The sign at the front is a vulgar extravaganza, the building at the back, a modest necessity. The architecture is what is cheap. Sometimes the building is the sign: the duck store in the shape of a duck, called 'The Long Island Duckling', is sculptural symbol and architectural shelter. Contradiction between outside and inside was common in architecture before the Modern Movement, particularly in urban and monumental architecture. Baroque domes were symbols as well as spatial constructions, and they are bigger in scale and higher outside than inside in order to dominate their urban setting and communicate their symbolic message. The false fronts of Western stores did the same thing: they were bigger and taller than the interiors they fronted to communicate the store's importance and to enhance the quality and unity of the street. But false fronts are of the order and scale of Main Street. From the desert town on the highway in the West of today, we can learn new and vivid lessons about an impure architecture of communication. The little low buildings, grey-brown like the desert, separate and recede from the street that is now the highway, their false fronts disengaged and turned perpendicular to the highway as big, high signs. If you take the signs away, there is no place. The desert town is intensified communication along the highway.

***

Maps of Las Vegas

A 'Nolli' map of the Las Vegas Strip reveals and clarifies what is public and what is private, but here the scale is enlarged by the inclusion of the parking lot, and the solid-to-void ratio is reversed by the open spaces of the desert. Mapping the Nolli components from an aerial photograph provides an intriguing crosscut of Strip systems. These components, separated and redefined, could be undeveloped land, asphalt, cars, buildings and ceremonial space. Reassembled, they describe the Las Vegas equivalent of the pilgrims' way, although the description, like Nolli's map, misses the iconological dimensions of the experience.

A conventional land-use map of Las Vegas can show the overall structure of commercial use in the city as it relates to other uses but none of the detail of use type or intensity. 'Land-use' maps of the insides of casino complexes, however, begin to suggest the systematic planning that all casinos share. Strip 'address' and 'establishment' maps can depict both intensity and variety of use. Distribution maps show patterns of, for example, churches, and food stores that Las Vegas shares with other cities and those such as wedding chapels and car rental stations that are Strip oriented and unique. It is extremely hard to suggest the atmospheric qualities of Las Vegas, because these are primarily dependent on watts, animation and iconology; however, 'message maps', tourist maps and brochures suggest some of it.

Main Street and the Strip

A street map of Las Vegas reveals two scales of movement within the gridiron plan: that of Main Street and that of the Strip. The main street of Las Vegas is Fremont Street, and the earlier of two concentrations of casinos is located along three of four blocks of this street.

The casinos here are bazaar-like in the immediacy to the sidewalk of their clicking and tinkling gambling machines. The Fremont Street casinos and hotels focus on the railway depot at the head of the street; here the railway and main street scales of movement connect. The depot building is now gone, replaced by a hotel, and the bus station is now the busier entrance to town, but the axial focus on the railway depot from Fremont Street was visual, and possibly symbolic. This contrasts with the Strip, where a second and later development of casinos extends southward to the airport, the jet-scale entrance to town.

One's first introduction to Las Vegas architecture is a forebear of Eero Saarinen's TWA Terminal, which is the local airport building. Beyond this piece of architectural image, impressions are scaled to the car rented at the airport. Here is the unravelling of the famous Strip itself, which, as Route 91, connects the airport with the downtown.

System and Order on the Strip

The image of the commercial strip is chaos. The order in this landscape is not obvious. The continuous highway itself and its systems for turning are absolutely consistent. The median strip accommodates the U-turns necessary to a vehicular promenade for casino crawlers as well as left turns onto the local street pattern that the Strip intersects. The kerbing allows frequent right turns for casinos and other commercial enterprises and eases the difficult transitions from highway to parking. The streetlights function superfluously along many parts of the Strip that are incidentally but abundantly lit by signs, but their consistency of form and position and their arching shapes begin to identify by day a continuous space of the highway, and the constant rhythm contrasts effectively with the uneven rhythms of the signs behind.

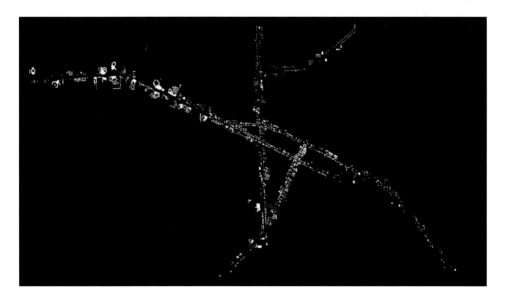

Map showing buildings in three Las Vegas Strips.

This counterpoint reinforces the contrast between two types of order on the Strip: the obvious visual order of street elements and the difficult visual order of buildings and signs. The zone *of* the highway is a shared order. The zone *off* the highway is an individual order. The elements of the highway are civic. The buildings and signs are private. In combination they embrace continuity *and* discontinuity, going *and* stopping, clarity *and* ambiguity, cooperation *and* competition, the community *and* rugged individualism. The system of the highway gives order to the sensitive functions of exit and entrance, as well as to the image of the Strip as a sequential whole. It also generates places for individual enterprises to grow and controls the general direction of that growth. It allows variety and change along its sides and accommodates the contrapuntal, competitive order of the individual enterprises.

There *is* an order along the sides of the highway. Varieties of activities are juxtaposed on the Strip: service stations, minor motels and multimillion-dollar casinos. Marriage chapels ('credit cards accepted') converted from bungalows with added neon-lined steeples are apt to appear anywhere toward the downtown end. Immediate proximity of related uses, as on Main Street, where you *walk* from one store to another, is not required along the Strip because interaction is by car and highway. You *drive* from one casino to another even when they are adjacent because of the distance between them, and an intervening service station is not disagreeable.

* * *

The Interior Oasis

If the back of the casino is different from the front for the sake of visual impact in the 'autoscape', the inside contrasts with the outside for other reasons. The interior sequence from the front door back progresses from gambling areas to dining, entertainment and shopping areas, to hotel. Those who park at the side and enter there can interrupt the sequence. But the circulation of the whole focuses on the gambling rooms. In a Las Vegas hotel the registration desk is invariably behind you when you enter the lobby; before you are the gambling tables and machines. The lobby is the gambling room. The interior space and the patio, in their exaggerated separation from the environment, have the quality of an oasis.

* * *

Architectural Monumentality and the Big, Low Space

The casino in Las Vegas is big, low space. It is the archetype for all public interior spaces whose heights are diminished for reasons of budget and air conditioning. (The low, one-way-mirrored ceilings also permit outside observation of the gambling rooms.) In the past, volume was governed by structural span; height was relatively easy to achieve. Today, span is easy to achieve, and volume is governed by mechanical and economic limitations on height. But railway stations, restaurants and shopping arcades only 3.5 metres (10 feet) high reflect as well a changing attitude to monumentality in our environment. In the past, big spans with their concomitant heights were an ingredient of architectural monumentality. But our monuments are not the occasional tour de force of an Astrodome, a Lincoln Center, or a subsidised airport. These merely prove that big, high spaces do not automatically make

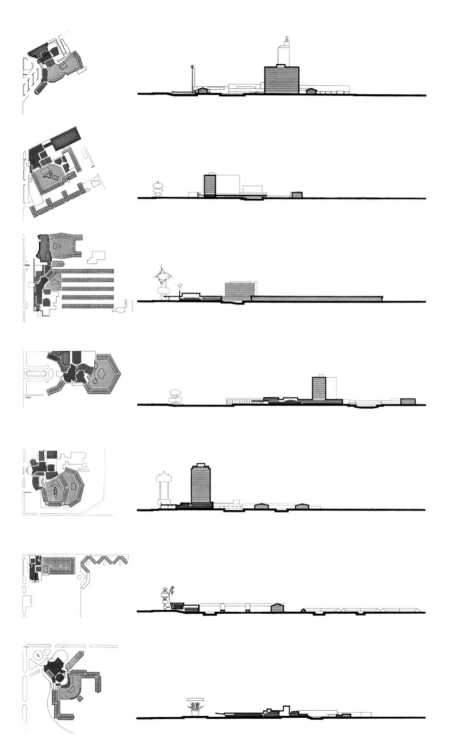

Casino typology.

Map of Las Vegas Strip showing every written word seen from the road.

architectural monumentality. We have replaced the monumental space of Pennsylvania Station by a subway above ground, and that of Grand Central Terminal remains mainly through its magnificent conversion to an advertising vehicle. Thus, we rarely achieve architectural monumentality when we try; our money and skill do not go into the traditional monumentality that expressed cohesion of the community through big-scale, unified, symbolic, architectural elements. Perhaps we should admit that our cathedrals are the chapels without the nave and that, apart from theatres and ball parks, the occasional communal space that is big is a space for crowds of anonymous individuals without explicit connection with each other. The big, low mazes of the dark restaurant with alcoves combine being together and yet separate as does the Las Vegas casino. The lighting in the casino achieves a new monumentality for the low space. The controlled sources of artificial and coloured light within the dark enclosures expand and unify the space by obscuring its physical limits. You are no longer in the bounded piazza but in the twinkling lights of the city at night.
★★★

Las Vegas Signs
Signs inflect toward the highway even more than buildings. The big sign – independent of the building and more or less sculptural or pictorial – inflects by its position, perpendicular to and at the edge of the highway, by its scale, and sometimes by its shape. The sign of the Aladdin Hotel and Casino seems to bow toward the highway through the inflection in its shape. It also is three dimensional, and parts of it revolve. The sign at the Dunes Hotel is more chaste: it is only two dimensional, and its back echoes its front, but it is an erection 22 storeys high that pulsates at night. The sign for The Mint Hotel on Route 91 at Fremont Street inflects toward the Casino several blocks away. Signs in Las Vegas use mixed media – words, pictures and sculpture – to persuade and inform. A sign is, contradictorily, for day and night. The same sign works as polychrome sculpture in the

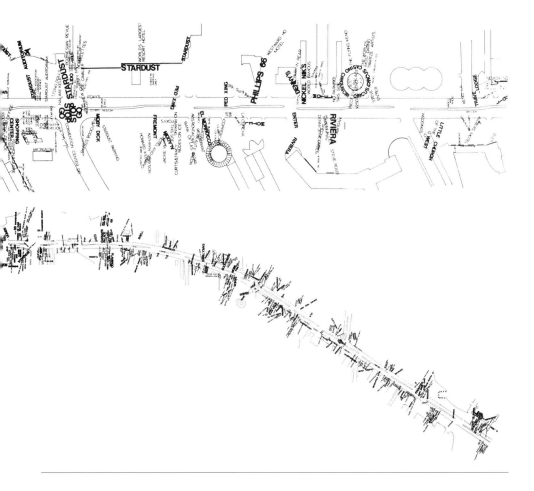

sun and as black silhouette against the sun; at night it is a source of light. It revolves by day and becomes a play of lights at night. It contains scales for close-up and for distance. Las Vegas has the longest sign in the world, the Thunderbird, and the highest, the Dunes.

Some signs are hardly distinguishable at a distance from the occasional high-rise hotels along the Strip. The sign of the Pioneer Club on Fremont Street talks. Its cowboy, 18 metres (60 feet) high, says 'Howdy Pardner' every 30 seconds. The big sign at the Aladdin Hotel has spawned a little sign with similar proportions to mark the entrance to the parking. 'But such signs!' says Tom Wolfe. 'They soar in shapes before which the existing vocabulary of art history is helpless. I can only attempt to supply names – Boomerang Modern, Palette Curvilinear, Flash Gordon Ming-Alert Spiral, McDonald's Hamburger Parabola, Mint Casino Elliptical, Miami Beach Kidney.'[3] Buildings are also signs. At night on Fremont Street, whole buildings are illuminated but not through reflection from spotlights; they are made into sources of light by closely spaced neon tubes. Amid the diversity, the familiar Shell and Gulf signs stand out like friendly beacons in a foreign land. But in Las Vegas they reach three times higher into the air than at your local service station to meet the competition of the casinos.

Inclusion and the Difficult Order

Henri Bergson called disorder an order we cannot see. The emerging order of the Strip is a complex order. It is not the easy, rigid order of the urban renewal project or the fashionable 'total design' of the megastructure. It is, on the contrary, a manifestation of an opposite direction in architectural theory: Broadacre City – a travesty of Broadacre City, perhaps, but a kind of vindication of Frank Lloyd Wright's predictions for the American landscape. The commercial strip within the urban sprawl is, of course, Broadacre City with a difference. Broadacre City's easy, motival order identified and unified its vast spaces and separate buildings at the scale of the omnipotent automobile. Each building, without doubt, was to be designed by the Master or by his Taliesin Fellowship, with no room for honky-tonk improvisations. An easy control would be exercised over similar elements within the universal, Usonian vocabulary to the exclusion, certainly, of commercial vulgarities. But the order of the Strip *includes*; it includes at all levels, from the mixture of seemingly incongruous land uses to the mixture of seemingly incongruous advertising media plus a system of neo-Organic or neo-Wrightian restaurant motifs in Walnut Formica. It is not an order dominated by the expert and made easy for the eye. The moving eye in the moving body must work to pick out and interpret a variety of changing, juxtaposed orders, like the shifting configurations of a Victor Vasarely painting. It is the unity that 'maintains, but only just maintains, a control over the clashing elements which compose it. Chaos is very near; its nearness, but its avoidance, gives ... force.'[4]

Image of Las Vegas: Inclusion and Allusion in Architecture

Tom Wolfe used Pop prose to suggest powerful images of Las Vegas. Hotel brochures and tourist handouts suggest others. JB Jackson, Robert Riley, Edward Ruscha, John Kouwenhoven, Reyner Banham and William Wilson have elaborated on related images. For the architect or urban designer, comparisons of Las Vegas with others of the world's 'pleasure zones' – with Marienbad, the Alhambra, Xanadu and Disneyland, for instance – suggest that essential to the imagery of pleasure-zone architecture are lightness, the quality of being an oasis in a perhaps hostile context, heightened symbolism and the ability to engulf the visitor in a new role: for three days one may imagine oneself a centurion at Caesars Palace, a ranger at the Frontier, or a jetsetter at the Riviera rather than a salesperson from Des Moines, Iowa or an architect from Haddonfield, New Jersey.

However, there are didactic images more important than the images of recreation for us to take home to New Jersey and Iowa: one is the Avis with the Venus; another, Jack Benny under a classical pediment with Shell Oil beside him, or the gasoline station beside the multimillion-dollar casino. These show the vitality that may be achieved by an architecture of inclusion or, by contrast, the deadness that results from too great a preoccupation with tastefulness and total design. The Strip shows the value of symbolism and allusion in an architecture of vast space and speed and proves that people, even architects, have fun with architecture that reminds them of something else, perhaps of harems or the Wild West in Las Vegas, perhaps of the nation's New England forebears in New Jersey. Allusion and commentary on the past or present, or on our great commonplaces or old clichés, are inclusion of the everyday in the environment, sacred and profane – these are what are lacking in present-day Modern architecture. We can learn about them from Las Vegas as have other artists from their own profane and stylistic sources.

Pop artists have shown the value of the old cliché used in a new context to achieve a new meaning – the soup can in the art gallery – to make the common uncommon. And in literature, Eliot and Joyce display, according to Poirier, 'an extraordinary vulnerability … to the idioms, rhythms, artifacts, associated with certain urban environments or situations. The multitudinous styles of *Ulysses* are so dominated by them that there are only intermittent sounds of Joyce in the novel and no extended passage certifiably in his as distinguished from a mimicked style.'[5] Poirier refers to this as the 'decreative impulse'.[6] Eliot himself speaks of Joyce's doing the best he can 'with the material at hand'.[7] Perhaps a fitting requiem for the irrelevant works of Art that are today's descendants of a once meaningful Modern architecture are Eliot's lines in 'East Coker':

> *That was a way of putting it – not very satisfactory:*
> *A periphrastic study in a worn-out poetical fashion,*
> *Leaving one still with the intolerable wrestle*
> *With words and meanings. The poetry does not matter …* [8]

Notes
1 R Poirier, 'TS Eliot and the Literature of Waste', *The New Republic* (20 May 1967), p 21.
2 A Colquhoun, 'Typology and Design Method', *Arena*, Journal of the Architectural Association (June 1967), pp 11–14.
3 T Wolfe, *The Kandy-Kolored Tangerine-Flake Streamline Baby*, Noonday Press (New York), 1966, p 8.
4 A Heckscher, *The Public Happiness*, Atheneum Publishers (New York), 1962, p 289.
5 Poirier, 'TS Eliot and the Literature of Waste', p 20.
6 Poirier, 'TS Eliot and the Literature of Waste', p 21.
7 TS Eliot, *The Complete Poems and Plays, 1909–1950*, Harcourt, Brace and Company (New York), 1958, p 125.
8 TS Eliot, *Four Quartets*, Harcourt, Brace and Company (New York), 1943, p 13.

From Robert Venturi, Denise Scott Brown and Steven Izenour, *Learning From Las Vegas*, revised edition: *The Forgotten Symbolism of Architectural Form*, excerpt from pp 3–72 © 1977 Massachusetts Institute of Technology, by permission of MIT Press. Images: pp 109, 113, 115, 117, 118–19 reproduced by permission of Venturi, Scott Brown and Associates, Inc. © John Izenour.

An Urbanism of Reform

Albert Pope

Albert Pope's classic book *Ladders* provided a structural reading of the evolution and dissolution of the American grid city. Houston-based Pope provides this original chapter as a further reflection on this city, but from the perspective of the persistent problem of the inner city in relation to the larger megalopolitan region. Using the idea of 'reform' as an architectural and urban design term rather than as a social project, Pope advocates looking at the city of the present rather than historical models in remaking the older centres of cities; and recent architecture production as focused on the public institutions of a metropolitan view of the city: libraries, museums and performance centres. Pope presents his project for the Fifth Ward in Houston to advocate reforming the inner city by focusing on the larger megalopolitan structure of the contemporary city, where the historical centre is just one node in a large polynucleated urban region.

Intractable social, political and economic problems provoke a familiar trajectory of bold initiatives followed by a train of ever-diminishing ambitions. Compromise follows compromise yet hope springs eternal in direct proportion to the growing cynicism of those who no longer care. Such is the trajectory of the 'inner city' as it has evolved in architectural and urban discourse over the past half-century. Beginning with the bold utopian transformation of inhumane slum conditions and ending with a resigned acceptance of market-driven gentrification, design-based reforms have followed a humbling, if not humiliating, line of retreat. What 50 years ago was the signature issue of a progressive urbanism – the wholesale redevelopment, not just of impoverished, substandard environments, but of the city itself – the inner city is now little more than a modest agenda of restoration based on obsolete 19th-century urban models.

Gentrification as Reform

Though it is not generally regarded as such, the last half-century of architectural and urban discourse pivoted around the transformation of the American inner city. By this I mean that the buildings that sparked the postmodern turn of the early 1970s were not a handful of detached, single-family houses realised on the bucolic back-roads of Megalopolis. What sparked the turn was the perceived failure of so many Modernist housing 'projects' built in inner-city neighbourhoods all over the United States. The unspeakable conditions in which these projects rose (and which they could not relieve) did more than any theoretician or designer could to promote an inquisition into the modern. The reaction against modern urbanism was both swift and strong enough to turn back the wave of progressive reforms that characterised architectural and urban discourse for nearly a century.

What ultimately emerged from postmodern urbanism was the return to an agenda of reform based upon monumental production – libraries, opera houses, theatres, museums – leaving the significant remainder of urban fabric to bureaucrats, market forces and to a burgeoning field of non-profits with little or no design intention. With regards to the inner city, postmodernism did not so much abandon reform through design as it returned reform to a basic, if not ancient, strategy. Postmodern urban reforms would be made, not by a redesign of the urban fabric directly – as in, for example, the case of Radiant City housing projects – but by monumental intervention whereby an exemplary (hierarchical) building would redefine an entire district serving as a catalyst for gentrification. This targeted approach to urban development has a long history; inasmuch as monuments have traditionally operated as catalysts for urban reform, the principle can be seen as the driving force of traditional urban development. This time-honoured urban tradition goes a long way toward explaining why the postmodern strategy of targeted, monumental intervention was adopted so quickly and so completely. Since its adoption in the early 1970s, the targeted intervention has become our exclusive approach to design in the inner city.

The beginning point of postmodern reform through monumental intervention is clear; the Centre Pompidou (1977) transformed the deteriorated Beaubourg district in the 4th *arrondissement* of Paris, turning it into what is perhaps the most significant tourist destination in the Western world. Throughout the following decade monumental intervention would continue to show modest success at urban reform. It was not, however, until the late 1990s that the postmodern monument would come into its own with the opening of the Guggenheim Museum in Bilbao (1997). Like the Centre Pompidou that preceded it, the Guggenheim is situated in a dense, pre-modern urban grid – the 1876 Extension of Bilbao by Alzola, Achúcarro and Hoffmeyer Architects. The museum formally terminates the Calle de Iparraguirre that frames the project within the street walls of the historical past. This placement of a hyper-modern building within the walls of a traditional urban fabric (as opposed to, say, an airport office park) is key to the building's success. In other words, targeted monumental intervention only works in the reform of a pre-modern urban context. To cite only the most recent examples of postmodern monumentality – the Casa da Música in Porto (2005), the Denver Art Museum (2006), the New Museum in New York (2007), the Wyly Theatre in Dallas (2008) and the MAXXI National Museum of the 21st Century Arts in Rome (2009) – is to cite the ongoing efficacy of targeted urban reform.

Reform for the Few

The problem with targeted, monumental intervention and the gentrification that it promotes is that it does not take into account the dramatic changes in urban infrastructure brought about by the rise of Megalopolis over the past half-century. The success of these targeted reforms is entirely due to the existence of traditional or pre-modern urban infrastructures like the gridiron streets of the American inner city. The most striking change that has come to the inner city over the preceding half century is not due to a 'new monumentality', however, but to changes that took place in the surrounding city. Once the hierarchical culmination of a vast metropolitan field, the inner-city grid now exists as one among many nodes that are otherwise absorbed into the extensive polycentric field – the conurbation of Megalopolis. In other words, the inner city no longer exists as the culmination of an open field of blocks and streets, but as one among many closed subdivisions loosely strung together into a distended horizontal network. And while the inner-city infrastructure was based on the traditional typologies of the block and the street, its new post-war surroundings are decidedly not. Megalopolis is not formed of blocks and streets, but is formed of an entirely different DNA.

No longer the undisputed centre of an urban hierarchy, the inner city is separated from the bulk of its urban setting by a fundamental shift in the form of urban infrastructure. Within this new context, the inner city is a historic relic, redeveloping its 19th-century thematic through the restoration or reconstruction of outmoded urban forms of gridded urbanism. Given these circumstances, reform through a targeted, monumental intervention takes on an entirely different meaning. In a megalopolitan context, monumental production is not the reform of the city, but the reform of an isolated historical district that in no way resembles the city at large. Far from universal reform, it is reform on a minor scale targeted at the remnants of historical urbanism that is destined for archaeologists, tourists and the privileged few who will ultimately inherit it. (While there are many things unknown about the evolution of cities, the outcome of gentrification is simply not in doubt.) If the wholesale tabula rasa urbanism of utopian Modernism can be seen as an attempt to reform the city in its entirety, the targeted intervention of postmodernism can be described as an attempt to reform the few.

Reform for the Many
As gentrification proceeds and blight pushes out to the first ring of 'suburban' development, the inner city will come to resemble nothing so much as the ossified structure of European cities where a privileged few occupy the historical centre that is otherwise preserved for the ever-expanding tourist industry – real urban culture on tour for those who must live elsewhere. As always, the less privileged are pushed to the periphery – the *faubourg* – where modernisation plays out with ruthless, unmediated efficiency. The *sublimation* of such modernisation – what was once called modern urbanism – is disdained as a tragic utopian dream, 40 years out of date. Yet, it is not difficult to argue that a regressive class structure is built into market-based gentrification. This leads us to immediately ask if there is not more for modern design to accomplish than targeted interventions intended to spur on the rehabilitation and reconstruction of 19th-century gridiron urbanism?

There is yet time for alternatives to the modest agenda of gentrification. The unsolved problem of the inner city forces us to move beyond 19th-century urbanism and confront the question of a modern infrastructure – infrastructure based on contemporary urban practices. If the inner city's gridiron urbanism is outmoded, then what, exactly, would constitute its reform today? If not the patching up of the gridiron infrastructure, what constitutes an upgrade to the present inner city? Here it must be remembered that Megalopolis distinguishes itself from the entire history of urbanism inasmuch as it is not based on a gridded formation of blocks and streets. Given that street grids have been extinct for some half-century, exactly what infrastructural form succeeds them? And can this alternative form be related to the problem of the inner city? Beyond the target intervention of the postmodern monument, is it not possible to project an alternative mode of urban reform – perhaps a return to the redesign of the urban infrastructure itself?

Broken City, Broken Form

All of these questions were played out in a design proposal for Houston's inner city. The site was chosen, not only because funding for inner-city projects was available, but also because it shared some structural similarities with the 'outer city', blurring the distinction between an outmoded gridiron infrastructure and a contemporary cul-de-sac infrastructure. The area is called the Fifth Ward and it is one of the poorest, most crime-ridden sections of the city of Houston. Comparable to the South Bronx, the Southside of Chicago, Watts and the Western District of Baltimore, the Fifth Ward is frequently characterised as a blighted slum. The Fifth Ward began proudly, as a 'Freedman's Town' founded in 1866 by the region's emancipated slaves. It is located adjacent to Houston's Central Business District yet it is a world apart from the corporate ethos that prevails downtown. For many decades the Fifth Ward served as the centre of the Houston African-American community. With over 100 churches and a concentration of black-owned businesses, the district reached its population peak in the years leading up to the Second World War. With sizeable rail yard and an active port facility on its southern border, the Fifth Ward was supported by good jobs all within walking distance. It was a destination in Houston commonly referred to as 'the Nickel'. Four members of Congress came from the Fifth Ward including Barbara Jordan and Mickey Leland. It was also the birthplace of George Foreman and Dr Ruth Simmons.

In the early 1960s things began to slide for the Fifth Ward as it did for the rest of urban America. As a result of containerisation, the port moved further out toward the gulf, rail traffic declined and jobs disappeared as the crime rate rose. At the same time that these economic ills appeared, the Fifth Ward was eviscerated by freeway construction. Major pollution in its southern section also came to light eventually leading to the declaration of a major Superfund Site. By the 1980s, the Fifth Ward was being referred to as the 'Bloody Nickel'. The 2000 census lists the Fifth Ward as a community of 21,640 people: 60 per cent African American, 37 per cent Hispanic and 2 per cent white. The majority of residents (51 per cent) have yearly incomes below $18,300; 67 per cent of the population rents, with a vacancy rate of 14 per cent. Some 55 per cent of the lots contain single-family houses, 71 per cent of the lots are valued at less than $25,000. One third of the lots in the Fifth Ward (32 per cent) are vacant.

Upgrading Infrastructure

The street plan of the Fifth Ward shows the present state of its gridiron infrastructure [see page 128, bottom left]. As an urban fabric, the grid pattern appears to be rent or torn. Very few streets are continuous and those that are tend to bypass the neighbourhood completely. Our intention in the reform of the district was not, however, to restore the gridded infrastructure to an 'original' state. What we wanted to do was to take the more difficult and more controversial task of upgrading the Fifth Ward to a distinctly modern or contemporary infrastructure. While no one would argue that such an upgrade is needed, there is much confusion as to what, exactly, a contemporary infrastructure actually is. If the grid is not the model for an upgraded infrastructure, then what is?

The reason for this confusion is that the urban grid is seen, not as a historically specific form, but as the very definition of the city itself. Without really thinking about it, we tend to see a grid of blocks and streets as the 'essential' quality of all cities that transcends any historical circumstances. Absent the grid, the city simply does not exist. This essential understanding of urban form obscures one crucial fact: that the gridiron is historically outmoded. Far from being essential, the gridded infrastructure of the inner city has not been produced over the last 50 years. While the gridiron underlies the urbanism that we inherit (and we have inherited a large amount of it), it is not the urbanism that we currently practise. A contemporary infrastructure – an infrastructure that stems from current urban practices – is the infrastructure of Megalopolis. While the rehabilitation and preservation of our historic legacy is important, it can hardly pass as urban reform. On the contrary, urban reform must engage not an isolated historical district, but the popular and predominant mode of urbanisation as it is practised today. For the past 50 years, that mode of urbanisation has been Megalopolis.

I have argued elsewhere[1] that Megalopolis is not 'sprawl', but possesses a historically unique structure based, not on the geometry of the grid, but on the geometry of the spine. Instead of restoring or reconstructing the grid, our approach to upgrading the Fifth Ward was to bring the spine-based forms of contemporary urban practices into the inner city. Through these upgrades, it is hoped that the amenities that make the spine-based cul-de-sac Megalopolis so desirable can be brought into the poorest section of the city. More important, perhaps, the qualities that make Megalopolis so attractive to its dwellers also make it attractive to its developers, fuelling a market-based upgrade of the Ward – a viable alternative to market-based gentrification.

Infrastructure

What we have learned from the experiments of urban renewal in the 1950s and 1960s is that upgrading the architecture of inner city is not sufficient. It can be argued that modern urbanism failed because it tried to reform urban slums by architecture alone instead of also reforming the infrastructure beneath. Urban renewal, and the new housing stock it requires, cannot succeed by brilliant architecture alone. One imagines that the projects designed for the Southside of Chicago, or the South Bronx, or for the slums of St Louis, could never have succeeded, even if they had been designed by the most brilliant architects in the world. The failure of modern housing projects is not simply due to architectural failure, but also to the failure of outmoded urban infrastructure upon which the projects were built. In hindsight, the obvious question to ask is what infrastructure can do in the inner-city environment that architecture cannot.

In response to these important, failed experiments in redevelopment, we attempted to invert the example of Cabrini Green and Pruitt-Igoe where architecture was everything and infrastructure was left untouched. In our proposal, infrastructure is everything and the architectural build-out could take on an infinite number of variations, both in space and over time, none of which we felt compelled to specify. The reason for this inversion was not simply to avoid past failures. In addition to being contrary, we wanted to stress that our proposal is not a masterplan and it is not a fixed urban composition; it does not project preemptive final forms. Like the infrastructure that historically preceded it, the Fifth Ward proposal seeks to identify the DNA of a new, uniquely contemporary aggregation through the specification of an aggregate unit.

Spine and Space

The characteristic that the broken street grid of the Fifth Ward shares with the infrastructure of Megalopolis that surrounds it is that it is fortuitously constructed of discontinuous, spine-like forms. Among the many qualities of spine-based urban production, this single characteristic stands out as primary; discontinuous spines produce an urban environment that is dominated by space rather than by form. In traditional urban environments, like the inner city, the logic of form (the logic of street walls and monuments) establishes the formal base line of the environment. In Megalopolis, however, space dominates form. This characteristic is made apparent by the simple act of driving a car through the contemporary Megalopolis. The buildings that appear out of the typical windshield occupy only a tiny fraction of the field of vision that is otherwise dominated by a super-abundance of space. In Megalopolis, space envelops and dwarfs architectural objects that are scarcely capable of breaking the horizon. By chance, this characteristic is not unlike the conditions we found in the Fifth Ward where a large number of empty residential lots, abandoned industrial sites and infrastructure rights-of-way contributed to substantial gaps in the traditional urban fabric. Because the Ward has been subject to so much disruption – particularly in the destruction of its building stock and the appropriation of its land for freeway construction – it in some ways possesses a spatial dominant similar to the spine-based development of the outer city. If one objective of upgrading the inner city is to reflect the qualities found in contemporary development, then the Ward's spatial excess can be seen to give us a head start.

Rather than employing a formal approach based on the megalopolitan spine, our designs for the Fifth Ward began with an approach that would emphasise its spatial characteristics. What we want to do in our upgrade of the Ward is to develop techniques of analysis and design that engage the spatial dominant. This was accomplished by a primitive diagramming technique that employed the simple vocabulary of point, line and plane illustrated in the accompanying diagrams. By way of commentary to the project panels that accompany this essay, I would like briefly to go through this vocabulary of point, line and plane in turn.

1-way

2-way

3-way

4-way

	4-way	3-way	2-way	1-way	% sw	% null
residential	42	22	3	3	70	30
park	7	23	2	2	34	66
educational	38	8	7	2	6	40
religious	39	23	4	5	71	29
commercial	37	22	2	4	65	35
industrial	3	12	3	4	22	78
parking	15	11	4	3	33	67
empty	24	19	3	6	52	48

SWITCH DISTRIBUTION. The switch field constitutes a unique index of the formal and spatial structure of the urban environment. The field can also be directly correlated to urban programmes. The first stage of this correlation is to count the switch numbers and classify them by type. After counting up the switches, it is possible to generate a ratio of switch to area for each programme category. This is further broken down into switch type. This ratio allows us to extract ratios from the existing Fifth Ward situation, and to apply them, with modification, to the New Town. For example, the calculations for the residential area are simple: 70% of a residential area is covered with intersections of all types. Subtracting from the total, 30% of the Fifth Ward residential area is open. Of the total number of intersections, 42% are four-way, 22% are three-way, 3% are two-way and 3% are one-way. These ratios are calculated for all programme areas and listed in the table above. The table shows an enormous variation in the 'continuity' of each programme area. This

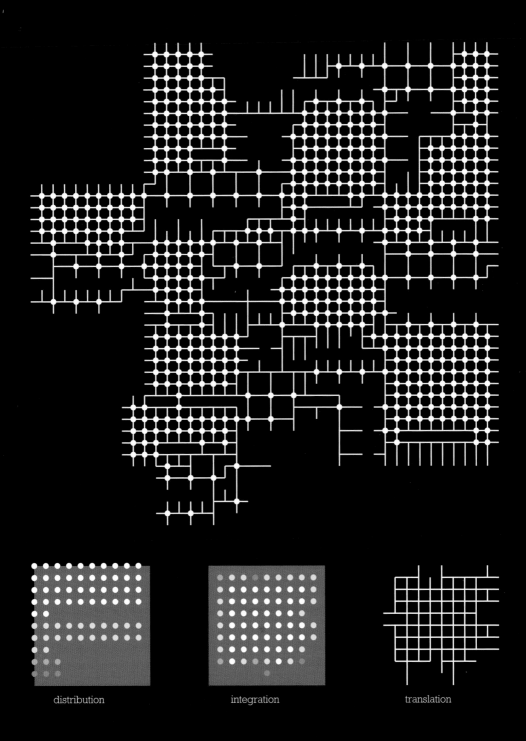

distribution   integration   translation

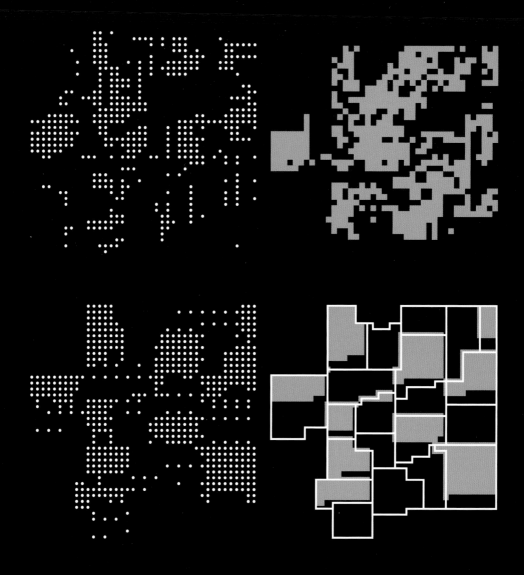

PROGRAMME AND CONTINUITY. Above left is a diagram showing the existing four-way intersections or switches in the Fifth Ward. Above right is a diagram showing the existing areas programmed as residential. The switch type and programme area are nearly coincident. Residential districts consistently show a high proportion of four-way intersections that provide maximum continuity among living areas. In the Fifth Ward, there are 547 residential blocks and 388 intersections. Of the 388 intersections, 230 (59%) are four-way intersections. By way of contrast, there are 471 industrial blocks, 107 intersections of which only 15 (14%) are four-way. What this told us is that programme areas have remarkably consistent degrees of continuity. This continuity can be measured in the form of a 'switch ratio'. It is possible to calculate the continuity or switch ratio and use it to generate alternate configurations. Below left shows the distribution of four-way switches in the final plan while below right shows the new programme area for residential which has the same continuity as what exists. All programmes were disposed in this manner leading to the development of the 'subgrid' indicated above left.

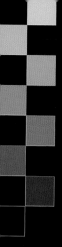

religious: area zoned to accommodate the 66 churches that now exist

education: area zoned for all educational institutions

residential: predominant residential use not limited by building type

park: area zoned for publicly owned and maintained park space

commercial: area zoned for retail and administrative enterprises

industrial: area once industrial, now abandoned, open space

parking lots: area once distributed lot by lot, now grouped

empty lot: area once abandoned and tax delinquent, now in reserve

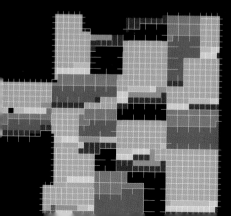

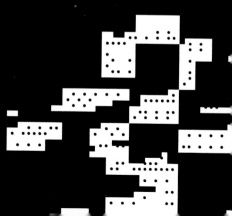

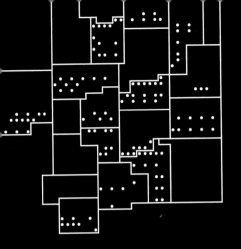

SUBDIVISION AND ONE WAY SWITCHES: POINTS OF SPACE. This diagram shows the relation of the subdivision boundaries and one-way switches (dead end streets). In Megalopolis, space is not contained by a form or framed by an edge, but rather emanates from a series of points. One-way switches mark the literal termination of form and the beginning of space. The switches on the left mark the subdivisions of the plan that are characterised as voids.

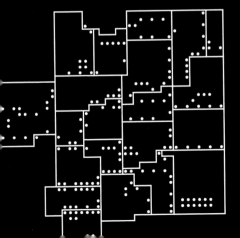

SOFT WALLS AND THREE-WAY SWITCHES. Fences and walls destroy the qualities of contemporary urban space. Three-way or 'T' intersections create invisible walls. Instead of constructing material boundaries, we have subdivided the Ward using 'soft walls' made of three-way intersections. Soft walls are not new, but they have never been subject to systematic deployment. The switches on the right are three-way switches which line up with the subdivision lines of the plan. These subdivisions are all created without the use of material walls.

Points: Continuity of Intersections

While the figure-ground diagram is a perfect method of diagramming cities dominated by form, it tells you almost nothing about an environment that is dominated by space. Instead of indexing building footprints, we chose instead to index street intersections resulting in a point field of relative continuities. To be clear, in marking intersections we were not marking infrastructural forms as much as we were marking the relative continuity of each of the Fifth Ward intersections. Referring to the diagram [see page 128, top], we started this analysis with all of the possible intersections of the Fifth Ward. Subtracted from this regular point field are only the intersections that remain as indicated by the street plan. A third diagram shows us all of the intersections that were either demolished or never built in the first place. There were roughly as many demolished or unbuilt intersections as there were active intersections. This absence of development is rarely registered, yet the diagram serves to underscore that what does *not* happen is just as important as what does, especially in urbanism.

From the list of all functional intersections, a further breakdown was made. Of the existing intersections, one subset consists of one-way intersections (which are dead-end streets), a second subset consists of two-way intersections (which are elbow intersections), a third subset consists of three-way intersections (which are the notorious 'T' intersections), and a fourth subset consists of all intact four-way intersections. When all of these intersection types are combined, a sophisticated point field comes into play whereby each point is weighted toward a lesser and greater continuity. What this means is that a field consisting of mostly one-way switches would have a much lower continuity than a field consisting of mostly four-way switches. Given that the points can be ranked on a simple one to four scale, a number or 'continuity index' can be assigned to each field. In this way, the differences between a gridiron pattern consisting of mostly four-way switches can be quantitatively distinguished from a cul-de-sac pattern consisting of mostly one-way switches. Despite the fact that it simply tracks the status of functional intersections (and is thus pure information), the diagram of the point field ultimately provides an entrance into form.

In breaking down the point field into the five switch types – null, one-way, two-way, three-way, and four-way switches – we began to see that combinations of switches not only made unique point fields, but that the switches themselves had distinct characteristics of their own. For example, we noticed that the generally open programmes had an abundance of dead-end streets terminating in what we are calling one-way switches. It made obvious sense that open spaces would be created by a combination of one-way switches and null points. As a result, we began to understand the one-way intersection as the location at which form stops and space begins. We began to think of one-way intersections as being, not the frame or edge of space, but points of emanation; for once, urban space becomes something other than the framed boulevards and parks of the 19th-century city. This observation led us to group programmes with lesser continuity and a greater percentage of open space together so that we could form a kind of spatial 'armature' for the new plan. The idea here is that space can be glue, not in the way it is in traditional cities where space is framed by urban blocks, but by using space as a medium by which to unify a loosely jointed set of objects. Thus, the new plan has a core that is not manifest

SPINE AS TYPE FORM

If Megalopolis were typologically determined, then the cul-de-sac form would be reproduced with very little variation. While the cul-de-sac is the dominant motif of the megalopolitan aggregate, it is not bound to the narrow variations of type that existed in traditional cities. The much broader range of variation available to megalopolitan aggregation is seen in the alternatives of the basic cul-de-sac form depicted in the accompanying diagrams. This range of variation is expanded into 'search spaces'.

SEVEN UNITS OF AGGREGATION

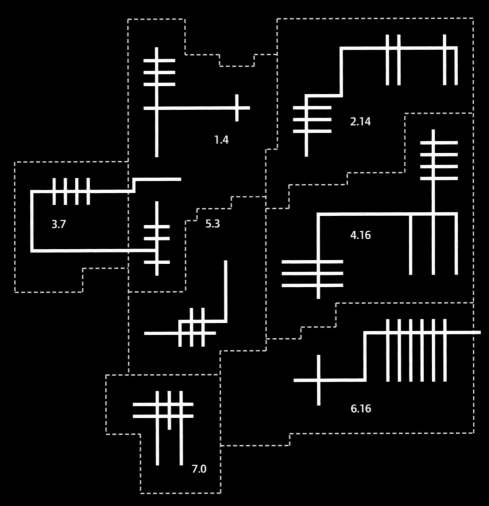

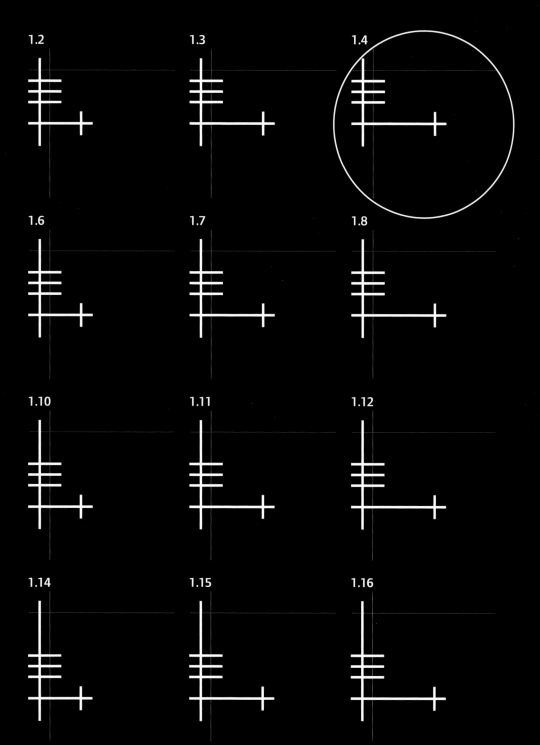

2.2 **2.3** **2.4**

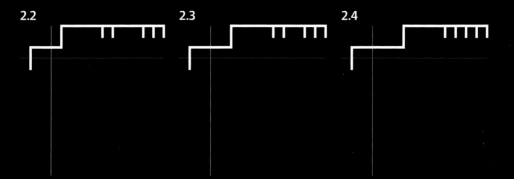

2.6 **2.7** **2.8**

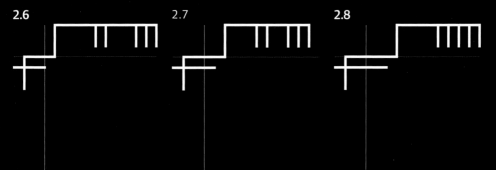

2.10 **2.11** **2.12**

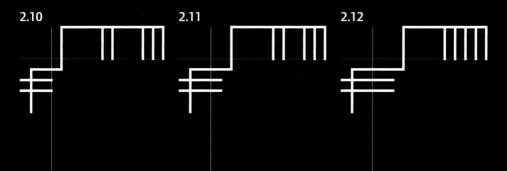

2.14 **2.15** **2.16**

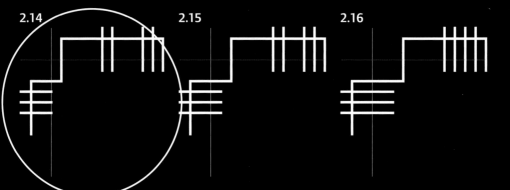

4.2 **4.3** **4.4**

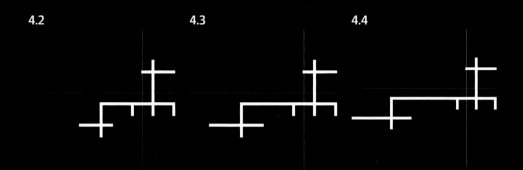

4.6 **4.7** **4.8**

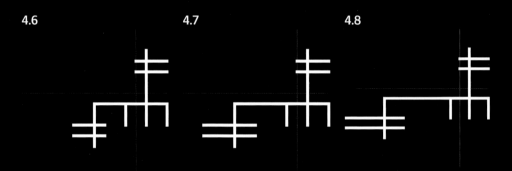

4.10 **4.11** **4.12**

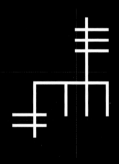

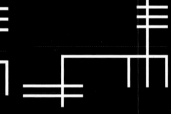

4.14 **4.15** **4.16**

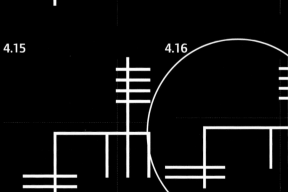

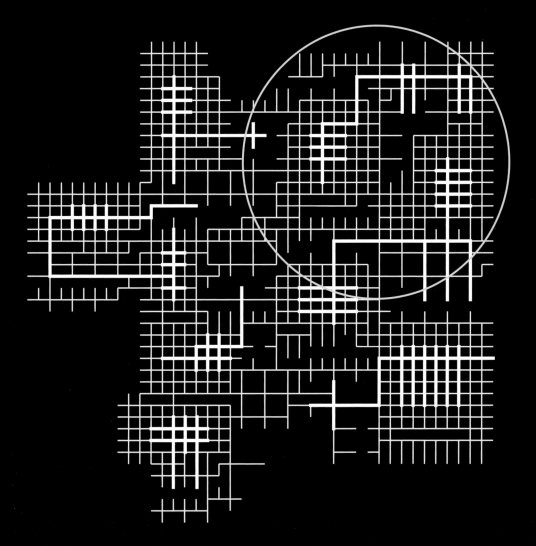

THE INTEGRATED MEGALOPOLIS. Most megaforms are megastructures; what this means is that most megaforms are closed, self-contained autonomous units that only anticipate their own extension. That a megastructure would be designed to anticipate another megastructure, in the manner in which a city block is designed to anticipate another city block, is practically unthinkable. As a result, megastructures create an archipelago morphology of closed islands. The implications of this failure to aggregate are significant. In the context of Megalopolis, megaforms are parts that do not make a whole, but are merely an accumulation of parts. This is significant because the very definition of a city is a whole that exceeds the sum of its parts. The absence of any such sum in Megalopolis throws the definition of a city into question. That question is not whether Megalopolis is a good city or a bad city, but whether it is a city at all. The parts described in the diagram above are open to the space that they create, and because this space is continuous, the potential for aggregation – for exceeding the sum of the parts – exists.

around an armature of form but around an armature of space – a unifying spatial matrix. As regards three-way switches or 'T' intersections, their remarkable characteristic was the ability to form invisible walls. Such 'soft' walls would be used to create the basic spatial subdivisions within the new plan. By the calculated distribution of three-way switches we could create the closed, cul-de-sac networks that make megalopolitan development so desirable without completely walling off the residential districts from their surroundings. The solution was to surround discrete residential areas by invisible walls formed of 'T' intersections. We tried to use these truncated intersections to make overt and explicit subdivisions within the environment without using material barriers.

Planes: Programmatic Surfaces

A preliminary subdivision of the Fifth Ward into discrete areas followed the existing gaps in the urban fabric. Taking a line of least resistance, we divided the Fifth Ward into three, seven and 21 subdivisions. These were nested divisions in the sense that one of the subdivisions into three, contained two of the subdivisions of seven and seven of the subdivisions of 21. What this allowed was a succession of simultaneously overlapping scales from small to large. As each of the subdivisions carried different programme mixes, the overlay of progressively larger areas worked against programmes being limited to isolated containers such as found in the typical zoning map.

These overlapping subdivisions were used to programme the project. Through the mapping of intersections and constructing point fields of differing degrees of continuity, we made an elementary discovery: that different programmes have a different number and type of intersections and each programme area has different continuities. We discovered, for example, that there are a lot more four-way intersections in residential neighbourhoods than in any other programme area. The logic was obvious: residential neighbourhoods, for example, need maximum penetration and interconnectedness. If you look at industrial development, on the other hand, it doesn't need a lot of penetration since the population is far smaller and access needs to be controlled. Industrial development needs a road in; it needs little bit of circulation around it and a lot of parking and storage and staging areas, but there is no need for a block structure and thus no need for many intersections. In other words, while residential areas have the highest level of continuity, industrial areas have the lowest. Following these basic correlations between continuity and programme, we divided up the rest of the programme areas of the Ward and calculated each of their continuities. We ultimately came up with a 'continuity index' for each programme area that allowed for a redistricting of use that was tied not to the present location of the existing programme area, but to its relative continuity. Furthermore, new street patterns could be extrapolated from the distribution and redistribution of a fixed number and type of points related to a given continuity index.

Being no longer tied to location, we could reprogramme the entire district secure in the knowledge that the penetration and interconnectedness of the infrastructure would be adequate for the defined programme areas. For obvious reasons, our strategy was to leave the residential infrastructure and building stock largely intact and distribute the rest of the programme around these denser areas in order to complement them with the necessary amenities.

Lines: the Subgrid and the Supergrid

The interaction between the dis/continuous point and the programmatic plane produces the configuration of the street pattern or line. The continuity required of each programme specifies a number of potential distributions of points that can then be directly translated into a set of lines [see page 133, bottom left]. In the illustrated scheme we have created two hierarchical levels of lines/streets to replace the typical cul-de-sac subdivision. The first set of streets – variations of the spine-form DNA of Megalopolis – grew out of an interaction between a variety of combinations between points and programmatic planes. This interaction was governed by the relative continuity (continuity index) of each programme area. The programmatic continuity, the number and type of points produced the first level of street hierarchy that we call a 'subgrid'. While the subgrid produces a spatial dominant, it is relatively continuous allowing the Fifth Ward to achieve a measure of unity while supporting a series of discrete subdivisions. Fixed firmly between the absolute continuities of the gridiron and the absolute discontinuities of the cul-de-sac, the new fabric of the Fifth Ward attempts to create both open space and open form at the same time [see page 129]. Borrowing qualities from both the gridiron and the cul-de-sac, the subgrid forms the base level of the new urban hierarchy.

The second set of lines, superimposed on the subgrid, is referred to as the supergrid. More figural than the subgrid, these lines are the direct descendants of the spine-based configuration of Megalopolis. Formed around the voids created by the subgrid, these figural spines anchor the open-ended, widely distributed subgrid. Derived from large sets of alternatives [see pages 136–9], these figures form the essential unit of megalopolitan aggregation whereby the megaforms that they ultimately structure are synergistically related to each other.

Holism and Urbanism

One of the problems with traditional architectural megastructures, including subdivisions, airports and shopping malls, is that they operate as closed architectural systems. Simply put, they are objects that do not anticipate other objects but present themselves as complete, in and of themselves. Often marketed as 'social condensers', they are nevertheless closed systems that have no urban intentions beyond the environment that they contain and control. What we were testing in the Fifth Ward plan is the *design megaforms in an aggregate fashion*. In Megalopolis we have spine-based forms that are layered up in a hierarchical succession, yet, like megastructures, each form is blind to the next and they're all blind to each other so there simply is no cumulative effect.

We instinctively know that the entity that we call 'city' is more than a certain quantity of buildings. We know that a city only exists when a whole emerges that is greater than the sum of its parts. Our expectations, if not our conscious awareness, assume a cumulative experience. Following this train of thought, one could argue that, absent a whole, the minimum definition of a city has not been met. If Megalopolis is nothing more than a quantity of parts – a spreadsheet accounting – that does not add up in any way, then the appropriate question is not whether Megalopolis is a good or a bad city, but

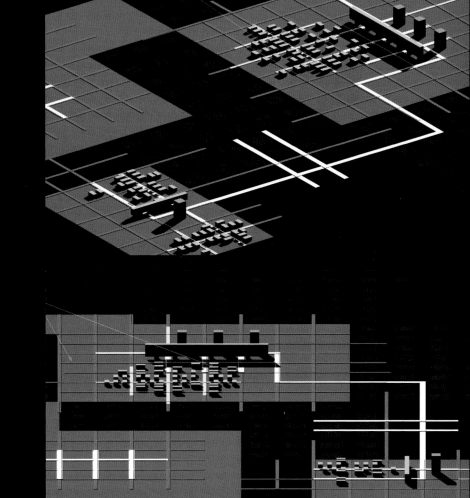

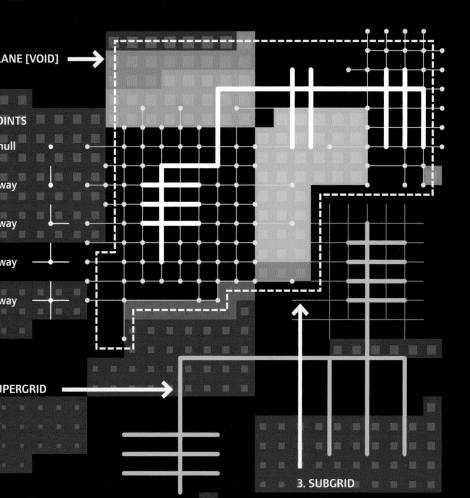

PLANE [VOID]

POINTS

- null
- way
- way
- way
- way

SUPERGRID

3. SUBGRID

whether Megalopolis is a city at all. The lack of cumulative effect in Megalopolis today may go a long way toward explaining why it is that we fail to recognise the legitimacy of contemporary urbanism. The atomised subject and the spine form that constructs it are nothing but quantities of parts that do not satisfy the minimal requirements of urban legibility. This absence of a whole can only be addressed by investigating the prospects of a coherent megalopolitan aggregation. In the Fifth Ward we are testing out the possibility of megalopolitan aggregation, an aggregation that could produce synergies out of isolated elements and get them to add up to something more – to add up to a city. [see page 143] We wanted to investigate the terms of a spatial aggregation and to anticipate the prospects of a whole that is greater than the sum of its parts.

Conclusion

In conclusion, the spine-based forms of the Fifth Ward proposal reject postmodern reform on a minor scale brought about by the gentrification of an outmoded urbanism. We contend that the restoration of historical enclaves is equivalent to preservation, not urbanism. Meaningful, broad-based reform is founded, not on the infrastructure that we inherit, but the infrastructure that we actively practise – an urbanism that we have practised for the past half-century. Compared with grid-based urban traditions, spine-based megalopolitan urbanism is not proven. For those who understand the city in essentialist terms, contemporary urbanism will never be legitimate, and our proposal for the Fifth Ward can only be seen as a destructive act. But while it may well stand as an example of destroying the city in order to save it, what is being destroyed is the fiction of an urban ideal that blocks our most pressing urban problems. Ultimately, the reform that we seek is not that of the inner city, whose importance diminishes with the continual growth of the immense conurbation that surrounds it. The reform we seek is of the enclave itself, whether historical, as most are, or modernistic. This will only happen through the acknowledgement that what exists 'outside' our essential urban enclaves is not an illegitimate urbanism or a suburbanism, it is the city itself.

Note
1   A Pope, *Ladders*, Princeton Architectural Press (New York), 1997.

The Pearl River Delta showing the shift of mud and
construction of levees, villages and cities from the 1950s to
the present. This is a small snapshot in time of a millennia of
water–land transformations in this delta.

Mega Urban Ecologies

Sharon Haar and Victoria Marshall

Through most post-Second World War history there were two very different trends in global urbanisation – the exodus of residences, business and commercial areas to a wide car-based megalopolis of the developed world and the implosion of megacities through massive rural to urban migration in the developing world. Sharon Haar and Victoria Marshall combine their research experiences in the Pearl and Yangtze River deltas in China to describe a new hybrid megaregional development containing both megalopolitan car-based sprawl and megacity implosion. Haar and Marshall examine how slight shifts in the superposition of the new megablock structure of Chinese urbanisation can better accommodate the historical hydrological network of the historical delta cities of China.

Introduction

China's explosion of urbanisation offers a redefinition of both the megacity and the megalopolis. Situated within a culture and state structure that privileges 'planning' – of cities, the economy and social relations – China's cities do not fit neatly into the category 'megacity' represented by cities of the Global South. While sharing many causal factors and statistical narratives with cities such as São Paulo and Mumbai, known for their intensive rural in-migration, in China the planning and design of both existing and, increasingly, new cities operates within different registers. Similarly, as China quickly builds a 21st-century infrastructure to support megalopolitan regions already firmly in place, Chinese cities do not cleanly follow the American patterns of suburban and exurban sprawl. Rather, Chinese urbanisation is a process that reorganises and radically transforms existing ecosystems into official ideals of nature and city. Two case studies, one an analysis of the New Administrative District in Shunde in the Pearl River Delta and the other an urban design proposal for Shaoxing in the Yangtze River Delta, will illustrate how large-scale, planned development in China is used to intervene in and control the informal production of the megacity, built atop and expanding upon the pre-modern aqua-urban network of two megadeltas.[1] Within these vast deltas we observe and analyse Chinese planners' attempts to integrate the dispersed urban elements of the new megalopolis created by duplication, replication and excess through an endless repetitive grid that threatens the intricate urban water–land interactions of two megadeltas.

Much of the contemporary understanding of Chinese urbanisation derives from the study of the spectacular explosive growth of cities such as Shenzhen in the Pearl River Delta and Shanghai in the Yangtze River Delta. Here we focus our attention on two lesser-known cities in these regions to illustrate more generic urban processes that are taking place throughout China. Structuring our discussion within a patch dynamic framework rather than a centre/periphery dialectic, we first analyse existing Chinese planning and design methodologies through the example of the New Administrative District of Shunde. We then shift our focus to an urban design proposition for a new town for Shaoxing referred to as a 'riverbank city'. In doing so, we understand these cities as part of larger urban ecosystems that include the uneven history of dynastic, colonial, communist and global dynamics. Until the 1960s the phrase 'urban ecology' was used as a metaphor rather than based on an underlying metabolism. Over the past two decades, a way of thinking about the actual ecological processes of the city has been absorbed into a larger concept of the 'sustainable' city, which assigns ecosystem processes a role alongside other urban systems, be they economic, cultural, social or political. Like all open, evolving systems, the sustainable city is not without its tensions. Of particular note are those that arise between economic goals and cultural traditions as well as developmental imperatives and existing ecosystem processes. These tensions become evident in the examples of Shunde and Shaoxing.

Our study asks whether it is possible to introduce disturbances into the mega-morphology of Chinese urbanisation in such a way as to interrupt its cellular, insular logic through the retention of existing and creation of new microclimates. We further seek to understand how current official concepts of sustainability can be supplemented by everyday resilient urban ecologies, operationalising the current 'culture debate' in China by updating the contemporary idea of harmony as 'balance' to be more consistent with the Confucian ideal of harmony as 'sustained by energy generated through the interaction of different elements in creative tension'.[2]

Megadelta

Shunde and Shaoxing sit within two of the 11 megadeltas in the coastal zones of Asia that are continuously being enlarged by sedimentation from rivers originating from the Tibetan Plateau.[3] Defined as an area of more than 10,000 square kilometres (3,860 square miles), megadeltas support huge conurbations along the coastline of the South China Sea and Bay of Bengal. Taking a long historical perspective, the megadelta cities of the Yangtze and Pearl Rivers are built on land that had been created or enriched with fertile topsoil made mobile through 2,000 years of upstream deforestation.[4] According to Mark Elvin, 'upstream deforestation almost certainly lay behind the rapid filling in of the Pearl River Delta in late-imperial times'. In addition, 'the growth of the deltas of the Yellow River on its various north and south courses, and of the Yangtze, must both have depended to some degree on the same effect', the site of what is now Shanghai, for example, was created by Yangtze River sediments in about the 13th century CE.[5] Humans, separated from the sea by a sea wall, washed delta land free of salt, transforming it into rice or fish ponds enclosed within polders.

The late-imperial megadelta was an agriculturally productive landscape a few feet above sea level, dotted with a network of cities strategically created as administrative centres that played an important role in administration and taxation. Cities 'belonged to the wealthy citizens such as administrative officers, merchant traders, and noblemen and their extended families, which strictly controlled it behind its walls, keeping most of the people from outside away'.[6] Global trading networks via ocean and land routes

The Qiantang River Delta (part of
the larger Yangtze River Delta)
showing the shift of mud and
construction of levees, villages
and cities from the 1950s until
the present – a small snapshot
from a millennia of water–land
transformations in this delta.

connected these cities with Afro-Eurasian networks of exchange from the 1st century CE.[7]
Until modernity the Yellow and Yangtze Rivers were much more important than the Pearl
River. The north, with its political centrality in Beijing, became disconnected from the
south, with its growing emphasis on trade. The development of treaty ports in the mid-
19th century marked a shift to new types of north/south entanglements. The Pearl River
Delta – at a great distance from the centre of politics – became the site of the first Special
Economic Zones after 'opening up' at the beginning of the 1980s. These experiments in
economic reform were later exported north to cities such as Shanghai, where the massive
influx of migrants needed to fuel economic growth met with more resistance.[8]

The Hukou registration system has controlled the movement of rural populations to
cities since 1958; at the same time, industrialisation and the move to a socialist market
economy has resulted in the vast expansion of Chinese cities and urban populations,
particularly along the coast. The by-product of these internal borders is a temporary
'floating population of workers who inhabit surplus housing of former work units,
within the densifying urban villages and dormitories built adjacent to new factories and
construction sites'.[9] The form of this large collective body becomes evident at Chinese New
Year when migrant mobility overloads the capacity of Chinese transport infrastructure.
Middle-class urban residents, for which Chinese urbanisation is designed, move around
all of this: shopping, trading, recreating and driving cars. Large-scale planned cities built
with only this population in mind, keep the floating population adrift.

Pre-modern delta settlement patterns were defined by a dyke-pond system of fish ponds, cultivated dykes and grid-like water patterns of flood storage and canal transport. The Pearl River Delta, in the southern subtropical zone, has a longer cropping period yet a shorter history of farming than the Yangtze River Delta. On the other hand, the Yangtze River Delta located on the southern end of the north subtropical zone has a shorter growing period as the water freezes in winter. The mulberry, sugarcane, banana and flower dyke-fish pond systems rationalise space proportion of dyke to pond[10] as a waffle-shaped terrain that is now being overwritten by the planned megacity's smoothening surfaces. Natural resources are channelled toward urban assembly zones where they are intermixed to produce massive volumes of goods for global export and internal distribution to the growing middle class, all facilitated by digital networks. This flow of goods is paralleled by the socio-spatial redistribution of people from farming to industrial manufacture. The term 'megadelta' needs to incorporate and engage this mixing of hard and permanent materials on top of muddy and silty earth combined and circulated by floating and permanent populations interconnected by mobile and digital networks.

Megalopolis/Megacity

In using the term 'Megalopolis' in the late 1950s Jean Gottmann was creating a 'place name' for a 'unique cluster of metropolitan areas' extending along the north-eastern seaboard of the United States from Boston to Washington, DC.[11] A megalopolis is not a single, expanding city but a stringing together of cities into one extended urbanised region. By contrast, a megacity is understood to be a metropolitan area of 10 million inhabitants, produced by massive hypergrowth, most commonly associated with the post-colonial cities of the Global South.[12] Although they are often conflated by virtue of their overlapping qualities associated with sprawl and density, a megalopolis and a megacity are not the same. Brian McGrath and David Grahame Shane see the 'sprawling global megalopolis and the imploding megacity' as 'the monstrous twin products of the "open" neoliberal world (dis)order'.[13] Yet, in China's megadeltas the distinction between the centrifugal and centripetal forces of megacity and megalopolis is less clear.

In the context of Chinese urbanisation it is Gottmann's description of the landscape the megalopolis encompasses that is most applicable. Travelling along the ground by rail or highway one experiences a continuous landscape of densely settled land; from the air, however, one sees: '… ribbons of densely occupied land along the principal arteries of traffic, and in between the clusters of suburbs around the old urban centers, there still remain large areas covered with woods and brush alternating with some carefully cultivated patches of farm land'.[14] He continues: 'We must abandon the idea of the city as a tightly settled and organized unit in which people, activities, and riches are crowded into a very small area clearly separated from its nonurban surroundings. Every city in this region … grows amidst an irregularly colloidal mixture of rural and suburban landscapes; it melts on broad fronts with other mixtures, of somewhat similar though different texture …'[15]

Gottmann's megalopolis was built along centuries of overlaid infrastructure that 'straddles state boundaries, stretches across wide estuaries and bays, and encompasses many regional differences'.[16] From the air in China one sees not just patches of suburbs and rural lands being transformed between old urban centres, but the lingering existence of rural villages that now sit within its densifying and sprawling cities. While some of these 'urban villages' represent the 'swallowing up'[17] of rural life by rapidly sprawling older cities (for example, Beijing and Shanghai), others are the result of the planning and rapid growth of new cities, most evident in the example of Shenzhen. Here the 'controlled anarchy of the urban villages contrasts vividly with the order and discipline that has characterized Shenzhen's development'. As former villagers capitalise on the increased value of their land, they produce megacity conditions the Chinese are at pains to control through planning.[18]

Two of the primary crises associated with the megacity – the pressures on people, transit, resources and housing produced by extreme density and the absorption of agricultural land brought about by extensive sprawl – underlie Chinese planning. The city-building enterprise in China comprises concerted attempts to avoid the unrestrained growth of slums and informal development present in the cities of the Global South. As Jose Castillo notes in regard to Mexico City, 'The use of the term megacity ... implied much more than just a quantitative aspect, applied to urban agglomerations of more than ten million inhabitants. The expression carried beleaguered associations with the most negative and problematic traits inherent in cities.'[19] In China, it is often the unregulated urban villages that provide the housing and support network for the large, unaccounted for 'floating population', suggesting that these cities are not just 'mega' by virtue of statistics, but also by the existence of unacknowledged informal urbanisation located in the former *danwei* (work units), on roofs, crammed into spaces that formerly housed one family, and tucked away behind walls and billboards touting new urban and suburban developments.

Despite the differences between the megalopolis and the megacity, in reality their form and lived experience often merge, as can be seen in the case study of Shunde, to the south-west of Guangzhou in Guangdong province.[20] Established as a county during the Ming Dynasty, Shunde is currently a city of 1.3 million inhabitants within a megalopolis of over 40 million. Since being chosen as a 'pilot city' in the 1980s, Shunde has seen vast influxes of private and public capital that have combined with strong pre-existing industries, agriculture and trade demonstrating – in microcosm – the globalising forces at work in the region as a whole. As the city expands, its small urban and farming villages, historical gardens and temples, and canal towns are literally encircled by a new global geography made up of industrial and technology parks, highways, residential developments, shopping malls, skyscrapers, government facilities, cultural and entertainment attractions, golf courses and restoration projects. Within the 'Old City', vestiges of urban village neighbourhoods cling to the back of mountains, hemmed in by new roadways and high-rise construction; adjacent to the 'New City', with its New Administrative District at its centre, farming villages are strung along canals and water systems, awaiting the moment when new suburban developments expand outward and erase them too. Highways and the electrical grid crisscross the fish farms and dykes with their cyclical rhythms of micro water-land interactions. Small pockets of residential and commercial buildings built by displaced farmers, now often factory workers, fill the interstitial spaces between 'old' and 'new'. This is the tense life of the megacity, rushing to avoid disorder.

In China the problem of the megacity is most often conceived as one of inadequate population and infrastructure planning not of design. Although neither Shunde nor Shaoxing are megacities, they sit within growing megalopolises, each of which contains statistical megacities. And they can be seen as part of a larger strategy to enlarge and develop new cities in advance of conditions that could lead to 'implosion'. The question is how does design – architectural, urban, landscape – interface with the larger, and in China, more important state-controlled project of planning, which typically preconfigures the land in such a way as to limit both the extent of intervention on the part of the designer and the ability to work within preexisting water–land interactions.

Megablock

The implications of Chinese large-scale planning imperatives to avoid the megacity can be seen throughout both the Pearl and Yangtze River deltas. At one extreme is the desire to organise uncoordinated urban development brought about by the decentralisation of planning, changing patterns of wealth and urban–rural hierarchies, localism and competition driven by market forces that lead to repetition of investment and infrastructure.[21] Tingwei Zhang notes that in a country where 'City planning ... means really planning a whole city', speed and concerns over national identity – seen in the social conflict between efficient growth and equitable distribution of resources – and political conflict – between power and democracy – lead to a frustrated and at times powerless planning profession.[22] Therefore, at the level of the city, nationwide, top-down physical planning principles are clearly in evidence. Here megablocks are the dominant motif of land development. Like New York's Commissioner's Grid of 1811 and the US Land Ordinance of 1785, in contemporary Chinese development the uniform parcelisation of land allows for its efficient sale. The Chinese megablock interlinks the scale of modern superblock development with the closed compound of the historic Chinese walled city. This 'megatypology', as Kjersti Monson labels it, 'is efficient for implementing rapid expansion since it allows the government to limit its hard investment to the planning and construction of a widely spaced pattern of major infrastructure only, shedding enormous chunks of developable land with approved use rights in single transactions, wherein the private owner will plan and build interior roads'.[23] Coming out of the institutionalised practices of China's Local Design Institutes, Monson notes, 'buildings within a superblock project tend to be standardized, streamlining the design process and reducing costs'.[24]

The strategy used by the designers of Shunde's New Administrative District – building new urban areas outside existing centres – is common as Chinese cities struggle to expand beyond physically constrained historic centres to accommodate massive urban growth. The superimposition of an urban grid measuring 300 metres x 300 metres (9 hectares) (984 feet x 984 feet (22 acres))[25] over pond-dyke systems has created a jarring clash between old and new. The urban grid places the new city hall across from a large public space flanked on either side by administration buildings sitting atop parking plinths hidden by a designed landscape. Despite the rapid rate of construction, environmental considerations are prioritised (according to the city's own brochures), so that an 'immense artificial green landscape' is simultaneously being grown. New convention centres and exhibition halls highlight the relationship of administration and economy, and new high-rise residential complexes, malls and entertainment centres are quickly built to support the district's burgeoning population. Unlike the congestion of the Old City, the New City welcomes the automobile: its six- to eight-lane roadbeds anticipate a move toward the use of the private car, forming a megagrid infrastructure system that contains individual megablocks.

The region's canal-focused villages illustrate a form of family-based, communal living that remains extant in many new residential projects but without the integration of productive land. The role of water as a symbol of the region's ecosystem is present in almost every new development, but particularly in residential projects where water courses through artificial streams, canals, ponds, fountains and play areas. Separated from the dramatic nature of a walled garden, these water elements provide what Keyang Tang calls 'a sort of cultural ritual to "get outside the city" while "returning to the past"'.[26] Here stripped of its functions as resource, and connector, water becomes a metaphor, an image rather than environment, and a stand in for sustainability. Separated from ecologically productive functions, its 'artificiality' is of a different nature than the artificial ecosystem of the aquaculture built within rather than on top of the delta.

Panorama of the New Administrative District of Shunde including the new city hall and administrative buildings in 2004. The cutting of the mountainside (left) creates fill for the new ground plane built on former fish ponds. In the foreground is a sales centre for a new residential development, now complete. To the right are new civic buildings under construction.

Megascene

Shunde's websites actively promote the city's 'Return to Nature', 'the Natural Watery Region', and 'Traditional Culture'.[27] To create the new ground plane for industrial agriculture, industrial and technology parks, and entirely new cities, large amounts of the mucky delta must be filled. The effect of this filling is evident, not only in the loss of productive agricultural land but also in the denuding and carving out of the area's hills and mountains which provide the material for the infill. Each block of the new city swallows numerous fish ponds with little attention to existing land divisions or waterways. Landscaping – requiring constant watering by mobile tankers throughout the cool night and tending by manual labour throughout the hot day – serves to augment the monumentality of the district's open spaces, roads and buildings, but does little to relieve the excessive scale of roadbeds. In the New Administrative District, the local ecosystem is reenvisioned as a scenography of sustainability, while in both urban and exurban housing developments water becomes the set-piece around which the megablock car-oriented lifestyle is constructed.

Preservation is also a developmental imperative necessitating the survival of parts of rural lifestyle and the building of new sites to selectively frame history and tradition. In Shunde, the 400-hectare (988-acre) Shunfeng Mountain Park sits at the juncture between the old and the new cities. Containing both historic and recreated features, the park conjoins Chinese and Western characteristics, with reference to Chinese historic landscape elements and a programme designed to be a 'leisure and body-building people's park' affording the qualities of a 'city-lung'.[28] Shunfeng Mountain Park provides the entire district with a landscape and heritage site in which views to and from it suggest a history of urban and landscape construction deeply tied to long-standing religious and cultural traditions. Stanislaus Fung in his reading of the traditional text on Chinese Gardens, *Yuan ye*, within both a traditional Chinese and a Western philosophical context, offers an alternative way to understand the potential of such a monumental restructuring of tradition: 'The borrowing of views is discussed in *Yuan ye* as eventful encounter and depends on the notion of tradition, here conceived not as a tradition of stylized or designed objects but as embodied practices of daily living.'[29] Such 'embodied practices of daily living' may present opportunities for urban design to create new identities in physical and mediated space in a context where official history and tradition are carefully curated.

Shift

According to Elvin, before the Southern Song Dynasty, the breach of a tidal barrier resulted in significant erosion of the northern shoreline of Hangzhou Bay. In the 12th century shoreline stabilisation was therefore needed to protect the inhabitants from incursions by the tide. Sea walls were built on both sides of the river. At the same time deposition of sediment blocked the southern draining streams creating flooding upstream. All the while the path of the river periodically shifted between three 'mid-bay mountains', hills called the northern, central and southern cleft. Like a gigantic funnel, the bay intensified the force of the incoming tides and the outflow of the river provided a counter-force, depositing and moving sediments brought in by the muddy tide, flowing south from the

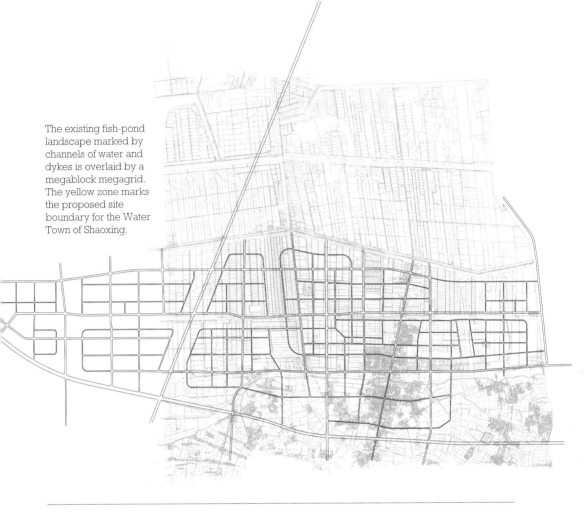

The existing fish-pond landscape marked by channels of water and dykes is overlaid by a megablock megagrid. The yellow zone marks the proposed site boundary for the Water Town of Shaoxing.

Yangtze River, located just to the north. The hardened edge of the sea walls bounced waves and deflected currents into unpredictable patterns of erosion and sedimentation. By the 17th century, 'the geometry was generating its own destruction'.[30]

Today the Qiantang River flows through the northern cleft, a path less than 200 years old, and the inflow and outflow of sediments are carefully and expertly harvested. New land for urban growth is created daily. In 2010 an urban design competition was launched by the City of Shaoxing to generate ideas for a 'Riverbank City'.[31] On the southern shore of Hangzhou Bay, 20 kilometres (12.5 miles) south-east of Hangzhou, the new city is part of the planning project for Zhejiang Province and is nested within the 'Regional Plan for the Yangtze River Delta', the first cross-province regional plan in China. In this enormous planning project, the port of Shanghai is being promoted as an 'International Gateway for the Asia Pacific Region'. A mental image of a gigantic bird – 'One Body and Two Wings' – locates Shanghai as the body and Nanjing and Hangzhou as the two wings. The social project of this gigantic bird aims for 'a well-off society in an all round way by 2015'.[32] All of this is to take place in a region that in the 18th century was referred to as the 'Chinese Netherlands', given its extensive polder landscape, much larger than its European contemporary.

The brief for this new city was similarly dynamic. The goal was to design a new town sub-centre, south of the main new town that is to be built within the next 10 years. To do this the design teams were requested to minimise large-scale public buildings and, at the same time, create centralising space and form. Feedback from Shaoxing planning officials reflected the codes and sustainable development tropes of central planning such as a call for two main streets and four main functions including main public facilities such as sports buildings, hospitals and cultural facilities, service centres, commercial facilities such as supermarkets, commercial complex, office buildings and green parks. Directives included requirements for at least 25 per cent of green land and water, an urban complex in the core area with a scale of 50,000 square metres (540,000 square feet) of built-up area and 20,000 square metres (215,000 square feet) of land area. Buildings, especially residential, were required to be in south–north direction and the two main roads could not be changed.

The competition entry titled 'Water Town' consists of three formal 'shifts' that open up the logic of the megablock. The first is the result of a happy error, where the new road grid does not align with the existing canal grid. This results in varying block shapes, divided by an interconnected water network that supports a bus-on-water. The second shift is the insertion of as many boat slips (lou) perpendicular to the canal grid inside the megablocks as possible. The lou is unique in Shaoxing and its surrounding areas; it serves as a boat slip for daily commuting, for loading, to wash clothes or vegetables etc. As it only has one end that connects to an outer water body, and the other one is a dead end, no boats pass by. The third shift is a rotation of the core of the city within the water network, which creates open triangular water spaces, grand views and reference to an adjacent low-rise and dense walled fishing village called Lihai. These formal moves follow the rules of the megablock and at the same time serve to replace the redundant inner road infrastructure of the megablock with an infrastructure of water. The water body is designed on the patterns of slow water flow and social water use in the region.[33]

Emphasis is also placed on the design of new microclimates. For example, a boat pavilion provides a cool shelter for commuters waiting for the morning bus-on-water as well as an environment for groups of elderly residents to socialise. Each pavilion is also a sensing device, tracking slow ecosystem change as well as announcing the fast coming and going of the boat. The project of slowly opening the contained and stagnant fresh water to the push and pull of saline water by the ocean and the river is mediated by everyday observations of fish and plant health. In this city, gates, valves and weirs are a shared resource, operated remotely. Like an urban game, residents can modulate water flows, pushing high bacteria content water into constructed wetlands as well as pulling salt water into fishing hot spots. A second microclimate example is a roof-top plaza in the Central Business District. Tilted to create a viewing plane toward a canal that passes under an elevated highway, the plaza is designed as an energetic environment for youth. Below the plaza is a mat of shopping accessed by pedestrian malls and narrow streets. Monumental office and hotel buildings, each designed with a charismatic shape to encourage affection in the residents, punctuate this intimate retail base. At night the illuminations of

Facing south, this night view of the
competition entry shows the shift
of the Water Town in relation to
the alignment of the megablock
megagrid surrounding it.

The water of the Tibetan Plateau meets the North and South China Sea and Bay of Bengal in nine megadeltas. From east to west: Yellow, Yangtze, Pearl, Red, Mekong, Chao Phraya, Irrawaddy, Ganges-Brahamputra and Indus (not shown on map).

skyscrapers as well as streetlights present environmental measures such as evaporation and transpiration. Colours that slowly change affect our mood, therefore while some lights sense rain, for example, others respond to human senses via text messages. The skyline from within the city and when viewed from afar acts as a kind of sensual measuring device, spatialising body–climate interactions as spectacular local weather events.

Microclimates triangulate existing natural processes such as the cycle of the moon, plum rains, tides and typhoons with everyday life circulation patterns such as commuting by boat, passing through the city on the six-lane highway and relaxing in the youth plaza, mixing these with environmental measures such as water, sound and air quality. They are considered prompts, as potentially famous views, given that ideas of what is considered spectacular may change over time or alternatively may become fixed in a long duration. In this design strategy, desire – to shop, trade, make, relax, meet, travel and sleep – acts as a sensorial and environmental support system making the city a place where one becomes more familiar with the 'strange stranger'[34] that is nature. These views offer an alternative to the 'money shot' that often frames an urban design project through a singular lens of creating an extremely high value product. When built, the views of the Water Town can be reproduced via mobile phones and digital cameras in everyday life, creating an image mixing space where residents continue the project of building the digital representation model of the city.

These microclimates engage the Confucian ideal of harmony and the contemporary ecological theory of resilience, prompted by the 'Culture Debate' occurring among Chinese urban residents after partially recovering from the shock of rapid change since the 1980s. According to Zha Jianying, this debate includes, among other topics, a renewed interest in Confucianism, Daoism and Buddhism.[35] Ecologists used to believe that natural systems have an equilibrium-seeking force and that disturbance is not natural; however, contemporary ecology now engages a non-equilibrium framework of ecosystem dynamics, understanding that disturbance is natural. When the classical Confucian ideal of harmony is viewed side by side with this non-equilibrium framework, some productive resonance occurs that can move the desire for a scientific approach to ecosystem management towards an ecological model that includes humans. These could open formal planning moves of conservation and preservation towards options that engage everyday life micro-practices of socio-natural interactions as discussed above. Chenyang Li states that the 'notion of harmony does not presuppose a given, fixed underlying structure in the world; if the world is to have a structure, it is a result of the harmonizing process, rather than a precondition for harmony. We may call this radical notion of harmony "deep harmony" as opposed to the kind of harmony seen as conforming to a pre-existing structure in the world ... Deep harmony in this sense is a self-generating harmony.'[36] The non-equilibrium frameworks of ecosystem dynamics as well as the microclimates of the competition entry engage this generative, nonlinear and integrative imagination of change.

Conclusion

The questions raised in this paper are meant to point to areas for further investigation, not as indictments. The city and people of Shunde, for example, are living the experiment of 'creating a future with urbanisation' where 'the future lies in the past',[37] a difficult task that begins to take into account the need to balance economy, culture and ecosystems, but remains lacking as it negates the megadelta within which it is built. In Shaoxing, residents are living the experiment of the expanded port city, as the 'International Gateway for the Asia Pacific Region', an image that continues to separate water from land. In the unfolding urbanisation of China, urban ecosystems and the larger ideal of sustainability will have to be understood as more than 'greening'. This will necessitate a conceptual move from the metaphoric to the metabolic within mediated and sensorial dimensions.

Can other scales be evoked beyond those claimed by the discipline of urban design to create sustainable Asian megadeltas? A more nuanced embrace of harmony could become a meaningful way for Chinese residents themselves to engage and participate in shaping the culture debate at the local urban scale. Could microclimate changes prompt formal design projects of conservation and preservation? At another scale, political scientists and environmental activists are shifting our attention from the land to the sea, speculating on how ocean space can become a space for co-operation for human ecological security.[38] Similar dialogues are occurring around mountain space, in the context of shrinking Himalayan glaciers. Can the 11 Asian megadeltas become the sites for new human hydraulic interactions that are responsive to changes in their headwaters and midstream water-sharing projects? Understanding megadeltas in the context of both their hydrological and urban histories may offer a way to conceive the future megalopolis as a resilient system in this stretched environmental frame. However, without deeper consideration of the flow and everyday life of *all* people in and out of these regions, the cultural, economic and social implications of the megacity being created today hinder the success of the sustainable Chinese urban project.

Notes

1 Megadelta is a generic term given to the very large Asian river deltas: the Huanghe (Yellow), Changjiang (Yangtze), Pearl, Red, Mekong, Chao Phraya, Irrawaddy, Ganges-Brahmaputra, and Indus. This term was developed by the Asia-Pacific Network for Global Change in 2004 as a conceptual model toward establishing capacity building networks among fluvial and coastal specialists of the Asia Pacific regions, especially those from developing countries. http://www.megadelta.ecnu.edu.cn/main/default.asp (last accessed 7 June 2011).

2 Chenyang Li, 'The Confucian Ideal of Harmony', *Philosophy of East and West* 56 (October 2006), p 589.

3 Intergovernmental Panel on Climate Change, *IPCC Fourth Assessment Report: Climate Change 2007*, Working Group II: Impacts, Adaption and Vulnerability. http://www.ipcc.ch/publications_and_data/ar4/wg2/en/ch10s10-6.html (last accessed 7 June 2011).

4 M Elvin, *The Retreat of the Elephants: An Environmental History of China*, Yale University Press (New Haven), 2004, p 35.

5 Elvin, The Retreat of the Elephants, pp 23–4.

6 Sun Shiwen, 'The Institutional and Political Background to Chinese Urbanisation', *AD: New Urban China*, 78 (September/October 2008), p 23.

7 Tansen Sen, 'The Intricacies of Premodern Asian Connections', *The Journal of Asian Studies*, 69 (November 2010), p 992.

8 See TJ Campanella, *The Concrete Dragon: China's Urban Revolution and What It Means for the World*, Princeton Architectural Press (New York), 2008.

9 Partha Mukhopadhyay, 'Beginning a Conversation on Chinese Urbanization', in A Gurung, B McGrath, Jianying Zha (eds), *Growing Cities in a Shrinking World: The Challenges of Urbanism in India and China*, Macmillan (New Delhi), 2010, p 130.

10 Gonfgu Zhong, 'Ecological Models and Characteristics', in Gongfu Zhong, Zengji Wang, and Houshui Wu, *Land-Water Interactions of the Dike-Pond System*, Presses Universitaires de Namur (Namur, Belgium), 1997, pp 17–19.

11 J Gottmann, *Megalopolis: The Urbanized Northeastern Seaboard of the United States*, The Twentieth Century Fund (New York), 1961, p 4.

12 B McGrath and D Grahame Shane, 'Metropolis, Megalopolis and Metacity', in C Greig Crysler, S Cairns and H Heynen (eds), *The SAGE Handbook of Architectural Theory*, Sage Publications (London), forthcoming.

13 McGrath and Shane.

14 Gottmann, *Megalopolis*, p 5.

15 Gottmann, *Megalopolis*, p 5.

16 Gottmann, *Megalopolis*, p 7.

17 See R Mangurian and MA Ray, 'Rural Urbanism: Thriving under the Radar – Beijing's Villages in the City', in *Distributed Urbanism: Cities After Google Earth*, ed G Wilkins, Routledge (New York), 2010; B McGetrick and Jiang Jun, *Urban China: Work in Progress*, Timezone 8 (Hong Kong), 2009.

18   Campanella, *The Concrete Dragon*, p 41.
19   J Castillo, 'After the Explosion', in R Burdett and D Sudjic (eds), *The Endless City*, Phaidon Press (New York), 2008, p 174.
20   Research in Shunde was conducted in autumn 2004 as part of a team of faculty and students in University of Illinois at Chicago's Urban Planning and Policy Program and School of Architecture hosted by the city and its local development company to work on proposals for new residential developments in Shunde's New Administrative District.
21   Zhang Jie, 'Urbanisation in China in the Age of Reform', *AD: New Urban China*, 78 (September/October 2008), p 33.
22   Tingwei Zhang, 'Challenges Facing Chinese Planners in Transitional China', *Journal of Planning Education and Research*, 22 (2002), pp 71, 75.
23   K Monson, 'Stringblock Vs Superblock: Patterns of Dispersal in China', *AD: New Urban China*, 78 (September/October 2008), p 47. Here we use the term 'megablock' rather than Monson's 'superblock', first because of the enormous shift in scale and, second, in order to look at the way individual 'blocks' are linked into larger systems.
24   Monson, 'Stringblock Vs Superblock', p 47.
25   Monson notes megablocks may reach 20 hectares; developments of this kind can be seen in Shunde's expanding suburbs.
26   Keyang Tang, 'Chinese Public Space: An Indefinite Map', trans D Mair, in Li Xuesi, Zhang Fan, Li Xuanyi (eds), *Here for a Chinese Appointment Pavilion of China at the 12th International Architecture Exhibition – La Biennale di Venezia*, Exhibition Catalogue, China Arts and Entertainment Group (Beijing), 2010, p 87.
27   See: http://newcity.shunde.gov.cn/ (Shunde Information Center, last accessed 6 March 2009), http://www.shunde.gov.cn/newen/ (Shunde People's Government of Foshan, last accessed 6 March 2009), and http://www.shunde.cn/en/ (Shunde Information Center, last accessed 6 March 2009).
28   Quotations from promotional materials are taken from the four-volume report: *Shunde New City: Planning, Operation, Industry and Culture* provided by Shunde's planning department.
29   S Fung, 'Here and There in Yuan Ye', *Studies in the History of Gardens & Designed Landscapes*, 19 (1999), p 44.
30   Elvin, *The Retreat of the Elephants*, p 150.
31   The urban design firm TILL was invited to participate with Zhejiang University.
32   http://www.chinadaily.com.cn/m/hangzhou/e/2010-06/29/content_10032712.htm (last accessed 7 June 2011).
33   The number of bridges created by these shifts was the reason the entry did not proceed to the second round. They were considered too expensive.
34   T Morton, *The Ecological Thought*, Harvard University Press (Cambridge, MA), 2010, p 38.
35   CCTV Dialogue Edition 283.2010 http://bugu.cntv.cn/language/english/dialogue/classpage/video/20101010/100640.shtml (last accessed 7 June 2011).
36   Chenyang Li, 'The Ideal of Harmony in Ancient Chinese and Greek Philosophy', *Dao: A Journal of Comparative Philosophy*, 7:81 (2008), pp 91–2.
37   Shunde promotional materials.
38   Sanjay Chaturverdi, 'Common Security? Geopolitics, Development, South Asia and the Indian Ocean', *Third World Quarterly* 19:4 (1998), pp 701–24.

Ecology of the City
A Perspective from Science

Steward TA Pickett

> Paralleling Aldo Rossi's turn from the architecture *of* rather than architecture *in* the city, ecologist Steward Pickett argues for designers to understand ecology *of* rather than *in* the city. In fact Pickett underlines his main point: cities and other urban ecosystems are equally biological, social, built and geophysical. While ecology – and even the plural ecologies – has been used commonly as a metaphor in design, here Pickett points out the problem of employing ecology in only a limited metaphorical way. Instead, partnership with ecological science, especially new theories, models and knowledge, can only result in better designs for sustainable cities.

This chapter examines the nature of ecology in relation to the other concepts that frame this book: urban and design. The chapter asks: what is ecological science? Ecology, as a science, represents a dialogue between conceptual constructs about how the world works and observations of the material world. Second, ecological science has changed over time, so that contemporary knowledge is quite different from that available in the past. Unfortunately many designers may have outdated textbook knowledge of ecological science. Furthermore, although science is empirically based, it is rich in metaphor. Metaphor is the first entry into science for other disciplines. Hence, to use ecology it is important to recognise both the power and the limitations of metaphor. Because there is a rich empirical world behind metaphor, technical concepts and models are important for applying ecological science.

The ecology of urban areas is evolving. Although ecological science, especially in North America, has ignored urban systems, that situation is changing. In addition, as ecologists probe urban systems more deeply, they have progressed from primarily studying natural system analogues such as forested parks and vacant lots, to an approach of ecology *of* the city. Ecology of the city considers the entire urban system, requiring engagement with social sciences and with urban design. The ecology of the city is poised to engage an emerging mode of urban systems – the metacity.

Ecological Science

Ecology is the study of the interactions of organisms with one another and with the environment, and the transformations of matter, energy and information that are mediated by organisms. While the science originated to explain the physiology, genetics, structure and behaviour of organisms in context, it also includes landscapes and ecosystems. Indeed, understanding organisms is impossible without examining their linkage to larger systems. The idea of system is key.[1] A system consists of parts, but the system has properties that emerge from the interaction of the parts.

There are many kinds of ecological system. An ecosystem comprises a specified volume of the Earth, where organisms and the physical environment interact.[2] There is no fixed spatial scale for ecosystems. An ecosystem may be located *within* a rotting log in a forest. A larger instance of an ecosystem is all the animals, ranging from moose to insects, mosses, bacteria and fungi, and the soil, water and air in a northern bog. In all ecosystems, a physical complex of resources, wastes, conditions and signals interacts with organisms. Energy enters the system and waste heat exits. In most ecosystems, materials flow across the boundaries.

Ecological landscapes are areas that are internally heterogeneous. Some define ecological landscapes to exist on the human scale – that is, to the order of hundreds of metres.[3] Others characterise landscapes as an observation strategy defined by spatial heterogeneity and its consequences.[4] This broader definition of ecological landscape is used here. While the ecosystem concept emphasises the metabolic transformations that organisms generate, the landscape concept emphasises the spatial interactions of organisms and fluxes.

Landscapes consist of patches that differ from one another in physical, chemical and informational conditions. For example, a landscape may consist of patches of shrubs and the leaf litter that accumulates beneath them, and a surrounding soil matrix that is crusted with a mixture of bacteria and small mosses. The shrub and crust patches support different amounts of nutrients and water, and hence differ in hospitability to other organisms. Some landscapes facilitate movement of phenomena, such as fire or disease, while other landscapes retard the spread of physical disturbance agents or organisms. Information such as territorial defence calls or temperature fluctuations can move between landscape patches.

Urban areas are ecosystems too,[5,6] so the ideas above apply to cities. Urban is a broad term that contrasts with wild or natural resource management areas. In this broad sense, urban includes suburbs and exurbs. Urban ecosystems contain organisms, physical conditions and entities, and the interactions among them. Of course, humans and their institutions and artefacts are additional components.[7] Indeed, urban ecosystems consist of a biological component, a social component, a physical component and a built component.[6] It is clear that although the parts of an urban system can be examined independently, the parts cannot be separated from one another. Cities and other urban ecosystems are equally biological, social, built and geophysical.

Understanding ecology as a science and its evolving urban approach suggests that contemporary ecology needs and can support improved connections with urban design. I assume the following things about design: 1) It has a different culture than science, in which intervention and social benefit are central; 2) Creativity is important in design; 3) Analysis of site history and conditions, and the generation of forward-looking models are standard activities; 4) Following Vitruvius, urban designers are concerned with firmness, commodity and delight; finally, 5) Urban designers are interested in landscapes in a way similar to ecologists – as a heterogeneous spatial context in which dynamic flows of matter, energy, organisms and information occur. Urban ecologists can benefit from the commonalities, and complement the differences.

Ecological Science has Changed

Many people became aware of ecology through the environmental movement. However, ecology dates from the late 1800s.[8] Ecology emerged as a synthesis between botany and zoology, with input from the physical sciences. Early ecology focused on the distribution of climates, soils and organisms, the dynamics of collections of species, the transfer of energy through feeding relationships, and the physiology and structure of adaptation to contrasting environments.

Ecology has evolved since its inception.[9] For example, although the ecosystem was defined in 1935,[10] it did not become a specialty until the mid 1950s.[8,11] Earlier studies emphasised distribution and abundance of organisms, while ecosystem ecology emphasises the transformation of matter and energy. Other shifts have been stimulated by new perspectives. For example, although the science of evolution is older than ecology, an evolutionary ecology, in which natural selection is an explanatory tool, did not arise until the 1960s. This helped shift from focusing on patterns to focusing on processes. Ecosystem ecology also shifted from studying fixed states of nature to the processes controlling nutrient and energy flows.[12] New scales of observation also emerged. As remote sensing became available, ecologists developed landscape ecology to put communities and ecosystems in their spatially extensive context.[13] Such coarse scale spatial heterogeneity exposed new relationships, and highlighted humans and their artefacts. A temporal expansion also occurred, with longer data runs accumulating as research sites aged,[14] allowing ecologists to discover the impermanence of ecological assemblages and the importance of natural disturbances.[15,16] Because the patterns were dynamic, emphasis shifted to understanding processes. This mirrors the change from design of cities – top down masterplanning – to design in cities that is concerned with processes in which a place participates.

Ecology and Empirical Diversity

The pluralisation of the term ecology is unfamiliar in science. In the introduction, Brian McGrath uses ecologies to refer to diverse urban habitats within and among cities. In this sense, ecology refers to a model of structure and interaction in a city or patch which might differ from the models of other places due to contrasts in topography, hydrology, climate, biota, disturbance regimes, etc. Likewise, the exchanges of energy, material, organisms and information within the urban landscape and with the surrounding non-urban landscape may differ among places. Each of these biophysical, social and political situations could be represented by a model – 'an ecology'. Each model would call for designs that accounted for its particulars.

The pluralisation of ecology is rampant in the design world, and some uses may be different from the sense of a detailed model of urban structure and processes suggested by McGrath. However, rarely are the assumptions behind pluralisation addressed.[17] One interpretation might focus on the diversity of the field as a whole. The specialities of ecology occupy a gradient from emphasis on the physical aspect of ecological systems to the biological side. Ecologists who focus differentially along this gradient cluster separately; but they share the concerns captured in the definition of ecological science presented in the Introduction of this book. Because scientists emphasise unification, ecologists do not pluralise their field. However, within the search for generality and unification, both diversity and specificity have a home.

The concern of ecologists for diversity and difference generates plurality of conceptualisation and models. There is no single theory of ecology. However, Scheiner and Willig[18] propose general principles that apply throughout the discipline. Within this theoretical structure there are constituent theories, so that the theory of ecology is a nested hierarchy.[19] Within most general theoretical principles are nested constituent theories, which cover ecology's conceptual gradient. Within the constituent theories the hierarchy is divided into ever more narrow and specific models. Ecologists do not speak of 'ecologies' when referring to the large realms of the subject or to their specific models.

Ecology as a Metaphor

Ecological science as a dialogue between conceptual constructs and the material world and facilitated by models, contrasts with ecology as metaphor.[19] Metaphor communicates between scientific specialties that have little in common and generates new models in ecology.[8] Ecological 'succession' theory owes its founding metaphor to the transitions in monarchies. The technical term 'disturbance' startles to highlight natural perturbations that had been ignored by ecologists.

Metaphor also communicates scientific knowledge to society. However, ecology is often used metaphorically for aspects of the natural world that people value. Indeed, the metaphors chosen may reflect people's assumptions or values.[20] For example, ecology can stand for fragility in the natural world, or alternatively, for stability. In design, ecology as metaphor can represent the relationship of specific buildings or landscapes to their larger contexts.

Metaphor both within and outside science has risks.[20] Specific assumptions and networks of ideas are implied by different metaphors. Once science introduces a metaphor, however, other tools take over. Science goes beyond metaphor by specifying those assumptions and ideas. Clearly articulated theories and models embody the assumptions, specify the networks of ideas and causal connections, generate hypotheses and organise observations. Models are explanations of the material world. They identify the parts and interactions in the system of interest, the spatial and temporal boundaries of the system and the possible outcomes of interaction. Models can be physical, such as an artificial stream, quantitative as in the case of a differential equation, or conceptual and qualitative. Models in science are used differently from those in design, where models propose forms that *should* be.

The role of metaphor emerges from the fact that all ecological concepts have three dimensions:[2] 1) a core technical definition; 2) metaphorical connotations; and 3) the models by which the concept is applied to the material world. The same ecological term may stand for each of these dimensions. Although conversation may begin with metaphor, for substantive exchange, these questions must be answered: what is the core concept used? What are the model assumptions and structures? What values are implied by the metaphor? Clarifying different pathways through these multiple dimensions can be a productive way forward.

Summing up Ecological Science in its Definition

I indicated earlier that ecological science has changed over time. The current state of ecology is highlighted in a new definition:[12]

The scientific study of the processes influencing the distribution and abundance of organisms, the interactions among organisms, and the interactions between organisms and the transformation and flux of energy, matter, and information.

This new definition is not the standard one found in many textbooks. This definition allows an evolutionary, organismal perspective but also includes nutrient and energy flows. It recognises new kinds of observational realms such as landscapes or global connections. It acknowledges new scales of interest, ranging from hours to millennia, and from microbes to regions. It accommodates pattern, but is also process oriented. Finally, it requires a systems approach, with multiple interactions and feedbacks.

A new ecological paradigm complements the contemporary definition. Contemporary ecology makes assumptions contrary to those held by earlier generations.[21,22] Whereas earlier generations focused on equilibrium conditions, contemporary ecologists acknowledge that ecological structures and processes can be transient. When the older ecology examined dynamics, it assumed deterministic change and a stable end point. In addition, traditional ecology sought explanations within the boundaries of systems, while contemporary research recognises causes and influences that arise beyond system boundaries. Finally, most ecologists in the past assumed humans to be an outside influence, and therefore investigated systems and explanations that did not involve humans.

The new ecology does not assume these conditions will always hold. The old assumptions can be special cases. However, a new paradigm or set of background assumptions allows ecology to take a more open-minded approach. Humans are recognised as components of ecological systems, which suggests the need for dialogue with urban designers. The corollary assumption, that bioecological processes are part of urban systems may help advance the dialogue between ecologists and designers.[23] This may become a key principle for design.

Misuse of Ecology in Masterplanning

Ecology as a scientific discipline generates empirical knowledge about the role of organisms and the transformations they mediate in the material world, while serving as a source of sometimes contradictory metaphors for the public, other scientific disciplines and urban-oriented professions.[20]

Misuse can reside in both the empirical and metaphoric realms. Empirical knowledge can be misused by taking ecological data to be normative, or applying the incorrect model. Although ecological science embodies such generalisations as 'no natural system grows without limit', how such knowledge might be used by society as a norm[24] is a social negotiation. Another principle posits limited resources, which is key to natural selection. This principle has been misused to suggest that competition is the only mechanism of selection, and hence that unbridled competition should drive human society. However, this neglects knowledge that cooperation within groups of organisms can be selected.[25]

There is also the potential to misuse ecological metaphors. Larson[20] analysed metaphors surrounding the issues of sustainability. While he acknowledged the utility of metaphor for generating interest and action, it is clear that metaphor also disguises values in what is often presented as purely scientific discourse. Metaphor obscures the conceptual or quantitative models of a system. Interdisciplinary work must therefore go beyond metaphor. For such a transformative step, rigorous technical definition and various kinds of explanatory models are required. Hence, the full toolkit of ecology, as in any other discipline, includes not only metaphor, but also meaning and model.

One fault in using metaphor to communicate ecology is that the science may have moved beyond the models from which a metaphor originated. An example comes from the science of evolution. In the 19th century, a common metaphor was 'nature red in tooth and claw'. This image embodied two of the core ideas of natural selection – that the resources for organisms are limited in their availability, and that competition between an overabundance of progeny must ensue. The emphasis on competition was adopted in social sciences and in politics to justify the erroneous 'natural' hierarchy of races, and the unfettered industrial and colonial machinations of the late 1800s. 'Social Darwinism' is a catchphrase for this misuse of a biological metaphor.

The organismal metaphor for biological communities has also been superseded. The first theory of change in plant communities was proposed in 1916[26] by Frederic Clements, who considered plant communities to be organisms. Thus, communities were expected to have a deterministic life cycle, and a stable end point or climax. Organisms have a blueprint for development, and pass deterministically juvenile, through mature, to senescent, skipping no phases. This metaphor was compelling, matching everyday experience and what was then cutting edge biology. However, the idea was controversial from the start, and other leading ecologists argued that the directionality of change and the necessity of a particular trajectory were far from universal.[27]

Meanwhile, the idea that communities were organisms with a life cycle had been adopted by the sociologists at the University of Chicago. Thus a faulty metaphor from the science of ecology was transferred to the social sciences and through them, to urban masterplanning.[28] Other analogies influenced the transfer of naturalistic images to city planning. These included the early 20th-century concern for management of limited natural resources in the United States, exemplified by the exhaustion of the Midwestern pine forests and by the dust bowl. The science of ecology had been used in framing management approaches to natural resources. Why not also apply it to the conservation of neighbourhoods and the rejuvenation of blighted urban areas? Jennifer Light[28] demonstrated the persistence of the life cycle metaphor and its policy implications for masterplanning into the 1960s. Ironically, the life cycle and organismal approaches to natural vegetation had been replaced through empirical and theoretical critique over that same period.[29]

Ecology In Versus Ecology Of the City

When ecologists first studied cities, they focused on sites that were analogous to the places they studied elsewhere. Vacant lots were like meadows. Large forested parks invited familiar methods, and allowed comparisons with the numerous studies of forests outside cities. Wildlife populations were documented in urban green patches. Such an approach is ecology IN the city. It neglects much of the urban fabric.

The contrasting approach is ecology OF the city.[30,31] In this approach, the entire urban area is relevant to ecological processes, including reciprocal relationships among organisms, the physical environment, resources, waste streams, environmental regulating factors, human individuals, households and institutions. An early version of ecology of the city was urban metabolism. Budgets of materials in air and water, and the pools and pathways through which solid materials such as food, building material and wastes flowed were exemplified by Hong Kong.[32] This echoed the pioneering social focus on urban metabolism, for example by Karl Marx, because it related the budgets to human well being.[33]

Ecology of the city has evolved since it was adumbrated as metabolism in the 19th century. Ecosystem ecology has matured to examine how budgetary flows are related to the identity of biological species and the heterogeneous structure of both the substrate and the biological community within ecosystems.[34] Likewise, the ecology of the city becomes a more expansive urban ecological science. A metabolic focus is maintained to examine the flows of energy and matter in the system, the linked transformations of these fluxes, and the involvement of organisms along with the physical structures and legacies that organisms generate. The legacies of organisms include soils, organic matter, coarse woody debris in streams and on land, and the woody structure of shrubs and trees. Studies of the urban ecosystem now routinely ask about species identity, spatial heterogeneity and dynamics of vegetated patches within an urban system, and the interaction between biotic composition, heterogeneity and fluxes. Ecology of the city still allows focus on the conspicuous green patches within urban areas. However, it also focuses on less conspicuous or undervalued places. More radically, the ecology of the city treats the city-suburbs-exurbs jointly as an ecological system.

These physical and biological processes and entities are ineluctably linked to social structures and processes. Indeed, in the urban ecosystem, to mention a biophysical focus entails its connection to social, cultural and economic processes.[35] In other words, the ecology of the city, while describing both social and biophysical phenomena, attends to the array of feedbacks and reciprocal influences between these two realms. Social processes alter, divert and shape flows of energy, matter and information. Such a network of structures and interactions is the essence of the ecology of the city. Many different models are required to capture its complexity and dynamism. Consequently, a rich array of ecologically framed models constitutes the knowledge of urban ecology. Those trained in the science of ecology would most probably call them the complementary models that constitute the ecology of the city. Designers may call them ecologies.

Toward An Ecology of the Metacity

The contemporary approach to ecology of the city links to a new understanding of city form.[36] New forms of cities are emerging globally. In the 1970s, Lynch[37] could speak of 1) the cosmological city, 2) the city as machine, and 3) the organic city. Shane[38] has alerted urbanists to the heterogeneity within each of these classical city models, and showed how the components can be recombined as urban actors and their goals change. On the global stage, cities exhibit new combinations of existing components, new components and new governance and social arrangements.[39,40]

Informal settlements explode near old colonial cities, capitals have been established *de novo*, new 'ecocities' are established on the fringes of old cities, or in the countryside or coastal margins, classical industrial cities collapse and shatter, commuting and telecommuting shift the timing, direction and volume of traffic. Bubbles of housing value and reorganisation of financing leave new developments unoccupied, and lead to the gutting and demolition of new houses. Consumerism drives a succession of shopping malls and commercial centres. Informal and formal economies mix and intermingle based on food, drugs and entertainment, sometimes threatening the stability of entire nation states. In such a world 'the city' is not a given.[41] It is a huge, changing, slippery thing. Changing terminology suggests how fluid the urban realm has become: city, metropolis, megalopolis, hypercity and metacity. This series of terms captures increasing size and density, establishment of multiple centres and shift of density from centres. The UN[39] introduced the term 'metacity' to indicate a city form that had more than 20 million residents, was larger than a megalopolis, was polycentric, and had diffuse governance. The term seems to be mainly structural.

Ecology of the city suggests a different perspective on the conurbations now engulfing the world. In ecology, 'meta' has been used to indicate something more inclusive than a certain ecological structure. Hence, a metapopulation comprises a number of isolated, discrete populations of a species that are connected by migration.[42] In a metapopulation, individual populations can grow, persist, decline or become extinct. New populations are established, sometimes in new patches, and sometimes in a patch that had been vacated. Thus, a metapopulation is a spatially heterogeneous, dynamic, differentially connected system. A similar concept applies to *communities* of different species.[43] A community may rise and fall at a site, it may be obliterated or establish in a new location. Exchanges of species, information and resources across the matrix of patches will affect and be affected by the spatial changes in the communities. In other words, 'meta' in ecology is about dynamics and flux across heterogeneous space.[44]

This concept from ecology reinforces the idea of the metacity. In fact, McGrath's use of this term in the Introduction is manifestly more dynamic and process oriented than the descriptive coinage by the UN.[39] The metacity provides a bridge between ecology of the city and urban design. As urban design has focused more on specific sites that are linked to their larger social and ecological contexts, and as it has recognised the dynamism of buildings and landscapes, as opposed to the traditional architectural view of monumental permanence, so too it finds justification in the metacity. Exploring the ecology of the metacity suggests a shared future for research and designs for the dynamic, patchy, networked and adaptive cities of the future.

This paper was developed with support of the National Science Foundation for the Baltimore Ecosystem Study, Long-Term Ecological Research Program (DEB 1027188), and for the Research Coordination Network on Urban Sustainability (RCN 1140070).

Bibliography

1   FS Chapin, III, PA Matson and HA Mooney, *Principles of Terrestrial Ecosystem Ecology*, Springer-Verlag (New York), 2002, p 436.

2   STA Pickett and ML Cadenasso, 'Ecosystem as a Multidimensional Concept: Meaning, Model and Metaphor', *Ecosystems*, vol 5, 2002, pp 1–10.

3   RTT Forman, *Land Mosaics: The Ecology of Landscapes and Regions*, Cambridge University Press (New York), 1995.

4   TFH Allen and TW Hoekstra, *Toward a Unified Ecology*, Columbia University Press (New York), 1992.

5   MJ McDonnell, AK Hahs and JH Breuste (eds), *Ecology of Cities and Towns: a Comparative Approach*, Cambridge University Press (New York), 2009.

6   STA Pickett and JM Grove, 'Urban Ecosystems: What would Tansley do?', *Urban Ecosystems*, vol 12, 2009, pp 1–8.

7   GE Machlis, JE Force and WR Burch, 'The Human Ecosystem. 1. The Human Ecosystem as an Organizing Concept in Ecosystem Management', *Society & Natural Resources*, vol 10 (4), 1997, pp 347–67.

8   JB Hagen, *An Entangled Bank: the Origins of Ecosystem Ecology*, Rutgers University Press (New Brunswick), 1992.

9   SE Kingsland, *The Evolution of American Ecology, 1890–2000*, Johns Hopkins University Press (Baltimore), 2005, p 313.

10   AG Tansley, 'The Use and Abuse of Vegetational Concepts and Terms', *Ecology*, vol 16, 1935, pp 284–307.

11   FB Golley, *A History of the Ecosystem Concept in Ecology: More than the Sum of the Parts*, Yale University Press (New Haven), 1993.

12   GE Likens, *The Ecosystem Approach: Its Use and Abuse*, Ecology Institute (Oldendorf-Luhe, Germany), 1992.

13   MG Turner, 'Landscape Ecology: The Effect of Pattern on Process', *Annual Review of Ecology and Systematics*, vol 20, 1989, pp 171–97.

14   GE Likens (ed), *Long-term Studies in Ecology: Approaches and Alternatives*, Springer-Verlag (New York), 1989.

15   STA Pickett and PS White (eds), *The Ecology of Natural Disturbance and Patch Dynamics*, Academic Press (Orlando, FL), 1985.

16   EA Johnson and K Miyanishi (eds), *Plant Disturbance Ecology: The Process and the Response*, Elsevier Academic Press (Burlington, MA), 2007, p 698.

17   M Mostafavi and G Doherty (eds), *Ecological Urbanism*, Lars Müller (Cambridge), 2010.

18   SM Scheiner and MR Willig, 'A General Theory of Ecology', *Theoretical Ecology*, vol 1, 2008, pp 21–8.

19   STA Pickett, J Kolasa and CG Jones, *Ecological Understanding: The Nature of Theory and the Theory of Nature*, second edition, Springer (New York), 2007, p 233.

20   B Larson, *Metaphors for Environmental Sustainability: Redefining our Relationship with Nature*, Yale University Press (New Haven), 2011, p 301.

21   STA Pickett, VT Parker and PL Fiedler, 'The New Paradigm in Ecology: Implications for Conservation Biology above the Species Level', in PL Fiedler and SK Jain (eds), *Conservation Biology: The Theory and Practice of Nature Conservation, Preservation, and Management*, Chapman and Hall (New York), 1992, pp 65–88.

22   DB Botkin, *Discordant Harmonies: A New Ecology for the Twenty-First Century*, Oxford University Press (New York), 1990.

23   AW Spirn, *The Granite Garden: Urban Nature and Human Design*, Basic Books (New York), 1984.

24   E Ostrom, *Governing the Commons: The Evolution of Institutions for Collective Action*, Cambridge University Press (New York), 1990.

25   DS Wilson, *Evolution for Everyone: How Darwin's Theory Can Change the Way We Think About Our Lives*, Delacorte Press (New York), 2007.

26   FE Clements, *Plant Succession: An Analysis of the Development of Vegetation*, Carnegie Institution of Washington (Washington DC), 1916.

27   WS Cooper, 'The Fundamentals of Vegetation Change', *Ecology*, vol 7, 1926, pp 391–413.

28   JS Light, *The Nature of Cities: Ecological Visions and the American Urban Professions 1920–1960*, Johns Hopkins University Press (Baltimore), 2009.

29   EA Johnson, 'Succession, An Unfinished Revolution', *Ecology*, vol 60, 1979, pp 238–40.

30   STA Pickett et al, 'Integrated Urban Ecosystem Research', *Urban Ecosystems*, vol 1, 1997, pp 183–4.

31   NB Grimm et al, 'Integrated Approaches to Long-Term Studies of Urban Ecological Systems', *BioScience*, vol 50, 2000, pp 571–84.

32   S Boyden et al, *The Ecology of a City and its People: The Case of Hong Kong*, Australian National University Press (Canberra), 1981.

33   JB Foster, 'Marx's Theory of Metabolic Rift: Classical Foundations for Environmental Sociology', *Americal Journal of Sociology*, vol 105, 1999, pp 366–405.

34   CG Jones and JH Lawton (eds), *Linking Species and Ecosystems*, Chapman and Hall (New York), 1995.

35   CL Redman, JM Grove, and L Kuby, 'Integrating Social Science into the Long-Term Ecological Research (LTER) Network: Social Dimensions of Ecological Change and Ecological Dimensions of Social Change', *Ecosystems*, vol 7, 2004, pp 161–71.

36   BP McGrath et al (eds), *Designing Patch Dynamics*, Columbia University Graduate School of Architecture, Preservation and Planning (New York), 2007, p 160.

37   K Lynch, *Good City Form*, MIT Press (Cambridge, MA), 1981, p 512.

38   DG Shane, *Recombinant Urbanism: Conceptual Modeling in Architecture, Urban Design, and City Theory*, John Wiley & Sons (Hoboken, NJ), 2005, p 344.

39   United Nations, *Urbanization: Mega & Meta Cities, New City States?*, UN-Habitat: State of the World's Cities 2006/7 Report, 2007.

40   United Nations Population Fund, *State of World Population 2007: Unleashing the Potential of Urban Growth*, United Nations Population Fund (New York), 2007, p 100.

41   NE McIntyre, K Knowles-Yanez and D Hope, 'Urban Ecology as an Interdisciplinary Field: Differences in the Use of "Urban" Between the Social and Natural Sciences', *Urban Ecosystems*, vol 4, 2000, pp 5–24.

42   I Hanski and ME Gilpin, *Metapopulation Biology: Ecology, Genetics and Evolution*, Academic Press (San Diego), 1997, p 512.

43   MA Leibold et al, 'The Metacommunity Concept: A Framework for Multiscale Community Ecology', *Ecology Letters*, vol 7, 2004, pp 601–13.

44   STA Pickett, ML Cadenasso and CG Jones, 'Generation of Heterogeneity by Organisms: Creation, Maintenance, and Transformation', in M Hutchings, EA John and AJ Stewart (eds), *Ecological Consequences of Habitat Heterogeneity*, Blackwell (New York), 2000, pp 33–52.

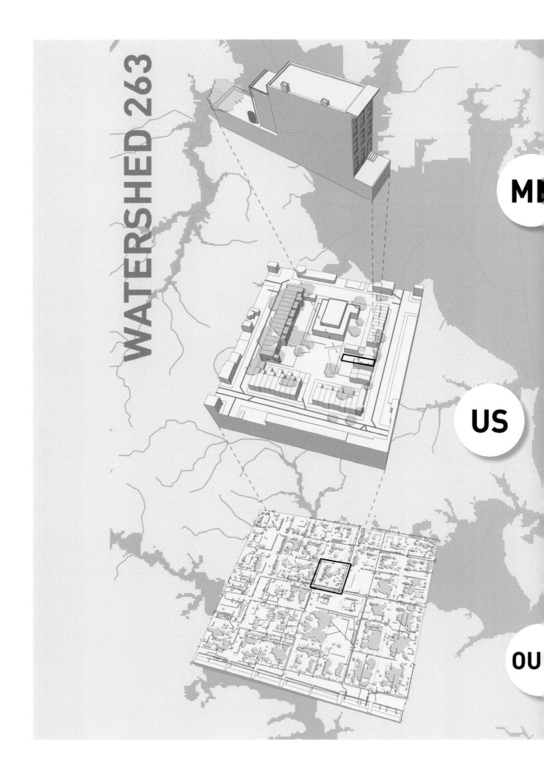

ME

US

OU

ROWHOUSE BACKYARD RAIN BARREL

R COURT SAND FILTER DETENTION TANK

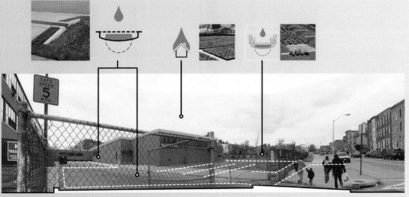

STREET CATCHMENT BIO-FILTERS

From the architecture to the ecology of the city: ecologists and urban designers collaborate in the Baltimore Ecosystem Study in developing alternative strategies for water management based on private, shared or public efforts. Courtesy of urban-interface. © Brian McGrath.

Mark Robbins, detail from *Orders*, photograph
and installation, Plaza San Francisco, XV Quito
Biennale: *Visible Cities*, *Quito*, *Ecuador*, 2006.

People as Infrastructure
Intersecting Fragments in Johannesburg

AbdouMaliq Simone

> This essay is framed around the notion of *people as infrastructure*, which emphasises economic collaboration among poor residents of the megacity. While infrastructure is commonly understood as large physical structures for the movement of information, vehicles, water and energy sources, Simone's notion of *people as infrastructure* 'indicates residents' needs to generate concrete acts and contexts of social collaboration inscribed with multiple identities rather than in overseeing and enforcing modulated transactions among discrete population groups'. This chapter includes the introduction and conclusion of a longer ethnography of inner-city Johannesburg, where Simone identifies these human infrastructure networks as models of a new 'Infracity' in urban Africa.

The inner city of Johannesburg is about as far away as one can get from the popular image of the African village. Though one of Africa's most urbanised settings, it is also seen as a place of ruins – of ruined urbanisation, the ruining of Africa by urbanisation. But in these ruins, something else besides decay might be happening. This essay explores the possibility that these ruins not only mask but also constitute a highly urbanised social infrastructure. This infrastructure is capable of facilitating the intersection of socialities so that expanded spaces of economic and cultural operation become available to residents of limited means.

This essay is framed around the notion of *people as infrastructure*, which emphasises economic collaboration among residents seemingly marginalised from and immiserated by urban life. Infrastructure is commonly understood in physical terms, as reticulated systems of highways, pipes, wires or cables. These modes of provisioning and articulation are viewed as making the city productive, reproducing it, and positioning its residents, territories and resources in specific ensembles where the energies of individuals can be most efficiently deployed and accounted for.

By contrast, I wish to extend the notion of infrastructure directly to people's activities in the city. African cities are characterised by incessantly flexible, mobile and provisional intersections of residents that operate without clearly delineated notions of how the city is to be inhabited and used. These intersections, particularly in the last two decades, have depended on the ability of residents to engage complex combinations of objects, spaces, persons and practices. These conjunctions become an infrastructure – a platform providing for and reproducing life in the city. Indeed, as I illustrate through a range of ethnographic materials on inner-city Johannesburg, an experience of regularity capable of anchoring the livelihoods of residents and their transactions with one another is consolidated precisely because the outcomes of residents' reciprocal efforts are radically open, flexible and provisional. In other words, a specific economy of perception and collaborative practice is constituted through the capacity of individual actors to circulate across and become familiar with a broad range of spatial, residential, economic and transactional positions. Even when actors do different things with one another in different places, each carries traces of past collaboration and an implicit willingness to interact with one another in ways that draw on multiple social positions. The critical question thus raised in this ethnography of inner-city Johannesburg is how researchers, policymakers and urban activists can practise ways of seeing and engaging urban spaces that are characterised simultaneously by regularity and provisionality.

Urbanisation conventionally denotes a thickening of fields, an assemblage of increasingly heterogeneous elements into more complicated collectives. The accelerated, extended and intensified intersections of bodies, landscapes, objects and technologies defer calcification of institutional ensembles or fixed territories of belonging. But does this mean that an experience of regularity and of sustained collaboration among heterogeneous actors is foreclosed? We have largely been led to believe that this is the case. Thus, various instantiations of governmentality have attempted to emplace urbanising processes through the administration of choices and the codification of multiplicity. The potential thickness of social fields becomes the thickness of definitions and classifications engineered by various administrations of legibility and centres of decision making.[1] Once visible, the differentiated elements of society are to assume their own places and trajectories and become the vectors through which social power is enunciated.

In this view, urban spaces are imagined to be functional destinations. There are to be few surprises, few chances for unregulated encounters, as the city is turned into an object like a language.[2] Here, relations of correspondence are set up between instances of two distinct and nonparallel modes of formalisation – of expression and content.[3] Particular spaces are linked to specific identities, functions, lifestyles and properties so that the spaces of the city become legible for specific people at given places and times. These diagrams – what Henri Lefebvre calls 'representations of space' – act to 'pin down' inseparable connections between places, people, actions and things.[4] At the same time, the diagrams make possible a 'relation of non-relation' that opens each constituent element onto a multiplicity of relations between forces.[5] In this multiplicity of connotations, it is always possible to do something different in and with the city than is specified by these domains of power while, at the same time, acting as if one remains operative inevitably only within them.[6] This notion of tactics operating at the interstices of strategic constraints is a recurring theme in the work of Michel de Certeau.[7]

In other words, the disposition of regularities and the outcomes of collaborative work in the city can be open ended, unpredictable and made singular. The truncated process of economic modernisation at work in African cities has never fully consolidated apparatuses of definition capable of enforcing specific and consistent territorial organisations of the city. State administrations and civil institutions have lacked the political and economic power to assign the diversity of activities taking place within the city (buying, selling, residing, etc) to bounded spaces of deployment, codes of articulation, or the purview of

left: Outside Wimpy-Park Station, Johannesburg, South Africa.
right: View of the Central Business District from atop Carlton Centre, Johannesburg, South Africa

designated actors. According to conventional imaginaries of urbanisation, which locate urban productivity in the social division of labour and the consolidation of individuation, African cities are incomplete.[8] In contrast to these imaginaries, African cities survive largely through a conjunction of heterogeneous activities brought to bear on and elaborated through flexibly configured landscapes. But it is important to emphasise that these flexible configurations are pursued not in some essential contrast to non-African urban priorities or values but as specific routes to a kind of stability and regularity that non-African cities have historically attempted to realise. Consider the incomplete, truncated or deteriorated forms and temporalities of various, seemingly incompatible institutional rationalities and modes of production – from the bureaucracies of civil administration to the workshop, the industrial unit, subsistence agriculture, private enterprise and customary usufruct arrangements governing land use. All are deployed as a means of stabilising a social field of interaction. In part, this is a way to continuously readapt residents' actions to engage the open-ended destinations that their very collaborations have produced.

For example, the transport depot in Abidjan is full of hundreds of young men who function as steerers, baggage loaders, ticket salespersons, hawkers, drivers, petrol pumpers and mechanics. There are constantly shifting connections among them. Each boy who steers passengers to a particular company makes a rapid assessment of their wealth, personal characteristics and the reason for their journey. This reading determines where the steerer will guide prospective passengers, who will sell their tickets, who will load their baggage, who will seat them, and so forth. It is as if this collaboration were assembled to maximise the efficiency of each passage, even though there are no explicit rules or formal means of payment to the steerers. Although each boy gives up control of the passenger to the next player down the line, their collaboration is based not on the boys adhering to specific rules but on their capacity to improvise.

Such a conjunction of heterogeneous activities, modes of production and institutional forms constitutes highly mobile and provisional possibilities for how people live and make things, how they use the urban environment and collaborate with one another. The specific operations and scopes of these conjunctions are constantly negotiated and depend on the particular histories, understandings, networks, styles and inclinations of the actors involved. Highly specialised needs arise, requiring the application of specialised skills and sensitivities that can adapt to the unpredictable range of scenarios these needs bring to life. Regularities thus ensue from a process of incessant convertibility – turning commodities, found objects, resources and bodies into uses previously unimaginable or constrained. Producer-residents become more adept at operating within these conjunctions as they deploy a greater diversity of abilities and efforts. Again it is important to emphasise that these conjunctions become a coherent platform for social transaction and livelihood. This process of conjunction, which is capable of generating social compositions across a range of singular capacities and needs (both enacted and virtual) and which attempts to derive maximal outcomes from a minimal set of elements, is what I call *people as infrastructure*.[9]

This concept is not meant to account for inner-city Johannesburg in its entirety. Many residents, battered by the demands of maintaining the semblance of a safe domestic environment, find few incentives to exceed the bounds of personal survival. But *people as infrastructure* describes a tentative and often precarious process of remaking the inner city, especially now that the policies and economies that once moored it to the surrounding city have mostly worn away. In many respects, the inner city has been 'let go' and forced to reweave its connections with the larger world by making the most of its limited means. Still, the inner city is embedded in a larger urban region characterised by relative economic strength, an emerging pan-African service economy, political transformations that have sought to attenuate the more stringent trappings of population control and a highly fragmented urban system whose regulatory regime was never geared toward high-density residential areas. This ensemble, in turn, has given rise to a markedly heterogeneous domain of people.

* * *

Infracity: Johannesburg and Urban Africa

On the surface, inner-city Johannesburg has many features in common with inner cities in the United States. Many of the economic and political mechanisms that produced American inner-city ghettos have been at work in Johannesburg, and these are only reinforced by the strong influence of US urban policy on South Africa. But large swathes of Johannesburg reflect the failures of strong regulatory systems and the economic and social informalities commonly associated with urban Africa. To this extent, inner-city Johannesburg is a kind of hybrid: part American, part African. Indeed, it is mainly Johannesburg's American features – its developed physical infrastructure, social anonymity and extensive range of material and service consumption – that have attracted large numbers of urban Africans. It is easy to show that changes in the global economy have substantially restructured and respatialised cities everywhere, often around residual pockets of ruin. The potential significance of reflections on Johannesburg, in contrast to other global cities, rests in how the city embodies, speeds up and sometimes brutalises aspects of urban life common to many African cities.

One such aspect is its urban residents' constant state of preparedness. Driven by discourses of war, contestation and experimentation, many African cities seem to force their inhabitants to constantly change gears, focus and location. Of course, there are some quarters whose residents have grown up, raised families and devoted themselves to the same occupation or way of life without moving. Yet even this stability is situated within a larger, more fluid arena where people must be prepared to exert themselves. There is the need to ensure oneself against a lifetime without work or the means to establish a family or household of one's own. There is the need to prepare for the possibility that even hard work will produce nothing.

There is the need to prepare for an endless process of trickery. Government officials trick citizens with countless pronouncements of progress while finding new and improved ways of shaking them down. Parents trick their children with promises of constant nurturing – if only they would sell themselves here or there, as maids, touts, whores or guardians. And children trick their parents with promises of support into old age – if only they would sell the land, the house in exchange for fake papers, airline tickets or a consignment of goods that just fell off the truck.

This sense of preparedness, a readiness to switch gears, has significant implications for what residents think it is possible to do in the city. Households do display considerable determination and discipline, saving money over the course of several years to send children to school, build a house or help family members to migrate. They are in a place, and they demonstrate commitment to it. At the same time, African cities are a platform for people to engage with processes and territories that bear a marked sense of exteriority. The reference of this 'exterior' has commonly been other cities, both within and outside the continent. Increasingly, it includes various interiors: rural areas, borders and frontiers. These interiors may also be symbolic or spiritual and involve geographies that are off the map, as demonstrated in popular descriptions of subterranean cities, spirit worlds or lucrative but remote frontiers. Cities straddle not only internal and external divides and national and regional boundaries but also a wide range of terrain and geography, both real and imaginary.

left: Street food vendor, Marshalltown, Johannesburg, South Africa.
right: Carlton Centre, Johannesburg, South Africa.

In many respects, then, Johannesburg not only displays and accelerates these tendencies by providing a rich urban infrastructure on which they operate, but it also stands as a receptacle, witness and culmination of this preparedness. The inner city is a domain that few want to belong to or establish roots in. But it keeps alive residents' hopes for stability somewhere else, even as it cultivates within them a seemingly permanent restlessness and capacity to make something out of the city. One has to canvass only a small sample of the stories of foreign migrants to see how many different places they have been within the recent past. One informant from Cameroon showed me a passport with stamps from Congo, Angola, Namibia, Zimbabwe, South Africa, Dubai, India, Malaysia, Thailand, Singapore, China, Brazil, Uruguay, Paraguay, Chile, Peru, Venezuela, Guyana, Trinidad and Argentina – all acquired over a seven-year period. The same holds true even for residents of South Africa, Lesotho or Swaziland who may never have left the region but whose trajectories through diverse rural towns and urban townships encompass a very wide world.

Increasing numbers of Africans are situated in what could be called half-built environments: underdeveloped, overused, fragmented and often makeshift urban infrastructures where essential services are erratic or costly and whose inefficiencies spread and urbanise disease. The majority of Africans still do not have access to clean water and sanitation. They are malnourished and, on average, live no longer than they did 20 years ago, even though the *raison d'être* of built environments would suggest a continuous trajectory toward the improved welfare of their inhabitants.

The international community has made a substantial effort over the last decade to help African municipalities to direct urban growth and restructuring. Here, capacity building centres on developing proficient forms of codification. Not only does the city become the objective of a plurality of coding systems, it is meant to manifest itself more clearly as a system of codes. In other words, it is to be an arena where spaces, activities, populations, flows and structures are made visible, or more precisely, recognisable and familiar.

Once this enhanced visibility is accomplished, urban spaces and activities are more capable of being retrieved and compared for analysis and planning. The emphasis is on the ability to locate and to define the built environment, specific populations and activities so that they can be registered. The prevailing wisdom is that, once registered, these phenomena can be better administered and their specific energies, disciplines and resources extracted. But it is clear that much of what takes place in African cities is fairly invisible: the number of people who reside in a given compound; how household incomes that can support only one week's survival out of every month are supplemented; or how electricity is provided for 10 times as many households as there are official connections.

In Johannesburg's inner city, the heightened emphasis on visible identities and the converse need of actors to hide what they are actually doing generates a highly volatile mix. But it is in this play of the visible and invisible that limited resources can be put to work in many possible ways. Throughout urban Africa, residents experience new forms of solidarity through their participation in makeshift, ephemeral ways of being social. At the same time, these makeshift formations amplify the complexity of local terrain and social relationships by engaging the dynamics of a larger world within a coherent, if temporary, sense of place. Sometimes this sense of place coincides with a specific locality; other times, and with increasing frequency, it is dispersed across or in-between discernible territories. In this economy of interpenetration, notions about what is possible and impossible are upended, and urban residents are ready to take up a variety of attitudes and positions.

Take, for example, African urban markets. They are renowned for being well run and for their multitude of goods and services overflowing whatever order is imposed upon them. In these markets, cooking, reciting, selling, loading and unloading, fighting, praying, relaxing, pounding and buying happen side by side, on stages too cramped, too deteriorated, too clogged with waste, history, energy and sweat to sustain all of them. Entering the market, what do potential customers make of all that is going on? Whom do they deal with and buy from? People have their networks, their channels and their rules. But there are also wide spaces for most people to insert themselves as middlemen who might provide a fortuitous, even magical, reading of the market 'between the lines', between stall after stall of onions or used clothes, between the 50 cent profit of the woman selling Marlboros and 5,000 freshly minted $20 bills stuffed into sisal bags with cassava and hair grease, tossed on top of a converted school-bus heading somewhere into the interior. For it is these possibilities of interpretation, fixing and navigation that enable customers to take away the most while appearing to deliver the minimum.

Throughout much of urban Africa, accidents, coercion, distinctly identified spaces, clandestine acts and publicity are brought together in ways that trip up each of these categories. The clandestine becomes highly visible, while that which is seemingly so public disappears from view. More importantly, the apparently fragmented and disarticulated collection of quarters and spaces that make up the city are opened up to new reciprocal linkages.

These linkages are sometimes the constructions of individuals who desire to master self-limitations as opposed to merely straddling divides. At other times, urban residents invent a range of practices – religious, sexual, institutional – capable of relocating individual actors within different frames of identity or recognition. This relocation enables them to understand their relationships with other actors and events in new, broader ways. Actors speak and deal with one another in ways that would otherwise be impossible. Such unanticipated interactions can be used to rehearse new ways of navigating complex urban relationships and to construct a sense of commonality that goes beyond parochial identities. Still, residents invest heavily in opportunities to become socially visible in ways that are not necessarily tied to formal associations. For example, throughout urban Africa, the proliferating neighbourhood night markets do not simply provide an opportunity for localised trade or for extending trading hours, but serve primarily as occasions to be public, to watch others and whom they deal with, and to listen to their conversations. The task is to find ways to situate oneself so one can assess what is happening – who talks to whom, who is visiting whose house, who is riding in the same car, who is trading or doing business together – without drawing attention to oneself, without constituting a threat.[10]

Inner-city Johannesburg raises the stakes on these realities and capacities. It does not use the residual features of its 'American side' to either resolve or make them more manageable, palatable or visible. With its well-developed communications systems, efficient yet pliable banks, and relatively easy access to daily comforts, Johannesburg would appear to have more sophisticated parallel (though often illegal) economies than other African cities. What the inner city provides is an intersection where different styles, schemes, sectors and practices can make something out of and from one another. In these respects, inner-city Johannesburg is the quintessential African city. Johannesburg becomes a launching pad not only for better livelihoods within the inner city but also for excursions into a broader world, whether Dubai and Mumbai or the pool halls of Hillbrow and the white suburb of Cresta only a few kilometres away. On the other hand, the density of skills, needs, aspirations and willingness brought to work in the inner city makes it a sometimes brutal place, where everything seems to be on the line.

Concluding Note
The intensifying immiseration of African urban populations is real and alarming. For increasing numbers of urban Africans, their cities no longer offer them the prospect of improving their livelihoods or modern ways of life. Yet the theoretical reflections that

underpin an ethnographic observation of inner-city Johannesburg point to how the growing distance between how urban Africans actually live and normative trajectories of urbanisation and public life can constitute new fields of economic action. In striking ways, the translocal scope and multilateral transactions displayed by these more ephemeral economic machines are similar to the operations pursued by the dominant transnational economic networks of scale. But they are just similar, not the same – for their similarity is generated precisely through the disarticulation of coherent urban space. In significant ways, both the global/regional command centres and the dispersed, provisional, quotidian economies of the popular urban quarters do not intersect.

With limited institutional anchorage and financial capital, the majority of African urban residents have to make what they can out of their bare lives. Although they bring little to the table of prospective collaboration and participate in few of the mediating structures that deter or determine how individuals interact with others, this seemingly minimalist offering – bare life – is somehow redeemed. It is allowed innumerable possibilities of combination and interchange that preclude any definitive judgement of efficacy or impossibility. By throwing their intensifying particularisms – of identity, location, destination and livelihood – into the fray, urban residents generate a sense of unaccountable movement that might remain geographically circumscribed or travel great distances.

Notes

1 H Lefebvre, *The Production of Space*, Blackwell (Oxford), 1991.
2 H Lefebvre, *Writings on Cities*, trans E Kofman and E Lebas, Blackwell (Cambridge, MA), 1996.
3 C Wolfe, *Critical Environments: Postmodern Theory and the Pragmatics of the Outside*, University of Minnesota Press (Minneapolis), 1998.
4 H Lefebvre, 'Reflections on the Politics of Space', trans M Enders, *Antipode* 8 (1976), p 33.
5 Lefebvre, 'Reflections', 33; Gunnar Olsson, 'From a = b to a = a', *Environment and Planning* A 32, no 7, 2000, p 1242.
6 J Rajchman, *Constructions*, MIT Press (Cambridge, MA), 1998.
7 M de Certeau, *The Practice of Everyday Life*, University of California Press (Berkeley), 1984.
8 This is a common assumption about the nature of urban Africa but one with its own histories and disputes. See DM Anderson and R Rathbone, 'Urban Africa: Histories in the Making', in DM Anderson and R Rathbone (eds), *Africa's Urban Past*, James Currey (Oxford), 2000.
9 This notion attempts to extend what Lefebvre meant by social space as a practice of works – modes of organisation at various and interlocking scales that link expressions, attraction and repulsion, sympathies and antipathies, changes and amalgamations that affect urban residents and their social interactions. Ways of doing and representing things become increasingly 'conversant' with one another. They participate in a diversifying series of reciprocal exchanges, so that positions and identities are not fixed or even, at most times, determinable. These 'urbanised' relations reflect neither the dominance of a narrative or linguistic structure nor a chaotic, primordial mix.
10 A Bayat, 'Un-civil Society: The Politics of the "Informal People"', *Third World Quarterly* 18, no 1, 1997, pp 53–72.

From AbdouMaliq Simone, 'People as Infrastructure: Intersecting Fragments in Johannesburg' in *Public Culture*, vol 16, no 3, excerpts from pp 407–29. © 2004 Duke University Press. All rights reserved. Reprinted by permission of Duke University Press. Images: p 174 photograph Mark Robbins © Mark Robbins; pp 177, 180, photographs Erick Gregory © Erick Gregory.

Bangkok
The Architecture of Three Ecologies

Brian McGrath

> This chapter, an essay first published in 2008 in *Perspecta* adapted here for length, employs Felix Guattari's three ecological registers – the environment, social relations and human subjectivity – as a framework to establish a method for analysing both the architecture and the ecology of the megacity. The title also refers to Reyner Banham's book on Los Angeles (see chapter pages 98–107), which opened up new ways of looking at how the territory of the city region provides different 'ecologies' for architectural expressions and social behaviour. Bangkok's three-dimensional sectional city centre of shopping malls and Skytrains also resonates with Alvin Boyarsky's chapter on Chicago (pages 48–59) and Shelton, Karakeiwicz and Kvan's analysis of Hong Kong (pages 72–85).

Carved gold-leaf wooden shutters frame scenes of paddy rice farming, grazing water buffalo and lotus gardens floating within an encrusted background of miniature diamond-shaped mirrors. These reflective surfaces evoking a bucolic, water-based life animate the raised colonnaded ambulatory of the *ubosot* at Wat Pathumwanaram in the heart of Bangkok. When saffron-robed mendicants circle the temple, the glimmering surfaces mirror the sky, trees, lotus gardens and worshippers in a kaleidoscopic mosaic of shifting reflections. The mirrored shutters also reflect a new urban panorama beyond the monastery precinct. Two of Asia's largest shopping malls bookend the temple just east of the new Siam Central Station, the main junction of Bangkok Transit System's first two mass-transit Skytrain lines.

Wat Pathumwanaram was constructed in the early 19th century by King Rama IV, as a royal retreat along the San Saeb Canal. With the expansion of the Kingdom of Siam and growing commercial contacts with Europe during the early 20th century, the Thai elite began to experiment with the architecture, landscapes, dress codes and decorum of colonial Europe in the Pathumwan district around the old monastery. Today, the monastery complex shares this long super block with four major shopping mall/mixed-use commercial complexes comprising the Central Shopping District of Bangkok. Surprisingly, the recent profusion of reflective and transparent architectural skins and surfaces resembles the aesthetic dematerialisation – if not spiritual dimensions – of Wat Pathumwanaram's glimmering illusionary shutters. Digital screen-printing as well as new glass and LED technologies create new luminescent images and reflections back to city inhabitants wandering through the malls or gliding above the city on the elevated Skytrain.

The collapse of histories, geographies and cultures at this corner of contemporary Bangkok frames this chapter as a vivid example of Félix Guattari's three ecologies: the environment, the socius and the psyche (Guattari, 2000). Unlike Reyner Banham's

Wat Pathumwanaram is dwarfed between Siam Paragon and the Central World office and shopping complex. The water gardens of the palace and temple have been replaced by underground parking, with a reflecting pool above.

topographical analysis of Los Angeles (see pages 98–107), here ecologies are understood as nested circuits of relationships between ecosystem processes and human consciousness. Furthermore, the embedded scales of Guattari's ecologies parallel Bangkok's Hindu-Buddhist cosmology. The *Traiphumikata*, Thailand's Theravada Buddhist canon, describes three worlds – one formless, one comprising form but no sensation, and finally the world of form and sensation – divided into 34 levels of existence (Khanjanusthiti, 1996). For eight centuries, Siam has constructed symbolic urban realms embodying modes of behaviour interpreting this cosmological model in architectural details, ritual space as well as in city planning and design.

Radical contemporary Buddhism now interprets the *Traiphumikata*'s super-mundane realms as psychological states in the here and now (Sivaraksa, 1988). The repeating cycles of human existence based on suffering, death, karma, merit making and rebirth can be understood best through meditation practices which still the body and mind in order to bring attention to reality as constant flux and change. Contemporary ecological thinking has also been radicalised through new open, non-equilibrium, disturbance models (see pages 162–71 and 272–81). Rather than seeing ecology as a closed system in balance, ecosystem science today conceives of the world as comprised of an open impermanent system of patches in constant flux (Pickett, 2005). The global context in which both contemporary Buddhism and disturbance ecology are imagined has radically shifted as well. For the first time in human history, the majority of people are urbanites. Nature can no longer be conceived as the wild 'other' of the city, isolated from human disturbance, and cities can no longer be conceived as closed human systems outside nature.

The following three sections intersect these new lines of thinking by reflecting on contemporary Bangkok's three embedded ecologies. *Liquid Perception* presents the Chao Phraya River Basin as the regional environment within which the historical, geological, topographic and climatic conditions of Siamese urbanism can be understood. *Transpolitanism* describes the Lower Chao Phraya Delta as a dynamic social construction, continuously transformed by a distributed network of human agents operating within fluctuating political, cultural, hydrological and market conditions. Finally, *Simultopia* revisits the mediated human ecosystem that comprises the commercial blocks surrounding Wat Pathumwanaram as an architectural expression of Bangkok's current collective psyche. While the scale of inquiry is expansive, it is my intention to portray architecture as the primary agent for situating the nested space of Guattari's three ecologies within a framework of sensate human perception, social experience and material existence. The chapter's spatio-temporal collapse seeks to understand ecosystem processes and connective logics across scale and time, rather than defining historically discrete or topographic limits to urban ecologies. Contemporary ecological frameworks – watersheds, human ecosystem and patch dynamics – are employed here in order to understand contemporary Bangkok as part of an emergent human ecosystem while Bangkok's three ecologies are presented as new design models for confronting the primary environmental, social and psychic dilemmas present in 21st-century architecture and urbanism.

Liquid Perception

Along the 14th parallel, day and night oscillate neatly between predictable 12-hour divisions, and months pass with little change in temperature. However, between May and October, a slight shift in atmospheric currents brings monsoon rains from the Indian subcontinent north, from the Indonesian archipelago to the mountain ranges ringing northern Thailand whose run-off feeds the Chao Phraya River Basin – and Bangkok sprawling across its flat, silted tidal delta. Seasonal cycles of precipitation rather than temperature extremes of winter and summer bring rhythm to life just above the equator, putting into motion human cycles of planting, harvest and migration, as well as shaping Siamese beliefs and rituals. The mountain rainforests release a sacred mixture of rain and nutrients which follows the historical topography of the capital cities of the Kingdom of Siam through fan-terraced floodplains at the foothills of the mountains in Sukhothai (13th century); converging at the island confluence city of Ayutthaya (14th–18th centuries); before finally depositing in deltaic Bangkok (18th century to the present). Siamese urbanity and domesticity evolved from an intimate association with climatic, topographic and hydraulic conditions. River, canal and lagoon based garden cities retained six months of rainwater for the following six dry ones, staging ceremonies and rituals in sync with attentive observation of hydrological cycles and variations.

The Siamese fluvial topography was overcoded by a feudal tributary power system. Upstream vassals and lesser kings sent annual gifts to the royal houses in the successively downstream capitals, from which auratic power was reflected back to village hinterlands (Winichakul, 1994). Honorific space materialised a Buddhist cosmology of distant kings

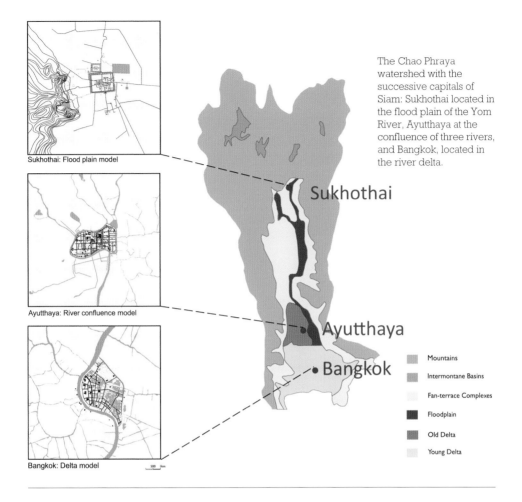

Sukhothai: Flood plain model

Ayutthaya: River confluence model

Bangkok: Delta model

The Chao Phraya watershed with the successive capitals of Siam: Sukhothai located in the flood plain of the Yom River, Ayutthaya at the confluence of three rivers, and Bangkok, located in the river delta.

Sukhothai

Ayutthaya

Bangkok

Mountains

Intermontane Basins

Fan-terrace Complexes

Floodplain

Old Delta

Young Delta

and river valley kingdoms comprising distinct watersheds. Power was primarily symbolic, as villages made decisions about land and water management locally. Contemporary life in a newly industrialised country follows the less predictable flows and fluctuations of global capital. Thailand's strategic Cold War alliance with America catapulted the kingdom's economy to a world stage, and new ideas and fantasies from abroad now freely mix with ancient myths and rites. When rice prices fall and word of jobs in Bangkok reaches small subsistence agricultural settlements, economic migrations trickle and then flood the capital city. Now, media flows in a reverse direction to the watershed, and television broadcasts from Bangkok infiltrate nearly every household in the kingdom.

Contemporary ecology is conceived around measuring the ecosystem performance through a watershed framework. In the Hubbard Brook Experimental Forest, ecologists developed a working ecosystem model by measuring the inputs and outputs in a hydrologically defined small experimental watershed in the White Mountains of New Hampshire (Bormann and Likens, 1981). In the Baltimore Ecosystem Study, experimental models derived from the Hubbard Brook, are being tested for the first time in urban, suburban and exurban sites. The social science model for this study, the Human Ecosystem Framework, links critical biophysical resources to social systems through the flows of individuals, energy, nutrients, materials, information and capital. In urban ecosystem science, both urban and rural patterns are recognised as recombinations of vegetative and built patches structured by watersheds identified as Patch Dynamics. Urban ecological structure and performance is understood through measuring inputs and outputs of flows through relatively small, bounded patches over time.

The discipline of Urban Design is now being added to this framework in order to create new dynamic design models of urban ecosystems. Much of the work points to a reassessment of the way river and water flows have been engineered to pass around and under cities rather than through them. A pre-modern, locally-controlled, human watershed ecosystem structured and sustained Siamese cities for centuries. Today, ministries in Bangkok manage the Chao Phraya River Basin's vast hydroelectrical and irrigation network. Remotely controlled modern dams and reservoirs replaced cities as locally controlled and maintained water retention systems. Water and floods were thought to be technologically controllable and manageable in contrast with the complexities of indigenous Thai socio-hydrology and urbanism.

Transpolitanism

From his floating research lab, a pontoon boat, Terdsak Tachakitkachorn documents urbanisation patterns along the Mae Khlong River, one hour west of Bangkok. The farmers' stories, together with historical documents and maps, convey the difficulties of transforming a swampy delta jungle into a network of individual households, markets and villages. Small irrigation canals feed raised-bed orchards, while houses line natural levees along rivers and larger navigable canals (Tachakitkachorn, 2005). Where these house-lined waterways intersect, informal markets formed, first floating retailers, then formalised into waterside market districts. Market cities grew at major intersections between canals and rivers. The muddy jungle marsh of the Lower Delta of the Chao Phraya was transformed into an extension of the island Capital City of Ayutthaya through the construction of short-cut and transverse canals beginning in the 17th century. By the mid-19th century, this agri-urban linear urban settlement pattern stretched for hundreds of miles along the water distribution channels of the Lower Delta. This landscape became the verdant setting for the relocation of the capital of Siam to Bangkok in the late 18th century.

Bangkok's Outer Ring Road, a giant elliptical expressway, stretches 90 kilometres (55 miles) north/south, and 30 kilometres (18 miles) east/west, passing over and through this dynamic patchwork of orchards, rice fields, fishponds, industrial, residential, commercial and leisure spaces of the Lower Chao Phraya Delta. The Bung Tong Fishing Hut is a long covered wooden deck built over an expansive grid of fishponds along the expressway 20 kilometres (12 miles) east of Bangkok. The Ring Road provides both high visibility and easy accessibility for the fish farm, restaurant and recreational fishing huts, while providing easy transport for the one million fish farmed here every year. Danai Thaitakoo employs remote sensing to measure regional land cover change and conducts excursions around the Outer Ring Road to survey changing land use practices. Danai interviews rice, fruit, fish and shrimp farmers as they respond to falling prices and increased costs. The new economy of the Ring Road now consists mostly of land speculation for new industrial estates, housing subdivisions and commercial complexes. Labour-intensive rice transplanting and orchard farming has disappeared in Greater Bangkok in recent decades, as labour costs have risen. Some farmers grow turf instead of rice or sell topsoil for the lawns and golf courses of the housing developments. Others hollow the land to harvest topsoil producing fish farms, easily flooded in the subsiding delta.

Terdsak and Danai's research follows decades of work by social scientists from the Thailand Cornell Project and the Kyoto University Center for Southeast Asia Studies. The Cornell researchers studied the transformation of the rice-growing community of Ban Chang to the east of Bangkok since the mid-19th century from their Cold War American vantage point of the middle of the 20th century. Social scientists Lucien Hanks and Lauriston Sharp were thrilled to see the invisible hand of Adam Smith at work in indigenous Thai urbanism long before the Americans arrived (Sharp and Hanks, 1978). In *Rice and Man* (1972), Hanks documents the socio-ecological change by interviewing villagers and examining archival records. Hanks identified the fear of abandonment and isolation as the immanent threats to this frontier rice-growing village along San Saeb Canal, but what continually fascinated the group most was the economic *transformative* capacity of Thai agri-urbanism as evident as one farming village changed from shifting, to broadcasting and finally to transplanting cultivation and slowly became incorporated into the extended networked market economy of Greater Bangkok.

Sociologist Richard O'Connor has demonstrated how in Thai society, a person can choose his or her affiliations creating fluid extended household structures rather than a fixed nuclear family model. For O'Connor, Thai groups are fluid and overlapping. This fluidity is not incidental but integral to the organisation of society (O'Connor, undated). Thai *transpolitanism* adapted from centuries of both Indic and Chinese contacts and diasporas, resistance of English, French, Dutch, Portuguese, Spanish and American colonialism in South-East Asia, and more recent global alliances through contemporary global trade and tourism. Contemporary research and the Cornell Thailand Project both demonstrate the dynamic and adaptive socio-ecological capability of Thai urbanism. The deltaic network city of greater Bangkok points to an alternate way towards modern social development, one that allows for multiple options and mobility at the individual and household level.

Simultopia

The grand opening of Bangkok's glittering newest shopping mall, Siam Paragon, was broadcast throughout the kingdom in December 2005. The mall replaced the verdant Siam Intercontinental Hotel, torn down in 2002 on royally owned land next to the gardens of Srapatum Palace, just west of Wat Pathumwanaram. The grand entrance of the mall is a faceted glass 'jewel' meant to glitter like diamonds in the day and glow with the colours of gems – from ruby, sapphire, emerald to topaz – in the evening. Inside Siam Paragon are car showrooms, luxury restaurants along an indoor canal and Siam Ocean

Bangkok's eastern periphery is dominated by rice fields irrigated and connected by trunk canals, some built during the Ayutthaya kingdom. Following construction of new highways, many rice fields are being replaced by housing subdivisions and factories. Fish farms dominate the south-eastern fringe. Bangkok's west bank consists of canals which follow the old meanders of the Chao Phraya, before short-cuts were dug by Ayutthaya's kings. Orchards prevail in this part of the city, making it very attractive for new home buyers. Shrimp farms dominate the south-western coastline, replacing mangrove forests.

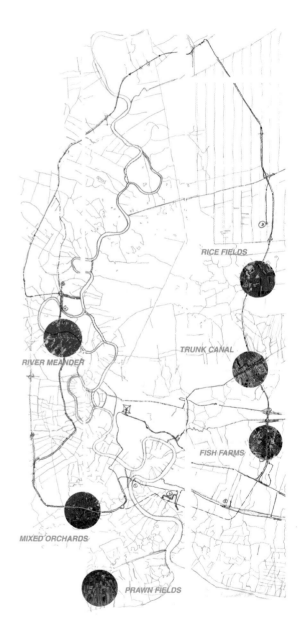

RICE FIELDS

TRUNK CANAL

RIVER MEANDER

FISH FARMS

MIXED ORCHARDS

PRAWN FIELDS

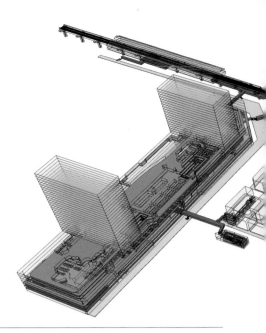

Siam Paragon is set back from the three levels of Siam Central Station. A raised public plaza connects directly to the Skytrain mezzanine level. Central World Plaza constructed a raised walkway from Siam Station to Ratchaprasong Intersection.

World, the largest aquarium in South-East Asia. The mall's nine different sections: Luxury, Fashion and Beauty, Digital Lifestyle, Living and Technology, The Exotic East, Dining Paradise, Paragon Gourmet Market, Paragon Department Store, and the Paragon World of Entertainment, draw 100,000 visitors a day and make Bangkok a shopping destination eclipsing even Hong Kong and Singapore.

While the spiral ramps to Siam Paragon's 4,000-place car park loom above Wat Pathumwanaram's western flank, the expansive construction site of Central World Plaza rises to the east. According to the project architects, Altoon and Porter, Central World Plaza was redeveloped as a mixed-use centre that includes a seven-storey high, 350-metre (1,150-feet) long digital Media Wall, with the capability to project multiple LED images, ticker tape and lasers. The new high-tech face of the greatly expanded centre looks out on a revitalised plaza – which, like Times Square in New York, serves as the gathering space for the annual New Year's countdown, and in the cool winter months as enormous German beer gardens, complete with fountains and gardens. The mall offerings that flash across the big screens are a variety of retail 'rooms' or precincts, an Olympic ice rink, bowling, a fitness centre, a convention centre, high-rise hotel, 50-storey office space and multiple entertainment spots. The redesign turned the eight-storey mall inside out by moving the vertical circulation including stairs, escalators and elevators to the interstitial space between the wall of the building and the media screen, which hangs from the existing facade.

The catastrophic Asian economic crisis of 1997 began with a real estate bubble, bank failures and currency speculation in Thailand. Between 1985 and 1995, Thailand was the world's fastest growing economy, and huge, glittering commercial buildings symbolised the promise of national prosperity. After 1997, they turned into the counter symbol of economic depression, as hundreds of commercial developments in central Bangkok fell idle due to bankruptcy, shoppers disappeared, and the city became known for its haunting hollow concrete shells. Here these fears of isolation and abandonment became manifest prominently in the symbolic heart of the modern city. Following the crises, a national

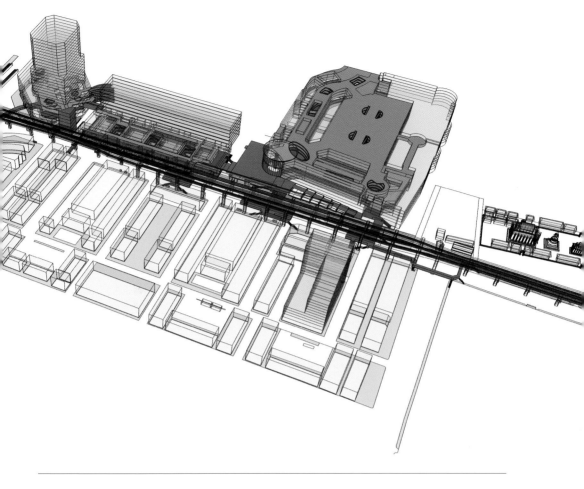

soul-searching took place, with King Rama IX supplying a message of Buddhist self-sufficiency, and a new political party named 'Thai love Thai' – led by telecommunications billionaire Thaksin Shinawatra – achieving government control. The social change the new political philosophy of Thaksin ushered in – unrestrained, credit-based optimistic consumerism – was the opposite of the King's concept of social moderation. Thaksin made shopping a national duty at all levels of society.

Simultopia is an ambiguous term coined to give meaning to the complex experience of place in late capitalist megacities. While *-topia* means place, *simul-* implies both the Modernist dream of *simultaneity* – the ability to understand multiple actions in one place – as well as *simulation* and Baudrillard's concept of the *simulacra* which refer to copies without an original (Baudrillard, 1994). *Simultopia*, therefore, describes the mediated experience of contemporary space, both the experience of speed, movement, transparency and simultaneity that captivated historical Modernist aesthetics, and revisionist notions of the phenomenology of place which grew in reaction to the 'placelessness' of Modernist technological space. In this sense, *simultopia* resonates between the simulacra and the vast knowledge embedded in Bangkok's Theravada Buddhist scriptures and practices. *Simultopia* dreams of inventing new paradigms for inhabiting space as different layers of reality and embraces a philosophy of the new and the now, to understand a world of changing perceptions and experience, rather than symbolically fixed representations and signs of place.

Conclusion: Attentive Circuits

According to Ronald Bogue, the philosopher Henri Bergson found himself split into two individuals, one the automata, an actor in his role one, and one the independent spectator who observes the other as if on a stage (Bogue, 2003). For Bergson, time and memory are not inside us, but it is the interiority that we are in, in which we move, live and change. The actual and the virtual, physical and mental, present and past are inseparable ongoing coexistences. Theravada Buddhist meditation practice, likewise, enables the attainment of such perception by the development of a separate consciousness surveying centred, sensorimotor existence from a floating, detached, non-reacting vantage point. This practice is most ideally developed in isolation – the most learned priests in Sukhothai were in the forest monasteries to the west, while in modern Thailand, wandering ascetic monks still seek enlightenment in the forests, equipped only with a tent-like umbrella and an offering bowl, or make their rounds in the small streets leading to Rama 1 Road as the malls open and commuters from Ban Chang file off water taxis on San Saeb Canal.

According to Bergson's concept of *attentive recognition*, when we consciously reflect on an object, we summon up a remembered image and superimpose it on the perceived object. Bergson carefully analysed the connection between recognition and attention (Bergson, 1988). To recognise an object is to revive a past memory of it and note its resemblance and presupposes a reflection, an external projection of an actively created image onto an object. Attentive vs automatic recognition do not differ qualitatively, in both we summon up a memory image and project it onto the object. In attentive recognition, the object and each memory-image we summon up together form a circuit. As we pay closer attention to the object, we summon up memory-images from broader and more distant past contexts. Deeper, reflective attention represents a higher expansion of memory and deeper layers of reality. An architectural understanding of circuits of recognition, attention, reflection and memory is evident in the great monastery architecture and planning of Siamese cities.

Bangkok seems poised between these two conditions of automatic and attentive reflection. How can architecture make contemporary sensate environments in a world that is more and more mobile, fast-paced and mediated? Contemporary architecture provides a wide array of attention-grabbing forms as well as new materials and technologies. The question ecosystem science poses for contemporary architecture, is how can this newly attentive urban citizen be directed to larger systems and processes to create new urban models based in new urban experience. The opportunity to connect these worlds, these ecologies, is ever present. In the heart of Bangkok, it is the water gardens of Wat Pathumwanaram and Khlong San Saeb beside and behind giant shopping malls deploying water and media as themes and signs. But along the Outer Ring Road, every few minutes another bridge crosses a canal and passes over a water-based world connected only by the vertical posts of huge billboards. These are the sites in which to create the architecture of Guattari's Three Ecologies.

References

- Banham, R, *Los Angeles: The Architecture of Four Ecologies*, Allen Lane (London), 1971.
- Baudrillard, J, *Simulacra and Simulation*, University of Michigan Press (Ann Arbor), 1994.
- Bergson, H, *Matter and Memory*, Zone Books (New York), 1988.
- Bogue, R, *Deleuze on Cinema*, Routledge (London and New York), 2003.
- Bormann, FH and GE Likens, *Pattern and Process in a Forested Ecosystem*, Springer-Verlag (New York), 1981.
- Guattari, F, *The Three Ecologies*, Athlone Press (London), 2000.
- Hanks, LM, *Rice and Man*, Aldine Publishing (Chicago), 1972.
- Khanjanusthiti, P, 'Buddhist Architecture: Meaning and Conservation in the Context of Thailand', Dissertation, University of York Institute of Advanced Architectural Studies (York), 1996.
- O'Connor, RA, *Hierarchy and Community in Bangkok*, undated unpublished paper in the collection of the Thailand Information Center.
- Pickett, STA, Lecture at Columbia University Graduate School of Architecture, Planning and Preservation, 2005.
- Sharp, L and L Hanks, *Ban Chan: Social History of a Rural Community in Thailand*, Cornell University Press (Ithaca), 1978.
- Sivaraksa, S, *A Socially Engaged Buddhism*, Thai Inter-Religious Commission for Development (Bangkok), 1988.
- Tachakitkachorn, Terdsak, 'A Comparative Study on the Transformation Process of Settlement Developed from Orchards in the Chaophraya Delta', Dissertation, Graduate School of Science and Technology, Kobe University (Kobe), 2005.
- Winichakul, T, *Siam Mapped*, Silkworm Books (Chiang Mai), 1994.

From Brian McGrath, 'Bangkok: The Architecture of Three Ecologies', excerpt from *Perspecta* 39, The Yale Architectural Journal, 2007, pp 12–29, by permission of Brian McGrath. © Brian McGrath. Images: p 185 photograph Brian McGrath, 2005, © Brian McGrath; p 187 drawing Brian McGrath, assisted by Seher Aziz and David Reidel, © Brian McGrath; pp 190–1 Danai Thaitakoo and Brian McGrath, 2006, © Brian McGrath; pp 192–3 Brian McGrath and Yuttapoom Paojinda, Central Shopping District 3-D model constructed by Chulalongkorn University Faculty of Architecture students: Chaiyot Jitekviroj, Kobboon Chulajarit, Krittin Vijittraitham, Nara Pongpanich, Pornsiri Saiduang, Ratchawan Panyasong and Yuttapoom Paojinda. With the assistance of Chulalongkorn faculty: Mark Isarangkun na Ayuthaya, Terdsak Tachakitkachorn and Kaweekrai Srihran. © Brian McGrath.

Sustainable Megacity Visions from São Paulo

Carlos Leite

Carlos Leite offers both a framework for understanding the larger global discourse on the megacity, and an outline of visions to understand São Paulo as a model for the sustainable megacity of the future. The major challenges facing the megacity are: mobility, housing, environmental issues, exclusion, governance and opportunities, and Leite offers a list of 'massive changes' to face those challenges. These include: creating compact cities inside the megacity (again a variation of the urban archipelago idea of Ungers, see pages 36–47), repopulating downtown, making a city for people, not for cars, looking beyond government for solutions, and seeing the city as an intelligent 'system of systems' through innovation. This last suggestion points to the final section of chapters, 'The Metacity'.

In 1930, the economist John Maynard Keynes foresaw that humanity, after a hundred years of development, would face the problem of how to use the new leisure and freedom from pressing economic concerns, that science and economic gains would bring; how to live well, 'knowingly and pleasantly'? Now, only 18 years before the centenary of the scenario proposed by Keynes, it may be more appropriate to ask ourselves the great question of the 21st century: how do we create a sustainable urban world? After all, if the 19th century was the era of nations, the 20th the century of empires, this is the century of the city, and cities constitute the key sites for the socio-ecological innovation that needs to occur. This chapter maintains that sustainable solutions might come from unexpected places, such as the connections and linkages of the marginal, void and underutilised multiple localities of megacities such as São Paulo.

Megacities

One hundred years ago, only 10 per cent of world population lived in cities. Currently, the figure is more than 50 per cent, and by 2050, it will be more than 75 per cent. The city is where human exchanges are made, from large and small businesses, to social and cultural interactions. But it is also the place where there is an excessive growth of slums and informal work: it is estimated that two in three people are living in slums or sub-housing. This is also the stage for dramatic changes where cities with more than 10 million people emerged, concentrating much of the world population in the megacities of the 21st century.

São Paulo's high line:
the Minhocão, 'big
earthworm', during
weekdays, an expressway
for 7 million cars.

Most megacities have concentrated poverty and serious social and environmental problems from the lack of investment in infrastructure and sanitation. The importance of megacities in the national and global economy is disproportionately high. According to the UN, in the future we will have many and new megacities – from the 16 existing in 1996, there will be 25 in 2025, many of them in the developing world.[1] In this explosion of inequality, the 'planet of slums', according to Mike Davis, concentrates 2 billion inhabitants and grows 25 per cent per year.[2]

At the same time, new territorial configurations are emerging, such as the megaregions: the BosWash stretch (from Boston to Washington, via New York), Chongqing, China, or the megaregion of SãoRio (São Paulo-Rio de Janeiro), according to a recent provocative study by Richard Florida, the economist-guru of the Creative Class concept. He demonstrates that in the coming decades the global world will focus growth and innovation in a few spectacular places, peaks of excellence, the 40 most creative megaregions (SãoRio is already the 26th in his ranking). These 40 megaregions are the drivers of world economy: they concentrate a fifth of the world population, two-thirds of the GNP, and, incredibly, 85 per cent of the innovation.[3]

Economists, from Paul Krugman and Edward Glaeser to Hernando de Soto, the Peruvian economist and founder of the Institute for Liberty and Democracy, predict that the growth of cities is the economic model of development future. This is because megacities concentrate the greatest transformations of our time, generating an unprecedented demand for utilities, raw materials, products, housing, transport and jobs. It is indeed a great challenge for governments and civil society, which requires strong changes in public administration and forms of governance, forcing the world to review the standards of comfort typical of urban life – from excessive use of the car to carbon emissions.[4]

Major challenges lie ahead, since in the next two decades the cities from underdeveloped or emerging countries will concentrate 80 per cent of the urban population of the planet. The reality already signals this boom – Lagos, Nigeria, for example, has had a population increase of 3,000 per cent since 1950. In other words, against all bets set in the late 20th century, cities have not died, nor entered into decline. Quite the contrary, cities have never looked so crowded. In a planet increasingly digital and virtual, never have so many sought physical encounters, never before have cities been so attractive.

The more advanced innovations in information technology and distance connections become, the more cities become attractive. We will see that one thing only reinforces the other and physical interaction spurs innovation like never before. Cities are 'the' agenda of the 21st century and the challenges are: sustainable development, socio-territorial inclusion and intelligent management.

It is in the megacities of the future that the world needs to reinvent itself, dividing wealth to achieve a well-balanced and more equitable pattern of development. More sustainable patterns are necessary, not only in the face of environmental challenges, but also in social and economic areas – which can no longer be measured in financial indicators, but in human development and ecological footprints.[5]

If we look at the history of cities, we can see that they have always been the place of innovation, but also the locus of the contradictions and conflicts in their societies. It would be a naive thought that the technological innovations of the 21st century alone would provide greater social inclusion and sustainable democratic cities. An examination of São Paulo reveals the potential for social and cultural innovations necessary for the coming century.[6]

São Paulo

São Paulo today is paradigmatic of a megacity constituted of multiple localities in the global world. It is both a world city linked to global networks, and a local city, where everyday space is often manifested as unjust and unqualified. According to Saskia Sassen, São Paulo is one of 10 'world cities' integrated into the network of global cities. In truth, the city presents opposing realities in contradictory ways. On one side are spaces defined by new financial capital and linked to new information technologies, which in turn are tied to the global economy. On the other side, so-called banal spaces appear in a fragmented territory exposing all of the local deficiencies. We are confronted with a 'glocal' megacity, the repository of an urban area that faithfully portrays contemporary society, with all the contradictions of our time.[7]

In this way, the potential of São Paulo lies in its vast territory full of an array of contemporary mutations. Paulistas live in an era of accelerated transformation. Territorial dynamics have never been so dramatically unleashed in the history of cities. When architecture is inserted into this context it is lost within the larger scale territorial transformations. The megacity materialises in its fragmented territory as points of rupture without traditional city consciousness. The consequences of the rapid transformations in the post-industrial megacity are varied and heterogeneous. Complex, unfit spaces emerge in cities, residues of older productive areas: vacant lots, urban dysfunctions. Transformations in architecture are present in the territorial environment and vice versa.

São Paulo contradictions in numbers:

- Population: 19.8 million
- Area: 3,120 square miles (8,080 square kilometres)
- Density: 6,400 people/square mile (2.6 square kilometres)
- Population growth: 0.5% per annum (5% during the 1970s)
- Population in 1900: 0.2 million (grew 27,000% in 100 years)
- Urbanised area growth: 40,000% in 100 years
- % Population living in slums: 20% (1.3% in 1973)
- GDP: $US 381 billion (= Austria)
- GDP/person: $US 19,050 (= South Korea)
- Human Development Index: 0.828 (= Slovenia)
- Metro network: 45 miles (71.5 kilometres) (5 million passengers daily)
- Number of cars: 7 million

---

overleaf: São Paulo and its symbol: Paulista Avenue, the formal megacity at its cradle of power.

São Paulo downtown: modernity
superposes and neglects the old
centre (Viadutos Building by João
Artacho Jurado, 1961).

- Murder rate: 35 per 100,000
- Energy generation: 100% renewable (hydropower and waste)
- Climate change policy since 2009: 2005-12 30% GHG emissions reduction
- Headquarter for more American companies than any other city outside US
- Most crowded air space in Latin America and the Southern Hemisphere
- Highest per capita helicopter ownership

São Paulo constitutes a territorial palimpsest, where successive generations always built over what existed, making the city mutable and polynucleated. The megacity, the outcome of almost 500 years of progressive negation of history, now confronts the challenge of restoration.

Global society enters the 21st century with parallel concerns including a strong inclination towards environmental preservation and recycling existing resources. United Nations Agenda 21 makes new demands on the territorial realm that architecture can no longer avoid in its new principled context.

The future transformation of environments – on the scale of the territory and of the building – is set within this new demand for sustainable development. Like other resources, existing built environments cannot continue to thrive without recycling and transformations. It makes more sense to transform existing and under-utilised spaces rather than to ignore or replace them.

Within this extremely complex situation, architecture continues to be a fundamental alternative for the transformation of the territory: an essential instrument of spatial intervention. The challenge to contemporary architecture is its confrontation with the existing city, beginning with its infrastructure, without negating it.

Theoretical and conceptual analyses, in both international discussion and in the local territorial context, should cultivate methodological debate regarding urban interventions but not cancel out the innocent nature of local actions. While many cities around the world promoted the large-scale redesign of downtown areas, this was until recently rejected in São Paulo. The city centre has finally turned to urban requalification processes. In spite of the delay, and perhaps taking advantage of it, requalification in São Paulo can deal with contemporary reality in a more coherent manner without committing the errors of earlier processes of discarding obsolescent districts of the city.

Finally, the impossibility of operating a total process of urban design in a megacity of this immeasurable territorial scale seems clear. Today it is evident that instead the potential of government power is to use urban design to stitch together territorial logics and to requalify disconnected public spaces. On the one hand, to design everyday spaces, to promote the best use of banal space, and on the other, to make possible urban connections and the linking of fragmented metropolitan territory: to use the potential of empty spaces to promote links that articulate the territory and effect a restorative urban planning process.

Can the megacity territory in a process of accelerated large-scale global transformation be confronted by local actions? In this sense, can urban design still assist the rescue process of immense historical but degraded areas without creating scenic simulacra? At the other end of the problem, can large urban projects be configured as an instrument for the re-articulation of fragmented territory, on an immeasurable scale? Should planning be managed as an instrument for the legitimisation of the illegal, although real, sectors of the city such as informal urbanisation in environmentally protected areas? Finally, how can an urban project confront wastelands, *terrains vagues*, without constituting itself as an instrument of omnipresence, but rather as a possibility for the re-articulation of the territory?

Several environmental problems are evident in São Paulo, with its high number of vehicles and buildings. With approximately 7 million cars, the city discharges 5.6 tonnes of pollutants per day into the atmosphere – 90 per cent from vehicles. The impact of this, especially in the winter, is a climatic inversion that keeps air pollution at the lower strata intensifying respiratory diseases.

Although the city provides 92 per cent of the households with water supply, only 65 per cent are connected to the sewerage system. As a result of this lack of domicile collection, plus industrial sewage and storm water, the conditions of the two main rivers in the city are precarious. What could be an opportunity for leisure and water transport in the water bodies of the megacity, are perceived by the *Paulistas* as degraded open sewers.

The deficit of green space in the city is observable by the green area ratio per inhabitant. São Paulo has only 7 square metres (75 square feet)/inhabitant, while the minimum suggested by the World Health Organization (WHO) is 12 square metres (130 square feet)/inhabitant. In comparison, Rio de Janeiro has 60 square metres (645 square feet)/inhabitant, Curitiba 55 square metres (600 square feet)/inhabitant, and Brasília 120 square metres (1,300 square feet)/inhabitant.

São Paulo is aggravating this problem by devastating the Atlantic tropical rainforest, that stretches from the city to the ocean, at an alarming ratio. Since 1990, the Atlantic tropical forest has lost 1,700 hectares (6.56 square miles).

If this continues at the same pace, there could be notable problems of water contamination and deforestation of the surrounding watersheds of the reservoirs in the southern part of the city, mostly by the illegal formation of informal settlements in supposedly environmentally protected areas.[8]

Urban Interventions
When it comes to the realisation of major urban interventions, São Paulo is lagging behind other world cities. Buenos Aires, its closest neighbour, has with Puerto Madero succeeded in creating a high-end development on brownfield industrial land, which attracts business and visitors, despite its lack of integration within the city.

Sites identified by the city authorities for urban regeneration, *operações urbanas* (urban interventions), include areas often – but not always – adjacent to existing transport infrastructure.

But who wins and who loses in these projects? How are these projects delivered? What institutional arrangements impact on design quality and the creation of sustainable environments? How many jobs are created? And for whom? These are the questions that São Paulo's political, design and development communities need to address to formulate a new urban policy and to deliver a strategy to implement high quality urban design that works with the grain of the city.

São Paulo's high line: the Minhocão, 'big earthworm',
at the weekend, a concrete beach for Paulistas.

Many of the international success stories in the regeneration of large-scale sites
– such as redundant ports, railway, manufacturing and transport areas – suggest that
considerable levels of public investment and management are necessary to make them
work. In Brazil, the private sector has historically taken the lead due to the lack of public
funding or involvement in urban regeneration. Yet, a long-term perspective is a prerequisite
of sustainable planning as opposed to the short-term returns on investment required
by any commercial operator. The establishment of a delivery vehicle – an administrative
structure with strong public as well as private sector representation – that manages and
implements the project from inception to realisation is critical to its success in promoting
economic development and generating new activities.

The compact city model, with its reduced energy footprint that promotes intensification
of well-connected inner-city sites, has become the central objective of many European
cities. Urban containment, smart growth and sustainable development within a defined
urban footprint are central components of this new urban vision that not only drives
the identification of individual sites – often highly contaminated areas near the centre –
but also shapes policies that promote sustainable living such as the introduction of the
Congestion Charge in London or the Vélib public bicycle in Paris. This approach has driven

São Paulo's borders: at the southern border, the informal occupation of an environmentally-protected territory encompassing water and green belts.

the development of a new urban hub at Paris Rive Gauche on the eastern edge of the city – coordinated by SEMAPA (Société d'Economie Mixte d'Aménagement de Paris) – which has attracted 60,000 jobs, counterbalancing Paris's better-known financial centre at La Défense in the west. Urban containment as a smart growth urban policy, has to work within more defined limits: urban territory occupation should be rational, careful and sustainable.

Paris has developed its urban interventions within a clear regional and metropolitan perspective of economic restructuring that prioritises the international service sector, while London has focused some of its spatial policies on the creative industries through the actions of the Mayor's London Development Agency. These interventions were instrumental elements of a successful marketing strategy that has promoted the city as tourist destination, placing it in competition with world capitals.

The evidence from these projects points to the development of new management tools and the involvement of a wider range of social agents to better define successful urban regeneration. A key element is public transport, a critical component of sustainable urban development. The success of the King's Cross development and the London 2012 Olympics site in the Lower Lea Valley are also highly dependent on their location next to major rail-based transport hubs that will create higher density clusters of a polycentric nature. In Milan, the viable redevelopment of ex-industrial sites at La Bovisa and La Bicocca into major office and residential neighbourhoods was predicated on their proximity to the city's extensive public transport network. In common: high densities are very welcome if connected to a transit-oriented development model (TOD).

By analysing international case studies, it becomes clear that the state has played a key role in their implementation, despite the high level of private sector investment. Even in the United States there is evidence of substantial public investment – at federal, state and city level – to implement infrastructure, transport, public spaces and cultural institutions in major urban projects. Another lesson is that solutions to urban problems depend on the involvement of local actors, civil society and the active participation of government at many levels. On balance it can be observed that highly centralised traditional planning tools, which regulate land, use and urban development – as they are currently implemented in Brazil – have become obsolete.

Reinvention

São Paulo's strategic plan – the Plano Diretor Estratégico – is a case in point. The PDE 2000 determined that 20 per cent of its built-up area should become sites for *operações urbana* (urban interventions). To date these have been the subjects of repeated criticism with piecemeal results, which lack a comprehensive vision of urban design. There is no vision for a sustainable urban model with clear environmental objectives, nor has there been any public debate about public space and rebalancing the role of public transport and the private car in the city's future.

The crisis of contemporary Brazilian urbanism reflects the weakness of the system of large-scale 'strategic masterplans', which wrongly assume that all urban problems can be solved by one single instrument. The successful strategy for city-level 'urban interventions' must be considered as an instrument of structural transformation, built on a partnership between the public and private sectors. It is a process that requires the participation of landowners, investors, residents and representatives of civil society, which identifies particular urban areas for transformation as part of a wider metropolitan strategy. To be implemented successfully, such a strategy requires a series of medium- and long-term measures, including land tenure reform, evaluation of real estate potential, strict land use regulations and public space interventions.

Since the 1990s, the São Paulo experience has failed to deliver an effective and democratic urban vision for the city. The major reason for this failure is the absence of a proper management and implementation vehicle that takes into account the full social and economic costs and benefits of projects of this scale and complexity. Any intervention of this sort must embrace the various actors and agents involved in the production of city space, constructing a communal fabric that values the individual citizen. Yet, this approach assumes public engagement to achieve a shared objective. Demolition of entire pieces of city and their replacement by 'model' projects will do little to improve the lives of existing urban dwellers, and will simply cause displacement and erosion of its existing social and urban fabric.

Given the extreme levels of social inequality found in most Brazilian cities we would argue that a more subtle and sophisticated approach to urban regeneration is necessary: one that is based on a collective effort and broad participation, and that aims to promote local development and social inclusion. To this end we would suggest that São Paulo adopts a new system for the implementation of its urban interventions founded on the following principles: the necessity for a clear political commitment to implementation, innovation and inclusion through a metropolitan masterplan that integrates the development potential of urban sites with public transport provision; the establishment of a legal framework that promotes social inclusion and public participation (by creating a participatory management forum for individual urban projects); the establishment of an independent local development agency to implement specific urban projects, that includes all key stakeholders and is responsible for project management and delivery, inward investment, funding and project financing; the development of an integrated mobility plan that optimises public transport use incorporating metro, bus, bicycle and pedestrian movements and minimises private car dependency; the establishment of a metropolitan-wide development fund that can capture value of future return on investments; the promotion of a sustainable environmental approach that integrates the remediation of water and river systems with redevelopment of brownfield land; the proposal of mixed-use centres that provide housing and employment and support the 'new economy'; and the identification of special conservation areas across the city that take into account the historic value and architectural merit of buildings and spaces.

Massive Changes

Envision São Paulo's sustainable urban future by imagining it composed of many cities inside the megacity, each with different territorial contexts, densities, qualities, issues, opportunities and demands through a smart city management.

The top challenges would be: mobility, housing, environmental issues, exclusion, governance and opportunities.

Massive Change 1: compacting cities inside the megacity

We could create sustainable city development through a network of well-connected compact nuclei. Compact, dense and mixed-use city cores would be connected by an efficient mobility system incorporating collective transport, urban design that encourages walking and cycling, and new forms of individual transport. The compact city model optimises the use of urban infrastructure and promotes greater sustainability – energy efficiency, better use of water resources and reduction in pollution. Residents have increased opportunities for interaction and a heightened sense of public safety, since the compact city provides the best sense of community (proximity; mixed uses; collective use spaces).[9]

Massive Change 2: repopulating downtown

We could connect downtown densification and urban sprawl with social housing, repopulating downtown through the reactivation of existing empty buildings and stopping peripheral sprawl

São Paulo's borders: at the northern border, the informal occupation of an environmentally-protected territory, the forest over the hill.

over protected environment (green and water). We should remember that in megacities like São Paulo, the main task would be in opening opportunities for the informal sector to give access to the formal system of housing ownership. According to Hernando de Soto, 'the lack of an integrated system of property rights makes it impossible for the poor to leverage their informal ownerships into capital, which would form the basis for entrepreneurship'.[10]

Massive Change 3: city for people, not for cars (aka, let's create new city smart cars)
We could imagine the city for people and not for cars. Leaving more street space for people will improve livable and sustainable cities, so the challenge for future urban mobility is using less space. Bruce Mau, who founded Institute without Boundaries, has pointed out: 'the radical success of the car has brought about its failure: all the world embraced traffic. New personal mobility projects should deliver maximum freedom with minimal impact in cities'.[11]

São Paulo classic contrast: one territory, two cities. The Paraisopolis slum (city of heaven) juxtaposed against Morumbi walled condominiums reveals the lack of any social sustainability.

Massive Change 4: we could go beyond governments
This is the century of the city. Citizens are creating new forms of city management and replicating good practices: NGOs, networks, wikis, sharing, city information centers. The 21st-century informal city is a welcome component of the megacity society if we deliver systems of integration through projects for different slums drawn up by respected architects with the participation of local community leaders. 'São Paulo agglomerates more than 1,500 slums and an immense challenge to transform them into districts integrated within its territory. This is a reality common to almost all megacities on all continents. Creating a network of successful experiences, resulting from the ideas of architects and urbanisms, represents a good way forward and a good model for the universalization of necessary and possible practices.'[12]

Massive Change 5: we could think of the city as an intelligent system of systems through innovation
We redefine *Smart Cities* as arrived at not only through new smart technologies, but more importantly by the face-to-face social contact of different persons working and living together. The smart city challenge asks how we could go beyond governments'

dominating decision-making. If this is the century of the city, how are citizens creating new forms of city management and design? We think of the city as an intelligent 'system of systems' and are seeking to make cities more instrumental, interconnected and intelligent by managing land and mobility information and creating efficiently operating systems, which mitigates waste and respects the planet's resources as well as human dignity.

Urban Design Ecologies?

Smart compact megacities concentrate: diversity, opportunity, knowledge, culture density as well as informal city of 21st-century externalities.

They consume less, optimise infrastructure, generate innovation and wealth and connect polycentric networks through efficient mobility systems.

They are the engines of the new economy by generating development with sustainability.

They are the major agenda of the 21st century.

Want to be sustainable? Live in a megacity.

Notes

1   R Burdett, D Sudjic (eds), *The Endless City* (London School of Economics and Political Science and the Alfred Herrhausen Society/Deutsche Bank), Phaidon Press (London), 2008.

2   M Davis, *Planet of Slums*, Verso (London and New York), 2006.

3   R Florida, *Who's Your City: How The Creative Economy Is Making Where You Live The Most Important Decision Of Your Life*, Basic Books (New York), 2008.

4   EL Glaeser, *Cities, Agglomeration and Spatial Equilibrium*, Oxford University Press (New York), 2008.

5   P Hall and U Pfeiffer, *Urban Future 21: A Global Agenda for 21st Century Cities*, E & FN Spon (London), 2000.

6   R Koolhaas, *Keynote Lecture on Two Strands of Thinking in Sustainability: Advancement vs Apocalypse*, Ecological Urbanism Conference, Harvard University, 3 April 2009.

7   S Sassen, 'South American Cities and Globalisation', in *Urban Age Selection of South America Conference Essays*, Urban Age/LSE (London), 2008.

8   Carlos Leite, 'Urban Renewal and Sustainability', *Domus*, vol 911, pp 2–5, 2008; and 'Building the Unfinished: Urban Interventions in São Paulo', in W Siembieda and V del Rio, *Contemporary Urbanism in Brazil*, University of Florida Press (Gainesville), 2009, vol 1, pp 311–12.

9   R Rogers, *Cidades para um Pequeno Planeta*, Gustavo Gili (Barcelona), 2001.

10 B Mau, J Leonard, Institute without Boundaries, *Massive Change*, Phaidon (London), 2004, pp 127.

11 Ibid., p 37.

12 http://cidadeinformal.prefeitura.sp.gov.br

Essay derived from Carlos Leite, Nadia Somekh, 'New Forms of Metropolitan Governance. Instruments for Regeneration', in Ricky Burdett, 'Cities and Social Equity' report, *Urban Age*, London School of Economics (London), 2010, vol 1, pp 62–619. © 2012 John Wiley & Sons Ltd. Images: pp 196, 200–1, 202, 205–6, 209–10, photographs Tuca Vieira © Tuca Vieira.

Frugality and Urban Life

May Joseph

This chapter by May Joseph, a theatre director and professor of performance and global studies, offers the performative as an essential 'ecology' of urban design. Drawing from anthropologists such as Marcel Mauss, and sociologists such as Erving Goffman, by looking at everyday informal human practices, rather than urban form, we can see the megacity as present in a wide array of urban situations. The present predicament of the megacity is the result of a Cold War world order, where cities were divided into capitalist first, socialist second, and developing third worlds. It is the presence of the residue of second and third worlds in a 'first world' city such as New York that animates Joseph's unique reading of the 'frugal city'. In the context of worldwide financial crises, frugality is an important urban design ecology as cities of all shapes and forms look for more sustainable futures.

> 'Everybody sacrifices a little.'
>
> Mayor Michael Bloomberg[1]

The modern metropolis is bound neither by moats nor city walls, neither by asceticism nor excess. Its perpetual proliferation of desire and restraint is a condition of immersion in a landscape of reciprocity, of what people create and what they take away from a city. In 2008, the notion of frugality made a resounding comeback on the streets of New York City. People spoke of frugality as though it were the new excess. 'Be frugal' was a motto among many parents at Greenwich Village School PS 41 in 2009. The fashion and merchandising markets promoted frugality as a way for the times. This new frugality is a catchy sentiment. Its roots lie in earlier discourses on parsimonious consumption. Frugality is an international and interlocking phenomenon, grounded in earlier economic convulsions, particularly in former Second and Third World milieus. It has become, for the first time since the Great Depression, part of the American cultural fabric.

Living in New York City is a commitment, and frugality is implicitly part of its motto. New York's voraciousness is part of its lure. Flesh and bone impacts concrete, glass, steel and speed, generating the movable landscape of pleasure and abstinence. Yet somewhere at the heart of the tension between pleasure and denial, between enjoyment and rejection of the city's myriad opportunities, is a hierarchy of notions structured around the idea of more and less. Everything in a city dweller's life ultimately reduces to these two simple principles: more or less. Too much money, too little space. Too much distraction, too little time. Too many people, too little privacy.

In a city as diverse as New York, where everyone who enters its realms has a stake as a citizen of the city, the relationship of more to less assumes a complex set of adjustments and deferrals, best encapsulated by the term frugality. Frugality is an economic condition

Stations of the Cross, East Village, New York, 1996. Residents perform a passion play.

and social practice. However, for an immigrant urban dweller, a nomad or sojourner, the condition of frugality becomes more than an economic necessity. It becomes an aesthetic of everyday life, a way of being in the city of one's future – an urban aesthetic that is very modern, very urban and very New York.

New York is a system of desire, sacrifice and enjoyment woven into the intricate economy of immigrant labour that enables the city to perpetuate its fiction as the pleasurable city, the city that never sleeps. For immigrants and the underclass of New York, pleasure is experienced through an elaborate network of checks and balances, both psychic and material. This ecology of need and satiation, this frugality, is a fundamental principle that revolves around want, deferral and learning not to want.

Chinatown in Manhattan is noticeably populated by foreign banks. The idea of saving money, or sending all one's earnings back home to China or Bangladesh, precedes the immediacy of pleasure satiated by spending. For immigrants labouring at the peripheries of urban markets, the luxury of being in the metropole is often burdened by unseen kinship systems extending halfway across the globe.

The complexity of urban living unites the principles of frugality and perpetual desire. To live in a city involves sacrifice, with scarcity an operating principle determining the value placed on the object of desire. Scarcity always conceals the desire to acquire, to consume.

99¢ Dreams, Jamaica Queens, New York, 2004. Outlet store
sign at the last stop of the F train, Jamaica Center.

Frugality as Urban Aesthetic

Frugality in the 20th century was mobilised within the First, Second and Third World
arenas as a structuring concept that simultaneously expressed the different economies of
expenditure across the global divide. Urban expressions of state ideologies of frugality in
the West and in decolonising countries produced particular experiences of 20th-century
modernity. Socialist cities such as Dar es Salaam and Cairo in Africa, and Sarajevo in
the former Yugoslavia, are linked by the stark International Style of architecture with
Marxist cities in the Third and Second World imaginaries. Often marked by post-war
socialist housing, signs of urban decay, eroding residential structures and 19th-century
graciousness converted into 20th-century overcrowded housing, these cities bear an aura
of frugality through the public staging of urban neglect.

Frugality in the post-colonial era of the 1960s was a Modernist project. It emerged
as a result of the three-world system and a bifocal logic of excess or scarcity, capitalism
or socialism. Operating on this transnational logic, frugality manifested the negative side
of expenditure, the underbelly of conspicuous consumption. Frugality and democracy
formed linked rhetorics of the modern city, as right to the city and the rights of the
individual blurred the boundaries between needs and rights. Less space, more housing.
Less horizontal expansion, more verticality. Less spending, more thrift.

The history of frugality in mid-20th-century Western market economies suggests a
variety of other relations between abstinence, enjoyment and expenditure. In the United
States, frugality links with a notion of restraint, old wealth and measured spending that
denotes expendable capital. Here, the frugal city – the city that combines mass housing
with minimal expenditure – redefined Bauhaus style as proletarian. In communist Europe,
the minimalism of Bauhaus aesthetic merged with the frugality of socialist policies and
generated a new post-war framework of uniform housing that was rational, devoid of

character and productivity-driven. The resulting mushrooming of mass housing in the form of micro-cities, familiar in the urban United States as public housing complexes and in Third World cities as the sign of modernisation, created new conceptions of frugality in relation to economic need and aesthetic minimalism.

During the 1970s, the ecological and environmental movements – connected expressions of frugality – invoked images of a depleted earth. Vegetarianism and the popularity of books such as Frances Moore Lappé's *Diet for a Small Planet* (1973) marked a self-conscious move towards a selective frugality through the exclusion of meat but not, ironically, a prohibition on cars. The vegetarian represented a rejection of a certain kind of meat-eating culture of excess in the United States, while maintaining contradictory relations to consumption through dependency on the oil economy and car culture.

Frugality had a wider currency as a socialist aesthetic and state ideology during the first three-quarters of the 20th century in many Third World cities that imagined themselves as 'Second World' cities. The principle 'less is more' shaped relationships of exchange in cities like Prague, Dar es Salaam, Belgrade and Moscow during the Cold War. Frugality operated under a different logic in American cities, where ecological and environmental arguments against consumption gave rise to lifestyle choices such as vegetarianism and recycling. This subsequently became commodified in the 1980s and 1990s. Sentiments of 'less is more', linking frugality to urban concerns, were also mobilised in New York City in the 1970s during the energy crisis and the 1975 blackout of the city.

In a Second World context such as Tanzanian socialism, frugality was a means of addressing a post-independence transition crisis. The post-colonial city became a space of self-invention. In Dar es Salaam, as in Eastern European cities like Riga or the former East Berlin, the physical layout of the capital city mirrored the ideology of the state. Socialist housing, public monuments and statues commemorating the socialist state and its citizenry delineated the main transport arteries and junctures linking the city to its extremities of socialist flats and communal developments.

Frugality as a state policy of self-reliance, or Ujamaa, articulated in the 1967 Arusha Declaration in Tanzania, aimed at a redistribution of resources via the restructuring of education, physical culture and public housing. Through the strategic use of public spectacles like youth camps, national holidays, national parades and public dance performances on the streets of the city, frugality became institutionalised as a human-scale proposal essential to the recuperation of a post-colonial economy.

A Performance of Duty

Modern cities embody elaborate forms of frugality. They are economic, visual, tactile and visceral. The frugal is an obsessive condition. It is an insatiable desire that vicariously distorts urban need. In the rhetoric of policy, frugality was a concept associated with China's Chairman Mao's experiments with self-subsistence and mass education in the Yunnan province. In 1960s Tanzania, the first post-colonial Tanzanian head of state, Julius Nyerere, theorised a policy of economic restraint as a way to cope with the economic stranglehold of Western dependency and debt. In the African context, frugality emerged as an economic policy, a public commitment and a social issue during the first decade of post-colonial Tanzania – both a social philosophy of enforced daily practice and a necessary way of life, represented by spare shop windows and few luxury goods.

With the official demise of the three-world logic in 1989, the concept of a post-modern frugality has gained informal legitimacy. Articulated in the West through environmentalism, ecological movements and rhetorics of anti-consumption, Western frugality has come full circle to an earlier moment of anti-consumption, one laid out in pioneering sociologist Max Weber's analysis of the Protestant ethic and filtered through the excessive 1980s. Postmodern frugality is a layering of histories of anti-consumption, both capitalist and socialist. In his treatise on Protestant ethics, Weber advocates austerity as a way of socially managing the desires of the unruly body. Austerity becomes an expression of Calvinist rationalism. It is a response to the temptation that wealth might present in the guise of 'sinful enjoyment of life' and 'living merrily and without care'. But as a performance of duty in a calling, austerity is not only morally permissible, but actually enjoined.[2]

Weber points out that the emphasis placed on the ascetic life was bound to the development of a capitalistic social order. A revulsion against the ways of the flesh in early Puritan society supported the rational acquisition of wealth as much as it abhorred its irrational expenditure and consumption. This intrinsic contradiction within capitalist productive ethics fuels a fundamental urban tension. In Weber's terms, it is the contradictory site of capital accumulation through the ascetic compulsion to save, combined with the temptation of wealth itself as desire for worldly enjoyment.[3] Such an emphasis on 'the ascetic importance of a fixed calling' provided the justification for a utilitarian way of life, one in keeping with Weber's modern specialised division of labour.[4] If asceticism, Weber suggests, suited the mechanisms of capital, then enjoyment detracted from productivity, the goal of capital. Asceticism was harnessed to notions of the civic in the Puritan ethic, forging conceptions of the Puritan urban that were decidedly anti-consumption and anti-pleasure. The city was a place of industry and productivity, yes, but it was also a licentious threat to the capitalist enterprise because it encouraged hedonism.

While Puritan asceticism was a social aesthetic linked to the capitalist enterprise – and by extension, to the founding of the capitalist city – its artistic equivalents of minimalism, frugality and Modernist simplicity merged discretion with extravagance in the American city. This basic contradiction – between excess and austerity, enjoyment and restraint, corpulence and thinness – underwrote the logic of modernity, operating in temporal/spatial disjunctions of the city.

In Weber's theorising of modern urbanity, the medieval city represented a perfect fusion of fortress and market, an enclave of militantly competent citizens.[5] The geography of the medieval city organised labour and leisure in structurally distinct social categories. Social identities and urban possibilities were closely interwoven. Guilds organised by trade, such as merchants and artisans, coexisted with other autonomous civic institutions for urbanites. At the core of this emergent social restructuring was an elaborate network of urban rights – the legal, cultural and sociopolitical network through which civic citizenship in the medieval city operated. These systems of urban rights made available new ideas of

Street vendor and furniture store murals, Jamaica, Queens, New York, 2007.

civic unification. For Weber, a city can develop only under special conditions and has its own internal logic. It is a self-contained system of laws and spatial regimes. Its network of social relations is an aggregate of economic, religious and political institutions. In conceptualising the crucial elements of a city, Weber argues that a settlement has to display the following: a fortification, a market, a court of its own, autonomous law, a related form of association, and at least partial autonomy and autocephaly.[6]

The shift in geography from the medieval to modern city was also a shift in human flows. By the 19th century, changing notions of speed, distance and temporality had rapidly introduced a mercantile modernity to the European city. From Henri Pirenne's medieval cities, with their nascent notions of municipality and communal organisation, to Max Weber's patrician and plebeian cities, with their evolving sense of civic participation, the geography of the city redefined how people conducted themselves within urban space.[7]

The 19th-century city saw the slow dissolution of the strict boundaries of the geography of place, as the marketplace, court and fortress expanded their mercantile and civic interests in multiple ways. Industrial cities such as Dickens's London or colonial Madras embodied this rapidly diminishing distance between fortress and marketplace. In Manhattan, the World Financial Center's engulfing of Castle Clinton signified this shift in emphasis from security to finance.

The Stranger, Frugality and Pleasure

The pleasures of the street, as the French poet Charles Baudelaire's *flâneur* demonstrates, and the reticent German sociologist Georg Simmel's adventurer independently proffers, are a productivity of another sort. The street in their writings contributes to the wealth of non-ascetic urban mental life, at once profoundly modern and in tension with the logic of its Puritan counterpart. As both Baudelaire and Simmel observe, the exponential expansion of populations in 19th-century Paris and Berlin demanded new ways of perceiving reality. Changing, and often conflicting, conceptions of excess and restraint shaped ideas of enjoyment in the emerging modern European city.

For Baudelaire, 'every age had its own gait, glance and gesture'.[8] And the urban body of the 19th century was an amalgamation of the frugal and the excessive, of spiritual and material reality. Baudelaire's meditation on the *flâneur*, who strolls the city with the express intent to absorb its varieties, elaborates upon the imaginative spheres of enactment of the urban body. He observes that corporeality and optical perception must be imaginatively fused to comprehend the sensorial regimes that constitute the modern moving body in the street. The three-dimensional scoring of living 'style' through spatial as well as temporal aspects such as fashion and memory, offers a barometer of modernity that 'Time imprints on our sensations.'[9] Modernity's body is at once an architectural construct and a moving display, Baudelaire observes. It sets itself against a changing urban *mise-en-scène*. The moving body becomes a densely layered event of flesh, musculature and bone upon which an even more elaborate set of structures is imposed, in the way of fashion, gestures and mannerisms, offering glimpses into modes of self-invention and self-interpretation. The *flâneur* is of the crowd, immersed in it, but at the same time individuated in the sense of the meditative self. The modernity of the 19th-century *flâneur* lies in the self-reflexive realisation of everyday life through the spatiality of the body.

Implicit in the Baudelairean vision of the *flâneur*, however, is the sense of cultural sameness structured into the feeling of solitude caused by urban modernity and its resultant distancing. The Baudelairean *flâneur* is a stranger in a city he knows well, Paris in the 19th century, as much as his strangeness is caused by the density of migration to the city he inhabits with such intensity. He is also a cosmopolitan traveller, always with an eye on capturing scenes of everyday life on the world stage. Scenes from the 'garrisons of the Cape Colony and the cantonments of India' give one a glimpse of the array of experiences the true *flâneur* imbibes of the imperial world. In the *flâneur's* world, strangeness has textures and depths as varied as the global 19th-century market: 'And now we are at Schumla, enjoying the hospitality of Omer Pasha – Turkish hospitality, pipes and coffee.'[10]

As in Baudelaire, the modern individual in the city is the mediating point for Georg Simmel. Individuals and urban social relations hinge upon the category of exchange, which always involves some tinge of sacrifice, whether it is through deferral of desire or a burst of extravagance that will require payment in the long term. For Simmel, however, the crucible of modern individualism, the city, was also the scenario of unexpected encounters with strangers. The stranger was at once a central aspect and a sign of the city's chaos. The migrant, the immigrant and the traveller all embodied a realignment of fundamental social relations that could alter notions of culture and community in unforeseen ways and destroy existing social relations articulated around the familiar and the insular.

Writing in the same city, Berlin, at the same time, Ferdinand Tönnies similarly echoes an anxiety around the 19th-century expansion of *Gesellschaft*, or society, at the expense of *Gemeinschaft*, or community, as urbanisation and modern individualism reshaped the relationship of people to their rapidly changing environments and, in turn, sense of context and experience of place. Nostalgic for supposedly binding forms of community embedded in a fast-disappearing folk culture, Tönnies articulates a rising sense of alienation at the end of the 19th century. For Tönnies, the psychic disruptions wrought by industrialisation had introduced indifference as the scourge of modern urban life. 'But our souls, our feelings,' he laments, 'are indifferent to the great mass of people, not only to those who are unknown to us, the strangers, but also to those whom we know reasonably well.'[11] This spectre of indifference, whose sign was that of the stranger and the immigrant for Simmel as well as for Tönnies, is crucial to the narrative of what makes the city possible. And it is one of the axial points around which ideas of the civic continue to be articulated.

The Manhattan Way of Life

Cities conjoin frugality, perpetual desire and the complexity of urban living. They involve sacrifice. Financial scarcity in particular shapes urban desire. Today, this catastrophic combination threatens the very way of life in New York City, as regular visitors to soup kitchens surge, unemployment statistics escalate and New York's populations brace for more bad news on the job front. People who once earned comfortable middle-class incomes find themselves dangerously on the brink of bankruptcy. Two-income households careen under the stress of both householders losing their jobs. Neighbourhoods that ballooned in the days of subprime loan mortgages have fallen vacant, bringing chaos to vulnerable populations. For immigrant urban dwellers, or those located in uncertain jobs, the challenges of living in New York are further exacerbated by the stress of families left behind, sometimes halfway across the globe. In such a climate of restraint, frugality has temporarily established itself as a way of being in the modern metropolis. The Manhattan way of life is a formidable yet hopeful array of deferred and innocuous pleasure.

Notes
1   'Mr Bloomberg's Gloomy Budget', *The New York Times*, Editorials/Letters, 1 May 2009.
2   M Weber, *The City*, Free Press (Glencoe, IL), 1958, p 173.
3   Weber, *The City*, p 173.
4   Weber, *The City*, p 163.
5   D Martindale, 'Prefatory Remarks: The Theory of the City', in Weber, *The City*, p 53.
6   Weber, *The City*, p 55.
7   H Pirenne, *Medieval Cities*, Doubleday (Garden City, NY), 1956, p 39; Weber, p 55.
8   C Baudelaire, 'The Painter of Modern Life', in *The Painter of Modern Life and Other Essays*, Garland Pub (New York), 1978, p 14.
9   C Baudelaire, 'The Painter of Modern Life'.
10 C Baudelaire, 'The Painter of Modern Life', p 19.
11 F Tönnies, *Community and Society*, Transaction Books (New Brunswick, NJ), 1988, p 239.

Design, Sustainability and the Global City

Christian Hubert and Ioanna Theocharopoulou

The discussion of urban design and the megacity hinges on the issue of sustainability. Christian Hubert and Ioanna Theocharopoulou's chapter on design, sustainability and the global city begins with an important critical historical overview of the often-contested word 'sustainability'. From this clarification of the concept of sustainability, the authors present how the term can be used to identify important emerging urban design strategies in the megacity, in what they refer to as the 'global South'. But given recent economic events putting in crisis the finance-led urban development parameters of the 'global North', the case studies they show might become universally applicable.

The greatness of past civilisations is usually identified with the permanence of their monuments, even if these are only ruins. Empires eventually fall, but the fragments that remain evoke a powerful will to endure. To *sustain* its own structures, to endure without giving way, to bear up over time, is a measure of Architecture. Yet the scales of human time are minute in relation to the geological eras of the Earth. And the past 200 years – a brief instant in Earth's time – have been characterised by constantly accelerating change, not concerns for resilience or longevity.

Like all living species, we struggle to *sustain* ourselves in a world of danger and opportunity – to find the means to survive and to multiply. But in the course of their brief history of expansion, their unchecked transformations of the environment have given good reason to believe that these are *unsustainable* – that human societies are precipitating changes to the planetary matrix that will diminish their own capacities for further growth, or even survival. For human habitation to be *sustainable*, it cannot use up the resources or foul the very requirements for life. For many ecologically minded thinkers, human societies must use natural cycles of renewal as models – and entrain with their rhythms. The vast flows of energy and material that humanity has set in motion are subject to even greater environmental forces. They must work together.

In legal terminology, to *sustain* something is to uphold it as valid, as true, legal, or just. Injustices are thus by definition *unsustainable*. They may in fact persist, but they cannot be endorsed. Systems of exploitation, cruelty and violence must be excluded *de jure* from all projects that lay claim to *sustainability*.

All of these dimensions come into play in contemporary usage of the term 'sustainability'. The concept hovers between categories of science and art, between social, political and economic interpretations, between concepts of law and justice. Sustainability has been called on to connect human values to scientific analysis and projection, and to aspirations for global policy agreements as well. Small wonder that the definitions of the concept itself are contested and appropriated for different purposes.

In addition, contemporary design culture has produced an entire set of secondary expressions: 'eco-design', 'green design', 'ecological design' and 'sustainable design', that not only trade on the ambiguities of the more general term, but also add further contradictions internal to the concept of 'design' itself, with its conflicting claims between consumption, commercial interest and social purpose. Inundated by 'greenwash' and corporate 'messaging', sustainability tends to become a marketing buzzword, with its scope and political dimensions trivialised. In the next section we propose a reading that engages the rich, complex and fascinating background to the question of sustainability and the built environment, especially in its application to the contemporary city.

A Brief History of the Concept of Sustainability

If our understanding of sustainability is to be extended beyond a narrow technical sphere of 'green' invention and expertise, we need to take into account the rich history of related terms and the broad cultural debates about our relationship to nature and the environment that began taking form in the 19th century. While a great deal of new scholarship is needed to address the intersection between design and the broader history of ideas about nature and the environment, this section seeks to provide a general background or map to today's questions of sustainability by highlighting some important precursors and related ideas.

Over the course of the 19th century, the transformations of the natural environment resulting from industrialisation and modernisation processes provided the subject matter for many writers, poets and explorers at large, some of whom began to offer radical new visions for considering natural space. Ralph Waldo Emerson (1803–1882) and Henry David Thoreau's (1817–1852) writings belong to our basic understanding of the concept of sustainability. Works such as Emerson's 'Nature' (1836), Thoreau's *Walden; or, Life in the Woods* (1854), and his less well-known 'Walking' (1861) were enormously influential in establishing a uniquely American cultural appreciation of wild 'nature', and remain important to this day.[1]

George Perkins Marsh (1801–1882) challenged his epoch's attitudes to nature and argued for a better management of resources. He is considered by many to be the first 'environmentalist' in the West by treating man as an 'active geological agent' who could 'upbuild or degrade'.[2] His 1864 book, *Man and Nature; or, Physical Geography as Modified by Human Action*, argued that humanity plays a large and lasting role in environmental change, and that this can potentially be catastrophic and irreversible. Marsh argued that the ancient Mediterranean civilisations collapsed due to environmental degradation, particularly through deforestation, and that similar trends were already evident in the United States. As David Lowenthal writes in his introduction to a recent edition of Marsh's book, 'Anyone who wields an ax knows its likely impact, but no one before George Perkins Marsh had gauged the cumulative effects of all axes – let alone chainsaws.'[3]

John Muir's (1838–1914) lyrical writings and life-long activism, helped found and shape the modern environmental movement. Muir helped to create a public consciousness about the preservation of wild nature. At a time when millions of acres of forest were being exploited and abused by hunting, lumber, stock and mining interests, Muir helped to establish the concept of 'preservation' as a major American cultural and political value. He campaigned to create the first 'national parks', an idea endorsed by President Theodore Roosevelt, and his writings are credited with inspiring public support for the establishment of Yosemite National Park in 1890 and expansion of the park in 1906.[4]

The power of photography added new force to the arguments for preservation. Between 1870 and 1878, William Henry Jackson (1843–1942) served as official photographer for Ferdinand Vandeveer Hayden's US Geological Survey of the Territories, which established his reputation as one of the most significant interpreters of the American landscape and the natural wonders of the West. Similarly, Carleton E Watkins, one of California's early commercial photographers, created some of the first and most important photographs of the Yosemite region.

Unlike Muir, Gifford Pinchot (1865–1946), the first Chief of the United States Forest Service, argued that natural resources had to be managed in economically efficient ways, that this could be done scientifically, and could be profitable for the state as well.[5] Pinchot was generally opposed to the preservation of wilderness simply for the sake of preservation, a fact perhaps best illustrated by his support for the damming of the Hetch Hetchy Valley in Yosemite National Park, which Muir had fought hard to preserve. The eventual flooding of the valley in the 1920s to create a reservoir was a major environmental controversy in the Western United States.

Gradually the transformative and often destructive effects of human intervention, especially through technology, became the dominant theme of environmental thought. Aldo Leopold's (1887–1948) books, especially his *A Sand County Almanac: and Sketches Here and There*, published shortly after his death, renewed public interest in ecology and land conservation and influenced the development of modern environmental ethics as a choice between development and conservation. 'Like winds and sunsets, wild things were taken for granted until progress began to do away with them. Now we face the question whether a still higher "standard of living" is worth its cost in things natural, wild, and free.'[6] Echoing Thoreau's 'in wildness is the preservation of the world', Leopold wrote: 'Wilderness is the raw material out of which man has hammered the artifact called civilization ... The rich diversity of the world's cultures reflects a corresponding diversity in the wilds that gave them birth.'[7]

While wilderness and the problems of its protection and management continued to preoccupy one dimension of the environmental imagination, the industrial city informed another aspect of what today are considered issues of environmental justice and sustainability. To 19th-century reformers, the squalid conditions of the urban poor were not only unjust, but they too were a major component of environmental degradation. By the mid-19th century, reform movements, first initiated in Britain, sought to better provide for the poor in the growing industrial cities of North America.

In parallel to Marsh's discovery of the effects of human civilisation on nature, British art historian John Ruskin's (1819–1900) *Unto This Last*, first published as a series of essays and then in book form in 1862, is now considered as a proto-environmental indictment of the effects of unrestricted economic growth and industrial expansion on both nature and humanity. Critical of the capitalist economists of the 18th and 19th centuries, this book had a very important impact on the philosophy of Mahatma Gandhi – who translated it into Gujarati in 1908, under the title of *Sarvodaya*, meaning 'well being of all' – as well as on designer and artist William Morris, and sociologist and planner Patrick Geddes.

In America, a particularly striking and influential exposé was the work of Danish-born American journalist Jacob A Riis. Using the new technology of the mechanical flash, Riis was able to photograph dark building interiors as well as city streets at night. His photographs of the appalling conditions in the tenements of New York from the late 1880s had a massive impact on public opinion. The publication of his 'How the Other Half Lives', which first appeared as an article in *Scribner's Magazine* in 1889 and in book form in 1890, sparked the first significant debates to address issues that linked poverty to the environment which continue to inform the discussion of sustainability today.

Riis's work drew attention to the explicit links between social and environmental issues, as in his exposure of the state of New York's water supply. His story 'Some Things We Drink', in the New York *Evening Sun*, included six photographs (later lost). Riis wrote: 'I took my camera and went up in the watershed photographing my evidence wherever I found it. Populous towns sewered directly into our drinking water. I went to the doctors and asked how many days a vigorous cholera bacillus may live and multiply in running water. "About seven", said they. My case was made.'[8] The story resulted in the purchase by New York City of areas around the New Croton Reservoir, and may well have saved New Yorkers from an epidemic of cholera.

These steps towards environmental protection of cities were an attempt to combat some of the insalubrious aspects of urban life by establishing a stronger relation with 'nature' – a precursor to subsequent ideas of 'greening' cities. The 'evils' of the city took the form of poverty and disease, whose causes were equally social as environmental. The concept of 'Garden Cities' was developed as an antidote to the ills of the city, as an alternative that combined the best of both town and country, in both its ecological and its social effects. Ebenezer Howard's *To-morrow: A Peaceful Path to Social Reform* appeared a year prior to the publication of Riis's article in England (1898), and was reissued during 1902 as *Garden Cities of To-morrow*. A stenographer by training who had travelled to the US and had read Edward Bellamy's then controversial utopian novel *Looking Backward* (1888), Howard put forward a dynamic diagram of a ring-shaped city in the midst of gardens and surrounded by agricultural land. Although it has often been misunderstood as a precursor to suburbs, the 'garden city' had reverberations all over the world, and was particularly influential in the design of colonial and post-colonial capitals during the early part of the 20th century.

A near contemporary of Howard's, Scottish sociologist, historian, geographer and town planner Patrick Geddes (1854–1932), was particularly interested in the relationship between social processes and spatial form, and the ecological dimensions of economic development. Geddes studied town and city planning as a means of improving social conditions and everyday life. Geddes's work remained primarily on a theoretical level, but was extremely inspiring to planners and designers in the early part of the 20th century.

Geddes was acquainted with George Perkins Marsh's work, and later alerted Lewis Mumford to it.[9] Geddes was a pioneer of ecological city planning. Writing to Mumford from Calcutta in 1918, he proposed breaking with conventional drainage 'all to the sewer', and substituting 'all to the soil'.

The Garden City concept was a creative inspiration to both Frank Lloyd Wright (1867–1959) and to Le Corbusier (1887–1965), who proposed their own versions of the reconciliation of town and country in projects for new urban forms. Frank Lloyd Wright called for a radical dispersal of the city in his *Broadacre City*, a project he began in 1934 and worked on until the end of his life. When Wright published 'Broadacre City' in his book *The Living City* a year before he died, he inserted Emerson's essay 'On Farming' as an appendix.[10] Le Corbusier famously proposed towers in the park, in his 'Ville Contemporaine pour trois millions d'habitants' of 1922, designed with Pierre Jeanneret. 'The whole city is a park', Le Corbusier wrote, 'there are gardens, games and sports grounds. And sky everywhere, as far as the eye can see'.[11]

The vast cruciform office towers at the centre of the 'contemporary city' were bordered by two low-rise residential housing types. The *bloc à redents* (set-backs in plan) and the *bloc à cellules* arranged as perimeter blocks, were designed with maximum access to gardens: in the first instance each apartment had views to surrounding gardens, whereas in the second, the apartments were placed around vast rectangular garden courts. The latter were 'proposed as a "green" urban form, suitable for dense inner-city development'.[12] It is important to remember that besides Wright and Le Corbusier, at the core of modern architecture was a faith in the power of design to transform the lives of ordinary people. Throughout the 20th century, and especially during the 1920s and 1930s, architects in the industrialising cities of the North believed in promoting social reform through housing.[13]

After the Second World War, as the environmental movement developed an increasingly global or planetary focus, critiques of technology came to distinguish between its benign creative potential and its destructive uses. The visionary designer Buckminster Fuller (1895–1983), whose work on lightweight and easily deployable structures found more military applications than civilian ones, adopted the expression the 'Spaceship Earth' to emphasise the idea that we live on a *finite* planet, with limited resources for life support. His expression was to become even more memorable when the iconic colour pictures of the Earth taken from the Apollo spacecrafts first appeared.

These images served to dramatise the fragility of the Earth's environment, and they fuelled the environmental movement of the late 1960s as well as the first Earth Day (21 March 1970). Fuller's domes inspired some of the utopianism of the American design 'counterculture', while simultaneously representing the global reach of American official culture at the Montreal Expo in 1967. Domes from the 1960s and early 1970s served as their builders' personal manifestos and demonstrated their connection to the environment.[14] Lightweight and portable structures also informed the Edenic images of the British group Archigram as in their famous 'Walking Cities' diagrams from 1964, the 'Cushicle' from 1966, etc.[15]

Eagle Street Rooftop Farm, Brooklyn, New York. A 560 square metre (6,000 square foot) organic vegetable farm atop a warehouse owned by Broadway Stages and installed by Goode Green in Greenpoint, Brooklyn with the Manhattan skyline beyond. The farmers at Eagle Street Rooftop Farm supply food to an on-site market, through a CSA (Community Supported Agriculture) programme, and to local restaurants. The Farm also hosts educational and volunteer programmes in partnership with Growing Chefs, a food education non-profit organisation.

The same period highlighted the destructive effects of human technologies on the Earth's environment, especially in the use of toxic chemicals. Rachel Carson (1907–1964) documented the harmful effects of pesticides in her book *Silent Spring* of 1962. Opposition to the Vietnam War would underline the deliberate use of defoliants, napalm and other products of the chemical industry for warfare, while accidents such as Love Canal in the US, elevated concern about environmental pollution and led to the founding of the Environmental Protection Agency in December 1970.[16] In Canada, the opposition to environmental destruction would lead to Greenpeace, the historic non-governmental organisation founded in the early 1970s, whereas in Europe the environmental movement led to the formation of the first 'green party', *Die Grünen*, the German Green Party, in 1979.

The latter part of the 20th century saw significant doubts emerge as to 'limits to growth' and the depletion of resources, such as fossil fuels, especially in the light of the oil crisis of 1973. EF Schumacher published a book entitled *Small is Beautiful* that same year, providing an alternative vision to unending growth, and President Jimmy Carter installed solar panels on the roof of the White House. Schumacher would visit Carter in the White House in 1977. The panels were removed in 1986, reportedly for roof maintenance during the Ronald Reagan administration, and were never replaced. With the highest per capita consumption of resources, the United States came increasingly to be seen as an obstacle to equitable international agreements on environmental issues. A highpoint of American intransigence was expressed by George Bush I at the 1992 Earth Summit, when he flatly insisted that 'The American lifestyle is not up for negotiation.'[17]

'Sustainability': The United Nations and The Environmentalism of the Poor
On the other side of the Atlantic, the accelerating threats to the environment due to industrialisation led to the first United Nations Conference on the Human Environment, also known as *The Stockholm Conference*, convened in Stockholm in June 1972. This conference marked a turning point in the development of international environmental politics. It was followed in 1983 by the World Commission on Environment and Development (WCED). The commission was created to address the growing concern 'about the accelerating deterioration of the human environment and natural resources, and the consequences of that deterioration for economic and social development'. The commission's report, *Our Common Future*, was published in 1987 and is generally known as the *Brundtland Report*, after the name of the commission's chairperson, the former Prime Minister of Norway Gro Harlem Brundtland. It formalised the use of the term 'sustainability' as a global policy objective and grappled with guidelines for 'sustainable development', which to some might seem an oxymoron.

Under Brundtland's leadership, the commission sought to address environmental issues, uneven development, poverty and population growth within a broad framework of global equity. The report recognised the depletion of resources and the continued presence of poverty as obstacles to long-term global stability and explicitly addressed intergenerational equity, in a call to 'meet the needs of the present without compromising the ability of future generations to meet their own needs'. The Brundtland Report also

Primary School Extension, 2003, Gando, Burkina Faso, by Diébédo Francis Kéré. Drums and singing accompany a group of women smoothing the clay floor of the primary school extension while children look on. 'To achieve sustainability, the project was based on the principles of designing for climatic comfort with low-cost construction, making the most of local materials and the potential of the local community, and adapting technology from the industrialized world in a simple way.'

addressed equity within generations and regarded widespread poverty as a significant contributing factor to environmental degradation.

But for some of its critics, this amounted to 'blaming the victims', by failing to stress that the ever-increasing consumption of goods and resources by the wealthy developed nations is just as damaging for the planet as poverty in the developing world, if not more. Despite its holistic intentions as a 'global agenda for change', the project set forth by the Brundtland document has been an object of ongoing contention between developed economies and developing ones, between the (rich) 'global North' and (poor) 'global South'.[18] A 'political equator' roughly divides the planets into 'haves' and 'have-nots' expressed in the succinct words of one (Southern) observer, 'the first lesson is that the main source of environmental destruction in the world is the demand for natural resources generated by the consumption of the rich … The second lesson is that it is the poor who are affected most by environmental destruction.'[19]

The differences between the two political hemispheres have strained any single definition of sustainability as well as efforts to establish international agreements on the environment. Global discussions of sustainability and human impact have been forced to grapple with these divisions while still addressing the planet as a whole.

Environmental movements have also reflected these divisions. The environmental movements in the North remain identified with the protection of untrammelled nature, to be carefully protected and lightly used for recreation, along with the promotion of 'green' technologies and renewable resources. The movements in the South tend to take the form of social conflicts over access to and control over natural resources, such as conflicts between peasants and industry over forest produce, or between rural and urban populations over water and energy. In many of these areas, where resources such as oil and natural gas are sold for export, locals gain little from the exchange. They continue to have to subsist burning charcoal or cutting down forests while their traditional sources of living that rely on their natural environments become more and more polluted and depleted, leading to social unrest.

But despite the differences between developing nations and developed ones, the overall impact of humanity on the planet continues to increase, and the fast-growing appetites for resource consumption in the emerging economies such as India and China have placed new stresses on global resources along with new potentials for geopolitical conflict. Today the global human impact is gauged to be so significant that geologists are adopting the 'Anthropocene' as the scientific term for the present epoch.[20] According to Paul Crutzen, the Dutch Nobel-Prize-winning atmospheric chemist who first used the expression in a scientific conference in 2002, the real value of the term is not so much in revisions to geology textbooks, but to focus our attention on the consequences of our collective action – and on how we might still avert the worst. 'What I hope', he says, 'is that the term "Anthropocene" will be a warning to the world.' Like the passionate controversies over evolution, the thesis that natural forces and human forces have become so intertwined that the fate of one determines the fate of the other, is both a scientific hypothesis and a contentious cultural one.

Sustainability and Megacities in the Global South

Although it draws on scientific study and prognosis, the concept of *sustainability* remains a fundamentally political and moral term, like *justice* or *freedom*, and, like them, it requires interpretation in its specific application. As a basis for policy, sustainability is an explicit attempt to promote 'environmental justice', whether intergenerational or intragenerational. The term addresses both physical and social issues, and controversies over its scientific dimensions are often political arguments in disguise. All these defining dimensions of 'sustainability' come to bear on the design and planning for cities today.

The majority of human populations already live in cities, and cities account for more than two-thirds of human energy consumption. They are places of the most rapid social change, and many of them are particularly vulnerable to climate change. The projected population growth in the coming decades will be *entirely* located in cities. The UN has coined the concept of 'urbanisation of poverty' to describe the rapid growth of urban poverty, and contemporary megacities are its most vivid expression.[21] These megacities are the emerging 'global cities' of the near future, the proving grounds for any viable new forms of sustainability.[22] Urban sustainability can be understood as the criterion for

Day Labor Station, 2007, by Public Architecture, a national non-profit design organisation. 'The Day Labor Station is a design campaign that addresses the needs of a community that traditionally has not had access to quality design environments. Our effort [has been] to humanize the laborers and elevate the debate about them, the spaces they inhabit, and the ways in which they exist in the fabric of the community.'

a contemporary 'Right to the City', to use Henri Lefebvre's term – to the material and social requirements for human well-being.[23] It is imperative that any projective thinking on cities address the complex of issues packed into the concept of sustainability. The risks and opportunities that hyper-rapid urbanisation presents call for negotiations between growth, change and resilience.[24] Sustainability in its fullest sense demands the recognition of inequalities and injustice and requires a vision of cities as places of social and environmental creativity.

But is sustainability an achievable or even coherent objective for design and planning? Can the same term be used to articulate a set of goals for relatively stable, well-established cities *and* for rapidly growing ones? For older cities, sustainability may primarily be a matter of doing more with less, in an effort to maintain a high standard of living with fewer resources, and being resilient to climate change. These cities can focus on relatively expensive forms of 'eco-efficiency', often explicitly linked to leisure activities. But for

Quinta Monroy Housing, 2003–4, Iquique, Chile, by Elemental Architects: Alejandro Aravena, Alfonso Montero, Tomás Cortese, Emilio de la Cerda. To settle the 100 families of the Quinta Monroy in the same 5,000 square metre (54,000 square foot) site that they have illegally occupied for the last 30 years, Elemental created a design condition that provided a supportive framework for self-building and expansion. Some 50 per cent of each unit's volume in this photograph is self-built.

many of the newer megacities, with their rapidly growing populations that consist primarily of the new urban poor, the challenges of sustainability are far broader and more pressing. They manifest themselves in every aspect of urban life: in the need for housing, jobs, energy, transport, clean air and water, sanitation, food, safety and education, to name just a few. It is here that the main dimensions of sustainability – environmental stewardship, adaptability to climate change, effective allocation of resources, and the claims of social justice – converge in the tensions between urban growth, waste and vulnerability. Perhaps urban sustainability is best considered not as a set of objectives, but as a dynamic of human action, one that enfranchises the poor, that employs tactics of material recycling in relation to social action, in a dynamic that can sustain itself over time.

The 'uncontrolled' growth of megacities highlights a central contradiction of sustainability, an idea 'which combines postmodernist pessimism about the domination of nature, with an almost Enlightenment optimism about the possibility to reform human institutions'.[25] Although modern technological civilisation remains committed to control, any attempt to control nature or the direction of society inevitably leads to unintended consequences, that frequently run counter to the initial goals of the intervention. The explosive growth of informal or extra-legal urban spaces – the *favelas*, the townships, the 'mega slums' such as Mumbai's Dharavi – these large pockets of *other* cities, with their own economies, distinctive populations and resistances to formal authority, poses a significant challenge to formal urban planning.

Instead of state plans and capitalist property development, the new megacities require a different set of design tools that promote the active participation of the population and mobilise capacities for feedback loops between inhabitants and local leaders. These methods thrive on transparent local political governance. The initiatives of activist city governments by radically innovative city leaders in cities such as Curitiba, Bogotá and Medellín show some of the achievements that are made possible by political imagination locally applied in the service of urban populations, in which the enfranchisement of the urban poor is directly addressed through environmental action.

Intellectuals have played an important role in some of these experiments. Mayor Jaime Lerner's initiatives in developing a rapid bus service in Curitiba, Brazil, while distributing bus tickets to the urban poor in exchange for their collecting garbage in the *favelas*, is a classic example of sustainable politics. Lerner's example has been admired worldwide.

Antanas Mockus, a Colombian mathematician, philosopher and politician of Lithuanian descent, left his post as the president of the National University of Colombia in Bogotá in 1993, to preside over the city as mayor for two (non-consecutive) terms, during which he became known for springing surprising and humorous initiatives upon the city's inhabitants.[26] Under Mockus's leadership, Bogotá saw major improvements: the homicide rate fell by 70 per cent, traffic fatalities dropped by over 50 per cent, drinking water was provided to all homes (up from 79 per cent in 1993), and sewerage was provided to 95 per cent of homes (up from 71 per cent). When he asked residents to pay a voluntary extra 10 per cent in taxes, 63,000 people did so. He is currently the President of Corpovisionarios, an organisation that consults to cities about addressing their problems through the same policy methodology that was so successful during his terms as Mayor of Bogotá.[27]

Enrique Peñalosa Londoño was Mayor of Bogotá from 1998 until 2001. During his mayorship he developed five megaprojects; the bank of lands, the District's system of Parks (including Bogotá's Bike Paths Network), the District's system of libraries, the TransMilenio mass transit system, and road construction and maintenance. The impact of Mockus and Peñalosa on the development of Bogotá is described in a documentary film released in October 2009 with the title *Cities On Speed: Bogotá Change*, 'the story of two charismatic mayors, Antanas Mockus and Enrique Peñalosa who, with unorthodox methods, in less than 10 years turned one of the world's most dangerous, violent and corrupt capitals into a peaceful model city populated by caring citizens.'[28] Sergio Fajardo Valderrama, a mathematician from University of the Andes, Colombia, was the Mayor of Medellín from 2003 to 2007. In 2009 Fajardo, along with Alejandro Echeverri, were announced the winners of the Curry Stone Design Prize, for their bold and ambitious public works plan for the city of Medellín.

Other innovative interpretations of the megacity include contemporary interest in Dharavi, not merely as a 'slum', but as a vast recycling workshop and a vibrant social and economic entity making it more resistant to proposals for politically and financially motivated 'clearance' or 'renewal'.[29] Teddy Cruz's documentation of cross-border exchanges between San Diego and Tijuana, with the relocation and improbable forms of adaptation of suburban homes 'south of the border', provides a model for architectural work that both accepts

Parque Biblioteca España, 2005–7, Santo Domingo, Medellín, Colombia, by
Giancarlo Mazzanti Architects. Parque Biblioteca España in Santo Domingo,
is located in a crowded hillside neighbourhood that was known for being a
violent area in the 1980s and 1990s. It mixes library space with the outdoors,
comprising a 'library park'. The Metro Cable system operates near the library.

informal activities and empowers their actors. The rebirth of Detroit as a post-industrial
farmland, the widespread interest in urban farming especially in poor neighbourhoods,
and civic responsibilities for shared water and waste resources, all point towards ways of
enabling both decrepit older and expanding cities to sustain the needs of their populations.

Urban sustainability needs to be planned, but more than that, *it needs to be imagined*.
Its actions need to be adopted by populations, to become an integral part of daily life.
It requires concerted behaviours. It needs to be transmitted through peer pressure, to
be 'crowd-sourced' through social networks. It is subject to risk, and its forms are not
obvious in advance. Sustainability is primarily a hope, a hope embodied in specific acts,
on wagers placed on a still uncertain future.

Notes

1   For an analysis of Emerson and Thoreau's ideas about nature, see the writings of Laurence Buell, such as his *The Environmental Imagination: Thoreau, Nature Writing, and the Formation of American Culture*, Harvard University Press (Cambridge, MA), 1995, and Emerson, Harvard University Press (Cambridge, MA), 2003. For a fascinating and by now classic discussion about ideas of nature and the formation of a uniquely American literary imagination, see L Marx, *The Machine in the Garden: Technology and the Pastoral Ideal in America*, Oxford University Press (New York), 1964, that points out the dialectical tension in American 19th-century literature between nature and technology. See also R Williams' essay 'Ideas of Nature' in *Problems in Materialism and Culture*, Verso (London), 1980, and W Cronon's 'The Trouble with Wilderness or Getting Back to the Wrong Nature' in *Out of the Woods: Essays in Environmental History*, University of Pittsburgh Press (Pittsburgh), 1997.

2   L Mumford, *The Brown Decades*, Dover Publications (New York) reprint, 1971, p 34.

3   D Lowenthal, *Introduction to Man and Nature*, University of Washington Press (Seattle) 2003, pp xv.

4   Roosevelt and Muir went on a four-day camping trip in the Yosemite wilderness in May 1903.

5   Gifford Pinchot's family had made its fortune from lumber and land speculation. His father, James, made conservation a family affair and suggested that Gifford become a forester. Gifford Pinchot made it a high priority to professionalise the Forest Service. He saw the Yale School of Forestry, which he and his father endowed in 1900, as a source of highly trained men.

6   A Leopold, *A Sand County Almanac: and Sketches Here and There*, Oxford University Press (New York & Oxford), [1949], 1987, foreword, p vii.

7   Leopold, *A Sand County Almanac*, p 188.

8   *The Evening Sun*, New York, 21 August 1891.

9   Lewis Mumford, together with the geographer Carl Sauer, led a score of scholars at a 1955 conference dedicated to Marsh's memory, at Princeton, called 'Man's Role in Changing the Face of the Earth'. For a fascinating analysis of Geddes's work and ideas, see VM Welter, *Biopolis: Patrick Geddes and the City of Life*, MIT Press (Cambridge, MA), 2001. For the filiations between Marsh, Geddes and Mumford, see 'The Forgotten American Environmentalist', in R Guha and J Martínez-Alier, *Varieties of Environmentalism*, Earthscan (London), 1997, pp 185–201.

10 FL Wright, *The Living City*, Bramhall House (New York), 1958. On the inside cover of this book, there is a large fold-out map in colour, illustrating the plan of 'Broadacre City'.

11 Le Corbusier, *The City of To-Morrow and its Planning*, translated from the French edition of *Urbanisme*, Dover Publications (New York), 1987, p 177.

12 K Frampton, *Le Corbusier*, Thames and Hudson (London), 2001, p 48. Le Corbusier, too, kept reworking his ideal garden city: in 1930 he proposed 'La Ville Radieuse' (the Radiant City), first exhibited at the Third CIAM conference in Brussels; in the early 1950s, he referred to his design for the city of Chandigarh in India, as 'la ville verte'. For a compilation of visionary urban proposals that includes an analysis of each project's 'green' footprint, from the Roman City to Masdar in contemporary Abu Dhabi, see *WORKac: 49 Cities*, Storefront for Art and Architecture (New York), 2009.

13 There is extensive literature on the Modernist architects' faith in a social agenda. For a concise overview, see K Frampton's *Modern Architecture: A Critical History*, Thames and Hudson (London), [1980], 1992.

14 Another 'countercultural' experiment that illustrates the interaction between environmental concerns and design culture is Arcosanti, Arizona, a self-contained town begun in 1970 by architect Paolo Soleri (born 1919), using a concept he called 'arcology' (from 'architecture' and 'ecology') designed to explore how urban conditions could be improved with a minimal amount of destruction caused to the earth. Arcosanti is an ongoing experiment: since 1970, well over 6,000 people have participated in Arcosanti's construction.

15 There is growing scholarship on the relationship between environmental concerns and design during the late 1960s and '70s. See for instance S Saddler's 'Drop City Revisited', *Journal of Architectural Education*, vol 58, no 1, 2006, and F Scott's 'Acid Visions', *Grey Room* 23, Spring 2006. For an excellent essay on the influence of the rhetoric of 'space' on designers, see P Anker's 'The Closed World of Ecological Architecture', *The Journal of Architecture*, vol 10, no 5, 2005.

16 Love Canal, a community east of Niagara Falls, New York, made headlines in the late 1970s when investigators discovered that an entire neighbourhood, including a school, had been built on a massive toxic waste dump. Beginning in 1947, the Hooker Electrochemical Company had used the clay-lined Love Canal as a dump for 43,000,000 pounds of chemical waste. The company then

installed a cover over the canal and sold the property to the Niagara School Board for one dollar, without specifying the kinds of chemicals it contained. As early as 1958 residents had complained of odd odours and noticed skin rashes. Yet the extent of the problem did not become known until 20 years later. In the 1970s, scientists found that the drinking water contained excessive levels of 82 industrial chemicals, seven of which were thought to cause cancer. The residents of Love Canal had an unusually high rate of cancer and birth defects. The list of subsequent industrial accidents and ensuing human suffering is unfortunately long and continues to the present day; Japan's March 2011 earthquake and tsunami, and the subsequent damage to three nuclear reactors is perhaps the most poignant example of our day. For an informed list of environmental 'disasters' see: http://en.wikipedia.org/wiki/List_of_environmental_disasters

17   Quoted in P Singer, *One World*, Yale University Press (New Haven), 2002, p 2. The text is an extended argument for the responsibility of the developed countries to take a global ethical viewpoint.

18   With the significant exception of Australia, most of the developed nations are North of a latitude line approximately at 30 degrees North. One graphic representation, that dips down to include Australia, is known as the Brandt Line after the former chancellor of Germany, Willy Brandt, who drew attention to it in the 1970s. Since 2005 architect Teddy Cruz has been working on the concept of 'The Political Equator' that he sees not as a flat line but 'an operative critical threshold'. Taking the Tijuana-San Diego border as a point of departure, Cruz noticed that there is a line running 'across [the] world atlas, forming a corridor of global conflict between the 30 and 36 degrees North Parallel. Along this imaginary border encircling the globe lie some of the world's most contested thresholds: the Strait of Gibraltar, where waves of migration flow from North Africa into Europe; the Israeli-Palestinian border that divides the Middle East, along with the embattled frontiers of Afghanistan, Iran, Iraq, Syria and Jordan; the Line of Control between the Indian state of Kashmir and Azad or free Kashmir on the Pakistani side; the Taiwan Strait where relations between China and Taiwan are increasingly strained ...' For more on this concept, see http://www.politicalequator.org/

19   Indian journalist Anil Agarwal, 1986, from 'The Environmentalism of the Poor', in *Varieties of Environmentalism: Essays North and South*, R Guha and J Martínez-Alier, Earthscan (London), 1997, p 3.

20   According to a report to the Royal Geological Society in London, 'Sufficient evidence has emerged of stratigraphically significant change (both elapsed and imminent) for recognition of the Anthropocene – currently a vivid yet informal metaphor of global environmental change – as a new geological epoch to be considered for formalization by international discussion.' J Zalasiewicz et al, 2008. The process of determining whether the Anthropocene deserves to be incorporated into the geologic timescale is ongoing.

21   D Mehta, 'The Urbanization of Poverty', *Habitat Debate*, vol 6, no 4, 2000.

22   Global cities, such as New York, London, Tokyo, Paris, Los Angeles and Singapore, are generally located in the developed countries of the North. They are nodes of network connectivity, financial transactions, liberal media flows and collective security. For the most part, their growth rates of 1 per cent or less per year are far slower than those of emerging megacities, which are located primarily in the developing countries in Asia and Africa, and whose growth rates are as high as 5 per cent per year. Surveys and projections indicate that all urban growth over the next 25 years will be concentrated in the latter group, which includes Mumbai and Delhi, Shanghai and Guangzhou, Karachi, Dhaka, Jakarta and Lagos. For more on this concept, see S Sassen, *The Global City*, Princeton University Press (Princeton), 1991.

23   In Amartya Sen's formulation, these are the 'capabilities that a person has, that is, the substantive freedoms he or she enjoys to lead the kind of life he or she values', For Sen, '... poverty must be seen as the deprivation of basic capabilities rather than merely as lowness of incomes'. See *Development as Freedom*, Alfred A Knopf (New York), 1999, p 87.

24   For some authors, large cities are by definition unsustainable, and their apparent ecological gains are usually externalised by exporting them to larger scales. See J Martínez-Alier, *The Environmentalism of the Poor*, Elgar Publishing (Cheltenham), 2002, p 153.

25   S Dresner, *The Principles of Sustainability*, Earthscan Press (London), 2002, p 164.

26   These included actions by Mockus himself, such as taking a shower in a commercial about conserving water, walking the streets dressed in spandex and a cape as Supercitizen.

27   For more information, see http://www.corpovisionarios.com/
28   For more information, see http://www.dfi.dk/faktaomfilm/danishfilms/dffilm.aspx?id=22407
29   Or even well-meaning proposals by Western designers. See for instance the recent 'Hands Off Our Houses', by M Echanove and R Srivastava, published as an op-ed piece in the *New York Times*, 31 May 2011. The essay described as misguided attempts to design a $300 house by Western architectural students. Instead, the authors, who run a non-profit organisation in the area claimed that 'A better approach would be to help residents build better, safer homes for themselves.' http://www.nytimes.com/2011/06/01/opinion/01srivastava.html?scp=2&sq=dharavi&st=cse

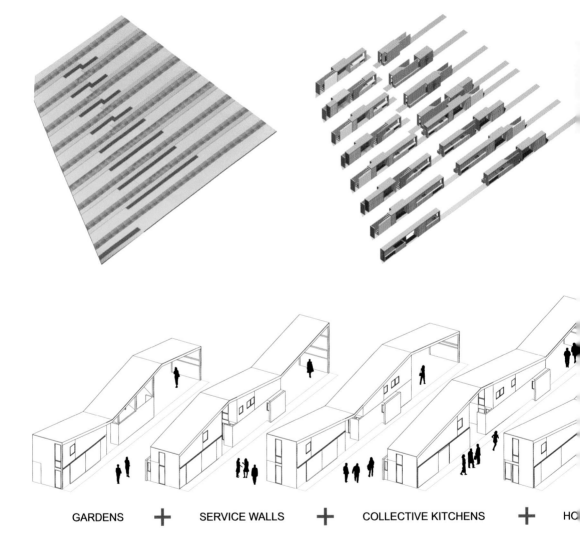

GARDENS ╋ SERVICE WALLS ╋ COLLECTIVE KITCHENS ╋ HO

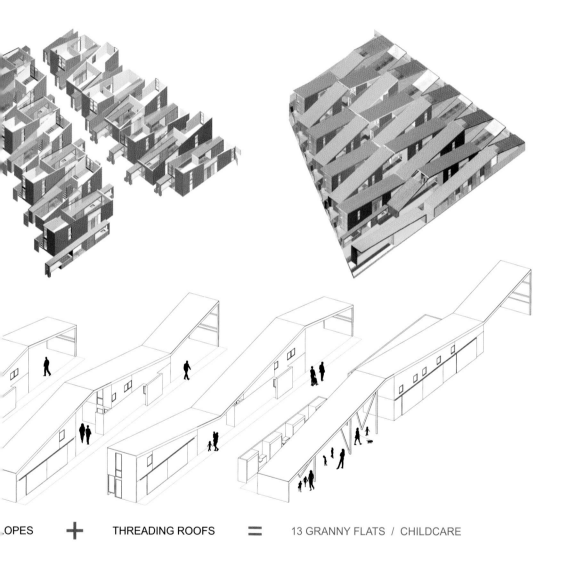

Casa Familiar in San Ysidro: neighbourhood-based community non-profit organisation becomes micro-developer, translating invisible socio-economic entrepreneurship into economic value. The tactical distribution of diverse housing building types within a small infrastructure of collective spaces allows the choreography of temporal socio-educational and economic community programming. Thirteen granny flats are threaded into a housing system where seniors are co-managers and co-producers of a childcare agency. Reproduced by permission of Estudio Teddy Cruz/Mark Gusmann Graphic Design © Estudio Teddy Cruz.

Situationist Space

Tom McDonough

Guy Debord's iconic 'Naked City' map describes the spatial logic of the influential art movement called the Situationist International (SI). SI's influence on urban design theory and practice can be seen from Bernard Tschumi's *Manhattan Transcripts* and design for Parc de la Villette to the recent work of Estudio Teddy Cruz. The map also serves as a social description of what ecologists Steward Pickett and Mary Cadenasso in this volume refer to as 'patch dynamics'. For us it will serve as the introduction of the metacity. With this map and with Situationism in general, we see what David Grahame Shane in this volume refers to as the fragmentation of the metropolis. Each fragment in Debord's map is described as having a specific atmosphere, and it therefore describes the 'psychogeography' of the city. Tom McDonough's essay, edited here from the longer original, provides an invaluable analysis of the spatial logics of Situationism as an introduction to the last section of this book. Cities are no longer just the physical manifestation of power or order, but the space of situations and events. Situational urban design must take account of the non-physical social and political ecologies of the city.

Proletarian revolution is the critique of human geography *through which individuals and communities have to create places and events suitable for the appropriation, no longer just of their labor, but of their total history.*

Guy Debord, *Society of the Spectacle*

In the summer of 1957 the MIBI (Mouvement Internationale pour un Bauhaus Imaginiste), an avant-garde group composed of various ex-Cobra artists and their Italian counterparts, published a singularly odd map of Paris entitled *The Naked City*, the creation of which was credited to G[uy]-E[rnest] Debord. The publication of this map was in fact one of the last actions taken by the MIBI, since this group had recently decided to join with the French Internationale Lettriste – of which Debord was the most important member – and the English Psychogeographical Society of London in order to form the Internationale situationniste. However, the map acted both as a summary of many of the concerns shared by the three organisations, particularly around the question of the construction and perception of urban space, and as a demonstration of the directions to be explored by the Internationale situationniste in the following years. Surprisingly little attention has been accorded this document, despite the fact that it has become an almost iconic image of the early years of the Internationale situationniste, appearing on dust jackets and as an illustration in several of the major books and articles on the group.

The Naked City is composed of 19 cut-out sections of a map of Paris, printed in black ink, which are linked by directional arrows printed in red. Its subtitle describes the map as an 'illustration of the hypothesis of psychogeographical turntables'. Appropriated by Debord, the term *'plaque tournante'*, which usually denotes a railway turntable (a circular revolving platform with a track running along its diameter, used for turning locomotives), here describes the function of the arrows linking the segments of the psychogeographical map. Each segment has a different 'unity of atmosphere'. The arrows describe 'the spontaneous turns of direction taken by a subject moving through these surroundings in disregard of the useful connections that ordinarily govern his conduct'.[1] Thus these 'spontaneous inclinations of orientation' that link various 'unities of atmosphere' and dictate the path taken by the given subject correspond to the action of the turntable, which links various segments of track and dictates the orientation of the locomotive. The implications of analogising the subject to a locomotive are, of course, founded on a certain ambiguity: although self-propelled, the locomotive's path is determined within strict boundaries, just as for the Situationists, the subject's freedom of movement is restricted by the instrumentalised image of the city propagated under the reign of capital.

It is immediately apparent that *The Naked City* did not function like an ordinary map. This observation is confirmed when its antecedents in the *Carte du Tendre* of Madeleine de Scudéry are examined. Cited in a 1959 article in the journal *Internationale situationniste*, the *Carte* had been created three hundred years earlier in 1653 by Scudéry and the members of her salon.[2] It uses the metaphor of the spatial journey to trace possible histories of a love affair. Key geographical features, through pathetic fallacy, mark significant moments or emotions (eg, the 'lac d'indifférence'). Positing this aristocratic diversion as an antecedent of *The Naked City* is another instance of appropriation, but despite their very different origins the *Carte* did illustrate the key principle of the psychogeographic map. That is, both maps are figured as narratives rather than as tools of 'universal knowledge'. The users of these maps were asked to choose a directionality and to overcome obstacles, although there was no 'proper' reading. The reading chosen was a performance of one among many possibilities (of the course of the love affair in the *Carte du Tendre*; of the crossing of the urban environment in *The Naked City*) and would remain contingent. The subject's achievement of a position of mastery, the goal of narrative's resolution, was thereby problematised.

The odd title, rendered in bright red capitals, was also an appropriation of the name of an American film noir of 1948. *The Naked City* was a detective story set in New York and filmed in a documentary style. Based on a story by Malvin Wald, the screenplay was a collaboration between the author and Albert Maltz.[3] (The title of the film, however, is itself an appropriation: originally entitled *Homicide*, the movie's name was changed to match the title of a book of crime photographs by Weegee, published in 1945.)[4] Although the reference to this Hollywood film of the previous decade may at first seem arbitrary, its purpose becomes clear when one examines the structure of the movie. As Parker Tyler explains it in *The Three Faces of the Film*:

> In *Naked City* it is Manhattan Island and its streets and landmarks that are starred. The social body is thus, through architectural symbol, laid bare ('naked')

... The fact is that the vastly complex structure of a great city, in one sense, is a supreme obstacle to the police detectives at the same time that it provides tiny clues as important as certain obscure physical symptoms are to the trained eye of a doctor.[5]

Just as the term turntable serves as a useful analogy for the 'spontaneous turns of direction' indicated on the map, so the title *The Naked City* serves as an analogy for the function of the map as a whole. It is no longer the streets and landmarks of Manhattan, but those of Paris that are 'starred': one quickly recognises, in the cut-out fragments, parts of the Jardin du Luxembourg, Les Halles, the Gare de Lyon, the Pantheon, etc. The act of 'laying bare' the social body through the city's architectural symbols is implicit in the very structure of the map. Freed from the 'useful connections that ordinarily govern their conduct', the users could experience 'the sudden change of atmosphere in a street, the sharp division of a city into one of distinct psychological climates; the path of least resistance – wholly unrelated to the unevenness of the terrain – to be followed by the casual stroller; the character, attractive or repellent, of certain places'.[6] So wrote Debord in his 'Introduction to a Critique of Urban Geography' (*Introduction à une critique de la géographie urbaine*) of 1955, two years before the publication of his version of *The Naked City*. For Debord the structure of Paris, like that of New York in the movie, was also a 'great obstacle' that simultaneously offered 'tiny clues' – only they were no longer clues to the solution of a crime, but to a future organisation of life in its presentation of a *'sum of possibilities'*.

Visually, *The Naked City* is a collage based on the appropriation of an already-existing document, composed of 19 fragments of a map of Paris. It is significant in this light that Debord, in the 1955 'Introduction to a Critique of Urban Geography', had discussed 'a renovated cartography': 'the production of psychogeographical maps may help to clarify certain movements of a sort that, while surely not gratuitous, are wholly insubordinate to the usual directives'.[7] These influences or attractions determine the habitual patterns through which residents negotiate the city. The complete 'insubordination' of such influences is realised in *The Naked City* by the fragmenting of the most popular map of Paris, the *Plan de Paris*, into a state of illegibility.
***

If the *Plan de Paris* is structured by description, which is predicated on a model of seeing that constitutes an exhibition of 'the knowledge of an order of places',[8] then a very different mode of discourse structures *The Naked City*. It is predicated on a model of moving, on 'spatialising actions', known to the Situationists as *dérives*; rather than presenting the city from a totalising point of view, it organises movements metaphorically around psychogeographic hubs. These movements constitute narratives that are openly diachronic, unlike description's false 'timelessness'.[9] *The Naked City* makes it clear, in its fragmenting of the conventional, descriptive representation of urban space, that the city is only experienced in time by a concrete, situated subject, as a passage from one 'unity of atmosphere' to another, not as the object of a totalised perception.

The Naked City and Social Geography

But the narrative mode does not fully account for the appearance of Debord's map. First, *The Naked City* does not cover all of Paris, as is expected of any 'good' map. Second, the fragments have no logical relation to one another; they are not properly oriented according to north-south or east-west axes, and the distance between them does not correspond to the actual distance separating the various locales. (Consider, for instance, the distance separating the Jardin des Plantes from its annexe, which are contiguous in the *Plan de Paris*.)

Debord explains these features in his article of 1956, 'Theory of the Dérive'. The fragments only represent certain areas of Paris because the map's goal is 'the discovery of unities of atmosphere, of their main components and of their spatial localization'.[10] Presumably not all areas in the city lend themselves to such spatial localisation; *The Naked City* names parts of the city (certain 'unities of atmosphere') instead of the whole ('Paris') that includes them. Through this synecdochic procedure, totalities like the Paris of the *Plan de Paris* are replaced by fragments like the components of Debord's map.[11]

But beyond the 'discovery' of such unities of atmosphere, the map also describes 'their chief axes of passage, their exits and their defenses'. The psychogeographical turntables of the map's subtitle allow one to assert 'distances that may be quite out of scale with what one might conclude from a map's approximations'.[12] Such distances become blank areas in *The Naked City*, gaps that separate the various fragments. The suppression of the linkages between various 'unities of atmosphere', except for schematic directional arrows, corresponds to the procedure called 'asyndeton': a process of 'opening gaps in the spatial continuum' and 'retaining only selected parts of it'.[13]

Structuring *The Naked City* through synecdoche and asyndeton disrupts the false continuity of the *Plan de Paris*. The city map is revealed as a representation: the production of a discourse about the city. This discourse is predicated on the appearance of optical coherence, on what Henri Lefebvre called the reduction of the city to 'the undifferentiated state of the visible-readable realm'.[14] This abstract space homogenises the conflicts that produce capitalist space; the terrain of the *Plan de Paris* is that of Haussmannised Paris, where modernisation had evicted the working class from its traditional quarters in the centre of the city and then segregated the city along class lines. But abstract space is riddled with contradictions; most importantly, it not only conceals difference, its acts of division and exclusion are productive of difference. Distinctions and differences are not eradicated, they are only hidden in the homogeneous space of the *Plan*.

* * *

Debord quotes Paul-Henry Chombart de Lauwe's 'Paris and the Parisian Agglomeration' (1952) in his 'Theory of the District in the 12th arrondissement of Paris' *dérive* of 1956.[15] Even more significant, *The Naked City* adopts the form of a map that appears in Chombart de Lauwe's report. This map, made by Louis Courvreur (a researcher working along with Chombart de Lauwe on the urban studies that contributed to the 1952 report), depicts 'the residential units of the "Wattignies" district in the 12th arrondissement of Paris'.[16]

In the 1952 report Chombart de Lauwe defines the elementary unit of the city as 'a group of streets, or even of houses, with more or less clearly defined borders, including a commercial center of variable size and, usually, other sorts of points of attraction. The borders of a neighbourhood are usually marginal (dangerous) frontier areas.'[17] It is important that these quarters are not 'given' urban districts clearly defined and logically linked one to the other. Rather, Chombart de Lauwe states that they 'reveal themselves ... to the attentive observer' in 'the behavior of the inhabitants, their turn of phrase'.[18]

Clearly dependent on these ideas, Debord also altered them in the fabrication of the psychogeographic map. For example, the notion of the quarter as the basic unit of urban structure is held in common by both Debord and Chombart de Lauwe; for both it is the site of social life and possesses a distinct character. (Chombart de Lauwe, in a telling naturalising metaphor, writes that each quarter has its own 'physiognomy'.) However, Chombart de Lauwe defines the quarter as a 'residential unit', giving it a preeminently functional role, whereas Debord defines it as a 'unity of atmosphere', which proves to be a much less empirical idea.

Chombart de Lauwe ultimately relies on the notion that quarters can be 'discovered', their existence proven, through more or less traditional research methods. Space is thought of here as a context or container for social relations – an idea that hypostatises both space and the social. But space does not simply reflect social relations; it is constitutive of and is constituted by them. That is, the quarter is not only the expression of the needs of its inhabitants, the spatial form of their social relations. As Rosalyn Deutsche has written, urban space is rather also 'an arena for the reproduction of social relations and as itself such a relation'.[19] Debord's psychogeography and its graphic representation in The Naked City take this into account, constructing 'unities of atmosphere' rather than 'discovering' them like physical, geographical phenomena that exist in a spatial context. The Naked City denies space as context and instead incorporates space as an element of social practice. Rather than a container suitable for description, space becomes part of a process: the process of 'inhabiting' enacted by social groups.

In this Debord takes up a position some distance from Chombart de Lauwe, but one that is quite close to certain ideas developed by Henri Lefebvre later in the 1960s. Lefebvre was also interested in the quarter as the essential unit of social life. Like Debord, he chose to study 'not the ossified socio-ecological forms (which are, by definition, inapprehensible), but the tendencies of the urban units, their inertia, their explosion, their reorganization, in a word, the practice of "inhabiting", rather than the ecology of the habitat'.[20] Although Lefebvre is here referring to the Chicago School of urban ecology, his distance from Chombart de Lauwe's functionalist model of urban sociology is equally clear. Against such a model he posits the notion of 'inhabiting' – what the Situationists called 'experimental behaviour' – a practice, as will be seen, mapped in The Naked City.

The Naked City and Cognitive Mapping
Debord's map images a fragmented city that is both the result of multiple restructurings of a capitalist society and the very form of a radical critique of this society. Its figuration

of a type of inhabiting is simultaneously related to and distinct from Fredric Jameson's 'aesthetic of cognitive mapping', perhaps most succinctly described in his classic article, 'Postmodernism, or the Cultural Logic of Late Capitalism'. Jameson concludes that the fragmentations of urban space and the social body create the need for maps that would 'enable a situational representation on the part of the individual subject to that vaster and properly unrepresentable totality which is the ensemble of the city's structure as a whole'.[21] These maps would allow their users to 'again begin to grasp our positioning as individual and collective subjects and regain a capacity to act and struggle which is at present neutralized by our spatial as well as our social confusion.'[22]

Certainly Debord also saw the 'spatial confusion' of the modern city as symptomatic of the violence inherent in capitalism's configuration of the space of the production and reproduction of its social relations. *The Naked City*, however, adamantly refuses the status of a regulative ideal, which is the goal of the cognitive map. If the latter is a means toward 'a capacity to act and struggle', the former is a site of struggle itself. In its very form it contests a dominant construction of urban space as homogeneous, appropriating pieces of the *Plan de Paris* and making them speak of the radical discontinuities and divisions of the public realm.

The cognitive map's normative function relies on the production of a spatial imagability that desires to assume what Rosalyn Deutsche has called 'a commanding position on the battleground of representation'.[23] The danger in this position is that the positionality of the viewer and relations of representation are sacrificed in order to obtain a 'coherent', 'logical' view of the city. Debord's map, on the other hand, foregrounds its contingency by structuring itself as a narrative open to numerous readings. It openly acknowledges itself as the trace of practices of inhabiting rather than as an imaginary resolution of real contradictions. Likewise, its representation of the city only exists as a series of relationships, as in those between The Naked City and the *Plan de Paris*, or between fragmentation and unity, or between narrative and description.

The Dérive and Social Space

Debord wrote in *Society of the Spectacle* that under advanced capitalism 'everything that was directly lived has moved away into a representation'.[24] As formulated by Lefebvre, the corollary to this in spatial discourse was that directly lived space ('representational space') had moved away into the space of the conceived and the perceived ('representations of space'). Social, concrete space had been completely denied in favour of mental, abstract space: '*the free space of the commodity*'.[25] However, this thoroughly dominated capitalist space was not seamless; in fact, it was full of contradictions, hidden only by a homogenising ideology. These contradictions made possible the struggle formulated by the Situationist project: the exploration of psychogeography and the construction of spaces that accommodated difference. Situationist 'experimental behaviour', their practice of 'inhabiting', were operations in dominated space meant to contest the retreat of the directly lived into the realm of representation, and thereby to contest the organisation of the society of the spectacle itself.

★★★

With the city as their 'theatre of operations' their primary tactic was the *dérive* (drift or drifting), which reflected the pedestrian's experience, that of the everyday user of the city.

The *dérive* took place literally below the threshold of visibility, in the sense of being beyond what is visible to the voyeur's gaze. As Debord describes it, the *dérive* replaced the figure of the voyeur with that of the walker: 'One or more persons committed to the *dérive* abandon, for an undefined period of time, the motives generally admitted for action and movement, their relations, their labor and leisure activities, abandoning themselves to the attractions of the terrain and the encounters proper to it.'[26] In allowing themselves 'to be drawn by the solicitations of the terrain', persons on the *dérive* escaped the imaginary totalisations of the eye and instead chose a kind of blindness.

Operating in the realm of everyday life, the *dérive* constitutes an urban practice that must be distinguished, first, from 'classic notions of the journey and the walk', as Debord noted in 'Theory of the Dérive'. The *dérive* was not simply an updating of 19th-century *flânerie*, the Baudelairean strolling of the 'man in the crowd'. This is not to say that they do not share some characteristics: both the *flâneur* and the person on the *dérive* move among the crowd without being one with it. They are both 'already out of place', neither bourgeois nor proletariat.[27] But whereas the *flâneur's* ambiguous class position represents a kind of aristocratic holdover (a position that is ultimately recuperated by the bourgeoisie), the person on the *dérive* consciously attempts to suspend class allegiances for some time. This serves a dual purpose: it allows for a heightened receptivity to the 'psychogeographical relief' of the city as well as contributing to the sense of 'dépaysement', a characteristic of the ludic sphere.

For the Situationists, however, the *dérive* was distinguished from *flânerie* primarily by its critical attitude toward the hegemonic scopic regime of modernity. As Griselda Pollock describes him (the *flâneur*, unlike the participants of the *dérive*, was an exclusively masculine type), the *flâneur* is characterised by a detached, observing gaze: 'The *flâneur* symbolizes the privilege or freedom to move about the public arenas of the city observing but never interacting, consuming the sights through a controlling but rarely acknowledged gaze ... The *flâneur* embodies the gaze of modernity which is both covetous and erotic.'[28] It is precisely these class- and gender-specific privileges that the *dérive* critiques in its refusal of the controlling gaze. The city and its quarters are no longer conceived of as 'spontaneously visible objects' but are posited as social constructions through which the *dérive* negotiates while simultaneously fragmenting and disrupting them.

The Situationists also located the *dérive* in relation to surrealist experiments in space. In his article on the dérive Debord cited 'the celebrated aimless stroll' undertaken in May 1924 by Aragon, Breton, Morise and Vitrac; the course of this journey was determined by chance procedures. The surrealists had embraced chance as the encounter with the totally heterogeneous, an emblem of freedom in an otherwise reified society. Clearly this type of journey was resonant for the Situationists. For example, in 1955 Debord discussed a similar trip that a friend took 'through the Harz region in Germany, with the help of a map of the city of London from which he blindly followed the directions'.[29] However, Debord would go on to critique the surrealist experiments for an 'insufficient mistrust of chance'. Perhaps, paralleling Peter Bürger's argument, Debord felt that these diversions had degenerated from protests against bourgeois society's instrumentalisation to protests against means–end rationality as such. Without such rationality, however, no meaning can be derived from chance occurrences and the individual is placed in a position of a 'passive attitude of expectation'.[30] Given that the Situationists were not interested only in the discovery of the uncanny, or the making strange of familiar urban terrain, but in the transformation of urban space, their mistrust of surrealist chance is understandable.

The blindness of the people on the *dérive* was a tactical practice, dependent upon neither spectacular consumption of the city nor upon factors of chance. This blindness, characteristic of the everyday user of the city who confronts the environment as opaque, was consciously adopted in order to subvert the rational city of pure visuality. The *dérive* was a tactic in the classic military sense of the term: 'a calculated action determined by the absence of a proper locus'.[31] Or, in the words of Clausewitz, a military theorist Debord greatly admired, the dérive as a tactic was an 'art of the weak'.[32] It is a game (Debord writes that the *dérive* entailed 'a ludic-constructive behavior')[33] that takes place in the strategic space of the city: '... it must play on and with a terrain imposed on it and organized by the law of a foreign power. It does not have the means to *keep to itself*, at a distance, in a position of withdrawal, foresight, and self-collection: it is a maneuver "within the enemy's field of vision", as von Bulow put it, and within enemy territory'.[34] The *dérive* therefore does not possess a space of its own, but takes place in a space that is imposed by capitalism in the form of urban planning.

The *dérive* appropriates this urban space in the context of what may be called a 'pedestrian speech act', in that 'the act of walking is to the urban system what the speech act is to language'.[35] Through the conscious appropriation of the city, the Situationists force it to speak of the divisions and fragmentations masked by abstract space, the contradictions that enable political struggle over the production of space to exist at all. The fragmented space of the city, as actualised in the *dérive*, is precisely what is imaged in *The Naked City*, with its invention of quarters, its shifting about of spatial relations, and its large white blanks of nonactualised space, the whole segments of Paris that are made to disappear, or rather that never even existed in the first place. The *dérive* as a pedestrian speech act is a reinstatement of the 'use value of space' in a society that privileges the 'exchange value of space' – that is, its existence as property. In this manner the *dérive* is a political use of space, constructing new social relations through 'ludic-constructive behaviour'.

The Dérive and Representations of Public Space

This contestation over the signification of public space leaves unaddressed the question of the very status of this space in the post-war period. It has been argued that, with the increasingly rapid growth through the 1950s of mass media, the formerly contested realm of the streets was evacuated. It was after all precisely technologies of the home – first radio, then television – that were the conduits for spectacular society's attempts to domesticate fantasy. In this view, the dérive was doomed to being an anachronism. Indeed, some texts on the *dérive* and urban space seem curiously sentimental. For example, in the bulletin *Potlatch* in 1954 an article mourns the destruction of the rue Sauvage in the 13th arrondissement: 'we lament the disappearance of a thoroughfare little known, and yet more alive than the Champs-Elysées and its lights'. Despite the qualification that 'we were not interested in the charms of ruins',[36] it is easy to agree with Benjamin Buchloh that, with the rise of technologies for controlling the domestic interior, the street 'would increasingly qualify as an artistic attraction, in the manner that all evacuated locations (ruins) and obsolete technologies appearing to be exempt from or abandoned by the logic of the commodity and the instrumentality of engineered desire had so qualified'.[37]

* * *

The Situationists' antipathy toward the 'charms of ruins' was precisely an acknowledgement that these 'norms of abstract space' that construct the public domain as evacuated were not 'charming' at all. But these representations were not impervious to contestation; in fact, the coherence of the city's signification was constantly threatening to break down. This was due to the fact that, despite the spectacle's hegemonic power, the production of the city remained a social practice, one that could not be fully instrumentalised. Contrary to the projections of spectacular society, which posited the city as a natural, timeless form, it existed only as 'an environment formed by the interaction and the integration of different practices'.[38] The *dérive* as a practice of the city reappropriated public space from the realm of myth, restoring it to its fullness, its richness and its history. As an important tool in the Situationists' struggle over who would speak through the city during the 1950s, the *dérive* was an attempt to change the meaning of the city through changing the way it was inhabited. And this struggle was conducted, not in the name of a new cognitive map, but in order to construct a more concrete collective space, a space whose potentialities remained open-ended for all participants in the 'ludic-constructive' narrative of a new urban terrain.

Notes

1   From text printed on the reverse side of *The Naked City*: A Jorn, 'Quatrième experience du MIBI (Plans psychogéographiques de Guy Debord)', reprinted in Gérard Berreby (ed), *Documents relatifs à la fondation de l'Internationale situationniste: 1948–1957*, Editions Allia (Paris), 1985, p 535.

2   The map was published in 1654 in her *Clélie: histoire romaine*, Slatkine Reprints (Geneva), 1973.

3   A Maltz and M Wald, *The Naked City*, Southern Illinois University Press (Carbondale and Edwardsville), 1979.

4   A Fellig (Weegee), *Naked City*, Da Capo Press (New York), 1975.

5   P Tyler, *The Three Faces of the Film: The Art, the Dream, the Cult*, revised edition, AS Barnes (South Brunswick, NJ), 1967, p 97.

6   G-E Debord, 'Introduction à une critique de la géographie urbaine', *Les Lèvres Nues* 6 (September 1955). Translated as 'Introduction to a Critique of Urban Geography', in K Knabb (ed and trans), *Situationist International Anthology*, Bureau of Public Secrets (Berkeley, CA), 1981, pp 5–8.

7   Ibid., p 7.

8   M de Certeau, *The Practice of Everyday Life*, trans Steven Rendall, University of California Press (Berkeley, CA), 1984, p 119.

9   L Marin, *Utopics: Spatial Play*, trans RA Vollrath, Humanities Press (Atlantic Highlands, NJ), pp 201–2. Although 'narrative' may not be the ideal term to describe the structure of *The Naked City*, it does convey the sense that the map is a representation of an event – or more properly, a sum of events, ie, the spatialising actions of the *dérive*.

10 G-E Debord, 'Theorie de la dérive', *Les Lèvres Nues* 9 (November 1956). Translated as 'Theory of the Dérive', in the *Situationist International Anthology*, p 53.

11   de Certeau, *The Practice of Everyday Life*, p 101.

12   G-E Debord, 'Theory of the Dérive', *Situationist International Anthology*, p 53.

13   de Certeau, *The Practice of Everyday Life*, p 101.

14   H Lefebvre, *The Production of Space*, trans Donald Nicholson-Smith, Blackwell (Oxford and Cambridge, MA), 1991, pp 355–6.

15   P-H Chombart de Lauwe, 'Paris et l'agglomération parisienne' (1952), in *Paris: Essais de sociologie, 1952–1964*, Les editions ouvrières (Paris), 1965, pp 19–101. For Debord, see 'Theory of the Dérive', *Situationist International Anthology*, p 50. This dependence is noted in passing by P Wollen in 'The Situationist International', *New Left Review* 174 (1989) p 80, n 40.

16   Chombart de Lauwe, 'Paris et l'agglomeration parisienne', pp 60–1.

17   Ibid., p 67.

18   Ibid.

19   R Deutsche, 'Alternative Space', in B Wallis (ed), *If You Lived Here: A Project by Martha Rosier*, Bay Press (Seattle), 1991, p 55.

20   H Lefebvre, 'Quartier et vie de quartier, Paris', *Cahiers de l'IAURP* 7 (1967).

21   F Jameson, 'Postmodernism, or the Cultural Logic of Late Capitalism', *New Left Review* 146 (1984), p 90.

22   Ibid., p 92.

23   R Deutsche, 'Men in Space', *Artforum* 28, no 6 (February 1990), pp 21–3. An expanded version of this article appeared as 'Boys Town', *Society and Space* 9 (1991), pp 5–30.

24   G Debord, *Society of the Spectacle*, Black & Red (Detroit, MI), 1977, p 1.

25   Ibid., p 166.

26   G-E Debord, 'Theory of the Dérive', *Situationist International Anthology*, p 50.

27   See W Benjamin, 'On Some Motifs in Baudelaire', in Hannah Arendt (ed), *Illuminations*, trans Harry Zohn, Schocken Books (New York), 1968, pp 172–3.

28   G Pollock, *Vision & Difference*, Routledge (London and New York), 1988, p 67.

29   G-E Debord, 'Introduction to a Critique of Urban Geography', translated in *Situationist International Anthology*, p 7.

30   P Bürger, *Theory of the Avant-Garde*, trans Michael Shaw, University of Minnesota Press (Minneapolis), 1984, p 66.

31   de Certeau, *The Practice of Everyday Life*, pp 36–7.

32   See K von Clausewitz, *On War*, trans M Howard and P Paret, Princeton University Press (Princeton, NJ), 1976.

33   G-E Debord, 'Theory of the Dérive', *Situationist International Anthology*, p 50. The ludic nature of the *dérive* is indebted to J Huizinga's *Homo Ludens; A Study of the Play-Element in Culture*, Beacon Press (Boston), 1950, a text originally published in 1937 and translated into French in 1951.

34   de Certeau, *The Practice of Everyday Life*, p 37.

35   Ibid., pp 97–9.

36   'On détruit la rue Sauvage', *Potlatch* 7 (3 August 1954); reprinted in *Documents relatifs à la fondation de l'Internationale situationniste*, 176. This article was followed up in 'La forme d'une ville change plus vite', *Potlatch* 25 (26 January 1956); reprinted in *Documents relatifs*, pp 234–5.

37   B Buchloh, 'From Detail to Fragment: Décollage Affichiste', *October* 56 (Spring 1991), p 100.

38   R Ledrut, 'Speech and the Silence of the City', in M Gottdiener and A Lagopoulos (eds), *The City and the Sign: An Introduction to Urban Semiotics*, Columbia University Press (New York), 1986, p 122.

From Thomas F McDonough, 'Situationist Space', excerpts from pp 59–77, *October 67* (Winter 1994). Notes have been renumbered. By permission of Tom McDonough. © Tom McDonough.

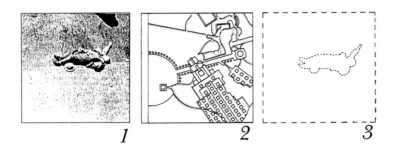

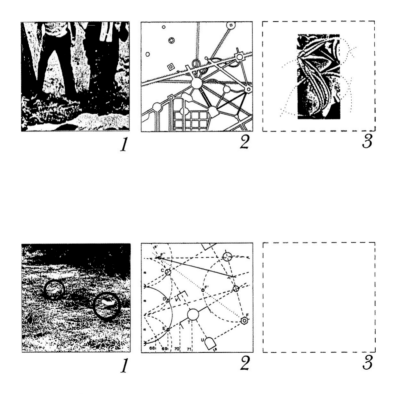

MT 1 'They found the Transcripts by accident. Just one little tap and the wall split open, revealing a lifetime's worth of metropolitan pleasures – pleasures that they had no intention of giving up. So when she threatened to run and tell the authorities, they had no alternative but to stop her. And that's when the second accident occurred – the accident of murder … They had to get out of the Park – quick. But one was tracked, by enemies he didn't know – and didn't even see – until it was too late.

THE PARK: *24 panels, 330 mm x 430 mm (13 in. x 17 in.). Pen and ink, charcoal and photographs on paper.*

The Manhattan Transcripts

Bernard Tschumi

Bernard Tschumi's *Manhattan Transcripts* appeared at the same time as Koolhaas's *Delirious New York*, and while the urban typologies – the block and the tower – are the same, their historical framework is completely different. Tschumi's historical sensibility locates his analysis of New York in his present, the 1970s, and Koolhaas looks back mostly to the inter-war period and New York's metropolitan peak. The *Transcripts* are a fiction, but to anyone who lived in New York during that period of economic restructuring, crime and hedonism, the scenes are familiar, and worth revisiting in this new era of economic uncertainty.

Foreword

Books of architecture, as opposed to books about architecture, develop their own existence and logic. They are not directed at illustrating buildings or cities, but at searching for the ideas that underlie them. Inevitably, their content is given rhythm by the turning of pages, by the time and motion this suggests. The books may read as sequences, but they do not necessarily imply narratives. They can be theoretical projects, abstract endeavours aimed at both exploring the limits of architectural knowledge and at giving readers access to particular forms of research.

Yet The Manhattan Transcripts *were first conceived in the context of live spaces – successive paper spaces (on a wall) that defined a real space (in a room). But their sequential nature still easily suggested a book. As in those film books in which the illustrations are enlargements of frames from the film, the* Transcripts *consist of frame-by-frame descriptions of an architectural inquest. By no means do they comprise a definitive statement; they are a tool-in-the-making, a work-in-progress.*

Although other forms of notation were devised in various stages of the total project (words, sounds, installations), the Transcripts *are composed mainly of drawings, for drawings are both key means and limitations of architectural inquiries. But two theoretical texts literally complement them. Both 'The Pleasure of Architecture' and 'Violence of Architecture' were written and published during work on the* Transcripts *and they unavoidably interlock with the present drawings, albeit with their own logic, for the logic of drawings will always differ from the logic of words. The introductory text simply outlines some themes and approaches.*

Introduction

The Manhattan Transcripts differ from most architectural drawings insofar as they are neither real projects nor mere fantasies. They propose to transcribe an architectural interpretation of reality. To this aim, they use a particular structure indicated by photographs that either direct or 'witness' events (some would say 'functions', others

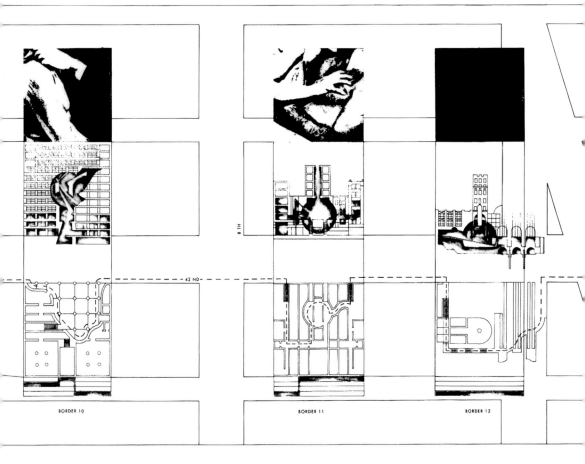

BORDER 10   BORDER 11   BORDER 12

MT 2 'Border Crossing … Derelict piers and luxury hotels, junkies and detectives, cheap whorehouses and gleaming skyscrapers had all been part of his world. So when he got out of jail, he thought he could pass safely from one to the next … But then he met her. To him, she was an enigma – bold, shy, wanton, and childlike in turn. From the moment he saw her he was a man possessed – possessed by a woman who was beautiful to look at, but lethal to love.'

THE STREET

Version I: *1 panel, 9750 mm x 600 mm (384 in. x 24 in.). Pen and ink, charcoal and photographs on paper.*

Version 11: *4 panels, 900 mm x 300 mm (36 in. x 12 in.). Pen and ink, pencil and photographs on paper.*

would call them 'programmes'). At the same time, plans, sections and diagrams outline spaces and indicate the movements of the different protagonists – those people intruding into the architectural 'stage set'. The effect is not unlike an Eisenstein film script or some Moholy-Nagy stage directions. Even if the *Transcripts* become a self-contained set of drawings, with its own internal coherence, they are first a device. Their explicit purpose is to transcribe things normally removed from conventional architectural representation, namely the complex relationship between spaces and their use; between the set and the script; between 'type' and 'programme'; between objects and events. Their implicit purpose has to do with the 20th-century city.

The *Transcripts* are about a set of disjunctions among use, form and social values. The non-coincidence between meaning and being, movement and space, man and object is the starting condition of the work. Yet the inevitable confrontation of these terms produces effects of far-ranging consequence. Ultimately, the *Transcripts* try to offer a different reading of architecture in which space, movement and events are independent, yet stand in a new relation to one another, so that the conventional components of architecture are broken down and rebuilt along different axes.

While the programmes used for *The Manhattan Transcripts* are of the most extreme nature, they also parallel the most common formula plot: the archetype of murder. Other phantasms are occasionally used to underline the fact that perhaps all architecture, rather than being about functional standards, is about love and death. By going beyond the conventional definition of use, the *Transcripts* use their tentative format to explore unlikely confrontations.

Programmatic Account

The first episode (*MT 1*) – 'The Park' – is composed of 24 sheets illustrating the drawn and photographed notation of a murder. The formula plot of the murder – the lone figure stalking its victim, the murder, the hunt, the search for clues building up to the murderer's capture – is juxtaposed with an architecture inextricably linked to the extreme actions it witnesses. A special mode of notation – the three-square principle – underlines the deadly game of hide and seek between the suspect and the ever-changing architectural events. Photographs direct the action, plans reveal the alternatively cruel and loving architectural manifestations, diagrams indicate the movements of the main protagonists. There, attitudes, plans, notations, movements are indissolubly linked. Only together do they define the architectural space of 'The Park'.

While *MT 1* finds its origin in New York's Central Park, *MT 2* – 'The Street' (Border Crossing) – is based on a typical street: 42nd Street. From the East River to the Hudson, there are over a dozen different worlds; from the Chrysler Building to the cheap whorehouses; from Bryant Park to the derelict piers. However, *MT 2* does not describe these 'worlds', but the borders that describe them. Each border becomes a space with the events that it contains, with the movements that transgress it. 'He gets out of jail; they make love; she kills him; she is free.'

In *MT 3* – 'The Tower' (The Fall) – home, office, prison, hotel, asylum find a common denominator in the lethal fall of one of their inmates. Such a manipulation of programmes has a side-effect: it inevitably questions the nature of the spaces that contain them. The set of drawings depicts someone's flight and subsequent fall through the full height of a Manhattan tower block, its 'cells' and its 'yards'. The drastic alteration of perceptions caused by the fall is used to explore various spatial transformations and their typological distortions. If Parts I and 2 of the *Transcripts* loosely matched the ambiguities of the plot with those of the architecture, Part 3 methodically discusses analogy, opposition and reinforcement within the relationship between programme and type.

In *MT 4* – 'The Block' – five inner courtyards of a simple city block witness contradictory events and programmatic impossibilities: acrobats, ice-skaters, dancers, soldiers and football players all congregate and perform high-wire acts, games or even the reenactment of famous battles, in a context usually alien to their activity. Disjunctions between movements, programmes and spaces inevitably follow as each pursues a distinct logic, while their confrontations produce the most unlikely combinations.

Reality

The architectural origin of each episode is found within a specific reality and not in an abstract geometrical figure. Manhattan is a *real* place; the actions described are *real* actions. The *Transcripts* always presuppose a reality already in existence, a reality waiting to be deconstructed – and eventually transformed. They isolate, frame, 'take' elements from the city. Yet the role of the *Transcripts* is never to represent; they are not mimetic. So, at the same time, the buildings and events depicted are not real buildings or events, for distancing and subjectivity are also themes of the transcription. Thus the reality of its sequences does not lie in the accurate transposition of the outside world, but in the internal logic these sequences display.

Such a departure from primary forms as generators does not mean a return to historicism and eclecticism, instead, it attempts to play with the fragments of a given reality at the same time as the rational structure of abstract concepts, while constantly questioning the nature of architectural signs. Those fragments of reality (as seized, for example, through the photographer's lens) unavoidably introduce ideological and cultural concerns. But, far from constituting learned allusions to the past, these fragments are to be seen merely as part of the material of architecture – as neutral, objective, indifferent.

Three disjoined levels of 'reality' are presented simultaneously in the *Transcripts*: the world of objects, composed of buildings abstracted from maps, plans, photographs; the world of movements, which can be abstracted from choreography, sport, or other movement diagrams; the world of events, which is abstracted from news photographs. At first, the respective importance of each level depends only on how each is interpreted by the viewer, since each level can always be seen against the background of another. In this sense, looking at the *Transcripts* also means constructing them.

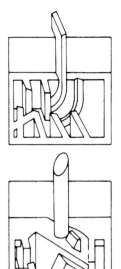

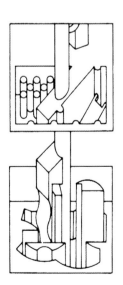

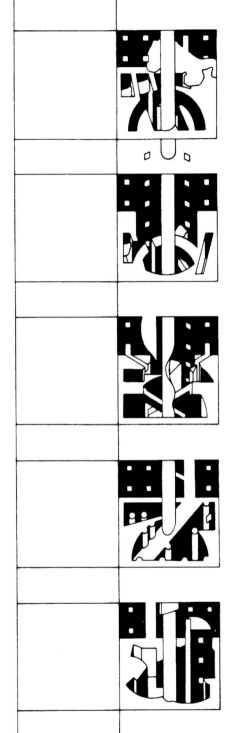

MT 3 'The Fall … First it was just a battered child, then a row of cells, then a whole tower. The wave of movement spread, selective and sudden, threatening to engulf the whole city in a wave of chaos and horror, unless … But what could she do … now that the elevator ride had turned into a chilling contest with violent death?'

THE TOWER: *10 panels, 600 mm x 1200 mm (24 in. x 48 in.). Pen and ink and transfer on paper.*

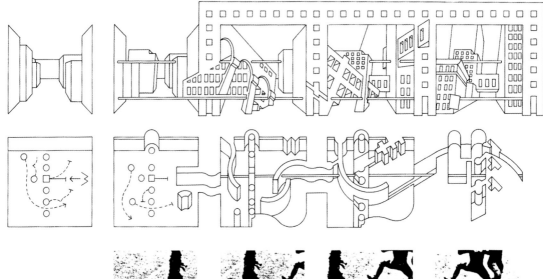

MT 4 'Here is the Block, with its loose yards and its ruthless frames – where well-dressed soldiers get rich on acrobats' habits … where fat football players send you up for knowing the wrong kind of strong-arm dancers … where everything you want belongs to somebody else, and the only way to get it is illegal, immoral, or deadly.'

THE BLOCK: *15 panels, 460 mm x 760 mm (18 in. x 30 in.). Pen and ink and photographs on paper.*

Reciprocity and Conflict

But it is the *Transcripts*' contention that only the striking relationship between the three levels makes for the architectural experience. So entangled are these levels with one another that at any moment they are perfectly interchangeable. Thus the *Transcripts* never attempt to transcend contradictions between object, man and event in order to bring them to a new synthesis; on the contrary, they aim to maintain these contradictions in a dynamic manner, in a new reciprocity and conflict.

Finally, it should be stressed that the implied programmatic violence of the *Transcripts* is there a *contrario*, to question past humanist programmes that strictly covered only functional requirements necessary for survival and production, and to favour those activities generally considered negative and unproductive: 'luxury, mourning, wars, cults; the construction of sumptuous monuments; games, spectacles, arts; perverse sexual activity'. The *Transcripts* also propose different readings of spatial function; they suggest that the definition of architecture may lie at the intersection of logic and pain, rationality and anguish, concept and pleasure.

Whether internally, within the logic of form, for example, or externally, within that of form and use, these disjunctive levels break apart any possible balance or synthesis. In their individual state, objects, movements, events are simply discontinuous. Only when they unite do they establish an instant of continuity. Such disjunction implies a dynamic conception posed against a static definition of architecture, an excessive movement that brings architecture to its limits.

Notation

The *Transcripts* are literally a work-in-progress, insofar as the method of work becomes increasingly precise and articulate in the later episodes, as if the search for new tools always passed through uncertainties, intuitions and shortcuts that, while accelerating certain discoveries, often hamper conceptual rigour.

The original purpose of the tripartite mode of notation (events, movements, spaces) was to introduce the order of experience, the order of time – moments, intervals, sequences –for all inevitably intervene in the reading of the city. It also proceeded from a need to question the modes of representation generally used by architects: plans, sections, axonometrics, perspectives. However precise and generative they have been, each implies a logical reduction of architectural thought to what can be shown, at the exclusion of other concerns. They are caught in a sort of prison-house of architectural language, where 'the limits of my language are the limits of my world'. Any attempt to go beyond such limits, to offer another reading of architecture, demanded the questioning of these conventions.

The insertion of movement or programme into the overall architectural scheme implied breaking down some of the traditional components of architecture. It soon became clear that such decomposition permitted the independent manipulation of each new part according to narrative or formal considerations.

For example, the plans of the Park, the section of the Street, the axonometrics of the Tower, the perspectives of the Park all follow (and occasionally question) the internal logic of their modes of representation. The compositional implications of an axonometric (an abstract projection according to the rules of descriptive geometry) are, as a result, widely different from those of a perspective with a single vanishing point.

A particular case is explored in the fourth episode of the *Transcripts*. As opposed to the plans, maps or axonometrics used in the early episodes, the perspectival description of buildings is concomitant with their photographic record; the photograph acts as the origin of the architectural image. The perspective image is no longer a mode of three-dimensional drawing, but the direct extension of the photographic mode of perception. One of the most common techniques of reproduction (of representation) is brought into the reality of the building, not as *trompe-l'oeil*, but as data.

The same applies to the movement notation. An extension from the drawn conventions of choreography, it attempts to eliminate the preconceived meanings given to particular actions so as to concentrate on their spatial effects: the movement of bodies in space. The early *MTs* introduce the idea of movement in general by freely improvising movement patterns, from the fugitive's to the street fighter's. The last *MT* analyses highly formalised movement diagrams of dancers, football players, skaters, army tacticians, acrobats.

Rather than merely indicating directional arrows on a neutral surface, the logic of movement notation ultimately suggests real corridors of space, as if the dancer had been 'carving space out of a pliable substance'; or the reverse, shaping continuous volumes, as if a whole movement had been literally solidified, 'frozen' into a permanent and massive vector.

Finally, each particular event or action of the *Transcripts* is denoted by a photograph, in an attempt to get closer to an objectivity (even if never achieved) often missing from architectural programmes. If other photographs are inserted according to specific rules of transformation, the combination inevitably suggests the idea of hybrid activities.

Here again, the photograph's internal logic suggests that it can function in varied ways. It first acts as a metaphor for the architectural programme, by referring to events or to people. Second, it can be read independently, for these photographs all possess their own autonomy, independent of the drawings juxtaposed to them. Finally, the events' allegorical content can powerfully disturb the neutral logic of the game's successive moves, introducing a purely subjective reading.

However, central to the *Transcripts* is the necessary interaction of each notation with the others. Their conflicting relationship is outlined in the following section.

Frames and Sequences
The Manhattan Transcripts are not a random accumulation of events; they display a particular organisation. Their chief characteristic is the sequence, a composite succession of frames that confronts spaces, movements and events, each with its own combinatory structure and inherent set of rules. The narratives implied by these composite sequences may be linear, deconstructed or dissociated. *MT 1* is linear, while *MT 2* only appears to be so; *MT 3* depicts two unrelated moments, while *MT 4* exhausts the narrative – it deconstructs

programmes in the same way that it deconstructs forms and movements; then it adds, repeats, accumulates, inserts, 'fades in', distorts and disjoins, always dealing with discrete, discontinuous moments, for each frame can always be exchanged for another.

At the same time, the *Transcripts'* sequences represent both time and consequence, temporality and logic. If *MT 1* and *MT 2* tend to favour temporality, *MT 3* and *MT 4* tend to favour logic. Yet the chronological succession of *MT 1* and *MT 2* is partly absorbed by a logical, atemporal structure. In *MT 3* and *MT 4*, the sequence has somehow been 'dechronologised', with emphasis placed on logic.

The temporality of the *Transcripts* inevitably suggests the analogy of film. Beyond a common 20th-century sensibility, both share a frame-by-frame technique, the isolation of frozen bits of action. In both, spaces are not only composed, but also developed from shot to shot so that the final meaning of each shot depends on its context.

The relationship of one frame to the next is indispensable insofar as no analysis of any one frame can accurately reveal how the space was handled altogether. The *Transcripts* are thus not self-contained images. They establish a memory of the preceding frame, of the course of events. Their final meaning is cumulative; it does not depend merely on a single frame (such as a facade), but on a succession of frames or spaces.

In *MT 1*, each set of frames determines the following by acting as a starting point modified by a rule of transformation (such as compression), or by the addition of a new 'existing' element (such as insertion). In *MT 2*, the work begins with an existing spatial sequence (the street). Then selected 'frames' are modified. *MT 2* also introduces the notion of transference, by which a space reappears as a kind of ghost-image, an after-image of an earlier organisation. *MT 3* starts with five variations on an archetypal sequence of spaces (rooms along a corridor), then progressively modifies them through the introduction (transgression) of movement patterns. On a second stage, it then performs what might be called a 'zooming' operation, as it suddenly focuses on one detail of the final operation and enlarges it to a new scale (the scale of communal courtyards as opposed to the earlier scale of single cells). In turn, these frames (which here coincide with the yards and their institutional use: prison, hotel, asylum, etc) are transformed (transgressed) by a further movement or event (a falling body) and lead to the final configuration of a continuous and vertical sequence of spaces. *MT 3* thus sees event and movement coincide in formal terms, even if the event's cultural implications inevitably differ from the significance of the movement pattern (which in this case is taken to be neutral). Finally, *MT 4* begins with a set of discrete frames (five 'real' architectural configurations, five 'real' movements, five 'real' events) and combines them in a set of autonomous and linear sequences (both transformational and programmatic), each with its own internal logic and rational rules (such as addition, repetition or disjunction). Only at the end are they all superposed and then deconstructed into something altogether different.

In any case, the *Transcripts* always display at least two conflicting fields: first, the framing device – square, healthy, conformist, normal and predictable, regular and comforting, correct. Second, the framed material, a place that only questions, distorts, compresses, displaces. Both are necessary. Neither is inherently special; neither communicates by itself. It is the play between them that does – their distance and its occasional transgression, when the frame itself becomes the object of distortions.

The frame permits the extreme formal manipulation of the sequence, for the content of congenial frames can be mixed, superposed, faded in, cut up, giving endless possibilities to the narrative sequence. At the limit, these internal manipulations can be classified according to formal strategies, such as:

> a repetitive sequence
> a disjunctive sequence
> a distorted sequence
> a fade-in sequence
> an insertive sequence.

Parameters that remain constant and passive for the duration of a sequence can also be added and transference can also take place, as in *MT 2*, where a given spatial configuration (the 'circle') repeatedly passes from one building to the next, regardless of the protagonists' moves. These internal strategies can apply equally to spaces, movements and programmes. In each case, new and unexpected combinations can always occur, as each sequence displays a separate existence, with a variety of *internal* relations and structures.

But, most important, and central to the *Transcripts'* aims, these sequences are also involved with one another, ie, in *external* relations. In *MT 4*, for example, a horizontal, internal relation occurs within each level. This relation may be continuous and logical; it can also jump from one frame to the adjacent and fully incompatible one, creating an internal disjunction. But there is also a vertical, external relation between the spatial movement and the programmatic level. This relation can, of course, be continuous and logical (the skater skates on the skating rink), but it can also be made unlikely and incompatible (eg, the quarterback tangos on the skating rink; the battalion skates on the tightrope).

The same applies to the formal and symbolic characteristics of the surrounding architectural spaces, which can either reinforce or contradict the events occurring within them. A classification may provide an overview of those internal and external relations. In abstracted terms (for *MT 4*):

Each horizontal sequence (made of five frames, notated A,B,C,D,E) is part of a simultaneous vertical relation that contains the three equal conditions of object, movement and event (notated 1,2,3). All combinations of the resulting matrix are then possible – from a repetitive A1A1A1A1A1 to an insertive E1(A1B1C1D1E1) – if the combinations are restricted to the 'object' level, and to A2B2C2, etc on the movement level. The vertical relations of object, movement and event can also be combined, from a 'functional' and homogeneous A1

> A2

> A3, where object-reinforces-movement

(which) reinforces-event, or vice versa, in a sort of architectural tautology favoured by most functionalist doctrines; or they can, alternatively, be fully disjunctive and heterogeneous, whereby A1

E2

B3 announces that there is no relation whatsoever between form, programme and movement. Further scrambling can be applied in the guise of a sort of post-structuralist questioning of the sign, whereby movement, object and event become fully interchangeable, an A3

B1

C2 occurrence

– where people are walls, where walls dance the tango, and tangos run for office.

These combinations are nothing but a form of editing, of montage, where stage and audience space are ultimately reversed, and action becomes its own representation. At the same time, the last *Transcript* eliminates all that is inessential to the architecture of the city. Spaces, movements, events are contracted into the only fragments absolutely necessary to outline the overall structure. Since each frame is isolated from the next, architecture can begin to act as a series of surprises, a form of architectural *jump-cut*, where space is carefully broken apart and then reassembled 'at the limits'.

Thus space can follow space, not necessarily in the order normally expected, but in a series of dramatic revelations that can announce a new spatial structure. Devices such as the insertion of any additional space within a spatial sequence can change the meaning of the sequence as well as its impact on the experiencing subject (as in the noted Kuleshov experiment, where the same shot of the actor's impassive face is introduced into a variety of situations, and the audience reads different expressions in each successive juxtaposition).

One last point: as opposed to logical transformations that proceed from rules inherent in the nature of the object, the *Transcripts'* sequences often proceed from 'subjective' moves. Although an objective rule is given arbitrarily (compression or superposition, for example), its implementation, articulation and final form depend upon the person who applies the rule. In other words, such sequences cannot result from a simple cumulative process of logical transformations for which instructions can be given to anyone.

In the same way, the pleasurable element of subjective arbitrariness enters into the selection of endless images of fighters or facades. (Rationally, only their essential characteristics need be defined.) Ultimately, the spatial relationships and physical dimensions of objects that change with each viewpoint are like movie shots from above that are intercut with those from below: reality is made infinitely malleable, so that emotive, dramatic or poetic attributes can change and unfold.

From Bernard Tschumi, *Manhattan Transcripts*, excerpt from pp 7–12, Academy Editions, 1995. The Publisher wishes to thank Bernard Tschumi and his office for their assistance in relation to this article. © Bernard Tschumi and John Wiley & Sons. Images: pp 248, 250, 253–4 produced by permission of Bernard Tschumi © Academy Editions/Bernard Tschumi.

The Fragmented Metropolis

David Grahame Shane

> David Grahame Shane's chapter, drawn from his global survey of *Urban Design Since 1945*, provides the context for the emergence of the metacity through the incorporation of new social actors who appeared with the fragmentation of the metropolis. Accompanying the article are Shane's illustrations from a lifetime of studying London – the quintessential fragmented metropolis. In this reprinting, a section on Colin Rowe and Fred Koetter's *Collage City* has been omitted since excerpts from the original text appear on pages 27–35 of this volume. In Shane's narrative, the car-based megalopolis is the instrument of fragmentation, and in the shards and ruins that followed both the Second World War and the subsequent car-based urbanism, pockets and patches of urbanity emerged that demanded new city models and created new urban ecologies. Tied to social movements such as civil rights, feminism, multiculturalism and sexual difference, these individual forces when aggregated, substantially limited the ability of the state to institute large-scale urban planning.

The success of the American model of the megalopolis and its peripheral growth, joining cities into linear networks around the world, seriously impacted the metropolis as the European powers lost their empires. Many people and activities moved from the metropolis to the suburbs of the megalopolis. Urban designers, who had wholeheartedly embraced and advanced the cause of megalopolis and the automobile, like Victor Gruen who helped invent the shopping mall, recognised that there were limits to the megalopolis. As global oil supplies were disrupted, sometimes by embargoes, sometimes by technical difficulties, states and cities had problems with their finances. The inner city became a place of poverty and urban riots as commercial interests faltered, the tax base shrank and drug gangs seized territories abandoned by the police, creating dystopian urban scenarios. Under these circumstances urban actors scaled back their grandiose plans for the metropolis. Designers also had to recognise that their giant megastructures imported from the megalopolis had to be scaled down and broken up into fragments in order to enable their development and finance in phases. Designers found that one way to achieve this in older cities was to use the traditional street and block as increments of urban development, also facilitating a more flexible link into the context of old cities. Modernist attempts to renovate old cities had inevitably involved the large-scale demolition of historic structures to accommodate cars, highways and parking. So much demolition gave rise to local opposition. UNESCO recognised the Historic Preservation movement with its World Heritage Convention (1972), an award system to protect special areas of cultural importance.[1]

This chapter presents the breakdown of the megalopolis as it interacted with the metropolis, creating a new hybrid: the fragmented metropolis. As it collapsed, the metropolis opened to reveal a Pandora's box of urban actors, who not only resisted the megalopolis but demanded to be heard, wanting protection for their urban villages in the megalopolis. The first part of the chapter focuses on the impact of urban activist Jane Jacobs, and on other examples of American and European community action in the 1960s and 1970s. Yet the basic theme of the destruction of the old in order to make the new is felt in fast-growing Asian cities today with equal force. Indeed the theme of urban villages, first met in connection with Le Corbusier and Chandigarh and later in Shenzhen, here re-emerges as a contemporary urban design issue. The servicing and incorporation of immigrants' informal, self-built settlements located close to the centre of globalising cities is a problem worldwide. American urban designers in the 1960s had to scramble to meet Jane Jacobs' challenges, inventing new rules for urban villages as special patches within the city, where different codes applied. This system of urban enclave design enabled urban actors to control a small fragment of the city, while not dictating rules for everyone else. The chapter studies the evolution of this fragmentary design ecology and how it became the new norm for global capitalist development as well as community activism. The chapter also begins to trace how this fragmentary mode of design worked for both shrinking European and American cities, and fast-expanding Asian cities after 1990.

New Urban Actors: Urban Villages and Jane Jacobs

In the year before her death, Jane Jacobs returned to New York to promote her last book *Dark Age Ahead* (2004).[2] The book accurately predicted an imminent financial breakdown of the American system of making cities, because it linked economic success to a mass suburbanisation that was becoming unsustainable not only economically, but also socially and ecologically. Jacobs' first book, *The Death and Life of Great American Cities* (1961),[3] has become the bible of community groups and activists worldwide because of its advocacy of local street life inside mixed-use, socially complex, small-scale, historic neighbourhoods. These same neighbourhoods often appeared as derelict slums to modern architects like Le Corbusier or planners like Robert Moses. Moses wanted to run a cross-island highway through Lower Manhattan to serve the suburbs. Jacobs became the articulate representative of all the repressed minorities who had no voice in the Modernist project, the Village 'peasants': the WASP, Italian, Jewish and African-American bohemian intellectuals and their blue-collar neighbours, the gays and lesbians of Greenwich Village, the mothers with families, the old people and children who all lived there together. Jacobs helped to organise the Friends of Cast Iron Architecture historic preservation society to protect the neighbouring 19th-century SoHo warehouse district, illicitly colonised by artists' lofts. Jacobs also warded off attacks from the prominent American architectural critic Lewis Mumford, who believed in moving people out of the slums of New York to rural retreats, expanding existing villages in the New York city-region.

Jacobs was well aware of what was at stake in terms of the decay of the metropolis as the megalopolis replaced public transport and public space with private cars and malls in the suburbs. Many writers, like Reyner Banham in his *Los Angeles: The Architecture of Four Ecologies* (1971),[4] revelled in the abandonment of the old city and demolition of

Downtown. The Village folk singer Joni Mitchell wrote a wistful and sad folk song about demolition and how 'they paved paradise and put up a parking lot' (*Big Yellow Taxi*, 1970). Ridley Scott captured the dystopic image of the future fragmented metropolis of Los Angeles in his film *Blade Runner* (1986), based on Philip K Dick's science-fiction novella *Do Androids Dream of Electric Sheep?* (1968). Countless noir comic books, like Frank Miller's *Sin City: The Hard Goodbye* (1991), updated Raymond Chandler detective stories in graphic novel format. Banham's Los Angeles had been described earlier by Robert M Fogelson as *The Fragmented Metropolis* (1967). Edward Soja echoed this historical theme in his *Postmodern Geographies* (1989) and his *Postmetropolis: Critical Studies of Cities and Regions* (2000). The urban geographer David Harvey in *The Condition of Post-Modernity* (1990) linked the urban fragmentation to the collapse of the modern Bretton Woods financial system based on nation states, and its replacement by a new system of global corporations that relentlessly sought profits but then had the problem of investing that profit in safe, urban enclaves to preserve its value.[5] In Mrs Thatcher's Britain and Ronald Reagan's America, huge urban fragments became feasible. The pioneer atrium and mall developer-architect John Portman's Renaissance Center (1977) in downtown Detroit perfectly represented this system of isolated fragments. This walled city within an abandoned city stood by the waterfront and highway, connected to its surroundings by a driverless monorail that was seldom used. The shock of the stark contrast between weed-strewn, still abandoned city blocks and this megastructural urban fragment or enclave still reverberates in the work of documentary photographers, such as Camilo Vergara in *American Ruins* (1999).[6]

Jacobs argued that dense cities, not spread-out suburbs, were the engines of world economic growth and important places of innovation. She loved the 'ballet' of her street in the Village, which different people used at different times in different ways over the course of 24 hours, a week, a month, the seasons and years. She praised the complexity of the interactions on the city's sidewalks in terms of cybernetics and feedback, as individuals randomly interacted with each other. She understood the role of urban actors at the micro scale and their role in creating the city, wanting to give the small people of the city a democratic voice in the top-down planning process of the metropolis as it fell apart (in the mid-1970s New York City barely escaped bankruptcy).

Jacobs' early journalism and advocacy of cities brought invitations to conferences on Urban Design at Harvard, where the Dean José Luis Sert (Le Corbusier's student, a member of the International Congress of Modern Architecture (CIAM) and Walter Gropius's successor) sought to establish the first course on Urban Design in the mid-1950s. Sert wanted to eclipse rival Team 10 member Louis Kahn's course on Civic Design at the University of Pennsylvania, begun in 1951. Sert hoped to give the Modernist vocabulary a new, more sensitive, small-scale lease of life through Jacobs' vision, but his own work in Latin America in that period remained tied to large plazas and broad pedestrian promenades. His later work, such as the Harvard University Holyoke Center (1965), successfully and skilfully married a Modernist slab building into a dense, small historic block close to Harvard Square. Jacobs' work connected with many urban designers' aspirations for a small-scale and active life on the street. The pioneer American mall designer Victor Gruen also lived in New York's Greenwich Village and befriended Jacobs, who endorsed his plan to pedestrianise the centre of Fort Worth (1955), surrounding it with a series of vast, multilevel car parks on a ring road and an underground service road for trucks (like many contemporary malls).

Sert, like Le Corbusier at St-Dié-des-Vosges and at Chandigarh, segregated pedestrians and automobiles in his designs for fragmentary new civic-centre malls, as in his scheme with Le Corbusier for Bogotá or his work with Paul Lester Wiener in Latin America. His student IM Pei took this idea and designed pedestrian malls in the suburbs, like the vast, single-storey Green Acres Mall in Long Island, New York (1956). Ernesto Rogers, the modern architect from BBPR in Milan and CIAM member, shared Sert's hope for a revival of Modernism while respecting the old scale and traditions of the central city. Rogers designed a heterotopic, mixed-use, precast and pre-tensioned, advanced concrete design skyscraper, the Torre Velasca in Milan (1958), housing a small shopping arcade, offices and luxurious apartments (a mixture that broke the Modernist taboo of segregating out all functions into separate buildings). Banham attacked the tower because it looked like the Gothic campanile of Milan Cathedral, with its many fins. Banham accused Rogers of 'betraying Modernism', while Rogers dismissed Banham as a 'lover of refrigerators' (a reference to his love of Pop icons and Los Angeles).[7]

Drawing of the streams and estates of London which formed the basis for the development of Georgian London's residential enclaves centred on squares.

Reinventing Urban Design: Special Districts, Enclaves and Urban Design Guidelines

These early European skirmishes between generations mark the collapsing of the old order of the imperial metropolis and different responses to the emerging megalopolis and American commercial dominance in the Cold War. Ernesto Rogers, as a professor at the Milan Polytechnic in the 1950s and editor of the magazine *Casabella*, described urban design as an emerging discipline with a long European tradition. As a discipline, Rogers argued the emerging field had its own rules, standards and codes, a specialised body of knowledge that formed the basis of decisions. Italian urban designers, because of the strength of the Italian Communist Party, were unusual in Western Europe in knowing about Soviet urban design. They were familiar with the super-scaled monumentality and grand plans for Moscow, while rejecting their monumentality as a reminder of Mussolini's Totalitarian era. Rogers' conception of urban design as a continuous tradition was influenced by the typological and morphological studies of the University of Venice since the 1930s under the leadership of Giuseppe Samonà. In the 1950s Rogers and his firm Banfi, Belgiojoso, Peressutti & Rogers (BBPR), worked in the centre of Milan and sought to contextualise their still-modern buildings. They added elaborate podiums with mixed uses, arcades scaled to surrounding 19th-century structures and short cuts through courtyards that honoured old lanes and paths. The firm tried to renew the architecture of the street and building facade within a small-scale Modernist vocabulary. Rogers saw architecture and the city as languages that had structural elements which defined their relationship and discourse within an urban context. Rogers' vision, like that of Le Corbusier, expanded in scale to include huge suburban superblocks, scaled like the industrial mills, factories and monuments of the industrial age that would inspire his student Aldo Rossi in the 1960s.

Rogers found a natural ally in his search for a new European urban architecture that could relate to the small scale of the historic city in *The Architectural Review*, a privately owned architectural magazine in London, for which Gordon Cullen wrote and illustrated a monthly column called 'Townscape' (later published as a book, *The Concise Townscape* (1961)).[8] The magazine's owner H de Cronin Hastings worked closely with the geographer Thomas Sharp and, like Cullen, loved the intimate, personal design scale of villages. These favoured places might be picturesque English villages like Blandford Forum, or Italian hill towns like Bergamo. Cullen saw Italian hill towns as the epitome of good urban design. He created a new language and system of elements for designing small-scale urban settings, describing 'urban rooms', 'enclaves', 'precincts', 'outdoor rooms' and 'passages' that allowed pedestrians to move elegantly and comfortably about the village through a series of urban enclosures. (Louis Kahn, in the breakaway Team 10 conference that ended CIAM at Otterlo, also spoke of urban 'rooms' and enclosures.[9] In his book and magazine articles, Cullen attacked the open plan and vast open spaces of modern urban design, occupied by no one and loved by few, especially in the British new towns.

Cullen created one brilliant drawing summarising his 'serial vision' of how a person moved through an ideal Italian village or hilltop environment. In this drawing, like a cinematic storyboard, sketches showed how, after entering the city walls through a city gate, a series of bounded squares led to the cathedral square and beyond to a

Mussolini-style semicircular plaza that opened out to views of the distant horizon and hills. Other sketches in *The Concise Townscape* showed that Cullen did not oppose mixing new buildings among the old, or limited access for automobiles, as long as bollards and cobblestones limited their speed and territory within a system of closed, urban fragments. In late drawings for Covent Garden, London (1971), Cullen included an underground highway and parking, although not opposing a nearby (LCC) proposal for a megastructure over the Strand, covering a proposed highway beside the Thames.

Kevin Lynch, in his *The Image of the City* (1960),[10] sought to provide a pragmatic base for Cullen's aesthetic preferences, which he knew from publications and shared students like David Gosling at MIT. Lynch interviewed over 1,000 inhabitants of central Boston just as a new elevated Central Artery cut off the business core from the waterfront and North End Italian community on its small hilltop site. At the same time, Gruen was busy demolishing another part of the West End of Boston for high-rise slab blocks set in a park in 1962. Lynch showed that the Boston inhabitants shared a fragmentary mental map of the central city that had distinct neighbourhoods or 'districts', enclaves that were bounded fragments with distinct visual and social characteristics. These were connected by, and organised around, main streets or 'paths'. In addition, people on foot used particular buildings as navigational devices or 'markers', especially church towers or tall buildings, and certain key street interchanges acted as 'nodes', interchanges within this system of 'paths'. In 1959, based on this research, Lynch and his associates from MIT advised a new urban development agency created to remodel the inner city – the Boston Redevelopment Authority (BRA) – on how to remodel around the elevated Central Artery, proposing a new public square and City Hall to the west and historic preservation of Quincy Market, the old waterfront, to the east. Sert's Harvard Urban Design graduate IM Pei won the subsequent urban design competition (1961) and Kallmann, McKinnell & Knowles won the competition for the new City Hall (1962). Ben Thompson (of Harvard) restored Quincy Market as a 'Festival Market' (1971–6) and finally the Central Artery was buried underground in the 'Big Dig' in the early 2000s.

Lynch demonstrated the power of fragmentary urban design when coupled with the BRA. While Lynch advocated the historic preservation of Quincy Market, he also argued for the destruction of Foley Square, a historic sailors' red-light district, but sought to preserve the nearby historic urban village of North Boston. This fragmentary patchwork combination of selective historic preservation and piecemeal modern intervention set a pattern for the redevelopment of many historic downtowns across America in the 1960s. In 1961 the New York City Planning Commission revised New York's basic Zoning Code (established in 1916, with the setback regulations that created the metropolitan image) to allow new towers on plazas, based on Mies van der Rohe's Seagram Building (1958) on Park Avenue. A rash of modern towers built on plazas to gain extra height ensued, resulting in the code being amended in the early 1970s. The later code revisions reverted to the street and the theory of Special Districts or patches in a city, instead of an overall masterplan. The first American, municipal Urban Design Department created by Mayor John Lindsay in 1967 wrote these new regulations. The department developed

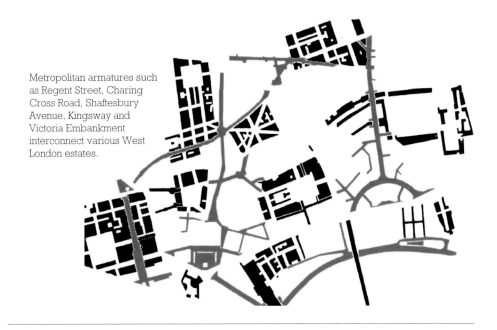

Metropolitan armatures such as Regent Street, Charing Cross Road, Shaftesbury Avenue, Kingsway and Victoria Embankment interconnect various West London estates.

the Boston idea of urban fragments as a micro-zoning tool, creating exceptional Special Districts. Legally these were based on the original 1916 Special District of Wall Street where preexisting skyscrapers broke the new setback codes and were 'grandfathered', or not penalised, because they predated the new regulations. Based on these Special Districts, the urban designers introduced Contextual Zoning Codes designed to protect the street armatures of Downtown and then Midtown and Fifth Avenue.

Jonathan Barnett explained in *An Introduction to Urban Design* (1982)[11] how Special Districts were originally intended to protect urban villages, like Chinatown and Little Italy, or the Theater District, but expanded with incentives to promote urban design goals, like the maintenance of the street wall on Fifth Avenue in Midtown or historic preservation in Greenwich Village. The system allowed for community input within a defined urban boundary from the bottom up. Barnett showed that the system was expanded to cover Battery Park City in the mid-1970s as a way of spurring development, creating a Special District that was controlled by an independent authority, financed by New York State. Here, new regulations created by Alexander Cooper (an Urban Design team member) and Stanton Eckstut in 1978 set urban design guidelines to create new streets and squares. The plan re-created a historic New York district or urban village, modelled on the Upper West Side neighbourhood, but at a new modern density under the influence of the Cornell Contextualists and European Rationalists. After the success of Battery Park City in the 1980s, Special Districts and urban design guidelines became the new norm of global development, along with independent state authorities that could aid development and finance (used, for instance, at Canary Wharf, London, Potsdamer Platz, Berlin or Pudong, Shanghai in the 1990s, not to mention Dubai or Saudi Arabia in the 2000s). Barnett went on to write *The Fractured Metropolis* (1995),[12] in which he extended the fragmentary analysis to the design of the city territory, studying the development of large urban fragments, malls, office towers, large housing estates, industrial parks and recreational areas scattered within the American landscape. Not all the later large urban fragments in Asia or the Middle East maintained the contextual design guidelines of Battery Park City. Pudong and Dubai, for instance, developed huge skyscraper towers on mall podiums in isolated megablocks beside wide boulevards set in parkland or desert.

* * *

Fragmenting the Metropolis: Fractal Design and Informality – The City Section

* * *

The isolation of the Special District system and fragmentary urban design also posed problems for urban actors. Fragments could be very isolated, like Canary Wharf in the London docks, which was disconnected from subways and highways during the 1990s, causing the bankruptcy of its developers. For many years after 1945 the racist South African regime pushed this logic of isolation and fragmentation to an extreme in its apartheid policies, with its segregated camps and townships. Eyal Weizman and others in *A Civilian Occupation* (2003)[13] have shown that a similar, but in some ways as brutal, logic has informed the vertical segregation of Jewish and Arab settlements in the Palestinian West Bank. Saskia Sassen, argued that every major global city, besides containing global financial service centres, like Canary Wharf, also contained its ghettos and immigrant enclaves that were essential as sources of cheap labour.[14]

In other situations the isolation of the fragmented metropolis could be turned into an advantage by developers of gated communities or theme parks, where only paying guests, registered inhabitants or their servants could gain access to a specific urban fragment. Walt Disney demonstrated in his Disneyland theme park in Anaheim, California (1954) how a planned urban fragment could serve to psychologically reassure anxious citizens in a fast-changing world. Thanks to television advertising, the fantasy Main Street of Disneyland attracted 12 million people in its first year of operation, and it continues to do so. Walt Disney World in Florida has attracted over 30 million people a year even in bad times. Nostalgic urban village vistas play a key part in marketing these theme parks to people who mainly live in suburbs or in fast-expanding cities in Asia, Latin America or Africa. These frozen urban vistas provide enclave developers, designers and occupants with a prefabricated urban image, as a stable and fixed stage set. This scenographic element served many marketing purposes for the developer. A similar picturesque strategy can be seen at work in the marketing of Dubai with its theme parks and malls throughout the oil-rich Middle East and Islamic world. In Britain, Prince Charles's re-creation of a small urban village on his private Poundbury Estate outside Dorchester (begun 1993) echoes the same theme of psychological reassurance through microcodes, like Battery Park City, but this time allied to the British tradition of picturesque urban villages, great estates and their powerful landowners.

Another advantage of the fragmentary system of urban design was that a known urban formula could be repeated in a different location, with further improvements built into the new fragment, creating an iterative fractal or evolving fragment. In the case of

Battery Park City and the World Financial Center, for instance, the success of the initial fragment was replicated around the world, in Hong Kong, Tokyo and Mumbai to name but a few cities. These enclaves came along with Special District designations, involving special tax regimes, legal exemptions, special authorities, special design codes and special housing enclaves. From Johannesburg in South Africa to Moscow, shopping mall podiums combined with skyscraper towers made new business districts in the centre and on the edge of existing cities. Housing towers could also be plugged into these commercial podiums, creating a new urban design type that was first pioneered in the Hong Kong new towns of the 1980s. This new hybrid urban fragment became a pattern that was endlessly repeated and altered by designers and urban actors for each site and time period, resulting in a repetitive fractal pattern that was never the same twice. A similar fractal pattern existed in the residential development of the 'Great Estates' of London in the 18th and 19th centuries … Brian McGrath's 'Manhattan Timeformations' at New York's Skyscraper Museum website shows that the evolution of skyscrapers as urban elements can also be seen as a genealogical, fractal pattern of repetition and constant innovation.[15]

The fragmentation of the metropolis opened the way for many urban actors to take control of their own, local urban environment, patch or enclave, emerging from their ghettos. The result was a mosaic of self-organising systems and urban patterns in place of one single dominant centre. The fragmentation of the metropolis also affected its former colonies (both Gandhi and Mao had stressed peasant villages as the basis of their nation's regeneration). Two years before *Collage City*, the United Nations first recognised the vast array of self-built shantytowns at the UN-HABITAT I meeting in Vancouver (1976). Here the British architect John Turner, Canadian economist Barbara Ward and her assistant David Satterthwaite organised a separate conference for the uninvited NGO representatives in a disused seaplane hangar. By the time of HABITAT III in Vancouver in 2006, the NGOs occupied most of the exhibition space in the conference centre. By this time self-built housing vernaculars had become recognised as what Fumihiko Maki called 'group forms' in his 1960 Tokyo Manifesto. These could be arranged around contours, like the Italian hill towns beloved by Cullen, as in the hilltop *favelas* of Rio de Janeiro, Brazil or the *ranchos* of Caracas, Venezuela. Or on the plains of Mexico City or Bogotá where barrios (neighbourhoods) could be laid out within government-provided superblock armatures that became the main commercial streets and access ways. Within the apparent chaos of the myriad of self-built houses simple rules applied, creating house types and conditions of access that Christopher Alexander, John Turner and many others saw as small-scale fractal systems generating complex, large-scale urban structures. BV Doshi tried to learn from this tradition in his Aranya, India, scheme of 1981, applying Turner's self-build ideas within the World Bank 'Sites and Services' setting.

Decaying Modernist megastructures, like the Sewoon Sangga Market (architect Kim Swoo-Geun, mid-1960s) in Seoul, South Korea, could form unexpected, hybrid and heterotopic urban elements in the fast-shifting dynamic of the fragmentary metropolis. Like Villanueva's de Enero estate in Caracas, Venezuela, small-scale shanties invaded the open spaces around the Modernist megastructure of the Sewoon Sangga Market, stretching two city superblocks. Built as a modern armature with an upper pedestrian deck over traffic to house a market by an old city gate, the upper levels of the block provided mass housing in a long, modern, panel-built structure. The market quickly expanded into the surrounding parking lots and became an informal shantytown of lanes and huts. Meanwhile various shops in the market expanded vertically up into the housing block to become small department stores. The large-scale clarity of the initial design soon became subverted by a million tiny moves that had their own fractal logic. Small urban actors created a new kind of hybrid structure that broke all the city's zoning rules, mixing housing, commerce, offices and industry and creating a complex vertical urban village and megablock hybrid section (soon to be demolished for a new Koetter Kim & Associates project, also with a hybrid section).

The Sewoon Sangga Market hybrid, like the now-demolished Walled City of Kowloon, Hong Kong, demonstrates the importance of the city section in fragmentary urban design ecologies. Alvin Boyarsky, in his article 'Chicago à la Carte' (1970)[16] and as director of the Architectural Association School (AA) in London, encouraged sectional experimentation in complex urban projects in the 1970s. There Zaha Hadid, while teaching with Koolhaas and Elia Zenghelis of OMA, won the Peak Competition in 1982 for a new facility at the top of the funicular on a spectacular site overlooking Hong Kong (AA graduate Terry Farrell eventually built a different facility on the site). Hadid's design opened up the centre of the Modernist megastructure, placing the hotel rooms in long thin bars above and below a new public space that looked down on the skyscrapers of Hong Kong. Within the sandwich of hotel accommodations, Hadid created a curved, drive-in entranceway on stilts that led to a reception foyer, with a bar and swimming pool floating above,

west end estates   millenium mile   city of london   olympic village   canary wharf   millenium dome   docks
parks   kings cross   shard   stratford rail
congestion   st. pancras high   koetter and kim proposal
pricing   speed rail

Layered drawing of modern London showing the Thatcher era dockland developments as well as the development plan for the 2012 Olympics.

layered london

looking down the mountainside onto the city. The spectacular three-dimensional ramp experience, while undeniably picturesque, was far removed from Cullen's concept of 'serial vision' in a historic urban village. Here the city section was activated in a novel way, creating a new, hybrid public space that could accommodate small-scale, potentially bottom-up innovations, as well as top-down codes.

Conclusion

The collapse and reformulation of the metropolitan urban design ecology under pressure from the megalopolis reflected a loss of state power and the rise of commercial forces in the marketplace as competing urban actors. The 1980s era of President Ronald Reagan and British Prime Minister Margaret Thatcher represented a shift away from the Bretton Woods agreements and American Marshall Plan that had supported the rebuilding of Europe, Japan and the 'Asian Tigers' after the Second World War. In the new era of neo-Liberal economics, the gigantic oil profits of global American oil companies and OPEC oil-rich nations powered the rise of international and global financial institutions that could recycle these profits in safe urban developments and enclaves.

American corporations had long enjoyed the economy of scale that came from a national market of approximately 150 million, where Britain, for instance, only had a population of approximately 50 million in 1945. American national corporations had the skills and brands to pioneer the global market, as the EU formed into a second trading block of a similar size. These large international markets required much energy and coordination, involving computational power and global communication systems on a new scale beyond even the US market. The scale of these global corporations was vast, perhaps serving 500 million worldwide, but they palled beside the size of the Asian markets. Both India and China had populations of around a billion people by the year 2000, with only one third living in cities.[17]

The emergence of India and China has challenged global energy, financial, industrial and electronics corporations to scale up their organisations by a factor of 2 if they want to be successful in just one market, say China, and by a factor of 4 if they enter both. By 2010 China is expected to have 7 out of 10 of the world's largest megamalls, all of them larger than the original American megamall, the Mall of America near Minneapolis (1992).[18] In the face of this challenge and the rise of India and China as global commercial powers, a massive transfer of organisational and information technologies is under way to set up the urbanisation of Asia in the 21st century. Large urban fragments – whether in South Delhi along Cyber Alley, in Beijing along the central business district (CBD) strip on the Second Ring Road, or in Pudong's Special Skyscraper District, capping Shanghai's high-rise towers – represent the global urban portals of this massive exchange. The Euro-American tradition of the fragmentary metropolis is being transformed here by the emerging outlines of the Asian megacity.

Koolhaas's dramatic China Central Television (CCTV) headquarters in Beijing stands as a monumental, corporate symbol of the Asian future of the city and as a supersized XXL piece of fragmentary urbanism. It is scaled as a spectacular public symbol for the one billion potential customers of the ambitious state media giant. It is a vast urban fragment, a 'city-within-the-city', with shops, hotels and offices, unflatteringly referred to by Beijing taxi drivers as the 'Trouser Building' (because of the constant view up into its crotch from the highway). This giant corporate urban icon, a megastructure worthy of a megalopolis, has its own irrational logic separated from its surrounding city within its enclave and plaza. Despite its connection to media systems and mass communications, the CCTV building stands as a monument isolated from the city. It is a monster of energy consumption and absurd structural display. Its complex interior arrangements are hidden in the singular megaform. This signature shape of dancing trousers soon gets lost on the city horizon among a forest of competing towers in this vast city. This apparently all-powerful, triumphant symbol of the informational city of the future disappears with a slither into the traffic flows of the CBD on the outer ring road of an emerging Asian megacity.

Notes

1   http://whc.unesco.org/en/convention/ (accessed 23 May 2012).
2   J Jacobs, *Dark Age Ahead*, Random House (New York), 2004.
3   J Jacobs, *The Death and Life of Great American Cities*, Random House (New York), 1961.
4   R Banham, *Los Angeles: The Architecture of Four Ecologies*, University of California Press (Berkeley), 1971.
5   RM Fogelson, *The Fragmented Metropolis: Los Angeles, 1850–1930*, Harvard University Press (Cambridge, MA),1967; EW Soja, *Postmodern Geographies: The Reassertion of Space in Critical Social Theory*, Verso (London, New York), 1989; EW Soja, *Postmetropolis: Critical Studies of Cities and Regions*, Blackwell Publishers (Oxford and Malden, MA), 2000; D Harvey, *The Condition of Post-Modernity: An Enquiry into the Origins of Cultural Change*, Blackwell (Oxford, UK and Cambridge, MA), 1989.
6   CJ Vergara, *American Ruins*, Monacelli Press (New York), 1999.
7   E Rogers, 'The Evolution of Architecture: Reply to the Custodian of Frigidaires', *Casabella Continuità* (June 1959), (republished in: *Editorali di architettura*, Einaudi (Turin), 1968, pp 127–36).
8   G Cullen, *The Concise Townscape*, Architectural Press (London), 1961.
9   DG Shane, 'Louis Kahn', in M Kelly (ed), *The Encyclopaedia of Aesthetics*, Oxford University Press (Oxford), vol 3, 1998, pp 19–23.
10 K Lynch, *The Image of the City*, MIT Press (Cambridge, MA), 1960.
11 J Barnett, *An Introduction to Urban Design*, HarperCollins Publishers (New York), 1982.
12 J Barnett, *The Fractured Metropolis: Improving the New City, Restoring the Old City, Reshaping the Region*, HarperCollins (New York), 1995.
13 R Segal, E Weizman (eds), *A Civilian Occupation: The Politics of Israeli Architecture*, Babel (Tel Aviv); VERSO (New York), 2003.
14 S Sassen, *The Global City; New York, London, Tokyo*, Princeton University Press (Princeton, NJ), 2001.
15 Brian McGrath's 'Manhattan Timeformations': http://www.skyscraper.org/timeformations/intro.html (accessed 23 May 2012)
16 A Boyarsky, 'Chicago à La Carte', in Robin Middleton (ed), *The Idea of the City: Architectural Associations*, Architectural Association (London), 1996. Article first printed in *Architectural Design*, vol 11, December 1970, pp 595–640.
17 D Satterthwaite, *The Transition to a Predominantly Urban World and its Underpinnings*, IIED, 2007.
18 On Chinese megamalls see: D Barboza, 'For China, New Malls Jaw-Dropping in Size', *The New York Times*, 25 May 2005.

Designing Ecological Heterogeneity

ML Cadenasso

Ecologist Mary Cadenasso has devised a new method of urban land cover classification that has great potential to provide methods for recognising, analysing, representing and designing ecological heterogeneity. This system, called HERCULES (High Ecological Resolution Classification for Urban Landscapes and Environmental Systems), recognises cities not as separate between built and vegetated landscapes, but as a patchwork of finely differentiated combinations of different land covers. Cadenasso's scientific framework helps urban designers out of the disciplinary impasse of dividing cities into buildings and green space. Rossi's architecture of the city, for instance, only addresses a classification system of property subdivision and buildings, while much landscape architecture just concerns itself with the space around buildings. Instead, ecologically speaking, the entire city is a socio-natural system which maintains significant environmental functioning.

Urban regions are characteristically heterogeneous, and this heterogeneity is composed of many different elements such as architectural form and building density, vegetation, types of infrastructure, economic activities and cultural expressions. These characteristics frequently shift within the scale of a single city block, giving rise to heterogeneity that is very finely scaled. Urban designers contribute to decisions about what elements will be present in the system and the amounts and configurations of those elements. In this way, urban designers play a large role in determining the spatial heterogeneity of urban systems. Linking the spatial heterogeneity of a system to the ecological functioning of that system is a central goal of ecological science. Studying urban systems through an ecological lens, however, is relatively new and ecologists are still learning how to quantify and map urban heterogeneity so that the link between heterogeneity and ecosystem function can be tested. This potential link between structure and function suggests that a collaboration between ecologists and urban designers could fruitfully advance our understanding of urban areas as integrated social-ecological systems.

What are Spatial Heterogeneity, Ecological Function and Patch Dynamics?

Spatially heterogeneity can be described metaphorically as a patchwork quilt. Each patch in the quilt is distinct from another because of colour, pattern, material or shape, for example. But patches do not have to differ from each other in all those characteristics – they could be the same size and shape and only differ in colour or they could be the same colour but distinct in shape. In addition, patches can repeat within the quilt.

For ecologists, spatial heterogeneity is the variation within a 'characteristic of interest' across space. There are two key elements to this definition. First, spatial heterogeneity is geographically explicit, meaning that it is variation that can be mapped. Second, the characteristic of interest is determined by the specific research question. There are many different characteristics varying across space and, as a consequence, many different ways to map the heterogeneity of a single area. A specific research question is needed to establish the characteristic of interest and the resulting depiction of heterogeneity required to address the question. For example, if a research question focuses on whether the density of trees and houses influences an ecological function, such as the maintenance of populations of tree-nesting birds across different neighbourhoods, then the characteristic of interest for this question is the density of houses and trees. After mapping the variation in the density of houses and trees in the different neighbourhoods, then the populations of tree-nesting birds can be quantified to determine whether the heterogeneity in house and tree is linked to biodiversity maintenance. Because the characterisation of spatial heterogeneity depends on a specific research question, there is no single description of spatial heterogeneity, and there may be alternative descriptions for the same area, each hypothesised to influence different ecological functions.

Mapping spatial heterogeneity results in an array of patches that differ from each other according to the characteristic of interest established by the research question. Typically, the patch array is contiguous, meaning that all space within the area belongs to a patch, or, returning to the quilt metaphor, there are no holes in the quilt. Though patch arrays can be mapped, they are not fixed in time. Patch dynamics refers to the changes in patches through time. Patches can change in two primary ways: 1) a shift in boundaries or 2) a shift in internal patch characteristics. These two types of changes are best illustrated by example. Returning to our previous example, if patches were initially established based on the variation in the density of houses and trees then changes to this density would influence the delineation of patches. Infill of housing would increase the density of buildings and the planting or removal of trees would change the tree density. If the change in density is consistent across the entire patch then the identity of the patch may shift as the internal patch characteristics are changed. Alternatively, if the building or tree density is changed in a portion of the patch, the boundary of that patch will shift as the patch is dissected into multiple patches with varying densities.

How is Heterogeneity Depicted in Cities?

Urban heterogeneity is typically depicted by land use classifications that map patches of land use such as residential, commercial, industrial, etc. This depiction of heterogeneity uses land use as the characteristic of interest that is varying across space. Land use classifications have been developed to standardise approaches and terminology. However, these standard classifications have constraints that limit their application to urban ecological systems. Specifically, they 1) were developed for application at the continental rather than urban scale, 2) separate built from non-built components in the landscape, and 3) confound structure and function, meaning that they assume that all residential areas that function as housing are structurally the same, for example. Research using land use as the descriptor of spatial heterogeneity assumes that the ecological function to be measured across this heterogeneity is somehow linked to land use.

The difference between land *use* and land *cover* is often ignored, but it is important for testing the link between spatial heterogeneity and ecological function. Land cover is a physical pattern and is focused on structural heterogeneity. In contrast, land use defines the land in terms of social and economic function, or how people use the land. Maintaining the distinction between land use and land cover allows land cover to be cast as an independent variable for explaining ecologically interesting functional variables such as biodiversity, nutrient retention and carbon storage. It can be argued that land use is not an ecological variable and knowing the land use of an area does not necessarily lend insight into its ecological functioning. For example, 'residential' is a *functional* land use class in these schemes. But all residential land is not *structurally* the same due to the fine scale variation in building density, vegetation and the amount of impervious surfaces. This unaccounted-for spatial heterogeneity may influence ecological functions such as surface water and heat retention within urban landscapes. As a physical descriptor of spatial heterogeneity, land cover may be more relevant to ecological processes than land use and would allow for testing links between structure and function.

In addition, most land use classification systems are designed to be used with remotely sensed images and are based on pixels. Though pixels can be large or small depending on data resolution, a pixel boundary is not inherently ecologically meaningful. Finer resolution data is increasingly available and yields greater detail. The logic structure of the classification approaches, however, remains based on land use. Therefore, whether the greater detail acquired by contemporary remote imaging technology leads to an increase in the understanding of system structure and function is an empirical question that needs to be rigorously evaluated.

What is HERCULES and How Does it Work?

As a response to the constraints imposed by the application of these pixel-based, land use, classifications for describing ecological heterogeneity in urban landscapes, I, together with my colleagues, developed a new classification called HERCULES (High Ecological Resolution Classification for Urban Landscapes and Environmental Systems). HERCULES takes advantage of the greater spatial resolution afforded by access to better imagery through low-flying aircraft, but it uses a different logic structure than previous land use classification systems. HERCULES focuses on land cover, not land use, and maps the heterogeneity of urban systems as patches hypothesised to have ecological meaning rather than pixels.

HERCULES allows the researcher to focus on the biophysical structure of urban environments and uses three recognised elements of urban heterogeneity: buildings, surface materials and vegetation. These three elements are divided into six features in HERCULES: 1) woody vegetation (shrubs and trees), 2) herbaceous vegetation (grass and herbs), 3) bare soil, 4) pavement, 5) buildings, and 6) building typology. The type and amount of vegetation, surface material and buildings is hypothesised to influence ecosystem function because of their differential influence on the amount and distribution of organisms, material and energy. For example, residential areas may have the same type and number of buildings (single structures at the same density) but differ dramatically by the number of trees in each area. This difference among residential areas may have consequences for ecological function such as the maintenance of biodiversity, the storage of carbon, or the uptake and release of nitrogen.

The human eye excels at recognising pattern. When told to study an aerial photograph of an urban region, people immediately see differences among contrasting areas, even though they may be unable, initially, to articulate the reasons for those contrasts. This powerful observation ability is used in HERCULES as the human eye delineates areas that have contrasting amounts or types of the six features described above. The process consists of two stages: 1) delineating patches and 2) classifying those patches according to the HERCULES classification scheme. Patches can differ from each other either due to a change in the type of element or a change in the proportional cover of the elements. For example, two neighbourhoods may have the same type of structure and the same amount of shrubs and trees but they might differ from each other in that one may contain a greater proportion cover of buildings than the other. A change in either proportional cover or type of element leads to a change in patch type. Once patches are delineated they can be classified. In HERCULES, patches are classified by the proportional cover of each of the first five features plus the building type. The patch is assigned to a category

	Coarse vegetation	Fine vegetation	Bare soil	Pavement	Building	Building type
	4	0	0	1	1	S
	4	0	0	0	0	N
	1	2	0	2	2	C
	0	1	4	0	0	N
	1	2	0	3	2	M
	2	4	0	0	0	N

Examples of patches classified using HERCULES. The proportional cover of coarse (woody) and fine (herbaceous) vegetation, bare soil, pavement and buildings is scored into five categories (0 = none, 1 = present–10%, 2 = 11–35%, 3 = 36–75% and 4 = >75%). Building types are identified as N = none, S = single, C = connected, or M = mixed.

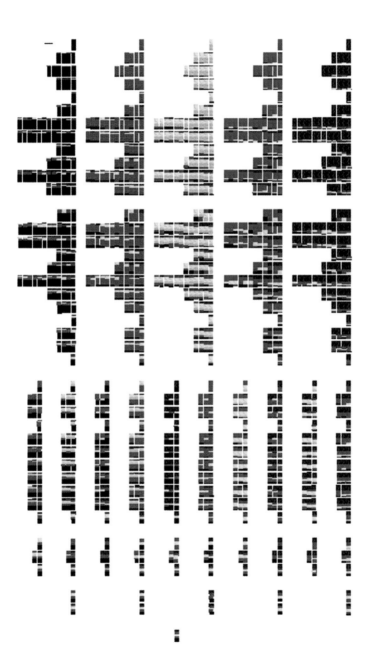

Classification chart of HERCULES patches (left)
present in the Baltimore region within the Gwynns
Falls watershed (right). The chart arrays patches top to
bottom from homogeneous to heterogeneous, and from
left to right from buildings to coarse vegetation.

of land cover for each of the first five features and a single letter to indicate the building type. The category numbers refer to ranges of per cent cover of the element present in the patch (0 = absent, 1 = present to 10% cover, 2 = 11–35% cover, 3 = 36–75% cover and 4 = >75% cover). These per cent cover ranges were selected in an effort to minimise the time needed to classify each patch. Generally a sampler can decide relatively quickly whether or not an element exists in the patch, and if so, how much exists using these broad categories. Therefore, the categories are arbitrary in that there is no ecological meaning associated with them. Examples of this classification are provided on page 275. The left-hand column contains thumbnails of different patch types and the top row contains the six elements of HERCULES. The digits and letters in the box indicate the classification of each thumbnail. For example, the top thumbnail is classified as 40011S. This six alphanumeric string describes the heterogeneity of the delineated patch.

Because the six elements are allowed to vary independently of each other, the resulting data set is a flexible descriptor of system heterogeneity that can be queried using any combination of the six features depending on the research question being addressed. For example, if the research focuses on the coarse vegetation in the landscape, the data can be sorted and analysed to emphasise the variation in that feature, independent of heterogeneity in the other features. Alternatively, if the research focuses on the density of buildings, the data can be re-sorted and analysed to address that question.

I have found, over several years of working with undergraduates, that once the criteria of HERCULES is explained, students delineate and map the patches in approximately the same place. The second step of classifying the patches by assigning the alphanumeric string, however, is a source of great variation among observers. To avoid this inconsistency, the classifying step has been automated through an object oriented classification approach. This approach uses high resolution digital imagery and other data, such as building footprints and light detecting and ranging (LIDAR) data, to group pixels into objects based on their similar reflectance and user created rules specifying three-dimensional shape and proximity to other features. The result is an image with all objects classified into one of the five feature types in HERCULES. This forms the base layer. The HERCULES patches delineated through visual interpretation can then be laid over the classified image and the types and amounts of features in each patch quantified. The result is no longer an alphanumeric string of code for each patch but rather a series of continuous cover percentages for each element present in the patch. This approach removes inconsistencies among samplers, quickens the pace of classifying the patches, and provides highly accurate, and repeatable, information for each patch.

Why Might HERCULES Change the Way We Understand and Design Cities?

HERCULES is a powerful tool to map and quantify the spatial heterogeneity of urban areas. By using HERCULES, the limitations of available pixel-based land use classifications are overcome because the HERCULES classification system 1) integrates human and natural components of the system, 2) recognises that features can vary independently of each other, 3) accounts for all combinations of elements in the area, 4) has greater categorical resolution, 5) does not confound structure and function, and 6) is based on land cover.

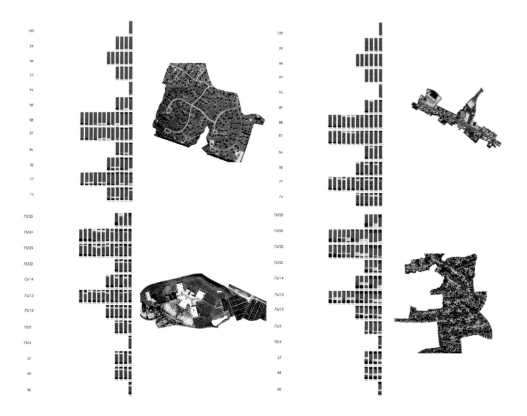

From the previous chart, families of land cover patches emerge, such as fine-vegetated dominant neighbourhoods on the upper left, pavement-dominated landscapes such as shopping malls on the lower left, building-dominated commercial strip on the upper right, and forest-dominated neighbourhood on the lower right.

Coarse Vegetation > 75%

Building 51-75%

Fine Vegetation 51-75%

Pavement and Building 36-50%

The bar charts represent the amount of HERCULES patches present in the Gwynns Falls watershed, mapped by land cover families. Upper left is coarse vegetation patches which are concentrated along river valley parks in the lower half of the watershed, and on protected hilltops in the upper watershed. Lower left shows the fine vegetation farmlands, new subdivisions, cemeteries and golf courses. Building-dominated patches (upper right) are not restricted to the centre of the city at the lower part of the watershed, but are also present in dense enclaves on the city's periphery. The lower right building- and pavement-dominated patches are along the old strip leading from the centre of the city to the suburbs.

Urban regions are integrated social-ecological systems. As such, they are comprised of built and non-built elements that interact and jointly influence ecological processes across fine spatial scales. HERCULES uses the amount and type of land cover elements, both built (eg, buildings) and non-built (eg, vegetation), as criteria to determine patches. This focus on land cover rather than land use is more ecologically relevant because land cover contains the elements that influence ecological processes. HERCULES is also more ecologically relevant because it uses patches rather than pixels. Different patches, meaning those with different types and amounts of land cover elements, can be compared to determine whether they also differ in a specified ecological process such as nutrient cycling.

The focus on land cover rather than land use opens the door widely for integrating our ecological understanding of cities with the design of those cities. Because designers frequently determine the type, amount and specific arrangements of land cover elements, they play a critical role in establishing the heterogeneity of a city. For example, an urban designer may determine the size, amount and materials used in buildings. They may also determine how multiple buildings are arranged relative to each other and relative to other built and non-built features of the system. These choices are frequently driven by visual variety and experience concerns for people using these spaces. These choices may, however, also influence ecological processes such as the movement of water, nutrients and organisms, and parameters such as temperature and moisture. Understanding links between design choices and understanding of how heterogeneity influences ecological processes can aid us in designing aesthetically interesting as well as sustainable, ecologically sound cities.

The Elementary City

Paola Viganò

This is the first English translation of the first chapter of Paola Viganò's important book _The Elementary City_. Viganò applies Van Doesberg's 'Neo-Plastic' critique of two dimensionality in art to architecture in urbanism, at both the building and territorial scales. Elementarism explores four-dimensional 'plasticism' in the field of time-space. 'The Elementarist sees life as not absolute but only relative, temporary, and transitory.' Also inspired by the detailed focus on everyday objects of Alain Robbe-Grillet's _nouveau roman_, Viganò uses the method of _stratigraphy_ to understand the prehistory and latent structure of urban landscapes, especially the everyday and banal ones of post-war Europe. This novel abstract reading of the strata of the everyday makes Viganò a pioneer of the metacity by not recognising limits between architecture and landscape, history and modernity, centre and periphery, city and territory.

Fragment/Detail

As at other points in the history of the city, many of the recent attempts to describe and design urban territory have relied on images of the fragment, of heterogeneity, of discontinuities between one thing and another. The idea of the fragment implies that a previously existing equilibrium has been broken or a previously unified, harmonious condition has ceased to exist. As a consequence, the contemporary city is judged negatively or instead, its fragmented condition is developed into a manifesto. But in its ordinary meaning, a detail is expected to be part of a whole: a whole that exists and is not imagined.[1] The fragment and the detail are provisional states through which each material of a city passes, over time, during which a detail of a whole becomes first a piece of wreckage, a fragment, the remains of something no longer there, and then becomes part of a whole again. The duration of the materials of a city as fragments and details is variable, depending on the distance in time at which we place ourselves and on the viewpoint we assume; and it is not an ontological condition but, to a significant extent, the result of an interpretation.

Understanding the material parts of cities as fragments has intensified our ability to note the differences between separated things and to see what it is that makes them separate, distinct, impossible to conflate. Different positions have resulted from this: the collector who observes the city as though it were a museum or a catalogue of pieces; the atopic approach taken by those who eliminate context and concern themselves with the syntax of decomposition and composition; and the ironic _bricoleur_ who re-uses and deforms excerpted parts from 'the liberating project of the modern'.[2]

In music Charles Rosen[3] describes how at the beginning of the 20th-century composition shifted from 'large pre-assembled pieces' organised within known, predictable sequences, to the 'note by note' organisation of pieces of musical syntax that were necessarily brief. Atonal music, composed note by note and disrupting previous rules of composition, gave way to serial music, which introduced new rules that made it possible to maintain a relationship between each note and the next. From Schoenberg to today, the whole development of contemporary music has concerned itself with searching for rules of aggregation that can take a fragment of sound and, making use of the concept of the series, integrate it into a melody: not denying its autonomy but iterating it and ascribing a place to it as part of a sequence.[4]

In a sense the city also went through this transition. The 19th-century city looks as though it was composed by making sequences of known elements: a city of details, put together in known ways. The contemporary city is less easy to decode, written as it is note by note: a city of fragments, endless parts that come to rest next to one another in random ways. Yet within this city that we interpret as fragmented and heterogeneous we also see that certain objects and particular materials repeat: car parks, shopping centres, detached housing developments, sports grounds, etc: materials that can be named and are finite in their forms, have precise, defined characteristics and are organised into various types of sequences.

Reflecting on urban elementarism requires us to move between those two extremes, from the fragment, to the detail, from an interpretation of the contemporary city as a composition of fragments, to another interpretation based on investigating the relationship between a whole and its parts and as in serial music, attempting to reorder them within a whole '... in which hierarchy is no longer based on the principle of identity by transposition but conversely on localised, variable deductions ...' and in which '... sound integrates itself more logically into a constructed form, on condition that the structures responsible for that form are founded on criteria of their own'.[5]

Elementarism, Deconstruction/Composition

The term 'elementarism' was used fairly frequently in the 1920s and the 1930s; in 1921 in *De Stijl* Theo van Doesburg published the *Appel à l'art élémentaire* signed by Hausmann, Arp, Pougny and Moholy-Nagy; and in 1926 and 1927, again in *De Stijl*, he published the fragments of an elementarist manifesto and added his own signature to those of the others.[6] According to Reyner Banham the word *elementarism* originates with Malevich, who used 'suprematist fundamental elements' as the basic components of his paintings.

Elementarism brings together multiple and apparently discordant contributions; van Doesburg's articles show a train of thought developing that draws on Neo-Plasticism, Constructivism and all of Dadaism, introducing elements that criticise the Constructivist aspects of *De Stijl* and that ultimately led to the departure of its most important protagonists.

For some, the elementarism in van Doesburg's painting, which was a new formulation of *Nieuwe Beelding*,[7] was 'the direct outcome of his experience with Van Eesteren';[8] but like so many other art movements of the early 20th century it was above all the evolution of a position that aimed to return to the origins of language by reducing its complexity and decodifying its forms, techniques and means of expression; in architecture this included investigating how colour could play a part in the deconstruction process. As van Doesburg moved away from his own Neo-Plasticist version of reductionism and embarked on the same reductionist path as much of the rest of European culture, by 1920 he was on a collision course with Oud who, unable to support van Doesburg's espousal of Dada, broke away from *De Stijl*; then Mondrian broke away in 1924 saying that '... van Doesburg's elementarist position (...) is a heresy that subverts the principles of the *Nieuwe Beelding* ...'.[9]

But van Doesburg was not simply replicating Dada; he was using it to enrich an investigation that had set itself the task of deconstructing language in order to reconstruct another that would not negate dissonance and could take upon itself the condition of complexity and chaos of the modern world. Like others at the time, van Doesburg (under the pseudonym IK Bonset) was interested in taking words and sounds apart and then re-assembling them: 'Dada is the need for a uniform reality of the world that is the outcome of dissonant, contrasting relationships.'[10]

Tone-on-tone composition enables contrasting elements to be put together without making any adjustments to them. In van Doesburg's counter-compositions this is expressed as horizontal, vertical and oblique lines; as juxtaposed heterogeneous materials in the collages by Schwitters and the Cubists; and in Van Eesteren's projects and urban plans, as equally heterogeneous urban elements such as houses, asphalt or footpaths. Van Doesburg wrote that in accepting the value of contemporaneity and its complexity, the elements used to construct each new elaboration must become the elementary structural components of a new world, to be rebuilt after another has been destroyed and its composition broken down into pieces.

After these investigations by van Doesburg and the art avant-gardes of the early 20th century, the idea of decomposing and deconstructing the world was taken forward in a very great number of different ways, eventually re-emerging in philosophy and the arts at the beginning of the 1970s as part of a new conceptualisation. 'The term *Deconstruction* which [Derrida introduces ...] goes back to Heidegger's task of "Destroying the History of Ontology. This Deconstruction does not seek to be a destruction, but a dissection and critical reappraisal".'[11] According to J Hillis Miller, Derrida's American disciple and an adherent of the New Criticism, deconstruction, or deconstructionism, or deconstructivism[12] means simply reading well: the art of reading attentively, close reading: *explication du texte*.

P Viganò, L Fabian. Layers re-elaboration of the survey carried out as part of preparing the plan for Prato (B Secchi, G Serrini, P Viganò, C Zagaglia, 1994–6). Layers: **a1** base, **a2** asphalt, **a3** gardens and towers, **a4** 4–5 floors; **b1** paved areas, **b2** retail activities (display and sales, shops open to the public, storage spaces), **b3** 2 floors, **b4** 1 floor; **c1** car parking, **c2** 1–2 floors, **c3** walls or retaining walls, **c4** 2–3 floors; **d1** 3–4 floors, **d2** 3–6 dwellings, **d3** 3 floors, **d4** pilotis; **e1** fences, **e2** 1–2 dwellings, **e3** 4 floors, **e4** more than 6 dwellings; **f1** services (culture, religion, entertainment, social and recreation, hospital, healthcare, sport, cemeteries, technical and administrative), **f2** dead-end streets, **f3** enclosures with greenery or hedges, **f4** unpaved ground.

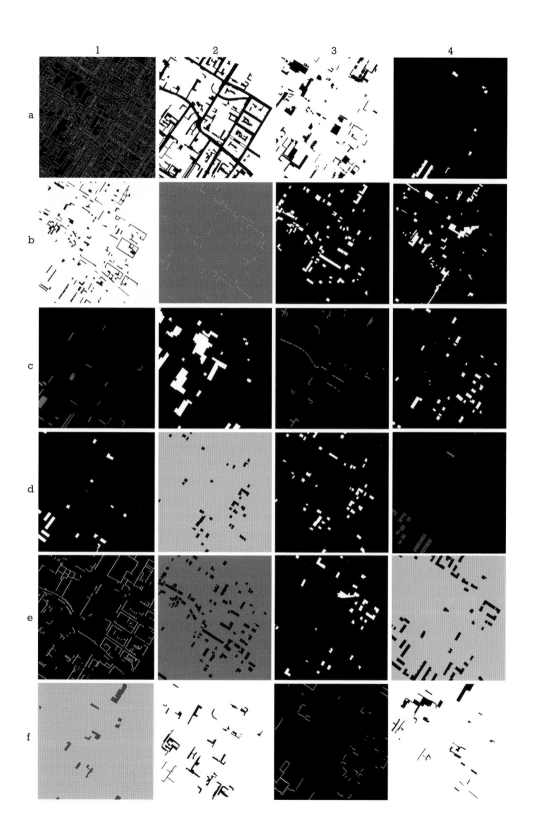

The act of close reading deconstructs, is hyper-precise, and assumes an ethical character that safeguards it from the risk of relativism inherent in any operation of deconstruction: '... An ethical moment is certainly inherent in Deconstructive close reading, since readers are expected to refrain from inventing anything and to focus on the textual structure'.[13]

Now that elementarism had been taken up ... deconstruction has been brought up to date, beginning from a technique of decomposition interposed between previously established categories and new representations. Some of the procedures now used to describe and survey the contemporary city and territory can also be seen as forms of close reading that consist of meticulously deconstructing a banal, everyday, 'obvious landscape'[14] into its most minute constituent elements (fences, unpaved paths, open-air storage facilities, access points for pedestrians and cars, pavements, asphalted areas, trees, houses) while suspending all judgement as to their aesthetic value (beautiful/ugly).

Exercises like these, used to describe the city, show that it is not only a place of difference, but also of repetition. They bring to light the two-sided, ambiguous nature of repetition: its potency,[15] which can reinforce the sense and meaning of the context in which it occurs, and the way in which it brings about 'the dissolution of the semantic identity of the sign',[16] for instance within heterogeneous communicative contexts, or as a result of changes that have come about in the internal structure of the discourse.

The space of the contemporary city, so paradoxically homogeneous because of the way in which identical objects repeat within it, is also very often the place where the meanings of these individual parts, and of all the parts as a whole, disintegrate; repetition is also the city of the 21st century.[17]

Surveying, Naming

The difficulty encountered in using predefined interpretative tools and analytical keys to decipher the territory of the contemporary has induced a great many scholars to go on the attack[18] and address the question; before architecture and urbanism were affected, anxious efforts to describe things had already been made in literature, cinema and photography. Surveying, walking and the practice of rapid surveying are all strategies of looking at the contemporary city that invest it with new possibilities for interpretation.

Walking is a process of appropriation of the topographical system: a spatial realisation of place. Because the walk implies that relationships exist between different locations, it becomes 'a space of enunciation'.[19] Jean-François Augoyard[20] proposes two figures of walking: the first, the *synecdoche*, is the rhetorical figure that nominates one part to stand for the whole that contains it; the second, the *asyndeton*, is the suppression of linking words such as conjunctions and adverbs; in the same way, in walking the *asyndeton* selects and fragments the space traversed. Commenting on Augoyard, de Certeau writes that these two figures of walking interact reciprocally: 'Synecdoche makes more dense: it amplifies the detail and miniaturises the whole. Asyndeton cuts out: it undoes continuity ...'.[21]

Surveying by walking is a form of deconstructing: naming objects and reporting what is seen at different scales and at different levels of abstraction, breaking down the city into its elements. An urban territory is the end result and the storehouse of practices and culture, and surveying it enables us to come close to its materiality. Ever since the surveys were made in the Renaissance as starting points for learning from the classical world, for a long time urban surveying has been at the centre of many of the efforts made to revisit previously consolidated theories or practices: Saverio Muratori's surveys of the minor buildings of Venice were his way of retracing the evolutionary process of Venice as an urban organism; the surveys of Robert Venturi, Denise Scott Brown and Steven Izenour were their way of learning from an existing environment to rediscover what they called 'the forgotten symbolism of architectural form', and for Rem Koolhaas, a retroactive survey of Manhattan made it possible to rethink the question of density and urban congestion.[22]

In the definition of 'places' given by Michel de Certeau, surveying by walking means getting involved with them, and with 'spaces' as 'places of practice'.[23] The most important works on how the space of the contemporary is used, and the role played by its various elements in representing the collective imagination, are those by Benjamin on the Parisian *passages*, Kracauer on the streets of Paris and Berlin;[24] Lefebvre, Raymond and others on the Parisian *habitat pavillonnaire*, de Certeau on the practice of everyday life, and more recently Roncayolo on the *boulevard-promenade* in Marseilles, and Jost on the *promenade* in Geneva.[25] The main thrust of these works is to describe the city and its different ways of life, beginning from the forms of their urban places, to construct a reading of urban spaces that overlays rhythms of use, practices and physical qualities in non-deterministic ways, carefully studying individual parts of cities and the possible ways of inhabiting, using, renewing, deforming and modifying them without separating words from things.

Reification of the world has led many to ask questions about the deposits we ourselves leave on things as we pass, the traces we leave on objects and that give clues to our own uses and practices: what is left behind by our decisions, choices, strategies and expectations.

In his preface to *L'Habitat pavillonnaire* Henri Lefebvre criticises the Corbusian approach to sociological positivism, and proposes Bachelard and Heidegger as alternatives. Habitat, he writes, is a matter of anthropology: attaching oneself to the ground, then detaching oneself, putting down roots and then pulling them up again. A dwelling consists of objects that form a characteristic whole within a society and signify the existence of social relationships (because they have both a practical function and a signifying function). The ways and means of habitat express themselves in language, above all in a spoken language that leaves no traces: 'Everyday life requires the perpetual translation, into ordinary language, of this system of signs that consists of the objects used for living, for dressing oneself, feeding oneself.'[26] Dwelling, finally, 'is expressed in an ensemble of works, products, and things that constitute a partial system: a house, a city, an agglomeration. Each of these things is part of that ensemble and bears the ensemble's distinguishing sign; each is testimony of the style (or lack of style) of the ensemble. Each has meaning and sense as part of the observable ensemble, and the ensemble offers us a social text. At the same time, habitat also expresses itself in an ensemble of words, of locutions.'[27]

Once we have acknowledged that this is a message with two aspects, one of words and the other of objects, it becomes important to describe not only houses, objects, clothes and behaviour in the minutest detail but also the tempos, the duration and the rhythms of life, whose observable expression is the amount of space taken up by each of them. The repetition of these everyday activities makes manifest their stability; their repetition generates rhythms that can be individually analysed.

Unlike Balzac, these objects and things and the ways in which we perceive them as they invade our perceptions and feelings cannot reproduce an ordered picture that shows correspondences between their various strata; man and his things can no longer be made to fit snugly together. There are only two ways to gain an understanding of them: through the ambiguity that is the principal characteristic of the modern and which we find in Perec's *Les choses*, in Robbe-Grillet's essay on the *nouveau roman*,[28] in the writings of Foucault, Baudrillard and de Certeau;[29] and by observing everydayness in places and spaces that would otherwise remain unobserved and unobservable.

This way of seeing the city, anticipated by Louis Aragon in 1926 in *Le Paysan de Paris* where he developed an exercise of perceiving the banality and everydayness of modernity, leads Henri Raymond, one of the authors of the study *L'Habitat pavillonnaire*, to overcome the early dismissiveness of the *habitat pavillonnaire* (the detached house), and see it instead as a place where space retains its elasticity and willingness to be transformed; where the act of organising a plot of land – a site – marking out its confines and enclosing them, is an appropriation of space and time. The *pavillonnaire* world is seen as a utopia, a waking dream: mythical in the sense that it relies on constantly evoking naturalness, the Nature myth, an ideological underpinning interpreted as an ensemble of representations that justify and explain a particular mode of social existence.

To observe and describe some of the material components of the contemporary city and explore them in greater depth goes back to an analogous approach and deepens it: for example, making observations of the street beginning from the different types of imagery that takes the street as its object, or by studying the spatiality of a city, such as by taking two underground stations in Tokyo and describing the materials of which they consist and the things that happen there; or by observing the detail of one piece of the *pavillonnaire* built fabric of Geneva, studying how it is physically made and the kind of people who live there.[30]

P Viganò and L Fabian.
Re-elaboration of the survey carried out as part of the preparations for the plan for Prato (B Secchi, G Serrini, P Viganò, C Zagaglia, 1994–6). Layers b2+d2+e2+e4+f1: mixed use.

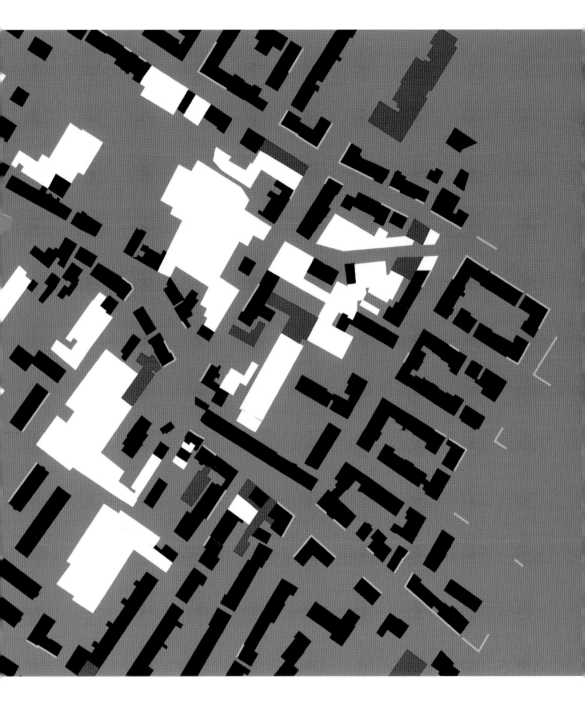

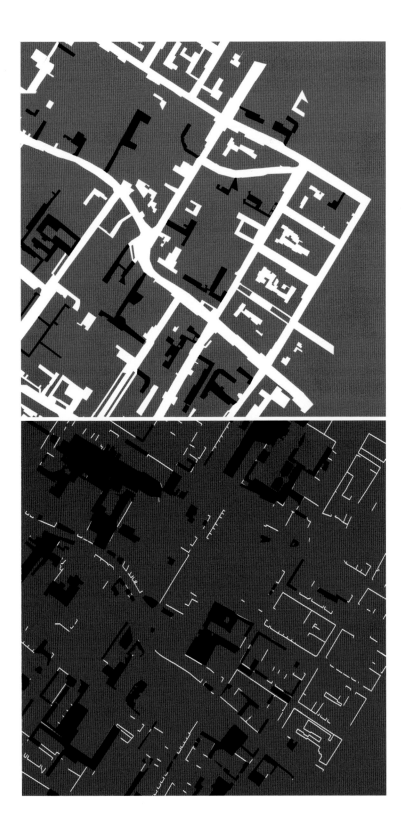

P Viganò and L Fabian. Re-elaboration of the
survey carried out as part of the preparations
for the plan for Prato (B Secchi, G Serrini,
P Viganò, C Zagaglia, 1994–6).

opposite top: Layers f2+a2: dead-end streets.

opposite bottom: Layers a3+c3+e1+f3: privacy.

above: Layers a2+b1+b2+c1+d4+f1:
permeability of space.

Urban Materials, Strata, Traces

Repetitions or recurrences that cannot at first be identified are often revealed by selecting a few urban materials that fall within a single layer or stratum (category): for example, fences, dead-end streets, blocks of flats, or detached houses with gardens, and trying to intersect some of them with one another: the detached houses with the fences or the blocks of flats with the fences, or the number of hours of sunlight received on each face of these particular houses in relation to the same faces of the building stock as a whole (which might of course show that there are no significant relationships at all between these strata).

This analytical and design-based conceptualisation that selects each stratum (layer) to be observed is not a banal oversimplification, nor an acritical return to 1960s structuralism. Rather, it attempts to identify urban ensembles that retain a sufficient degree of generality, that can be examined as a whole from different viewpoints, and that can be related to one another in various ways, bringing to light relationships between them that are not initially evident. In all cases – the illustrations in anatomical atlases, the stratigraphy drawings used by archaeologists, layered computer maps, or hypertexts that assign a thickness to each stratum – the layering process makes it possible to reorganise complex relationships within an ordered series of simple relationships: in archaeological terms, to construct a particular syntax in space/time.

By stratifying urban places we can read them. Elements distributed over a single surface provide a critical mass; they lend themselves to analysis; they form a surface that can be subjected to analysis;[31] 'the place is a palimpsest'.[32] Layering has been used as one possible way of ordering and organising the relationships between different urban materials and between materials and social practices: for example, for constructing a map of places used for socialising, and relating those places to the various times at which they are used by different parts of the population; or for exploring different modes of dwelling by observing how the open spaces of detached houses and blocks of flats are organised, how boundaries are given different treatments, whether fences are open, closed, high or low, which fences denote public space or private space, and how they interpret the concept of privacy in different ways. This type of analysis is synchronic when it tries to identify underlying structures, and diachronic when it passes through different temporal strata.

Just as the archaeologist attempts to interpret each excavated trace and associate it with the movement that produced it, the traces we uncover in urban places are clues that densely interact with the other traces of the deconstructed real world. In Derrida's interpretation, the meaning of each material belongs to the trace it has left in the past, and is the trace it will leave for the future. The present of the object is itself touched by this oscillation, this movement, making its meaning mutable and variable.

Designing by layers is a search for consistencies that are not global, but are capable of structuring an ensemble of fragments locally and in successive steps. It does not deny the fragment, but deals with it as a detail of one stratum, for example by transforming it into a topological detail. In this sense it resembles the work of the archaeologist: knitting together networks of consistencies according to a principle of not intervening,

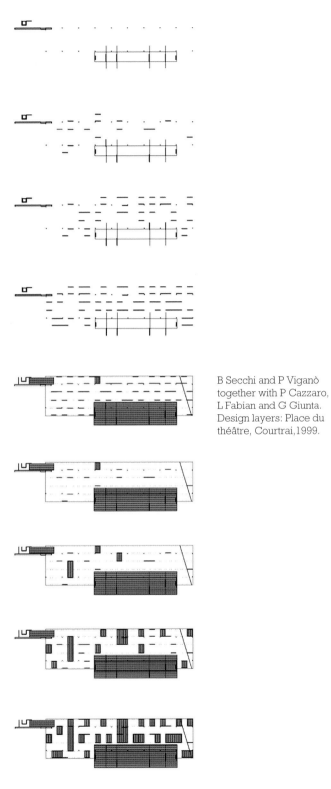

B Secchi and P Viganò together with P Cazzaro, L Fabian and G Giunta. Design layers: Place du théâtre, Courtrai,1999.

ie, bringing together a number of consistencies that do not reciprocally cancel one another out. In this way, designing by layers can underline the fragmentary character of the city and its territory; the degrees of consistency between its parts and the whole are only revealed insofar as they are taken apart.

Simple Materials, Complex Materials

Wittgenstein has pointed out how complicated it is to define 'the simple constituent parts of which reality consists '; 'What are the simple constituent parts of a chair? ' he asks. 'The pieces of wood from which it is made? Its molecules? Its atoms? "Simple" means: not composite. And this is the point: "composite" in what sense?'[33] All the same, he suggests, we can build up our image of reality by using unfocused concepts, for instance by defining, as I do, a footpath as a simple urban material, and a street – the footpath plus a cycle lane, a line of trees and a roadway – as a complex urban material.

In order to analyse these simple materials of the city – footpath, hedge, row of trees, roadway, sports ground – in 'technically pertinent'[34] ways, and group them to create more complex materials, for example pertaining to the layout of the city – park, street, sports complex – we can establish some rules of the game by creating sequences and setting them out on two axes. The first is a syntagmatic axis of elements that remain very stable over time – for instance, the position of a drainage channel at the edge of a road that varies so that there is no puddling in relation to the slope of the road surface, and which can take on a limited number of variations so that the road can function; the second is a paradigmatic axis that shows the great variety of ways in which that particular element can be constructed – the drainage channel can be made from concrete, stone, metal or other materials, can vary in cross-section, etc.

As the syntagmatic chain and the paradigmatic ensemble come together in a project for the city, it would be difficult not to enquire into the meaning of urban grammar and syntax. The game of deconstructing sequences and reconstructing them is not to be understood as two opposing ways of working; they are both simultaneously present within a project that lays down rules for the process of transformation of the city over time and in space, within given grammars and syntaxes more than in terms of finished compositions. Just as in music the note is no longer the unit, the project for the city becomes the spatialisation of complex segments; Stockhausen's *Gruppen* (1957), composed for three orchestras positioned in different parts of the performance space, works not with single notes but with blocks of sound (though at times this may be a single note) each of which in order to be identified must be defined in terms of its size, form, density and sound quality.

For some urban territories, compositional abacuses and matrices have been used to establish rules, sequences and variations for designing the open spaces that form parts of their urban plans. As specific forms of design, these abacuses and matrices establish short sequences that repeat in the city[35] and extend into projects for individual places, thus becoming associated with formalisations that go beyond merely making lists, and regulate the ways in which different objects can combine.

'How shall we establish an order for a finite collection of elements procured by chance or that the *bricoleur* finds in his storehouse?' asks Lévi-Strauss.[36] What exchanges are to be permitted so that the whole can form a system? According to Piaget '... we must understand that whilst the structure exists independently of the theoretician, it was the theoretician who created it'; if the field is mathematics he will use mathematical equations, but will use something else for other fields, 'so various different possible levels of formalisation exist, and will depend on the decisions of the theoretician'.[37]

The structure that enables us to pass from an accretion of objects to a system is not preordained or given, but is produced by a mental construct as the outcome of a project that only becomes precise and specific over time. This structure is created from elements '... but these are subordinated to the laws that characterise the system as such. These so-called laws of composition cannot be reduced to cumulative associations but confer to the whole, as it comes into existence, properties as a whole that are different from those of its elements'.[38]

In this way the concept of system can make reference to concepts of identity and belonging: that is, of the nameability and recognisability of each element and its belonging to a group, a whole, a family. There is no opposition between the system and its constituent elements; each plays its part in constructing the project.

The relationships established between the elements in various systems are dishomogeneous. Structuralist analysis makes reference to mother structures that give birth to various prototypes: algebraic structures, the prototype of which is the group and is characterised by a number of typical operations; ordering structures whose prototype, the grid or network, '... unites its elements using relationships of *"follow"* or *"precede"* ...'; and structures "... that are topological in nature and based on notions of closeness, continuity, and limit".'[39] For example, in an environmental system, the objective of guaranteeing and augmenting its biodiversity means that the elements of connection between the environments and within each of them must be identified. In designing such a system the importance is not only attributed to the large-scale natural elements whose role is to filter, concentrate and accumulate naturalness or to connect the various environments, but also to all diffused naturalness (for example, the micro-connections often associated with a very small-scale water distribution network). Constructing an environmental system in terms of how the territory functions ecologically also makes it possible to use fragmentary parts of open space. As in a mobility system, the structure of reference here is a grid into which the various patches are connected. A system of central places in the city is used to identify and propose an ensemble of places which for various functional, symbolic and representational reasons has been allocated a central role. As a whole these places do not necessarily define a grid so much as a topological structure of places that are also closely tied to the imagination and the mental geography of its inhabitants.

A project thus organised in terms of systems forces the structuring degree of a collage, the guiding metaphor for many contemporary projects, including those at the territorial scale: there may be no such thing as a city of fragments, but a city can be said

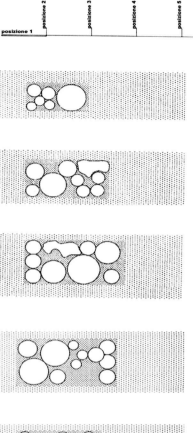

B Secchi, V Gandolfi, P Cigalotto,
M Santoro, P Viganò, S Rizzotti
and L Caravaggi (environmental
consultant). Grids and matrices for
designing open space in the plan
for Bergamo, 1992–5.

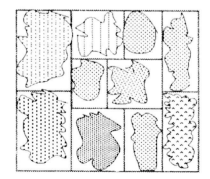

to exist that is a composition of fragments. Nevertheless the collage, with its emphasis on the fragment, is often integrated with a grid that becomes its structure of reference: an order imposed from outside.

The point of designing with systems is to define some levels of consistency and integration for all the parts of the city by superimposing multiple functional programmes and making them intersect, searching for non-global consistencies that relate to the attainment of an articulated ensemble of performances. The thing that unites the strategies of Tschumi, Koolhaas and Neutelings with designing with systems, as for example, our plan for Prato[40] is the analogy they all have with what Roland Barthes called 'structuralist activity'. For Barthes, structuralist activity 'constructs a "simulacrum" of reality using "operations" of "cutting-out" and "coordination". "Cutting out" is directed at selecting those elements to which it is desired to "give a current meaning", whilst "coordination" is directed at "discovering or setting their rules for association", so as to subject the simulacrum, and the elements of which it is composed, to "regular constraints in which what matters, more than formalism, inappropriately incriminated, is stability"; the latter of these two operations is a result of "the struggle against chance". '[41]

Compositional Modalities, Images

The idea of material, writes Michel Butor,[42] is inseparable from that of construction and composition. But the ways of putting together different materials are restricted to a finite number of images that belong to a historically and spatially determined disciplinary imagination.[43]

As in the theories of montage in the cinema of the 1920s, where extremely distant attitudes confronted one another from the dialectical Russian school of Eisenstein that made images collide to show the differences between things, to the American organic school, represented by Griffith, who followed the story line, to the radical position of Vertov, who refused to artificially depict nature and filmed Man in nature as a passer-by noticing his own reflection in the camera lens[44] – the organising principle of montage, of composition, is incorporated within a number of precise images and figures.

For a long time the images and metaphors used to describe and represent the city and its parts took as their reference the human body as a harmonious well-proportioned whole, or as the building: the house. Then the artistic avant-gardes of the early 20th century brought in a new family of images that emphasised mechanisation, new technologies, and the new as a value: from van Doesburg's Circulation City to Le Corbusier's metaphors in which the image of the machine organises the description of the modern city and the modern urban project. In the 1960s and 1970s the accent was placed on the idea of environments: infinite, transient architecture in which the city extends and causes itself to dissolve, as in Walking City by Herron and Chalk, or Superstudio's Continuous Monument. More recently Bernard Tschumi refused to use the term composition, because in his view only the terms *montage* and *assembly*, borrowed from the cinema, can convey how a project is constructed. In fact it is not only cinema that performs operations of assembly and montage; in a more general sense *mixage* might be the appropriate word to describe how the contemporary operates as a machine.

Often the contemporary city itself is taken as the location for producing new images through which it is represented and conceptualised. In general the fields of reference relate here to the new urban dimension: its particular density, its different composition, its new spatiality. Some of these images as collage city, patchwork metropolis, domino, jigsaw puzzle focus attention on a process of assembling individual pieces and defining weak or loose criteria that enable them to be positioned in relation to one another.

The use of terms like *assembly*, *montage* and *mixage* alludes to compositional operations that make use of existing urban materials; most of the materials of the project already exist as fragments and can be used to develop new compositions that attribute new meaning to them. It is difficult to avoid doing this and it brings a different, very significant light to bear on the ways in which each project is described and the possibilities of forming, deforming and re-using the materials of which it is composed.

Notes

1   O Calabrese, *L'età neobarocca*, Laterza (Bari), 1987.
2   M De Michelis, 'Scompaginamenti: Note sul frammento, la citazione, la decomposizione', in *La ricostruzione della città: Berlino – IBA 1987, XVII Triennale di Milano*, Electa (Milan), 1985, p 125.
3   C Rosen, *Schoenberg*, Marion Boyars (London), 1975. See also B Secchi, 'Città moderna, città contemporanea e loro futuro', in *I futuri della città: tesi a confronto*, Franco Angeli (Milan), 1999.
4   A Webern, *Der Weg zur Neuen Musik, Der Weg zur Komposition in Zwölf Tönen*, lectures given between 1932 and 1933 and published in 1960; P Boulez, *Penser la musique aujourd'hui*, Editions Gonthier (Paris), 1994.
5   Boulez, *Penser la musique aujourd'hui*, pp 43–4.
6   See T van Doesburg, *Scritti di arte e di architettura*, ed S Polano, Officina Edizioni (Rome), 1979.
7   van Doesburg, 'L'Elementarism e la sua origine', *De Stijl*, 1928.
8   van Doesburg, 'L'Elementarism', from the introduction by S Polano, p 23; it is worth remembering that the motto of Cor van Eesteren's Rokin project of 1927 was *Elementair*.
9   Polano, ibid., p 66; under the pseudonym IK Bonset, van Doesburg wrote Dadaist poems in *De Stijl* and edited the magazine *Mécano* (of which four issues were published between 1922 and 1923).
10 van Doesburg, 'L'Elementarism, p 395. The citation is taken from 'What is Dada', *De Stijl*, 1923.
11 PV Zima, *La déconstruction, Une critique*, PUF (Paris), 1994, p 34.
12 J Derrida, 'Invitation to a Discussion', *Columbia Documents of Architecture and Theory*, vol 1, Distributed Art Publishers (New York), 1993.
13 Zima, *La déconstruction*, p 87.
14 S Chermayeff, C Alexander, *Community and Privacy*, Doubleday Anchor Book (New York), 1963 (translated into Italian as *Spazio di relazione and spazio privato*, Il Saggiatore (Milan), 1968).
15 The power of repetition has always held a great fascination over every field of the arts as, for example, in literature, where the writings of Gertrude Stein can be taken as one example of many.
16 Zima, *La déconstruction*, p 54.
17 'The generic city is fractal, an endless repetition of the same simple structural module ...', R Koolhaas, 'Generic City', published *inter alia* in OMA, R Koolhaas, B Mau, S, M, L, XL, 010 Publishers (Rotterdam), 1995.
18 J Dewey, *Experience and Nature*, Open Court (Chicago), 1925.
19 M de Certeau, *L'invention du quotidien, 1. arts de faire*, Union générale d'éditions, collection 10–18, 1980 (from the Gallimard edition (Paris), 1990, p 148).
20 J-F Augoyard, *Pas à pas. Essai sur le cheminement quotidien en milieu urbain*, Seuil (Paris), 1979.
21 de Certeau, *L'invention du quotidien*, p 153.
22 S Muratori in *Studi per una operante storia urbana di Venezia*, Istituto Poligrafico dello Stato (Rome), 1960; R Venturi, D Scott Brown, S Izenour, *Learning from Las Vegas*, MIT Press (Cambridge, MA and London) 1972, 1977, R Koolhaas, *Delirious New York*, Monacelli Press (New York), 1978, second edition, 1994.
23 de Certeau, *L'invention du quotidien*, pp 171–2.

24   W Benjamin, *Passagen-Werk*, (ed) R Tiedemann, part of *Gesammelte Schriften* edited by TW Adorno, G Scholem, 1982, Einaudi (Turin), 1986; S Kracauer, *Strassen in Berlin und anderswo*, Suhrkamp Verlag (Frankfurt), 1964.

25   M Roncayolo, *Marseille, Les territoires du temps*, Editions locales de France (Paris), 1996; HU Jost, 'Promenades dans la ville', in F Walter (ed), *Vivre et imaginer la ville XVIII–XIX siècles*, Editions Zoé (Geneva), 1988.

26   H Lefebvre, preface to H Raymond, *L'habitat pavillonnaire*, 1 Harmattan (Paris), first edition, p 8.

27   Ibid., p 8.

28   G Perec, *Les choses*, Julliard (Paris), 1965; A Robbe-Grillet, *Pour un nouveau roman*, Les Editions de Minuit (Paris), 1963.

29   M Foucault, *Les mots et les choses*, Gallimard (Paris), 1966; J Baudrillard, *Le système des objets*, Gallimard (Paris), 1968 (translated into Italian as *Il sistema degli oggetti*, Bompiani (Milan), 1972); M de Certeau, *L'invention du quotidien*.

30   See the degree theses by G Canal, *La strada, per uno studio dell immaginario*, L Mascino, *Due stazioni della metropolitana di Tokyo: un esercizio di descrizione*, S Toffolo, *Formazione e trasformazione del pavillonnaire a Ginevra*, 1995–7, tutors B Secchi and P Viganò with H Jinnai and A Léveillé.

31   de Certeau, *L'invention du quotidien*, p 293.

32   Ibid, p 295.

33   L Wittgenstein, *Philosophische Untersuchungen*, Basil Blackwell (Oxford), 1953, from the 1995 edition, p 34.

34   L Benevolo, 'La percezione dell invisibile: Piazza San Pietro del Bernini', *Casabella*, no 572, 1990; B Secchi and P Viganò, *Un progetto per Prato*, Alinea (Florence), 1996.

35   For instance in the plans for Bergamo (B Secchi and V Gandolfi, 1992–5) and Prato (B Secchi, G Serrini, P Viganò, C Zagaglia, 1993–6).

36   C Lévi-Strauss, *Regarder, écouter, lire*, Librairie Plon (Paris), 1993 (translated into Italian as *Guardare, ascoltare, leggere*, Il Saggiatore (Milan), 1994, p 140).

37   J Piaget, *Le structuralisme*, Presses Universitaires de France (Paris), 1968; from the 1985 edition, p 37.

38   Ibid., p 38.

39   Ibid., p 55.

40   B Secchi, P Viganò, *Un progetto per Prato*.

41   F Infussi, *La costruzione del progetto norma: tecniche di 'traduzione normativa' e forme di piano*, Politecnico di Milano, December 1995, p 17.

42   M Butor, *L'embarquement de la reine de Saba*, La Différence (Paris), 1989, p 80.

43   O Soubeyran, *Imaginaire, science et discipline*, L Harmattan (Paris), 1997.

44   R Zancan (*Altri sguardi*, PhD seminar on Urbanism, IUAV, Venice, 1997), Sergei M Eisenstein (for example *Montage 37*, written between 1935 and 1937). Translated into Italian by P Montani in *Teoria generale del montaggio*, Marsilio (Venice), 1985.

Made in Tokyo

Momoyo Kaijima, Junzo Kuroda, Yoshiharu Tsunamoro

Using the innocuous method of the guidebook, Momoyo Kaijima, Junzo Kuroda and Yoshiharu Tsunamoro from Atelier Bow-Wow offer a provocative glimpse of contemporary Tokyo through their ethnographic survey technique of the here and now. By ignoring the historical, the monumental and focusing instead on the 'no-good, grade B architecture' of the city, they discover the DNA of the metacity. Kaijima, Kuroda and Tsunamoro pay their respects to the urban theories of Rossi, Rowe, Venturi and Scott Brown, and Koolhaas, and therefore reveal the synthetic nature of their urban design theory. Their book classifies the city of Tokyo into 'environmental units' which they term 'animated micro urban ecologies', and like good scientists they order the discoveries of the strange urban species nurtured in the hyper-dense environment of Tokyo based on category, structure and use.

The Appearance and Disappearance of Shamelessness

I'm often surprised when returning to Tokyo, especially when returning from Europe. Roads and train lines run over buildings, expressways wind themselves over rivers, cars can drive up ramps to the roof-top of a six-storey building, the huge volume of a golf practice net billows over a tiny residential district. Most major cities of Europe are still using buildings from previous centuries, and are not modernised in terms of renewing actual building stock. By comparison, almost all buildings in Tokyo have been built within the last 30 or 40 years, utilising contemporary technologies. These technologies have formed a background to the appearance of shameless spatial compositions and functional combinations, unthinkable in the traditional European city. What is it about this city of Tokyo, that can allow such unthinkable productions? How have we managed to arrive at such a different place to European modernity despite being equipped with the same building technology? But one week later, these sort of questions disappear from my mind, together with the feeling that something is wrong.

Changing our Surroundings into Resources

If we return to our everyday architectural life, architectural magazines and university textbooks are filled with famous works – east and west, old and new. Specialists, such as practitioners and critics, find their criteria by looking at overseas examples and Japanese classics. This is correct and necessary, but the values thereby gleaned judge this city as consumed by disgusting buildings. Yet, if our footsteps are actually embedded in such a pitiful urban landscape, the idea of using famous architecture as a criteria base would seem to be just an attempt to emulate good taste. Photographic books amplify a desire for an architecture which simply doesn't exist in our surroundings. In such a situation, suddenly architectural design no longer holds any interest; the future appears depressing.

If we can't try to turn 'disgusting' buildings into resources, then there is no reason to particularly stay in Tokyo. Surely we can start to think about how to take advantage of them, rather than trying to run away. Shamelessness can become useful. So let's start by considering that these shameless buildings are not collapsible into the concept of 'chaos', but are in fact an intricate reflection of the concrete urban situation.

Survey Beginnings

In 1991, we discovered a narrow spaghetti shop jammed into the space under a baseball batting centre hanging from a steep incline. Neither spaghetti shop nor batting centre is unusual in Tokyo, but the packaging of the two together cannot be explained rationally. Despite an apparent convenience in their unity, there is no necessity to hit baseballs towards the opposite hotel, sweat, and then eat at a spaghetti shop. Moreover, it is difficult to judge whether this combination is a kind of amusement machine, or strange architecture. This building simultaneously engendered the suspicion that it was pure nonsense, and expectation in its joyful and wilful energy. But we also felt how 'very Tokyo' are those buildings which accompany this ambiguous feeling. Having been struck by how interesting they are, we set out to photograph them, just as though we were visiting a foreign city for the first time. This is the beginning of *Made in Tokyo*, a survey of nameless and strange buildings of this city.

Da-me Architecture

The buildings we were attracted to were ones giving a priority to stubborn honesty in response to their surroundings and programmatic requirements, without insisting on architectural aesthetic and form. We decided to call them 'Da-me Architecture' (no-good architecture), with all our love and disdain. Most of them are anonymous buildings, not beautiful, and not accepted in architectural culture to date. In fact, they are the sort of building which has been regarded as exactly what architecture should not become. But in terms of conveying the reality of Tokyo through building form, they seem to us to be better than anything designed by architects. We thought that although these buildings are not explained by the city of Tokyo, they do explain what Tokyo is. So, by collecting and aligning them, the nature of Tokyo's urban space might become apparent. At that time there was a best-selling guidebook of Tokyo full of architect-designed works, but it did not show the bare Tokyo which we felt. It couldn't answer the question of what kind of potentials exist in this place we inhabit? What does it mean to think about and design architecture that has to stand alongside da-me architecture?

Flatness

The starting hypothesis for the survey is that in any city, the situation and value system of that city should be directly reflected through unique buildings. In the case of Tokyo, we suspect that da-me architecture contains hints to think about the city and architecture. However, the definition of da-me architecture was not necessarily clear from the beginning. We debated at length over each example as we collected them.

During these debates, we took care not to think about the city as a conceptual model. In the 1980s there was a background of chaos affirming theory and Tokyology, and the spatial expression of architectural works displayed confusing urban landscape as a metaphor. We were keen to get away from the attitude that the city can be summarised by metaphorical expression. Then again, from the very start, we avoided considering examples which can be read as stereotypical images such as stylistic eclecticism and contrast between pre- and super-modern. Although we agreed with the *Institute of Street Observation*'s emphasis on pleasure, we felt uncomfortable with the importance attached to modesty and wistfulness. We decided to try not to be influenced by nostalgia. The examples we stuck with were based more on particularity in the way they related directly to use. By treating the relation between elements as the major issue, we tried to see the object without preconditioned meanings and categories. We tried to look at everything flatly, by eliminating the divisions between high and low cultures, beauty and ugliness, good and bad. We thought that such a way of seeing is called for by the urban space of Tokyo, which is a gigantic agglomeration of an endless variety of physical structures. If we describe this agglomeration simply as confused or chaotic, or understand it with a predetermined story, then probably our own experience of Tokyo's atmosphere will suffer. Anyway, there are too many exceptions to be able convincingly to deduce each building's composition from the urban structure. So if we try to collapse da-me architecture into a typology, we will lose the interesting mongrel nature of the differing elements. Our flatness means something more specific.

Guidebook

The result of the observation also depends on the method of representation. If the method doesn't suit the observation, often the result can't be grasped. Therefore it is important to develop a method of representation which doesn't lose observational quality. The format we chose was that of a guidebook. Tokyo is a giant maze-like city without physical navigational aids such as axes or urban boundaries. Perhaps because of this, there are innumerable guidebooks on every facet of life in this city. Tokyo has already been edited to suit every possible objective. Even if they form a kind of software after the fact, in terms of organising the way the city is used, guidebooks can become a tool for urban planning. However, a guidebook doesn't need a conclusion, clear beginning or order. This seems suitable for Tokyo, where the scene is of never-ending construction and destruction.

Urban Theory by Architects

Much was learnt from the architectural and urban theories of our predecessors. From Bernard Rudofsky's *Architecture Without Architects*, we looked at the response between architecture and the environment in vernacular buildings. From Nikolaus Pevsner's *A History of Building Types*, we considered how he picked up arbitrariness and criticism in the selection of building types as material for thinking about architecture. From Aldo Rossi's *Architecture of the City*, we thought about the interdependent relationship between architecture and the city. From Colin Rowe and Robert Slutzky's 'Transparency: Literal

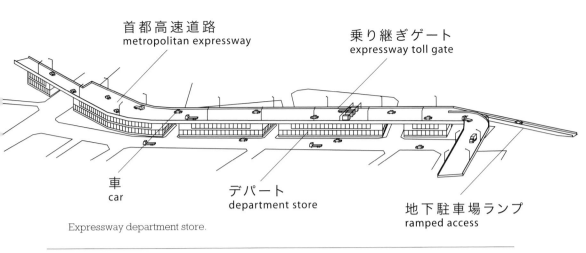

首都高速道路
metropolitan expressway

乗り継ぎゲート
expressway toll gate

車
car

デパート
department store

地下駐車場ランプ
ramped access

Expressway department store.

and Phenomenal', we learnt about how space evolves out of the overlapping of various design criteria. From Robert Venturi, Denise Scott Brown and Steven Izenour's *Learning From Las Vegas* we realised the power of placing 'bad architecture' within the line of architectural history. From Rem Koolhaas's *Delirious New York*, we delighted in the idea that the whole of the contemporary city is made up of a series of accidents, in accordance with inevitable changes to the overall urban plan. From Wajiro Kon's *Kogengaku Nyumon* (Introduction to Cultural Studies), we gained a love of observing the city before us, and an understanding where even the most subtle things start to hold meaning, sketch by sketch. From Terunobu Fujimori et al's *Institute of Street Observation* we discovered the joy of actually walking in the street and finding fragments ... allowing the imagination to take over and the communication of small urban histories. We were encouraged to think that each of these theories had been born out of discussing particular cities and architectures. They have concrete origins in a specific place, and yet in the end they lead towards an abstract level, which can open new architectural and urban awareness. What kind of awareness will be opened up by the buildings erected in Tokyo?

From 'Architecture' towards 'Building'

The buildings of *Made in Tokyo* are not beautiful. They are not perfect examples of architectural planning. They are not A-grade cultural building types, such as libraries and museums. They are B-grade building types, such as car parking, batting centres or hybrid containers and include both architectural and civil engineering works. They are not 'pieces' designed by famous architects. What is nonetheless respectable about these buildings is that they don't have a speck of fat. What is important right now is constructed in a practical manner by the possible elements of that place. They don't respond to cultural context and history. Their highly economically efficient answers are guided by minimum effort. In Tokyo, such direct answers are expected. They are not imbued with the scent of culture; they are simply physical 'building'. Moreover, Tokyo is really such a contradictory place, because it is in fact these buildings which most clearly reflect its quality of urban space, whereas the translation of issues of place through history and design seem fabricated – This is Tokyo.

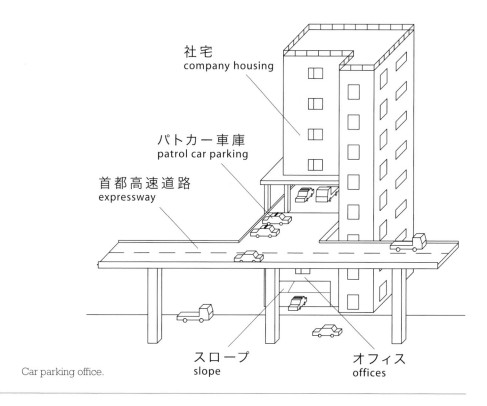

社宅
company housing

パトカー車庫
patrol car parking

首都高速道路
expressway

スロープ
slope

オフィス
offices

Car parking office.

Where cultural interest is low, interest in practical issues is high. Whether civil engineering structures, roof-tops, walls or gaps between buildings, all utilise whatever is at hand. What is important is the discovery of how to establish a secondary role for each environmental element. With this doubling up, it becomes possible to re-use spatial by-products. The material is not given, but is discovered through our own proposition of how to use it. It might be termed 'affordance' of the urban environment. Further to this, cross-categorical hybrids such as expressway-department stores can arise. In this example, the department store depends on the expressway for its structure. On the other hand, the expressway depends on the department store for its validity in such a busy commercial area. So neither can exist on their own – they are interdependent.

Such existence seems anti-aesthetic, anti-historic, antiplanning and anti-classification. It nudges the architecture of over-definition towards generic 'building'. The buildings of *Made in Tokyo* are not necessarily after such ends, but they simply arrive at this position through their desperate response to the here and now. This is what is so refreshing about them.

Adjacency and 'Environmental Unit'

Our interest is in the diverse methods of making and using coherent environments within the city, together with the urban ecologies seen there. This includes the unexpected adjacency of function created by cross-categorical hybrids, the co-existence of unrelated functions in a single structure, the joint utilisation of several differing and adjacent buildings and structures, or the packaging of an unusual urban ecology in a single building.

In Tokyo's urban density, there are examples of a coherency which crosses over categorical or physical building boundaries. It is something which differs from the architecture of self-sufficient completeness. Rather, any particular building of this kind can perform several roles within multiple urban sets. They cannot be specifically classified as architecture, or as civil engineering, city or landscape. We decided to name such coherent environments of adjacency 'environmental units'.

Furthermore, the external envelope does not serve to divide public and private, as in the traditionally understood idea of a facade. We are in a fluid situation, where rigid distinctions such as between shallowness and depth or front and back, are easily overturned by a shift in the setting of the ecological unit.

The magnificent Architecture of Architects retains distinctions between categories, rationalises physical structure, pushes preconceived use onto that structure, and tries to be self-contained. This is even though there are so many diverse ways to define environmental unities. It is a method that Modernism has passed down to us, and the precision of its ways is becoming stronger and stronger. Yet, everyday life is made up of traversing various buildings. Living space is constituted by connections between various adjacent environmental conditions, rather than by any single building. Can't we draw out the potential of this situation and project that into the future? If we can, it may be possible to counter the typical Japanese Modernist public facilities which are cut off from their surroundings and packaged into a single box. We can focus attention on the issue of how usage (software) can set up a network, where public facilities can be dispersed into the city while interlapping with the adjacent environment. Spaces for living can penetrate into various urban situations and thereby set up new relations among them. The possibilities for urban dwelling increase.

On/Off

We can find an overlapping of three orders which set up the 'environmental unit'. They are based on category, structure and use. If we take again the example of the hybrid between expressway and department store, the traffic above and the shopping below are simply sharing the same structure, but belong to different categories and have no use relation. In other words, it is only structural order which unites this example. Maybe it is not that the example is impossible to evaluate within the existing cultural value system, or the norm for architecture. Rather, the sense of unity is full of dubiousness which is the essential reason that this example is da-me architecture. We can say that when any of the three orders are operating, they are 'on', whereas when they do not take effect they are 'off'. This system starts to incorporate all the value poles which seem to form such an important role in the recognition and indeed the very existence of da-me architecture. We can recognise that the examples of Made in Tokyo almost always comprise some aspect of being 'off'. The only vacant endpoint to the chart that includes an aspect of 'off', is the position which might be filled by the continuous street facades of Paris. By contrast, the magnificent buildings of Architects are 'on', 'on', 'on'. Often, the Parisian streetscape and the Modern city are held to be in opposition, but the abundant examples of Made in Tokyo show that they are not necessarily bipolar. They simply exist within a score of on and off.

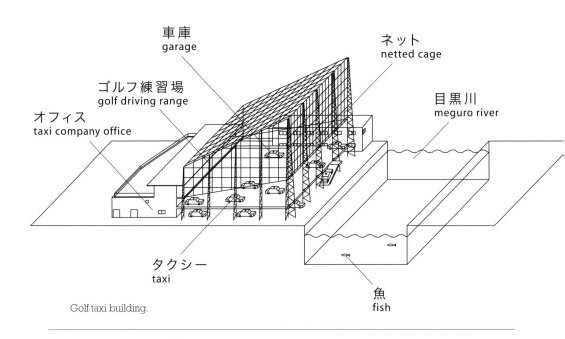

車庫
garage

ネット
netted cage

ゴルフ練習場
golf driving range

目黒川
meguro river

オフィス
taxi company office

タクシー
taxi

魚
fish

Golf taxi building.

Anyway, surely too much 'on' can't be good for our mental landscape. If we switch all three orders 'on', there is only one possibility for achieving satisfying architecture, but if we allow any or all aspects to be 'off', then suddenly the possibilities for variation explode to eight (two to the power of three). This establishes a huge release for designers. When we say that we can sense the pulse of Tokyo in the 'da-me architecture' which includes some aspect of being 'off', it means that even though the urban space of this city appears to be chaotic, in exchange, it contains a quality of freedom for production. The landscape of Tokyo is a random layering of different buildings corresponding with multiple social purposes. We hope in our design work to clearly represent possibilities for the urban future by being consistent with the principal findings of our research. The observations can only gain clarity once they have been studied through design and vice versa. Such interactive feedback between observation and design is one efficient method through which to contribute to the city through the scale of architecture.

Key Words

CROSS-CATEGORY
Even in the landscape of Tokyo, which is so often claimed to be 'chaotic', a certain environmental coordination made up of categorical crosses between architecture, civil engineering and geography, can be found. There is a clear logic in the way that differing activities are brought together by physical convenience such as scale and adjacency. We can see that part of Tokyo's dynamism is ordered through physical terms rather than the categorisation of contents. We start to recognise the unexpected interdependence of activities by looking at Tokyo in this kind of positive way – as a cross-category match of urban production.

AUTOMATIC SCALING

Because of inflationary land prices, there is a 'void phobia' in Tokyo, which elicits a reaction of 'what a waste!' when we see any unused space. Everywhere, the desire to find and fill gaps can be seen. What occurs in these openings is not usually related to the function of the host facility, but rather answers to a super-rationalism where the filling is matched to the gap simply according to size and proportion. Let's call the idea of the chance meeting of differing objects, purely given by measurements, 'automatic scaling'. At this point is born the kind of building with unexpected practicality of adjacency and connection, boldly ignoring and jumping beyond the history and social mode of the city. The knowledge, invention and imagination summoned in fully utilising these spaces to the extent of stubborn honesty, makes possible new urban relations.

PET SIZE

The city of Tokyo displays a whole range of sizes, but as a specific characteristic, items around the size of a vending machine can be pointed out. In Japan, vending machines are so abundant, but they are not nearly so visible in other countries. This difference may be due to the extent of public security in various cities, but it is also due to the nature of the sense of scale which exists in each location. For example, the urban code of Tokyo stipulates that neighbours must accept any new building work if it keeps 500 millimetres (20 inches) distance from the boundary. Of course everyone's site is too small, and so they try to build to the maximum possible extent. Tiny slivers of space between

Super car school.

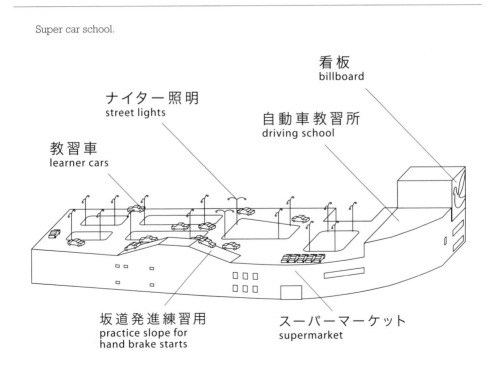

看板
billboard

ナイター照明
street lights

自動車教習所
driving school

教習車
learner cars

坂道発進練習用
practice slope for
hand brake starts

スーパーマーケット
supermarket

buildings, which can only be used by cats, are the result. With the high price of land in Tokyo, eventually these spaces become desirable for use. Maybe the vending machine is a kind of saviour in this situation. In particular, the very thin or very low proportions which can sometimes be seen are probably because of this tendency towards filling all gaps. Other types such as the karaoke box, car parking machines and signboards have also developed a unique size so as to be able to slip into these spare spaces. These items are a bit too small to be recognised as architecture, but a bit bigger than furniture. They are the kind of size which can exist in the corner of a room, or in the corner of the city, turning the urban environment into a 'superinterior'. The items' constant suppleness to fit their surroundings makes them like the pets of the city. So we can say that smallness = pet size.

LOGISTICAL URBANITY

If we wanted to show a visitor from another country the real Tokyo, then driving along the expressways would be highly recommended. Because the expressways were constructed in a hurry to be in time for the Tokyo Olympics, they are mainly sited over public land, parks, the palace moat and rivers. They allow views of a raw Tokyo like a rollercoaster plugged into the city. It is possible to glimpse parts of the mechanisms which support the huge logistics of transporting people and large numbers of physical objects. What Le Corbusier looked at with the planning for Algiers, and Marinetti proposed in his Futurist work, becomes actually constructed here, and linked to make an extensive network. In Japan, the 20 or so years between 1966 and 1988 saw the number of cars increase by 6.25 times, but the length of road only increased by 1.12 times. Transport infrastructure which allows physical distributions is like the blood vessel system connecting organs for the city. For Tokyo, which is on the brink of sclerosis, it is apparent that Radburn's planning theory of separating cars and pedestrians is completely impractical. By necessity, cars have entered into the realms of people. Previously, the criteria for comfort was seen as separation of the traffic space of cars and trains, and human space. But now a mixture between them occurs, which has become accepted as a new norm. The contemporary principle is about being able to imagine clearly how to connect to any particular location, and have easy access to the goal. Probably, the people of Tokyo have accepted the mixture of traffic space and human space, almost as a version of an 'urban regulation'.

SPORTIVE

Let's imagine a situation of being thrown into various environments with a single board under our feet. If that happens to be the big wave of the sea, then we are surfing. If that happens to be the slope of a snowy mountain, then we are snowboarding. And if that happens to be on the asphalt of the street, then we have added wheels and are skateboarding. The common vehicle of a single board helps us to observe differing environments and lets us perceive the reality of action as 'interaction with environmental information'. According to James Gibson, 'affordance' is the nature of the environment as defined by its relation to living beings. Contemporary urban sports are also based on the discovery of various values and meanings furnished in the environment through the movement of the body. By finding

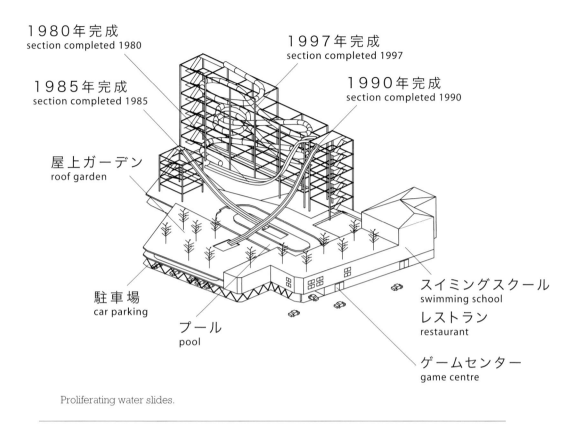

1980年完成
section completed 1980

1997年完成
section completed 1997

1985年完成
section completed 1985

1990年完成
section completed 1990

屋上ガーデン
roof garden

駐車場
car parking

プール
pool

スイミングスクール
swimming school

レストラン
restaurant

ゲームセンター
game centre

Proliferating water slides.

residual spaces inside the closely packed urban field, and using human action to turn those surfaces into sports fields, the elements of the city gain a whole new appearance. The body and the environment become inextricable, and the more urban elements are dragged into the sports scene, the more that particular sport goes wild. In their capacity to turn roof-tops, caged-in skies and boxed-in geography into broad sports fields, the buildings of *Made in Tokyo* exhibit the kind of fine play which should be enshrined.

BY-PRODUCT

Urban by-products – roof-tops, wall planes, under infrastructure and the abundant gaps between houses – are void spaces which generally avoid a predefined use being allocated to them. At the moment, the usual attitude is a kind of void-phobia which tries to paint over all trace of such spaces and they are considered only individually so that the meaning of their multiplicity is lost. However, these voids can become a breathing space within the over-dense urban environment of Tokyo, and can be recycled into a completely new use – the equation of by-product = void and its assemblies can become a tool for a future worm's-eye view urban planning.

URBAN DWELLING

Within the extreme density of Tokyo, real estate ideals – clean air, lots of greenery, no noise pollution, big rooms, plentiful sunlight from large south-facing windows – are like a faraway dream. Trying to approach such ideals entails huge cost: enormous monetary expense, or being pushed out to extremely distant suburbs. The uncontrollable spread of this situation is like a virus. Modern architects and city planners tried to counterattack the effects of this highly dense living environment by taking utopian ideas combining the rural and urban, and trying to project them into towers or onto Tokyo Bay. However, among contemporary urban dwellings, there exists an immunised type, which has adapted to the actuality of the current condition in its own attempt to overcome the urban disease.

MACHINE AS BUILDING

The city is our place for living. But if we zoom back, it can be seen as an organic structure like a machine or a creature breathing production and consumption. Although it is an analogy, if we think this way, then the city starts to need organs for power, transport, storage and discharge. In the case of a megalopolis like Tokyo, the load on such organs is enormous, and the organs required to look after them must also become huge. In reading these organs as built facilities, they can be readily seen in the area around Tokyo Bay. The most typical examples of these are almost-infrastructures such as power plants, rubbish incinerators and sewerage plants. Generally, they have been regarded as types of industrial building; because of modern architectural history's interest in them, they do not seem particularly strange to us now. However, in the latest infrastructure-related facilities of Tokyo, bizarre buildings which are really like large machines or instruments have appeared. These are what we have focused on for *Made in Tokyo*. According to Le Corbusier, 'the house is a machine for living in', but according to *Made in Tokyo*, the reverse 'machine as building' is also true. In other words, architecture as an analogy for machinery is possible.

URBAN ECOLOGY

Tokyo is an agglomeration of buildings, traffic infrastructure, civil engineering. Its landscape is said to lack visual control and is popularly thought of as chaotic or as 'white noise'. However, this kind of interpretation is based on mechanistic theory and semiotic systems. So, if we change this premise, a totally different interpretation of the city should be possible. Actually, despite these claims of chaos, Tokyo is interesting in its own way of functioning. It resembles the unstructured forms of the rainforest, within which there are many types of creature co-existing, with each constructing its own world. This is ecology, which understands the creature itself in relation to its living environment. If we stop using the metaphors of mechanistics and semiology and start using the metaphor of ecology, then it should be possible to discover layer upon layer of meaningful environmental unities, even within the landscape of Tokyo. This is a complex intertwining of people, the flow of things, elements of the environment and time; something which can never be obtained by the bird's-eye view. By walking around the reality of everyday life, we can

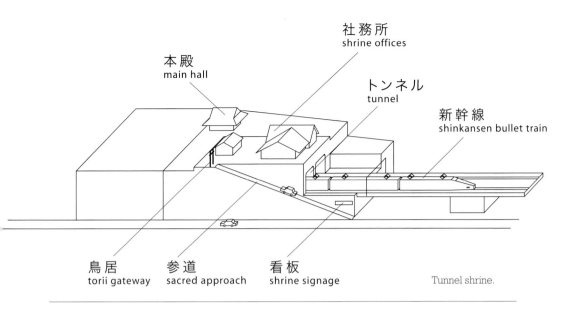

本殿
main hall

社務所
shrine offices

トンネル
tunnel

新幹線
shinkansen bullet train

鳥居
torii gateway

参道
sacred approach

看板
shrine signage

Tunnel shrine.

start to see an urban micro-ecosystem, or theatre of urban dwellers. Then, we can also start to form an image of a city accumulating from these variable happenings. This stage of connected action is brought into being by utilising every possible element from the surrounding environment. The completeness of any building and the categorical division between architecture and civil engineering becomes meaningless.

VIRTUAL SITE

The difference between convenience stores and other public building types such as libraries, museums and train stations is that there is an incredible number of them spread throughout the city, that they are made up of a small space of repeated design and that they have established a networking system. This network is supported by logistics systems that control informational and product exchange between merchants and their clients, known as POS (Point of Sales) Systems. In one sense, we can say that it is the network itself that makes one huge public facility. But this kind of network as software-architecture is invisible. It is only ever the parts, each individual shop, which can actually be experienced. Therefore, in terms of the network's strategy, there may be an issue of exactly where to locate the outlets, but there is no problem in terms of site specificity in the design of each shop. For example, there is essentially no difference in the layout of merchandise or the arrangement of the signage within any network. In fact it is the sameness of the specifications of the shop design that is the important software for the management of the convenience store.

From Momoyo Kaijima, Junzo Kuroda, Yoshiharu Tsunamoro, *Made in Tokyo*, Kajima Publishing Company, 2006, excerpt from pp 8–39. By permission of Kajima Institute Publishing Co. Ltd. © Momoyo Kaijima, Junzo Kuroda, Yoshiharu Tsunamoro. All images by permission of Momoyo Kaijima, Junzo Kuroda, Yoshihara Tsukamoto © Kajima Institute Publishing Co. Ltd.

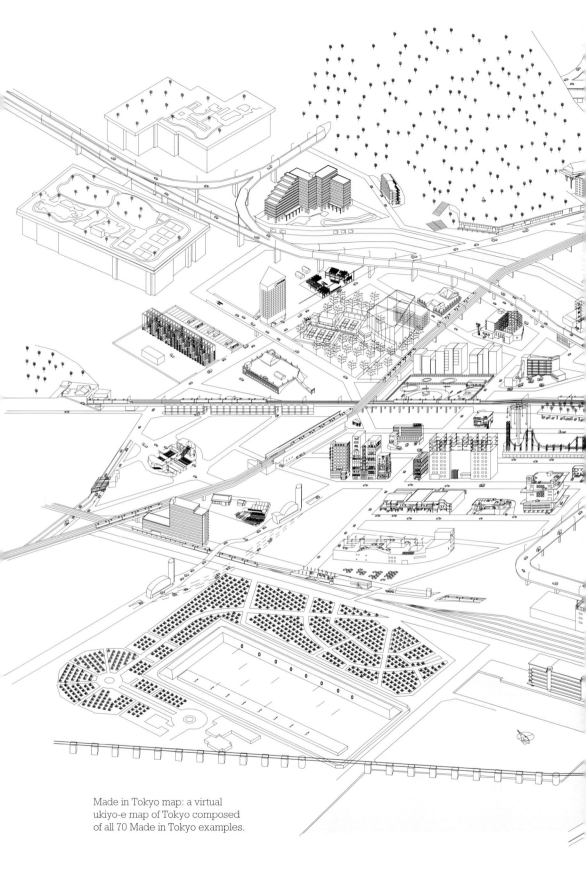

Made in Tokyo map: a virtual
ukiyo-e map of Tokyo composed
of all 70 Made in Tokyo examples.

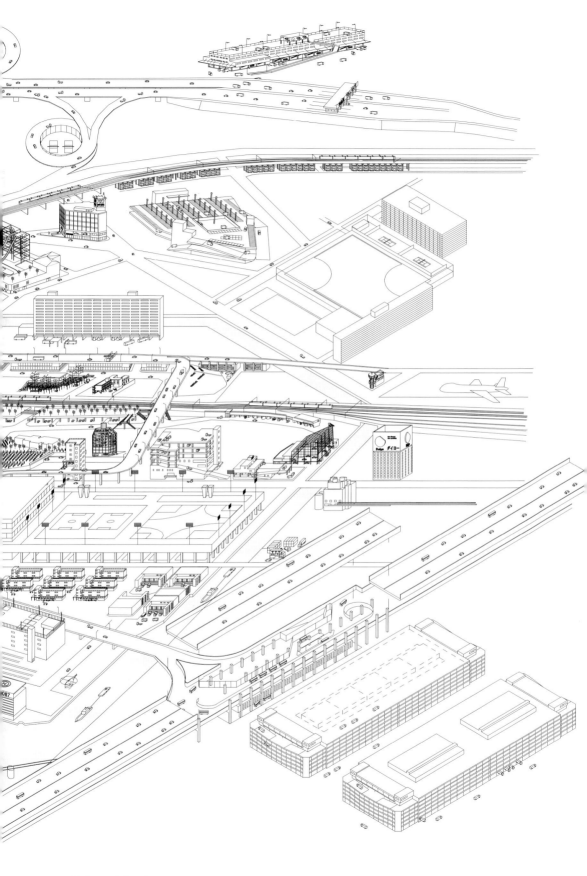

Index

Urban Design Ecologies is the seventh AD Reader. This reader series from John Wiley & Sons, the publishers of *Architectural Design* (*AD*), invites influential architectural thinkers and educators to compile anthologies on core topics of study for students of architecture and design.

Previous titles in the AD Reader series include:

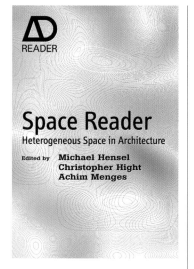

Space Reader: Heterogeneous Space in Architecture

Edited by Michael Hensel, Christopher Hight and Achim Menges

978-0-470-51943-1 (pb)
978-0-470-51942-4 (hb)

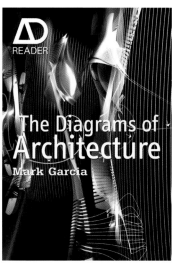

The Diagrams of Architecture

Edited by Mark Garcia

978-0-470-51945-5 (pb)
978-0-470-51944-8 (hb)

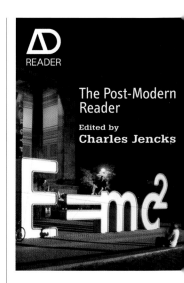

The Post-Modern Reader

Edited by Charles Jencks
(Second Edition)

978-0-470-74866-4 (pb)
978-0-470-74867-1 (hb)

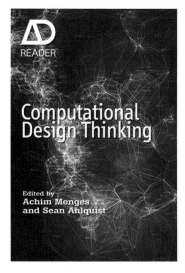

Computational Design Thinking

Edited by Achim Menges
and Sean Ahlquist

978-0-470-66565-7 (pb)
978-0-470-66570-1 (hb)

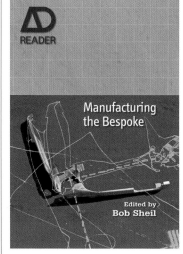

Manufacturing the Bespoke: Making and Prototyping Architecture

Edited by Bob Sheil

978-0-470-66582-4 (pb)
978-0-470-66583-1 (hb)

The Digital Turn in Architecture 1992–2012

Edited by Mario Carpo

978-1-119-95174-2 (pb)
978-1-119-95175-9 (hb)